Occasional Deconstructions

Occasional Deconstructions

Julian Wolfreys

State University of New York Press

Published by
State University of New York Press, Albany

For information, address State University of New York Press,
90 State Street, Suite 700, Albany, NY 12207

Production by Kelli Williams
Marketing by Susan Petrie

Library of Congress Cataloging-in-Publication Data

Wolfreys, Julian, 1958–
    Occasional deconstructions / Julian Wolfreys.
      p. cm.
    Includes bibliographical references and index.
    ISBN 0-7914-6225-0 (alk. paper) — ISBN 0-7914-6226-9 (pbk. : alk.paper)
      1. Desconstruction. 2. Literature, Modern—History and criticism. I. Title.

    PN98.D43W65 2004
    809'.04—dc22

                                             2003068659

10 9 8 7 6 5 4 3 2 1

CONTENTS

ACKNOWLEDGMENTS

Any statement of thanks will always resort to the formulaic. The attempt to add something "more" to the process only runs the risk of sounding even more like the same old thing. So, no more words, as I've already said too much, and can only say that the occasions of gratitude are many and sincere. Donald Ault, Joan Brandt, Mary Ann Caws, Claire Colebrook, Sophie Croisy, Thomas Docherty, Jonathan Dollimore, Kate Flint, Greg Freeman, Regenia Gagnier, Afshin Hafizi, Werner Hamacher, Terry Harpold, Kevin Hart, Susan Hegeman, James R. Kincaid, Peggy Kamuf, Roman Kazmin, Brandon Kershner, John Leavey, Martin McQuillan, J. Hillis Miller, Thomas Pepper, David Punter, Jean-Michel Rabaté, John Ronan, Avital Ronell, Nicholas Royle, Phil Wegner, Kenneth Womack, Fred Young—thank you all.

As the introduction discusses, several chapters in this volume were first given as conference presentations and the signs of their address have been retained, although all have been reworked extensively, largely as a result of received comments. A number of the other chapters, or parts thereof, have previously appeared in print; all have been substantially revised and extended for the purposes of the present volume. A significantly different version of chapter one appeared as "Justifying the Unjustifiable" in Julian Wolfreys, ed., *The Derrida Reader: Writing Performances* (Edinburgh: Edinburgh University Press, 1998); chapter two appeared in much shorter form as "Hollywood Gothic/Gothic Hollywood" in Andrew Smith and Geoff Wallace, eds., *Gothic Modernisms* (London: Palgrave, 2000); a much shorter, partial version of chapter three first appeared as "The Gothic and Liminal Lives of Mary Shelley" in Martin McQuillan, ed., *Muriel Spark in Theory* (London: Palgrave, 2000); a shorter version of chapter five, "Eternity and a Day or, 'an Endless Foreword': *Tout dire*," was first published as "Eternity . . . and a Day: an 'Endless Foreword',"in Martin McQuillan, ed., *Deconstruction Reading Politics* (Evanston: Northwestern University Press, 2000); chapter six first appeared in German, as "Der Spuk das Zitate" in Nils Plath and Volker Pantenburg, eds., *Anfuehren—Vorfuehren—Anfuehren: Das Zeitat in Literatur und Theorie* (Bielefeld: Aiesthesis Verlag, 2000) and, in another shorter version, in English, in *Mosaic* 35:1 (March 2002); a shorter version of chapter seven appeared as "Trauma and Testimonial Criticism" in Julian Wolfreys, ed., *Introducing Criticism at the Twenty-First Century* (Edinburgh: Edinburgh University Press); chapter ten first appeared in different form as "Letter to Martin McQuillan à propos of 'The New International'," in *Parallax*, Fall 7:3 (July–September 2001).

INTRODUCTION

Here is the enigma of this situation in which I get lost; but it is *this* enigma that erases the difference between calculative rationality and its other; and *this* enigma complicates and entangles all questions of decision and responsibility. One has to know, one has to know it. But, since the moment in which the decision is made is heterogeneous to knowing, I say it very firmly and unconditionally, but I inscribe this unconditionality on the trembling non-limit that I have just said. And I could, naturally, give a great many examples; it is the law of everything I write and of everything that happens to me *[qui m'arrive]*. Each time I write a text, it is "on occasion," occasional, for some occasion. I have never planned to write a text, everything I have done, even the most composite of my books, were occasioned by a question. My concern with the date and the signature confirms that.

Jacques Derrida

All metaphors are (by profession) equivocal. And there is scarce any word that is not made equivocal by divers contextures of speech, or by diversity of pronunciation and gesture.

This equivocation of names maketh it difficult to recover those conceptions for which the name was ordained; and that not only in the language of other men, wherein we are to consider the drift, and occasion, and contexture of the speech, as well as the words themselves; but also in our own discourse, which being derived from the custom and common use of speech, representeth not unto us our own concepts.

Thomas Hobbes

1

The purpose of *Occasional Deconstructions* is multiple, though all of its aims are closely related. Mobilizing a number of issues from Jacques Derrida's recent work around questions of ethics, politics, and identity, and addressing the ways in which these pertain to the necessary work of acts of reading attentive to the demands that the concerns of Derrida's text impose on one, the volume seeks to offer a number of reintroductions or reorientations to the text of Jacques Derrida and the idea or possibility of deconstructions. It does so initially through a critique of the received wisdom in the Anglo-American institution of higher education that deconstruction is some form of critical methodology, in order to show how the reader is more faithfully served in a reading of Derridean discourse by coming to terms with the idea that deconstruction is what happens, if it happens at all, in any form, and that the ethical demand of Derrida's work is to read those instances, or, as my title has it, occasional deconstructions, the occasions or instances in which textual logic comes apart at the seams, often by what Sarah Kofman has called the "syntax of the undecidable,"[1] foisting the impossible responsibility of decision on the reader. Telegraphing too hastily what is to follow, I pursue these issues through repeated engagement in Derrida's text concerning the various, nonsynonymous figures of ghosts, phantoms, spectres, haunting, the uncanny, and apparitions. Addressing these strange, disquieting tropes, and to telegraph the concerns of the particular chapters, I offer a series of readings of films and novels, biography, concepts of reading and love, questions of ethics and traumatic experience, and ontological and political matters. Thus, this book seeks, in one sense, to 'spectralize' the notion of deconstruction (a spectralization that is undeniably already at work in the very idea of deconstruction; deconstruction, if it can be defined, is *just this disquieting oscillation of the spectre*), in the face of the current antitheoretical or atheoretical climate in particular aspects of cultural studies and identity politics. *Occasional Deconstructions* suggests that the patient, necessary work of reading, in which response to the other and responsibility to the other has the chance of manifesting itself, is necessary to the always political and ethical tracing of the material and the historical, but how such a politics and an ethics comes to be figured cannot be determined ahead of the encounter with the other. Reading is, or should be, an encounter that gives place to an acknowledgment of the other; that giving place, a singular act oriented by the work of prosopopoeia, by which one is introduced to the other, however indirectly, can never be programmed; it is only a chance occasion.

Thus, the present volume is made up of nothing other than a series of occasional "introductions."[2] The figure of occasion is already announced in the title of this book, its function articulated in the first of the two epigraphs to this introduction; it will be considered again. However, we should begin by taking into account the ways in which the chapters that follow are "introductions." They are introductions not in the sense of being propaedeutic sketches gesturing toward particular practices, which in turn follow on necessarily from preliminary instruction. Rather, each chapter works through the problem of introducing into proximity with one another particular concerns and interests, which are, in turn, suggested by recent publications by Jacques Derrida, in order to witness what possible communication might take place in unexpected ways, what action occurs on the occasion of a chance "falling together" or "juncture" (to borrow from the *Oxford English Dictionary*'s definitions of "occasion") of disparate texts. Specifically, the chapters seek to address aspects of some of Derrida's more recent texts, and they attempt to do so in relation to material not usually seen in conversation with the text of Derrida. In addition, the occasions of these chapters, and the occasions from which they arose, offer the possibility of extending a number of debates now grown habitual, familiar, between particular discourses and Derrida's concerns, where it has been assumed that neither has anything to say to the other. Moreover, introductions are effected in response to an assumption that has occasionally been announced in recent years within particular academic circles, that Derrida has nothing relevant to say any longer. In this sense, there is a double operation at work in the figure of introduction, one of more possible significance than any tired rehearsal of introducing someone who, simultaneously, is too well known and hardly recognized, barely glimpsed, as yet. This double operation functions, if it functions at all, throughout the present text—as already suggested—by seeking to introduce Derrida to particular discourses, subjects, disciplines, and to introduce, in turn, those same discourses, subjects, and disciplines to the text that goes by the name of Jacques Derrida. Each so-called introduction is of course a separate occasion, and yet there emerges a sense that the introduction has already taken place, even if it has neither been received nor heard, and the occasions being remarked here are little more than so many untimely moments of belated recognition. In this fashion, introduction might be taken to be a figure, as well as the occasion, for reacquaintance, on the one hand a refamiliarization with what is unfamiliar, and, on the other, a defamiliarization with that which has been taken for granted, particularly with respect to specific dimensions of the reception of Derrida and the motif of so-called deconstruction.

If it is the case today that an understanding has been reached that (a) deconstruction is never single, that there are only deconstructions, and that (b) deconstructions, being irreducible to a methodology, a school of thought, an analytical or critical program, are *just what happen, if they happen at all,* how might one begin again to speak of deconstructions? If it is no longer possible, strictly speaking, to address or to teach deconstruction as either a method or coherent concept, much less a theoretical paradigm (even though there are some who do); it is also not enough to say that there are deconstructions-plural without careful qualification and caution.

This figure of plurality is, of course, dangerously seductive in its apparent appeal to community and consensus. It might be read, for example, as suggesting a progression in the thinking of an ontology of or, perhaps more accurately, *for* deconstruction. That is, implicit in the shift from single to plural is a movement in the developing subtlety and almost irresistible power of appropriative and recuperative modalities of thought. Unable any longer to identify directly in some ontological, hermeneutic, or other epistemologically coherent manner so-called deconstruction's sole identity or ipseity, such thinking manifests the tendency to shift to another procedure for getting at the desired conceptual organic unity or self-sameness. In this hypothetical scenario, so many deconstructions take on the guise of related species, belonging to a genus.[3] This can be understood, for example, as a combinatory assimilating the work of X and X and X under one name or, somewhat more loosely, determining by analogy a discernible resemblance between the "way in which X reads" and "the way in which X reads" (X comments on autobiography, and so does X; therefore, autobiography is a salient feature in locating resemblance, regardless of difference or heterogeneity).

The problem here is obvious, but necessarily in need of stating: in identifying various "species of deconstruction," one assumes a priori and as given deconstruction as genus, and, following Heidegger on the subject of the resistance of being to such thinking, elevation to metaphysical concept. To summarize: on the one hand, deconstruction-single identifies the genus and proceeds to prove its conceptual coherence by identifying or, more precisely, seeking out those aspects—the species—of the genus that prove the truth of the genus (which in this model is what Heidegger terms "species-enabling"); on the other hand, moving from the specific to the general, deconstructions-plural seeks to say "this (and this and this) is deconstruction." Such examples are read as typical and, operating in the ontological analysis *as if* they were species, prove the genus once more. From whichever side we approach the difficulty, it has to be admitted that both approaches to the question of determining deconstruction/s, whether pursued inductively or deductively, are plagued by an ontological reduction and a concomitant effort to downplay the difference by which any articulation of determination is possible in the first place.

Such being the case and returning to one of the initiating questions of the present project, how is one to consider responding when asked to speak of deconstruction, of deconstructions, or, even, to speak to "its" possibility (perhaps its impossibility)? This is the question that motivates this book, albeit indirectly. I say "indirectly" advisedly because any direct confrontation with the problem that I have previously outlined will have had the tendency, almost inevitably, to fall into modalities of determination or, equally, modalities of negation (which are, themselves, deterministic, and addressed in the chapter on "origins of deconstruction"): this is, this is not. Rather than proceed in such a fashion, and yet recognizing that it is important to address "deconstruction"—the importance, the necessity even, seems all the more marked because so many voices keep on insisting that deconstruction is dead, deconstruction is a thing of the past; and they do so, moreover, so frequently, that you might begin to wonder whether such statements, far from stating a truth, are actually engaging in some kind of proleptic speech act concerned with wish fulfillment. I seek to orient the act of response, understood as the volume in general, through readings and critiques, each of which are themselves responses, singular responses, and all of which share nothing in common so much as the fact that they have all been generated by "calls," demands, requests, injunctions, inquiries. Thus, a central focus of this volume is with the ontology and ideology of "the call" as a determinant in any academic work. In saying, however, that I resist any overarching thesis, it has to be admitted, of course, that there is discernible, as a common thread— what Derrida has called a *fils conducteur*—a sustained interest in the ways in which Derrida can be so suggestive for our acts of reading-as-response/responsibility, even while his own acts, in demanding such detailed attention, nonetheless resist any facile appropriation in the form of a supposed theory (such as deconstruction), which would then be apodictically applicable in some programmatic manner.

   The demands placed on deconstruction, those that involve identification or confession in some fashion, all desire, however sympathetically they might be framed, to "get to know" or become familiar with, to familiarize so-called deconstruction. The impulse is very much one concerned, again, with defining and refining, perhaps even reifying, the definition; otherwise, there is always a question of seeking allegiance: deconstructions *have to* locate their relationship to some master discourse (again, see the final chapter). However, it has to be asked what is it in the various requests or inquiries that motivates them in their own terms? It seems no longer enough to say that determinations of deconstruction from some other place (as though there were "some other place" where deconstructions will not, always already, have taken place) manifest a "will-to-ontologize," if it is possible to put it this way. The various general remarks concerning deconstruction, all of which I am in some manner rehearsing and restaging here, and which also haunt the chapters in this volume in various ways, are well known. The interest here, however, is to ask what remains unread, what is taken as given, what is occluded in the demands put on—and, equally, the resistance to—deconstruction, in particular specific ways. A demand can also, and all too often, be the symptomatic manifestation of a resistance. It articulates an imperative that the subject in question—Derrida, deconstruction—be subject to its laws, that it be called to account; and this arises, doubtless, because the place from which the demand comes to be issued is troubled by the possibility of its protocols being challenged, its procedures being transformed, once so-called deconstruction is admitted: hence the injunction, as proleptic resistance.

   With this as a recognition of a general procedure, and also recognizing and responding to what is always immanent in various demands, however hospitably couched their language might appear, I have sought to ask what is at stake in specific, singular instances: how does one respond when asked to write on the "origins of deconstruction" or to address the question of "deconstruction reading politics." What can be said in response to a call to address the very idea of a "New International"? What responsibility does the critic have when faced with a request to address the possibility of any relationship between Derrida and "revolutionary praxis" (whatever is meant by such a phrase, whatever its terms harbor)? What takes place in the request to analyze and account for hybrid genres, where such requests concern acts of historicization? How does one write an introduction to Derrida or to deconstruction? What does it mean to read after Derrida when, within certain aspects of academic publication, there appears to be a return to a nonreflective "pretheoretical" contentment that, ignoring its own epistemological orientations, seems content to pursue the most basic acts of summarizing plot, anthropomorphizing character analysis, and conducting an often reductive historicizing, as though it were understood what is meant by the term "history" (or, indeed, context). In every case, the question of reading becomes one of responding to the singularity of address, rather than simply assuming on the one hand a consensual role or, on the other, falling into the "ready-made" of a dialectic.

The following chapters all speak to the specifics of the issues just indicated; they are best described, in that way outlined in the opening paragraphs of this introduction, as occasional pieces, hence the title of this volume, *Occasional Deconstructions*. They were all written initially in response to requests to contribute to specific conferences and publications, which in turn required participants to consider particular subjects or topics, all in some way associated with the work of Jacques Derrida or the motif of deconstruction. In each chapter I sought, at the time of writing, not merely to produce one more piece of research or criticism but, instead, to engage and intervene, perhaps interrupt even, the various aphorisms and commands that frequently constitute Calls for Papers (CFPs). In each case, interruption takes place in a particular counterintuitive fashion, addressing the injunction rather than simply conforming to it in the hopes that interruption itself brings to a halt the work of interpellation implied in the numerous requests. As such, while these chapters have been significantly changed and expanded, I have thought it best to retain certain of the marks of the various occasions and the performances that they represent, especially as in most, if not all cases, each proceeds through readings of the aphorisms, titles, demands, and other forms of CFP. Thus, to identify some of these originating and instituting attempts at determination, the subjects of this book, broadly defined and already alluded to in telegraphic fashion, are film, biography, citation, spectrality, the origins of deconstruction, the notion of a "New International" and the Marxist response to *Specters of Marx*, "deconstruction reading politics," revolutionary praxis, the conventions of genres and practices, and those of identity constitution. Certain arguments or commentary recirculate, transformed in the process of differing contextualizations, but also indicative of the way in which no context is ever finite or closed. In each chapter, regardless of immediate address, the focus is on the construction of certain identities related to the term deconstruction, and the forms of ideological and ontological work that circulate around, and occasionally, in this strangest of names. How these identities come to be conceived is most starkly, often violently, revealed in the phrases by which someone, whether an individual or institution, seeks to call into being a collection of essays, papers, and so on. What I realize has most interested me in responding to such matters is not the staging of a more or less predictable defense of or apologia for Derrida or deconstructions, even though such an element is unavoidable (there is also a pleasure of sorts to be had from saying, repeatedly, no, that's not quite right, not exactly). Rather, I have sought to address what is articulated by or otherwise demonstrably immanent within the phrases that gather so much energy to themselves. The spectral transference of immanence in the institutional interpellation of the academic-qua-subject speaks of a form of inoculation, protecting against "contamination" (but of whom: the subject? The institution?), but also controlling reception. My consistent concern and interest throughout is to situate a response to whatever appears to be implicit in the different manifestations of CFPs, and to use these as singular texts, singular events, from which to move in a consideration of broader issues, where there is the difficult intersection between matters of rhetoric or poetics and politics and identity.

Each chapter involves an initial act of restaging arguments that are familiar, and, in this process, working at the structures and forms, and, along with these, the assumptions implicit within such constructs, so as to expose certain blind spots or limits. In this process, the restaging of the familiar, a certain repetition is as inescapable as it is necessary. Moreover, it could be said to be desirable because the act of repetition may produce an unexpected iterable event from within the very language that is being employed. Transformation has the chance—but it is only a chance, the merest of possibilities—of taking place, of happening, and of taking place differently. Repetition necessarily involves a kind of rehearsal, a rhythmic process by which something may come to take place. However, it has to be said that this "repetition" is not simply the formal, academic, or scholarly procedure of recasting in other words previously existing arguments or theses. Repetition also becomes part of an internal rhythmic gesture in the act of writing itself. There is a working of material as the praxis of a transformative critique, a certain performative destabilization within the constative commentary occasionally misread as belonging to a register or modality marked by everything from homage and imitation to parody and pastiche. There is also to be read a kind of "rehearsal of voices," a trying out if you will, of tones, styles, pitches, as response seeks to find the appropriate register or key in relation to its subject so as to acknowledge the singularity of what is being read.

While it is the case that such "rehearsing" could be, or has been, as just suggested, taken as imitation, pastiche, or even parody (whether intentionally or otherwise), such is the risk taken as a measured resistance throughout the volume to any form of institutional "calming down" of so-called deconstruction. Of course, institutionalization has always already begun, and with it the violence attendant on the process, which might best be understood as a forgetting of difference, a very necessary forgetting for the instituting of any institution (the institution of deconstruction as one more academic subject, as one form of theory). However, one has to be wary of such procedures, even though they appear to be inevitable in some cases. Calls for papers to be presented at conferences, requests for book chapters and essays in journals: all are the work of a certain scholarly or academic community. While there is nothing to be objected to in such functions of the institution, and certainly I would not wish to have done with these demands or have them done away with, it is worth observing that, as examples of the institution of a certain community, all, necessarily, engage in acts of "auto-immunity," of what Derrida calls in "Faith and Knowledge: The Two Sources of 'Religion' at the Limits of Reason Alone," the "auto-community, constituting [every community] as such in its iterability, its heritage, its spectral tradition." As Derrida remarks: "No community is possible that would not cultivate its own auto-immunity, a principle of sacrificial self-destruction ruining the principle of self-protection (that of maintaining its self-integrity intact), and this in view of some spectral sur-vival."[4]

The idea of the community immanent within any CFP or other related request preemptively incorporates within its body that which it is instituted to resist, hence its constant questioning of and interest in the very difference it would resist, as the means by which it maintains itself. The institutional act of maintenance relies on an assimilation (in the name of pluralism) of the difference, treating difference merely as a calculable differentiation about which there can be accord, which would signal the community as a community in ruins. And what motivates such accommodation is what might be termed a propaedeutic will, whether one speaks of "theory's" reception generally (assuming there has in fact been a reception), or, more specifically, the calculated reception, in which an account is made and a receipt—or recipe—written up, apropos of either Derrida or so-called deconstruction. The appeal of the propaedeutic is very great indeed.

Kant issues a caveat against its seductions in his "On the common saying: That may be correct in theory, but it is of no use in practice." Equally, one could cite Heidegger, concerning the institutionalization of thought as a "tendency-toward-the-institutional," as a modality within thinking governed by a kind of ontology-as-pragmatism. Here, in what is probably one of his most arch, and even funniest moments, Heidegger somewhat violently situates a critique of dialectical process apropos of the institution, in what might also be read as an apologia for phenomenology:

> Dialectic has its source in the same error committed by that which it wishes to remedy. It steps into an already constructed context, though there really is no context here, i.e., what is missing is the radical fundamental looking in the direction of and at the object . . . dialectic lacks radicality, i.e., is fundamentally unphilosophical, on two sides. It must live from hand to mouth and develops an impressive eloquence in dealing with readymade material. If it gains acceptance, the burgeoning Hegelese will once again undermine even the possibility of having a mere sensitivity for philosophy. . . . A year of reading and one can talk about everything, such that it really looks like something and the reader himself believes he's really got something. One ought to have a close look at the sophistry being pursued with schemata like form-content, rational-irrational, finite-infinite, mediated-unmediated, subject-object. It is what the critical stance of phenomenology ultimately struggles against. When the attempt is made to unify them, one treats phenomenology in a superficial manner. Phenomenology can only be appropriated through . . . demonstration and not in such a way that one repeats propositions, takes over fundamental principles, or subscribes to academic dogmas.[5]

The signs are here of an auto-immunity, a self-inoculation, despite the very anti-institutional polemic of Heidegger's critique. For, while the general tenor of the remarks point to the institutionalization of dialectic ("a year of reading," the systematization of thinking in terms of binary oppositions, and the subsequent "academic dogma" arising therefrom) and, therefore, to a failure to think, regardless of subject in terms simply of position and opposition, without accounting for or analyzing the conceptual operations of the terms making up the polar opposites; there takes place a fallback into dialectic, between, on the one hand, phenomenology, which is held implicitly to be antireductive and attentive to the question of singularity (it can "only be appropriated through demonstration" and not through the repetition of fundamental propositions), and, on the other, dialectic itself. The problem is not that Heidegger is wrong necessarily. Rather, there may be read here a certain precipitation from thought into unthought. The danger, the trap that Heidegger unwittingly both sets and springs, is in what might best be understood as an ineluctable slide from constative into performative, for the very academic purpose of illustration or representation, allied to a reliance on ontological assumption.

This of course has made itself more than manifestly evident in the reception of and resistance to Derrida. The most obvious signs of this is that deconstruction, difference, or any of the motifs associated with Derrida's writing and name (and including his name), have now been understood, considered enough. There is no longer any need to work with any patience with Derrida other than, yet again, in some pedagogical, propaedeutic manner, where whatever goes by the names *difference, supplement, deconstruction, writing, text,* and so on, are all subsumed within, subordinated to a form of technical competence and calculation. But what would happen—would anything happen?—if we were to substitute the word *reading* for any of these terms or figures associated with Derrida? What might a transformative notion of reading, always on the watch for institutionalization, and always seeking to read the signs of its violence, always wary of the tendency to reduce reading to a matter of *tekhne* (see the chapter on "guilty reading," particularly Suhail Malik's commentary on reading as technicity), be capable of disrupting? Reading to excess, reading to come, reading as response and responsibility to the *arrivant,* the *revenant,* these are the occasions when deconstruction might happen, if it happens at all. Reading might not necessarily figure as the occasion for deconstruction; it might, however, make available *occasional deconstructions,* as the chapters in this volume explore.

Part One

FALSE STARTS

Chapter 1

REFLECTING ON THE OCCASIONS OF INTRODUCTION: JUSTIFYING THE UNJUSTIFIABLE OR, BEGINNING AGAIN

Derrida's text leaves us with the infinite responsibility undecidability imposes on us. Undecidability in no way alleviates responsibility. The opposite is the case.

Drucilla Cornell

Sentences of the form "deconstruction is so and so" are a contradiction in terms. Deconstruction cannot by definition be defined, since it presupposes the indefinability or, more properly, "undecidability" of all conceptual or generalizing terms. Deconstruction, like any other method of interpretation, can only be exemplified, and the examples will of course all differ.

J. Hillis Miller

Ever since Jacques Derrida addressed himself to the problematic of introduction in relation to Hegel's "Preface" to the *Phenomenology,* everything that can be said on the subject of introductions has been said. Everything is exhausted, has become stale and familiar, especially, it has to be said, this chapter. And it's for that reason why this is not the introduction to this book, but is placed here, presumptuously, as the first chapter, a supplement to the introduction, stalled, a false start, and

also a series of reflections, backward glances, retrospective unlacings of
threads that are already worn and fraying in a number of places. Why
bother then? Why not just admit, in the words of the song, that I can't get
started? If there is ever a more unjustifiable gesture it is perhaps this
most untimely one, speaking of the occasion for introducing "Jacques
Derrida," after nearly half a century of such occasions. Indeed—and this
is not merely an overly neat fictive device to get me off the hook on which
I've already hung myself—at the very moment when I was completing
final edits and revisions to *Occasional Deconstructions*, I received an e-
mail inviting me to contribute to a book introducing, yet again, Jacques
Derrida. An uncanny event, the occasion of an unexpected arrival, to
which I am obliged to respond. In this chance instance, there is perhaps
the ghost of an answer to the otherwise unanswerable concerning the
occasions of introduction.

Is it possible to "introduce" a book addressing either Jacques Derrida
or deconstruction? Would it ever be possible to write such an "introduction"? What would that "introduction" look like? Can one ever do anything else apropos of Jacques Derrida, other than introduce his texts?
Does one ever get beyond introducing Derrida, and yet, paradoxically, failing all the while to do so? As a provisional response to such questions, I
would like to propose what might be construed as a somewhat scandalous
assertion: on the one hand, one can never introduce the work of Jacques
Derrida. Such a gesture is impossible if for no other reason than that Derrida's text exemplifies the condition of all thought, which is that it is irreducible to any attempt at totalizing recuperation. On the other hand,
however, one can never do anything, when writing in response to Derrida's work, other than to effect an introduction, albeit one in ruins. So:
one can never introduce the text of Jacques Derrida but one never does
anything except introduce the text of Jacques Derrida, and this is due to
the radically *occasional* nature of Derrida's writing. Let me borrow here
from the introduction to *Occasional Deconsructions*: the book you are
at present holding is nothing other than a series of occasional introductions, and if there is any justification for this, it is perhaps in the fact that
they seek to address much of the more recent work by Derrida and to do
so in relation to material that is not usually in conversation with the text
of Derrida. In this sense, there is a double operation at work in the figure
of introduction, one of more possible significance than any tired rehearsal of introducing someone who, simultaneously, is too well known
and hardly recognized, barely glimpsed, as yet. This double operation

functions, if it functions at all, throughout the present text by seeking to introduce Derrida to particular discourses, subjects, disciplines, and to introduce, in turn, those same discourses, subjects, and disciplines to the text that goes by the name of Jacques Derrida. Each introduction is a separate occasion, and yet there emerges a sense, as with that arrival of the e-mail mentioned earlier, that the introduction has already taken place, and the occasions being remarked here are little more than so many untimely moments of belated recognition.

Acknowledging this throughout, the present volume therefore seeks to situate itself in more or less indirect relation to the work of Jacques Derrida and to one particular, and particularly exhausted notion and motif, that of deconstruction, as so many responses to given occasions. It does so arguing, as it has been put in the "introduction" to *Occasional Deconstructions*,[1] that this is necessarily the only appropriate orientation—an orientation involving a series of more or less singular reorientations and disorientations *in* and *of* writing and reading—to the text of Derrida. This present chapter, being an improper "introduction," arises then, as I have already implied, as a response to the occasions, such as beginning a book or replying to requests that urge one to "begin" or to "start" thinking about particular subjects in relation to the more general "subject" of "deconstruction." There are always occasions on which introduction is called for, again and again, and yet which, in being called for, present one, not simply with the dizzying impossibility of any such act, but with the even more vertiginous possibility of impossibility. A subject is produced, projected in the name of generalizing and totalizing gestures, and this "subject" becomes subjected to the instituting act of violence that goes by the name of introduction. Thinking is thus institutionalized. The institutionalized subject imagines him- or herself as being hailed, being interpellated by the demand to spell out clearly, in the scenario imagined here, the work of deconstruction, yet in responding to this call, the subject finds such a project impossible.

What follows in this chapter therefore is little more—and, perhaps, a little less—than a concession to the genre of "the introduction," even though it introduces nothing other than its own failures. Or to put this another way: this therefore will not have been an introduction, recognizing as it does the aporia that appears before us, and which stops us dead in our tracks when we speak of the uncanny, disquieting singularity of the text of Derrida, particularly when that text is haunted by the ghosts of preface, preamble, prologue, beginning, opening. Instead, this is a response to the very idea, the illusory concept of "introduction." Order is disordered, and here we are under way in the "first" chapter, after any "introduction" should have been made, looking backward, in a gesture of retrospect that, far from offering any teleological comfort or promise, is premised on the apprehension that something has already opened.

The act of writing an introduction is, in general, out of the question, hopeless, unattainable, for it involves, in every singular example, justifying an absolutely unjustifiable act: such an act involves the violent delimitation of the singular in favor of the general. Supposing the possibility of introducing the work of a particular figure such as Derrida, whose own work has commented at length on the impossibilities of the genre and the act of introduction, is, arguably, even more unjustifiable and impossible. (Assuming for the moment that it is possible to suggest an impossibility beyond impossibility in general.) This act involves making a limited number of affirmations through the extraction of examples taken as synecdochic in their condition. Thus, you seek to represent the whole by the part, or by numerous parts, pretending all the while that such fragments are both authoritative examples and, at the same time, merely instances available for reassembly into some unified whole, which your prose, apparently subservient to the authority of the citation, nonetheless presumes to take responsibility for in the act of assembly (implying all the while that, somehow, the texts from which the various fragments came were not quite complete or clear enough, and that your function is to elucidate that which is unfortunately occluded). Proceeding in this manner, you would doubtless have to engage in acts of identification and determination, pointing to a number of problems in terms of your various justifications, all of which arise as a matter of course in making any affirmation or statement concerning your subject. All of which is, of course, unjustifiable. All of this is introductory in one sense; and yet the act of introduction is, inevitably, deferred, displaced.

Where then to begin? Perhaps it is a question of schematizing those affirmations, some of them at least, in the somewhat stark form of a list. Such a list might be composed, at least initially as the preliminary gesture of introduction, of statements, such as, "There is no such thing as deconstruction, if by this word one means a methodology or school of analysis." Or, one could say, "Jacques Derrida is not the originator of a critical methodology called deconstruction"; or one might also add, "That which Jacques Derrida writes is neither available for abstraction or reduction into a single, unified theory or methodology for the purpose of critical analysis." Strange affirmations these, it might be remarked, constituted as they are by negations. Another affirmation, another statement, equally singular in its counterintuitive orientation, is to be found in the words of J. Hillis Miller: "Deconstruction is nothing more or less than good reading as such."[2] This strange, enticing remark raises a question: If deconstruction is nothing more nor less than good reading *as such*, then why speak of deconstruction at all? It is impossible to respond to such a question; a definitive answer remains undecidable, although the impression is to be had that, traced within the statement is the ghost of an equation: deconstruction is good reading. We would still have to be wary of such a remark, given what appears as its positivist reassurance. Unless, of course, in reading the work of equation in the conjugation of the verb we were also to situate a simultaneous erasure. If deconstruction *is* (equivalent to) (good) reading, then deconstruction is no longer other than reading but, rather, the invisible alterity within reading, a necessary condition of reading, that which makes good reading good.

This doesn't appear to get the reader very far. Still, as odd as such comments might appear with regard to the very idea of introducing Jacques Derrida, and in an effort to avoid all the programmed excuses by which introductions conventionally proceed, it does at least seem that we have the beginnings of a list here. But a list is, of course, *just* a list, unless, of course, someone mistakes or desires to read the list as a taxonomically ordered series with a peculiar combinatory logic, or otherwise as a collection of aphorisms serving, again, the synecdochic function. Either way, the list is read for a certain accretive or projective force, there being a kind of incremental calculation under way in the textual machine. Such judgments are inevitably unavoidable. They arise as a result of the list-maker's inability to control the destination or reception of the inventory. As is well known, it is impossible to guess, much less direct, either delivery or reception.

Yet, the very idea of an "introduction," and of introducing, is itself never simply a starting point; it will also have been, to employ what appears here the most necessary use of the future anterior tense, a response, dictated from some other place, as well as being a responsibility. Such responsibility doubtless must involve an effort to justify what is unjustifiable, recognizing all the while in this what amounts to this inescapable condition of the arrival of a demand from elsewhere and, in that demand, a kind of negotiation between identities (the negotiation of equivalence and erasure in the same place). The idea of an introduction *just is* this idea of the negotiation, propelled by the act of imagining the possibility of the impossible, of responding, on the one hand, to particular singularities, while addressing, without the possibility of controlling, an imagined identity, such an identity being, in the hypothetical scenario on which I am speculating, what might be called *the Derrida reader*. Yet how can one predict who the Derrida reader is or might be? Is it not the case that anyone who believes they read Derrida already imagines him- or herself in this role? And are there not others, each in their own fashion, who receive this text without ever having read it? No position, no identity, can ever be ascertained certainly.

However, such an act of naming is not simply a moment of problematization, it also carries with it a chance—but never more than a chance—of a transformation, a translation of sorts. It can always act as a performative speech act: in this possibility, there can be imagined the Derrida reader who reads while claiming never to have "read" particular texts or authors, as will be seen in the discussion that follows. On the other hand, the Derrida reader may name a certain heterogeneous collectivity, an imagined figure of multiple singularities or, otherwise, a "singular plural" to borrow a phrase from a book by Jean-Luc Nancy.[3] Such a reader might be imagined, as Derrida has with respect to Joyce scholars, as "an infinite institution of people working as interpreters and philologists,"[4] all of whom will never have done with reading, and who recognize how reading is always to come. For this reason, one among many without doubt, one is always forced to come back to the question of beginnings, of the iterability implicit and necessary in starting again and again, and seeking in some manner to engage with the possibility of the impossible—the introduction. The introduction is impossible, but one will never get past its necessity. The Derrida reader is the one whom we imagine, like Derrida, will always have to begin reading again and again and who will, moreover, always be able to imagine the possibility of beginning one day.

To reiterate: the aporetic of the "introduction" as it is inscribed within, as the disarticulation of, any introductory act is this, therefore: one can never get beyond or have done with introduction, but one can never do anything else, if one comprehends how one always has to begin again, repeatedly, in the same place and yet also in a different place. What proscribes the apparently, supposedly, simple act of introducing or prefacing is, though, not merely the peculiar condition imposed in the effort to respond to Derrida's text. This is not merely a peculiarity with regard to Derrida, but belongs also to any response or approach to any text. To risk once more a repetition: one can never introduce, finally, but one cannot do anything other than introduce. Of course, Derrida has discussed and unfolded the problematic of the preface or introduction in *Dissemination*, among other places. Any material designated as prefatory or introductory belongs neither wholly to its subject nor remains completely "outside" that subject. It plays on, moves across, and, in the motion, inaugurates the dismantling of, the borders of any "outside" or "inside." The idea of any gesture of introduction thus may be said to take place, even in its performative displacement, in a liminal location and relationship to what is conventionally considered any corpus, any oeuvre. However, it has to be said that if one can never introduce even though one never does anything else (even though one also attempts to do so much else), then all that takes place, if it takes place at all, is this liminal, threshold motion, each time assuming a singular aspect, reiterating-deconstructing both the premises of its own auto-conceptualization, and any conceptual-ontological completion or unity (and, then again, with that, any ontology of the concept—of the concept of concept, even the concept of ontology—irreparably).

In tracing *and* enacting this strange motion or modality of *occasional thresholding*, where the threshold is *just* this enunciation of the occasion irreducible to any generalization, the preface or introduction still takes place under the injunction of presenting or re-presenting the thoughts, ideas, arguments, analyses, suppositions, and speculations that occur in some other text. What is understood here is that there can never be a true beginning but always, on the one hand, the orientation to what returns and, on the other, a violent, however faithful, gesture of dismemberment *and* incorporation. Introducing, it might be said, is the performative disfiguring named catachresis, masquerading as more or less mimetic fidelity. The preface or introduction disingenuously proposes that the subject or text being assembled or reassembled is, on the one hand, insufficient in some manner, incapable of presenting itself clearly, while, on the other hand, and as a consequence of incapacity, in need of rendering in some fashion to some neat, homogeneous, comprehensible, and finite model or genus, constituted through the act of introduction of so many species of the subject. With regard to "deconstruction" and the impossibility of any introduction, Derrida remarks that a *"Preface* would retrace and presage here a *general* theory and practice of deconstruction, that strategy without which the possibility of a critique could exist only in fragmentary, empiricist surges . . . . The preface would announce in the future tense ("this is what you are going to read") the conceptual content or significance of what will *already* have been written."[5] Tracing the disruption already at work as his own prefatory gesture, while analyzing its function, and thereby collapsing the distinction between any identification of the preface as either solely constative or performative, Derrida continues to note that "prefaces, along with forewords, introductions, preludes, preliminaries, preambles and prolegomena, have always been written, it seems, in view of their own effacement."[6]

What Derrida appears to show us here is the figure of a pen that, while it traces the outline of a text (while ostensibly miming what are taken to be the text's "principal" features), never present as such, also erases that gesture of outlining or describing in almost the very same moment or movement. This is the peculiar double logic, the supplementarity, of introducing. Introduction might, therefore be seen as a somewhat bizarre trope, as already implied by the figure of catachresis. It is tropological to the extent that the very premise of inauguration, institution, or even intuition (in that sense of looking into or contemplating some subject, rather than being suggestive, as is more conventional, of an unmediated apprehension) is related to what Derrida calls "a structure of reproduction," a structure that is also one of iterability *and* revenance. If this last figure seems a little excessive, we might recall here the rest of the quotation just indicated: "when the very *first* perception of an image is linked to a structure of reproduction, then we are dealing with the realm of phantoms."[7] As the very language of this false introduction demonstrates, the act of introduction is plagued with the traces of ghosts.

And so, I know that I will already have failed to write an introduction, that such an act is infelicitous *and* impossible; I cannot help failing and therefore, in seeking to be faithful to the injunctions of Derrida on the paradoxical conditions of any introductory act—as though one could start anew or start afresh without some ghost—I will betray Derrida in the process. Or, rather, perhaps it is the case that Derrida's haunting gifts, all the complexities of his thought, betray themselves and, in so doing, betray my perverse adherence to the convention of writing an introduction. This "introduction," already aware of its own problematic status *after Derrida* (so to speak, and with apologies to Nicholas Royle),[8] seeks to avoid being merely what it is, while also, and simultaneously, being no more than what Geoffrey Bennington describes as a series of "programmed excuses," a "point of departure" (one among many) and a *strategic* justification."[9]

So, while this introduction is not an introduction, while it is an introduction to the subject of introduction and not an introduction to this volume in any conventional sense, even though or, rather, *because* its excuses are wholly conventional—they are programmed, more or less obviously; they go "by the book," as the phrase has it—it nonetheless aims to be both singular and excessive. In locating itself in this place, and announcing itself as an introduction, it does not pretend to deliver any inaugural statement. This is not a summary or potted version of what follows; neither does it seek to "introduce" Derrida in any real sense, even though this is only what it ever does, such is the complexity with which one has to deal with regard to Derrida's text. Any act of writing *on* or *after* Derrida (and his work should always make any reader wary of the disruptive force of prepositions) can never be anything other than introductory, *while never being up to the responsibility invoked by such an unreasonable demand.* There cannot, therefore, be a question of joining up the dots, getting the complete picture, for all the reasons Derrida teaches us. There is no complete picture to be had (and, anyway, the dots always can be joined in different ways), and the effort to address the work of Derrida exposes, from all false starts, the fallacy of thinking and writing conceived as a mimetic or imitative act.

The singularity of this wholly unjustifiable "introduction" comes, then, from precisely the chances it has of exceeding the program to which it is most patently affiliated. Any chance for the singular articulation arises not in seeking to pretend to present any original thought or thesis, but only through the chance that, in proceeding predictably and with all the stale familiarity that it can muster, resistance might arise from the affirmation and self-awareness of "what the introduction does," thereby exposing what the limits of that act are, comprehending the "technical" aspects of the idea of the introduction conventionally comprehended, but otherwise taking place in an unthought manner. At the same time, however, in seeking to position itself self-consciously in some supplementary fashion, in coming "after" Derrida self-reflexively while situating Derrida's texts as yet to be read, always to come, this failed introduction aims at excessiveness and overflow. Such excess may be taken as performative to the extent that it attempts to proscribe ever moving beyond itself, beyond introduction, as though one could map out the terrain to be covered (as though one were not already lost in the landscape without the possibility of a commanding view of the lay of the land) in some propaedeutic manner, and then embark from the coordinates of some methodology.

I find myself in a double bind, spelled out in the opening epigraphs by Drucilla Cornell and J. Hillis Miller. Cornell alerts the reader to the inescapable responsibility imposed by Derrida's writing because of his attention to the question of undecidability. Miller speaks to the problem inherent in any attempt at generalization concerning the act of reading, taking the singular example of deconstruction (so-called), and the problems attendant on saying what deconstruction is, thereby stabilizing or normalizing it, taming it or otherwise making it conform to some program or notion of a critical methodology. (This is a problem that will be confronted in a number of different contexts throughout the chapters of this volume.) The question of deconstruction—if there can be said to be just one question, one inquiry that abides in the face of an excess beyond plurality—is nothing more nor less than the question of the example. Each example differs from each and every other example. This is the only general remark one can make with any confidence concerning Derrida's writing, Derrida's "procedures." Derrida can only be "introduced" if one begins by acknowledging that, in each and every example, his text gives attention to both the singularity and to an excess irreducible to an economy of textual polysemy. Yet Derrida is only responding himself to that excess named writing, a surfeit unaccountable to logical explanation. It is thus because of Derrida's response to singularity, to surplus and undecidability in every example, as that which makes the example's exemplarity available through reiteration, that writing any "introduction" is, at the risk of reiterating myself, just *so* impossible, so unjustifiable, even though this is precisely what I am seeking to justify.

The chapters herein—and, by extension and in principle, this very volume—seek to negotiate this double bind without resolving it. In each chapter, there is an address to the demand and responsibility involved in any negotiation between singularity and the temptation to generalize. The chapters seek to resist the lure of generalization and totalization by their attention to specific occasions, thereby resisting the very idea of any "introductory" gesture, any gathering or folding of the traces of incommensurable differences into a seamless whole. (Of course, this is not to say anything that is not already well known, but this necessary reiteration very much proves the point about the impossibility both of the idea of introduction and escaping any introductory mode.) They affirm their occasions, and, in so doing, resist, without being reducible to any simple dialectical or oppositional, negative function the idea that they can, through processes of reading, assimilation, and homogenization, become refigured as typical or representative of a particular approach, such as so-called deconstruction, even though it is the case that the title of the present volume plays on this very word, about which I feel so ambivalent, so divided. On the one hand, it is not a word I care for greatly. It is a word that has been overused, misused, misappropriated. This, we might say, is its history and its fortune or misfortune. On the other hand, it is a word that has retained a certain, occasional, strategic usefulness, indicating, at least for some, a certain excessiveness or violence in its very inscription. That it takes place in critical discourse and is therein misrecognized, suggests that it remains to be read, that it leaves in ruins the act of reading, and is, itself, if it is even this, the trace of a certain discourse in ruins, so to speak. Whatever the word might or might not be read as articulating, whatever it might be heard to announce, this often has, in truth, little enough to do with the work of Jacques Derrida; it certainly has little enough to do with the complexity and range of those writings that are signed by Derrida over some forty or more years. Each of the chapters here has a specific focus, responding to aspects of the work of Derrida, to the occasion of reading that Derrida makes possible, although it will be seen that particular interests overlap, particular motifs recur; the chapters constituting this volume are neither wholly singular nor wholly of a piece. They do bring together a number of issues that I take to be sustained, abiding concerns in Derrida's writing. However, this is neither to suggest, nor to be read as implying, that deconstruction-as-methodology either takes place or is otherwise assumed. All the chapters are just self-contained enough to offer a strong focus in their own right, retaining their disparity and heterogeneity from one another.

Arguably therefore, what Derrida makes possible is just this recognition of, and responsibility toward, singularity, a singularity that each of his publications bears witness to, although this is not always read, if it is read at all in particular instances. Derrida's writing bears a marked, and a remarkable, relationship to the singular, even though, arguably, it is also readable as sharing certain affinities with the work of, for example, J. Hillis Miller, Christopher Fynsk, Paul de Man, Peggy Kamuf, Geoffrey Bennington, Nicholas Royle, Jean-Luc Nancy, Philippe Lacoue-Labarthe, Tom Cohen, and others. (And there you have the beginnings of a list, where one might be tempted to enact a taxonomical gathering.) What might be understood as being shared among the texts signed by these names is a detailed and patient attentiveness to a refigured materiality, or to what Cohen has called "the facticity of the textual event itself . . . thematized on the level of inscription, sound, letters, signature, and other figures; not as 'formalist' elements of play divorced from the realm of experience and social change, [as is, and has been, so often charged, such indictments themselves the signs of misreading] but as active agents of transformation in the inner history of reading/writing itself."[10] Alternatively, but again citing Cohen, what is both misunderstood, poorly read, or remaining to be read every time the spectre haunting departments of English named deconstruction is invoked—one might substitute "theory" or "poststructuralism" here with instructive effect—is, quite simply, "a different sort of praxis . . . anti-mimetic, epistemo-political."[11] Similarity between critical voices, comprehended as "a different sort of praxis," one that resists the mimetic through an attention to the materiality of the sign and thereby posits alternative epistemological models of reading and writing, should not, however—and once again—not be raised to the level of a general principle or "theory." As Derrida comments on the question of singularity, relationship, and difference:

> What I share with Lacoue-Labarthe, we also share, though differently, with Jean-Luc Nancy. But I hasten immediately to reiterate that despite so many common paths and so much work done in common, between the two of them and between the three of us, the work of each remains, in its singular proximity, absolutely different; and this, despite its fatal impurity, is the secret of the idiom. . . . *The most urgent thing . . . would be to break with the family atmosphere, to avoid geneaological temptations, projections, assimilations or identifications*[12] (emphasis added).

Derrida's understanding of the respect and responsibility owed to singularity is of vital importance. The question of singularity is also the question of the idiom, that which is idiomatic in any and every act of writing. If deconstruction is anything, it is this: the irreducibility of the idiom to any abstractable formula and that, therefore, which will always already have left in ruins any ontologico-mimetic project in the name of criticism or reading, or any act of reading behaving according to the program of either an identity politics or the politics of identification. Avoiding the temptation to construct a methodology known as deconstruction from reading Derrida would belong to the effort of breaking with the "family atmosphere" about which Derrida rightly cautions.

At the same time, and following from the position articulated by Derrida regarding singularity, it should of course be stressed that Derrida's concern with singularity is not, itself, abstractable or available as a general theory or principle. Instead it emerges as a series of singular responses to, governed by the specific singularities, the irreducible idioms and occasions of encounters with the radically textualized other. Comprehending this, it may be said that Derrida does not so much "introduce" a theory of singularity. Nor does he raise singularity to the level of an absolute principle. Instead, it can be said that he "reintroduces" what is always already under way, that which often remains unread but makes possible the textual event. Derrida does not therefore merely "read" texts in any conventional sense; he introduces what we feel had been familiar, but now cast in an unfamiliar light. As he has pointed out in an interview, he claims never to have "read" certain authors at all. Of Joyce, Celan, and Blanchot, for example, Derrida has remarked that, while he has mobilized a word or two, here or there, as the occasion demands and as the operation of an analytical fulcrum, these authors remain to be read.[13] More recently, he has said of Plato and Aristotle: "I have constantly tried to read and to understand Plato and Aristotle and I have devoted a number of texts to them . . . I think we have to read them again and again and I feel that, however old I am, I am on the threshold of reading Plato and Aristotle. I love them and I feel that *I have to start again and again and again*. It is a task which is in front of me, before me."[14] (emphasis added)

Reading here is the impossible task, always to come and always introduced, begun repeatedly, though never completed. One is never capable of completing a reading. Indeed, beginning reading is only ever the verge of a possibility, a liminal place, from where one starts *again and again and again*. And so on, and so forth, etc. etc. Here, it has to be said, is the admission—the confession rather than the act of crossing any threshold—of the impossible secret of introduction. Once more: one can do nothing other than introduce oneself to reading, to reintroduce oneself to the other; yet one cannot introduce the other, finally, so as to have done with this act, and thereby move beyond the gesture of introduction. Thus, is introduction impossible. And so we are where we began: on the one hand, one can do nothing but begin the introduction, over and over; on the other hand, one can never, for one time only, complete, or even begin to complete an introduction. And what goes for Plato and Aristotle, goes for Derrida, too. The very idea of the introduction therefore introduces, admits one, forcing one to admit, to the experience of the aporetic, the undecidable. All one is left with, all that one has to admit is to come, is this singular experience, and its strategic justification.

As might be imagined, this is not all Derrida has to say on the impossibility of reading. Where he does attempt to speak of reading, he does so in a manner that does not seek to get to grips with the text, with the other, once and for all, thereby putting everything in order or in the right place, gathering everything up for the first and final time. Indeed, his understanding of reading, as already admitted, runs contrary to the conventional comprehension of what it means to read critically. Derrida's perception of the reading act is marked by a sense of chance and the ungovernable, in which something always remains behind and, therefore, to come, to be addressed. As an example of this, take the following passage from *Glas* in which Derrida seeks, in relation to a certain technicity or materiality of reading, the appropriate figure for "reading" the text of Jean Genet:

> I am seeking here the good metaphor for the operation I pursue here. I would like to describe my gesture, the posture of my body behind this machine. . . .
>
> So I am seeking the good movement. Have I constructed something like the matrix, the womb of his text? On the basis of which one could read it, that is, reproduce it?
>
> No, I see rather (but it may still be a matrix or a grammar) a sort of dredging machine. From the dissimulated, small, closed, glassed-in cabin of crane, I manipulate some levers, and, from afar, I saw that *[ça]* done at Saintes-Maries-de-la-Mer at Eastertime, I plunge a mouth of steel in the water. And I scrape *[racle]* the bottom, hook onto stones and algae there that I lift up in order to set them down on the ground while the water quickly falls back from the mouth.
>
> And I begin again to scrape *[racler]*, to scratch, to dredge the bottom of the sea, the mother *[mer]*.
>
> I barely hear the noise of the water from the little room.
>
> The toothed matrix *[matrice dentée]* only withdraws what it can, some algae, some stones. Some bits *[morceaux]*, since it bites *[mord]*. Detached. But the remain(s) passes between its teeth, between its lips. You do not catch the sea. She always reforms herself.[15]

The figure of the dredging machine might appear a curious choice initially for describing *how* one reads, but its figural force is undeniable. It is equally clear from this example that the figure is a singular and excessive one. Certainly, it resists domestication or appropriation. It is not wholly appropriate to the literary-analytical process it disfigures, and could only be translated into a figure for reading generally in the most violent manner, a violence already implicit in the singular, lawless example—I say "lawless" because, while the figure is readable as a figure for reading, reading that figure requires response to this idiomatic occasion while recognizing its relationship to the law of reading; were it absolutely singular, absolutely other, it would not be available for even a partial reading and thus its strange and estranging illicit force would be lost. So, while lawless, the figure of the dredging machine, which arguably invokes an act of writing as much as reading, is appropriate, it appropriates an act of reading to itself, because it wrenches us from our complacent notions concerning the habits, the *habitus*, of reading, the kinds of epistemological habitations concerning reading we habitually inhabit. That it is a figure of machinery, inhabited by and enclosing the apparently sovereign "I," suggests a certain estranging torque between habitation and the uncanny *[unheimlich]*, the more so because we do not have complete control over what is being dredged/read, and because the machine grasps what it will, leaving other matter behind, despite our place behind the controls, indicative in this case of an reading's irreducibility to any wholly anthropomorphic governance. The force of the image is such that the effect is best described not as metaphorical but as an example of catachresis, of catachrestic function, whereby the exchange of images—between reading/dredging, human/inhuman, familiar/unhomely—is so violently dissimilar and yet hauntingly recognizable as to defamiliarize, denaturalize, the assumed relationship. To imagine reading as dredging is to puncture any more or less mimetic correspondence through an analogical attention amounting to a performative act that materially countersigns the textual event, even while, in plying its speculative weave between the mechanical and the human, there is just enough sufficient dislocation to unnerve us, recalling Freud's well-known location of the uncanny in the response to the automaton, which is just human enough, but never quite human.

Derrida follows through his performative engagement in describing how, as the teeth (again, this plays on the human/inhuman, familiar/ uncanny, so typically at work at least since Kleist and Freud) scrape the seabed so, while random particles are picked up, other matter is dropped, something remains, and there is that which cannot be gathered in the first place. The act of gathering remains haunted by its own impossibility. No act of reading or writing can ever attain mastery over the object of its inquiry. It cannot do so for two reasons at least: (1) what reading or writing "pick up" cannot be determined ahead of the event of the textual encounter or the singular response to the other; and (2), whatever reading does gather, there is always that which remains, which are the remains of reading, the excess or supplement beyond the act of reading as the traces of an other writing, and the writing of the other. This is acknowledged most obviously in this passage from *Glas* where French words appear in brackets. Each carries within it an untranslatable, excessive supplement, a singular alterity, other possible phantom effects in sound and/or inscription, that no act of translation as reading or writing can recuperate, but which, prior even to Derrida's response to Genet, is always already at work, as the work of language. Furthermore, Derrida leaves the reader with what was there, so to speak, in the first place, the sea-text reforming itself, as though untouched by any act of reading, of dredging. Derrida teaches, among so many other things, that the condition of textuality is such that all boundaries and divisions assigned to a text are always overrun by, and from within, itself. Attending to this means that, in response to textuality, we acknowledge that what Derrida calls the "accredited concept, the dominant notion of a 'text'"[16] has to be extended and expanded. As is now well known, the text is always "a differential network, a fabric of traces referring endlessly to something other than itself, to other differential traces."[17]

Why reintroduce what is apparently so familiar from Derrida's writing? It seems to me that the idea of text as a differential network is both productive and transformative in radical ways. Rather than being simply available as something akin to a constative statement available to the critic for commentary on other texts—though this is, it has to be admitted, a necessary step in any act of reading or writing "after Derrida"—the notion of text as a fabric of traces has, as yet, not been received fully, as that which motivates and mobilizes any critical act that is also, simultaneously, performative. This is not to suggest that critics have not understood how or to what extent their own writings are composed of so many traces, or that any particular example of writing, while singular, is only both an instant and an instance of the gathering of intensities along so many lines of flight or flows. Instead, what I wish to propose is that the comprehension of the critical act can be transformed if one comprehends the extent to which, while Derrida claims never to have read certain authors, it is also the case that he has never written books as such. His writing is most intimately apprehended not as the pursuance or proving of a thesis so much as it is *occasional*; it operates through and as so many serial interruptions of the differential network. His published texts weave themselves out of that fabric of traces. So it should hardly be surprising that Derrida's interest in phantoms, spectres, ghosts, and phantasms, for example, is not limited solely to *Specters of Marx*. The traces of this interest extend back at least as far as *Disseminations*. Yet, reading after such traces, delimiting the differential network to those locations where the spectre, phantom, or ghost occurs, is, quite obviously to ignore, downplay, or, even on occasion, to sacrifice the work of other traces. One can neither introduce nor ever get beyond hopeless gestures of introducing Derrida's writing because it is resistant to all such thematizing maneuvers aiming at recuperation. As Derrida says of his own fragmentary writing in "The Deaths of Roland Barthes," "I value them for their incompleteness, even more than or their fragmentation, more for their pronounced incompleteness, for their punctuated yet open interruption"; such traces are "little stones, thoughtfully placed, only one each time, on the edge of a name as the promise of a return."[18]

Of course, Derrida is speaking here of the particular form of the essay from which these remarks are taken.[19] But, at the risk of a degree of violence always associated with citation, is it not possible to see, to hear, to read in this commentary, a statement of principle concerning the ways in which Derrida proceeds, negotiating between the event and the program? As Derrida remarks elsewhere, "the thread of repetition . . . splits singularity: as soon as a phrase is iterable, and it is so right away, it can break loose from its context and lose the singularity of its destined addressee. A technical machinery comes in advance to strip it of the unicity of the occurrence and the destination."[20] Taking this to be one possible scenario, working on the principle of the differential network as being composed of so many such open, interruptive placements, otherwise thought of as the "tangled web of these threads"[21] by which this volume is articulated, by which it got under way before it was thought of as such, each of the chapters works with, and works, recurrent threads, reworking them, reformulating, transforming, translating, in particular ways.

If anything can be said to connect these chapters—and this is a highly tentative, provisional connection, one in which the threads are frayed and separate or split off—then the connective tissues may be sought through attention to the constant, albeit discontinuous address to questions of rhetoric, tropes, motifs, and structures, to matters pertaining to elements of poetics and rhythms of reiteration, operating performatively within textual form, all of which may be identified provisionally as occasions. The focus on certain movements, rhythms (again), and resistances, and the concomitant attention to the double logics that inhabit writing and text, belong to an effort to respond to what Derrida has described as "the tension between disruption and attentiveness."[22] From this principle of response, a principle whose responsibility is to open reading to the singularity of the other through "reference . . . to the letter" with "patience [and] slowness,"[23] analysis proceeds, in Derrida's words, by trying "to find out how . . . thinking works or does not work, to find out the tensions, the contradictions, the heterogeneity within"[24] the singular examples herein considered. Such an effort must also necessarily inhabit in a not completely comprehensible or accessible manner one's own writing, rather than being merely the modality by which one questions or analyzes. This involves a "certain zone of disacquaintance, of not-understanding, [which] is also a reserve and an excessive chance—a chance for excess to have a future."[25] But at the same time that this must be the case, that I must in all responsibility recognize that what is remarked is also as true of my own text as it is of those on which I write, I have also to come to terms with the fact that I cannot control this or seek to have control over it in my own writing, I cannot employ it as a ploy within thought, as that which controls the reading from, as it were, the start. Were I to be able to master the procedure, program its effects, I would have given up on what the occasion makes possible, what might or might not occasionally take place, what might take place on certain occasions, as the unforeseeable result of occasions that will have arisen, if they arise at all.

All of which still gets me no further. I still have remaining in front of me the unjustifiable act, that injunction and double bind, of writing an introduction, of sorts, in the face of everything that mediates against such generalizing gestures. Like someone from a novel by Samuel Beckett, I can't go on, I'll go on.[26]

But this is also a way of giving to be read [donner à lire].[27]

Part Two

IDENTITIES IN RUINS

Chapter 2

UNCANNY TEMPORALITIES, HAUNTING OCCASIONS: *SUNSET BOULEVARD*

Cinema, like all other forms of writing, leaves something behind, something involving material effects that cannot be hidden.

Peter Brunette and David Wills

Keep it out of focus—I want to win the foreign picture award.

Billy Wilder

A word on the subject of the various figures of appearing—image, *morphe, eidos,* and especially phantasm . . . we come right back to . . . the "coming before" of the other in the I, i.e. as phantasm. But I would not free myself so easily of phantoms . . . I think that we are structured by the phantasmatic, and in particular that we have a phantasmatic relation to the other, and that the phantasmicity of this relation cannot be reduced, this pre-originary intervention of the other in me.

Jacques Derrida

I

Matters of structure and sequence are announced in and through the notion of "film," staging and representation also; and, through these, the projection of a certain economy or genealogy of cinema, having to do with what remains, what haunts, what retreats and returns, without either having vanished completely or, indeed, ever being there at all. Film is always caught up, even as it mediates, temporal loops, traces, and folds, as is well known. Film, it can be said, is always the scene in which haunting takes place, regardless of narrative concern, thereby revealing in the processes of apparition, arrival, revenance, and withdrawal, the subject's being "structured by the phantasmatic." Moreover, the ghostly condition of the filmic scene, as the revelation of our "phantasmatic relation to the other," articulates the irreducibility of this relation.[1] Film's possibility as everywhere an act of unfolding and staging of spectral relation is here explored through the traces of structures of inheritance, albeit structures that remain in *and* as ruins of themselves. The processes of uncanny transference, transport, transmission, and translation—addressed through the singular example of Billy Wilder's *Sunset Boulevard* are read for their occasional effects, for the ways in which they articulate the temporal disruption of the subject by the material effects of the otherwise immaterial interventions and calls of the other, leaving identity in ruins.

II

Sunset Boulevard (dir. Billy Wilder, 1950) concerns the life—and death—of Joe Gillis (William Holden), a struggling Hollywood screenwriter. It also focuses on the death-in-life of Norma Desmond (Gloria Swanson), a once-famous actress of the silent screen, and now parody of her previous incarnations, as she lives among her memories, delusions, and the remnants of a ghostly Hollywood past. Gillis, attempting to save his car from being repossessed, turns into the driveway of Desmond's rundown Sunset Boulevard mansion. At first, for some inexplicable reason, he is mistaken for an undertaker, the corpse in question being that of the actress's dead chimpanzee. However, on learning Gillis's real profession, Norma invites the writer to stay, to look over an unwieldy, melodramatic script retelling the story of Salomé, on which Norma Desmond has been working. Agreeing, Gillis finds himself also agreeing to stay at the house, ostensibly for convenience' sake, but, in reality, to avoid debt collectors. Once there, he finds it increasingly difficult to free himself from the claustrophobic situation into which he has been dragged. Eventually, following a love affair between the has-been actress and never-was writer, an evasive encounter between Norma and director Cecil B. De Mille, a series of melodramatic arguments, and a failed suicide attempt on the actress's part, Joe attempts to leave, only to be shot by the demented Desmond. The film opens, after the credits, with the image of Gillis's corpse floating in the mansion's swimming pool. An invisible narrator, the dead Joe Gillis, provides the incorporeal voice-over, in order to set the record straight, and to tell the "true" narrative of events, before the media can translate and thereby distort the reality, for which he believes he is the authorial voice. Thus, the film opens with a displacement that is also the sign of an unsuturable gap to which I will return—the disruption between sound and vision, the unseen and the seen, supposing, against all hope, that invisible sound will offer access to, or otherwise stand in for a narrative veracity in the face of all the visual distortions. *Sunset Boulevard* is a film predicated on, and also promising, the possibility of impossibility.

III

This chapter begins by addressing, most immediately, the interanimation between modernism and the various motifs, tropes, and images of the gothic in Hollywood narrative film. In particular, the purpose here is to explore Hollywood's sporadic engagement with modernism, and its more sustained interest in gothic narrative, through the example of Billy Wilder's *Sunset Boulevard*. Developing from this discussion of the movie as an exemplary occasion of the conjunction of differing filmic discourses and cultural identities, I wish to explore film as a fundamentally haunted medium, as already suggested. While the notion of the inescapably spectral condition of various forms of teletechnology is one heavily indebted to the texts of Jacques Derrida, it is also in the writing of Theodor Adorno that one finds the idea of film as spectral or ghostly medium indirectly anticipated. Adorno has remarked that film "resembles" "a subjective

mode of experience."[2] Comparing the phenomenological effect of cinema
with that of the urban subject's experience of and reflection on images of
nature (in a manner perhaps indebted to Walter Benjamin's own reflections on the auratic as marker of the "natural" landscape), Adorno suggests that "these images do not merge into one another in a continuous
flow, but are rather set off against each other in the course of their appearance, much like the magic lantern slides of our childhood. It is in the
discontinuity of that moment that the images of the interior monologue
resemble the phenomenon of writing."[3]

   In a gesture that establishes the fundamentally graphic, yet immaterial condition of projection—one that is, arguably, re-played, re-marked,
through the analogy with, and memory of, the phantasmagorical entertainments of childhood—Adorno's perception of the reception of discontinuous images in film, compared with the work of the magic lantern
slide show,[4] speaks to the phantasmatic condition, summarized by Derrida as so many "various figures of appearing,"[5] appropriate to the reading of film. Also interesting here is Adorno's comparison between
discontinuous motion and writing, which, once again, makes available
the comprehension of film as not merely a mimetic medium. That it *is* a
writing and, in being so, a medium marked by, and re-marking the marks
of discontinuity, delay, relay, return, and retreat, emphasizes the figure of
the trace and what remains invisible within and other than the image, or,
indeed, any supposedly mimetic manifestation. Wilder's film exemplifies
an unstoppable, if discontinuous, graphic flow as the uncanny "ghostwriting," a phantom force erupting from within narrative as a suspensive
modality. Wilder's movie therefore is available for reading as an instance
of modernist self-reflexion, even as it folds onto its narrative trajectory citations of Hollywood cinema. In engaging with such self-reflexivity, it
traces a certain modernist impasse signaled, on the one hand, in the gesture of the death of the author (in the figure of Joe Gillis) and, on the
other, in a romanticized addiction to an aesthetics in ruins.

   One name for such an aesthetic is, perhaps, the gothic. In considering questions of the gothic in relation to *Sunset Boulevard*, I will
start, albeit briefly, by acknowledging the direct or indirect influence of
German Expressionist filmmaking on the construction of mainstream
cinematic narrative shooting and editing in Hollywood. At the most obvious level, this influence is accounted for by the fact that a number of
film writers, directors, cinematographers, and other technicians had
left Germany, and, particularly, Berlin, for Hollywood in the 1920s and

1930s. Billy Wilder was, himself, an émigré filmmaker, born in Vienna in 1906, who worked as a writer among the various luminaries of the UFA studios in Berlin, such as Wiene, Lang, and Pabst, and who subsequently turned to filmmaking from screenwriting in Paris, before moving to the United States in 1934, at a moment when gothic narratives were enjoying particular commercial success in Hollywood. By the time Wilder emigrated, Carl Laemmle Jr. had produced, and James Whale had directed, some of the key films of the Hollywood horror genre in its first flush: *Frankenstein* was released in 1931, while *The Bride of Frankenstein* appeared in 1935, the year after Wilder's arrival in Hollywood. Laemmle had also produced for Universal Studios *The Mummy* (1932), with Whale's star, Boris Karloff, and *Dracula*, with Bela Lugosi (1931). Thus, the genre was well established. At the same time, however, because *Sunset Boulevard* is not in any immediate sense a "horror" film, it is necessary to stress the genre's own self-complicating, excessive, and modernist aspects, so as to situate Wilder's film in relation to what articulates it in somewhat occluded fashion.

David Skal has written one of the most interesting studies of early Hollywood horror movies, in particular the variations on the *Dracula* narrative, in his *Hollywood Gothic: The Tangled Web of "Dracula" from Novel to Stage to Screen*.[6] In this he offers a commentary on the necessity of treating the study of *Dracula*'s various manifestations from an interdisciplinary standpoint: "A completely straightforward academic history would simply not do the subject matter justice; the *Dracula* legend rudely refuses to observe conventional parameters of discussion and touches upon areas as disparate as Romantic literature and modern marketing research, Victorian sexual mores and the politics of the Hollywood studio system."[7] While this remark is directed solely at one narrative, it is, we would argue, applicable to *Sunset Boulevard* if not the entire Hollywood horror genre of the 1930s and 1940s with regard to the disparate discursive cross-contaminations of the kind that Wilder's 1950 film foregrounds in interestingly fragmented and self-reflexive fashion. At the same time as taking into account such matters of influence in passing, and seeking to move beyond the "straightforward" history of intertextuality, this chapter will address the persistent rem(a)inder, the indelible trace that recalls and projects itself as a spectro-cinematic, phantasmatic other in Wilder's movie of the silent screen, its power to signify, to speak from within narrative structure and, thereby, to haunt the "present" that is, supposedly the mise en scène of *Sunset Boulevard*. (Parenthetically, this should give us pause to consider whether Hollywood is, in fact, the site of haunting par excellence.)

What is of especial interest in the acknowledgment of influences and cinematic precursors here is, then, a somewhat more "spectral" influence in Hollywood film narrative, already intimated. The concern is with the haunting of narrative cinema by ghostly manifestations from Hollywood's past and Hollywood's European other, which effect has less to do with the obvious gothic contextualization of the film than with the work of cinema itself as a spectral medium. This haunting effect is inscribed at various levels in Wilder's film, whether the question is one of diegesis, the film's various 'styles' or intermixing of genres, the subsequent fragmentation that such cross-contamination makes happen, or the spectral determination to direct the reception of *Sunset Boulevard*'s narrative through the technological manipulation of certain of its images that mark the film as an exemplary modernist—and gothic—text. Indeed, bearing in mind the gothic and uncanny dimensions of the film, what is described as "interanimation" earlier in this chapter might better be expressed, with regard to Wilder's film, as "revivification." There is readable a filmic return of the dead to a flickering simulacrum of life, in specific relation to what Wilder's narrative appears to posit as Hollywood's decomposing corpse, if not of a kind of "living-on," an eerie survival beyond mere life in a disruptively uncanny fashion. This spectrographic registration of a palsied afterlife addresses how, in the words of Bernard Dick, all "movie-making is necromancy; it is literally bringing the dead to life."[8]

IV

That *Sunset Boulevard* offers a gothic narrative is well known. This is one of the acknowledged and established textual frameworks by which the film is haunted, which it is happy to acknowledge, and which has been subsequently commented on by critics, even though the film is not simply definable as gothic. In effect, the gothic is neither a single genre nor a single identity by which to comprehend this film. Rather, it is, itself, haunted, doubled and redoubled, divided into, and traced by several gothic manifestations, so that, in effect, the film traces, and is mediated by, multiple gothic modes drawn from literature, German

Expressionism, the silent screen, and Hollywood's adaptations of the Gothic novel, to identify only the most obvious. The identity of the gothic divides itself from and in itself, thereby haunting the very nature of the "gothic" through internal returns, transgressions, and arrivals or projections, from gothic's others, or, to put this another way, as the uncanny alterity within the very mode of the gothic. It is thus reasonable to suggest that the film cannot be read as though the gothic were unproblematically translated in any unified fashion by *Sunset Boulevard*, but, instead, that the film text fragments even as it is fragmented by a range of ghostly writings.

The most succinct assessment of the film's gothic aspect comes from Richard Corliss:

> *Sunset Boulevard* is the definitive Hollywood horror movie. Practically everything . . . is ghoulish. The film is narrated by a corpse that is waiting to be fished out of a swimming pool. Most of it takes place in an old dark house that opens its doors only to the walking dead. The first time our doomed hero . . . enters the house, he is mistaken for an undertaker. Soon after, another corpse is buried—that of a pet monkey, in a white coffin. Outside the house is the swimming pool, at first filled only with rats, and "the ghost of a tennis court." The only musical sound in the house is that of the wind, wheezing through the broken pipes of a huge old organ.[9]

This passage is cited by S. S. Prawer in his comprehensive study of Hollywood's indebtedness to German Expressionist horror films such as *Nosferatu* and the uncanny power of early Hollywood horror movies. One narrative aspect of Wilder's text being haunted by its European other is readable in the film's projection of a sense of fatality possessing its characters. Steve Seidman has discussed the influence of Berlin's UFA studio on Wilder in the German studio's use of expressive dramatic lighting, constant camera movement, the narrative interest in the workings of the psyche, and the related use of framing and lighting techniques to articulate the "inner life" of characters, and the exploration of the "darker aspects of human nature."[10] In this, Wilder manifests an indebtedness to the work of Murnau, whose own filmic techniques have been acknowledged by Alexandre Astruc as inscribing fatality within "the most harmless elements of the frame," a condition foregrounded most obviously throughout Wilder's film in the character of Joe Gillis. However, in

almost every aspect of *Sunset Boulevard* there is a similarly haunting uncanniness, perceivable as what Astruc (again speaking of Murnau) describes as a "diffuse presence of an irremediable *something* that will gnaw
at and corrupt every image" (emphasis added).[11] This "diffuse presence,"
this uncanny and unnameable *something*, is, we would argue, the effect
of the spectral.

Thus, Corliss's evaluative narrative précis is supported in its con-
tentions concerning the gothic frameworks by the film's nonnarrative
elements, which have been translated from their German context, and
yet which disturb in excess of the film's narrative. *Sunset Boulevard*'s
use of gloom and shade, stark lighting contrasts, and chiaroscuro effects, for example, impose themselves within the film in a fashion not
wholly consonant with the historical tale being told. While the story
may be read as concerning itself with the crisis between two different
manifestations of Hollywood, the "gothicizing" of the text creates a
temporal and aesthetic dislocation in the dialectic between the Hollywood of sound and that of silent image, so as to blur, and thus make impossible, any straightforward binary separation of the elements. Wilder
brings together two contesting, yet overlapping modes of Hollywood
representation (which are echoed at the level in the film's play in signifying codes between "horror" and "film noir"; in this context we might
recall Dickens's cross-contamination between comedy and gothic), only
to explore the limit of each text, the inability of each to address the
other. In this failure to communicate, a failure that can be read as a certain blindness of the gaze in the face of the screening of the other, there
takes place as the deconstructive work of *Sunset Boulevard* the concomitant opening of the aporetic, which the act of reaching the limit repeatedly unfolds in an abyssal fashion. And it is through this aporia that
the excessive, the hauntingly uncanny and gothic, project themselves,
retreating and returning, so that it remains undecidable exactly how to
read this film. What it is possible to read, however, is the blindness from
either side of Joe Gillis and Norma Desmond: neither comprehends
fully (if at all) that they are caught up in a ghost story, and, furthermore, that they are the ghosts, the spectral embodiments of two
repeatedly corpsing Hollywoods.

Wilder also works constant camera movement counterpointed by
moments of stillness in order to disorient in a manner reminiscent of
the film's European predecessors. There is, as well, the occasionally
skewed, emotive camera angle, and the estranging register of any one of

a number of protagonists' facial responses, lingeringly filmed. The camera pauses on expressions as the visible codes of emotional response, particularly those of Gloria Swanson, who plays faded silent star Norma Desmond, but it also hovers around the facial articulations, as instances of a silent, yet expressive visual "writing," of failed screenwriter Joe Gillis, and failed director/husband/servant Max von Mayerling (played by German director, Erich von Stroheim), along with other minor characters, such as the forgotten silent movie star played by Buster Keaton. As Ed Sikov puts it, and speaking in litotes, given the excessive character of the film's images, "Wilder chooses shots to express emotions."[12] The facial shot interrupts narrative with the inscription of a visual "stutter," imposing itself and remarking silently as the arrival of a suspensive modality from some other location. In this, the play of German Expressionist cinema and Hollywood's silent era is put to work, even as it can be read as returning from the past to disturb the film's present (a gothic motif itself on which *Sunset Boulevard* relies). Simultaneously, the shooting and framing of momentarily still faces turn the characters into viewers, doubling the gaze of the audience, and thereby returning to us in an uncanny fashion our own spectatorial—and spectral—role. Such "cinematographic enunciation"[13] is readable in the example of *Sunset Boulevard* as being haunted from within by an invisible, ghostly gaze, while, in turn, the audience is written as haunted in its response to the images that inscribe our emotional response to the narrative. We recognize the gaze as spectral inasmuch as we comprehend how the gaze always comes from somewhere else, how someone or something, that "diffuse presence," is always watching from some other place or, to complicate this, somewhere *other* than the place from where one watches another watching.

The phrase "cinematographic enunciation" refers to "an appropriation of the expressive possibilities of the cinema . . . enunciation involves a conversion of a language into a discourse. . . . Enunciation in fact constitutes the base upon which the persons, places, and times of a text are articulated."[14] In the case of Wilder's film, however, what occurs repeatedly is the play with and—concomitant dissolution of—fixed places and times. This occurs not only within the film in its acknowledgment of multiple cinematic and narrative frameworks, which are strategically alluded to only so as to effect their partial erasure and thereby make apparent the implicitly spectral nature of such referentiality (a representation in and of ruins), but, also, in the exemplary instance of the gaze between the world of the film and the world of the audience. Through the dislocating power of the gaze, the audience finds itself projected as one possible site of the other of the film in the faces of various characters, while, it is implied, the audience is itself transformed into a spectral phenomenon, haunting the ghostly characters on the screen. If *Sunset Boulevard* is a film concerned with various Hollywoods, and the crises that modes of representation come to face and, thereby, restage in and through the transformations of the various technologies of projection and representation, it is also a movie haunted by the fear of the loss of audience (the obsession, we might say, that haunts Norma Desmond; her "fan mail" is, after all, "ghost-written" by her servant, Max von Mayerling).

As already remarked, through the ways in which facial expression is shot, the film acknowledges not only early European, specifically German, cinema, it also enunciates its being haunted by the faces and techniques of the silent screen, as Hollywood's ghostly pasts catch up with, thereby disturbing from within, Hollywood's moribund present, a present that we understand is only ever an iterable series of flickering simulacra. These projections of otherness destabilize any concrete reality, presence, or its unequivocal representation through a staging of representation as, perhaps, a phenomenological apperception of sensibility irreducible either to any controllable semantic horizon or temporal location. The film thus opens for us a sense of uncanny ghostliness by reminding its viewers that there is always a "relation to a past that, never behind us, is hounding and calling up to us," as Avital Ronell suggests in her consideration of haunting.[15] Such hauntedness "allows for visitations without making itself at home . . . a relation has been opened to another text which manifests itself without presence yet with infinite nearness."[16] Thus, *Sunset Boulevard* is opened, and opens itself to our reading, by the constant, multiple projections of alterity that countersign the film with various traces of easily acknowledged frameworks, while neither settling, nor allowing the viewer to settle, into a cozy domesticated familiarity with such traces. To borrow from Ronell again, the film, in its sleepwalking irreality, is seen as constantly "taking dictation from a text of the Other."[17]

There are other aspects of the film that can be read as being traced by the shades of Hollywood's own gothic past, particularly in its striking use of the dilapidated, uncanny architectural mass that is Desmond's house. The German and Transylvanian castles of films such as *Frankenstein, The*

Bride of Frankenstein, and *Dracula*, while translated into the "rotten sumptuousness and sumptuous rot"[18] of a Sunset Boulevard mansion, haunt this house, making it all the more uncanny as we recognize that its shadows are their shadows, its "atmosphere" perhaps the most pervasive enunciation of haunting that Wilder's film manifests. As one critic has remarked, the house "is more ghostly than derelict."[19] As is well known, the idea of the house and the uncanny are always intimately connected, the one implicated in the other, at least since Freud, and the figural dislocation of the *un/heimlich*.[20] In the case of *Sunset Boulevard*, Norma Desmond's mansion is both gothic and uncanny, visually and atmospherically. It is gothic in its outward appearance, with its broken shutters, weed–strewn tennis court, unkempt vines, and, internally, with overdecorated, baroque, even exotic rooms. The house is unhomely to the extent that it is always already depicted as only ever the remains of a house. A house in ruins, its aesthetics are those of what we might call the phantom-picturesque.[21]

On pausing to look at the house, Joe Gillis appropriately remarks that the house recalls nothing so much as Dickens's Miss Havisham "in her rotting wedding dress." Typically for a hack screenwriter, Gillis conflates gothic house with equally gothic character, as figures for time simultaneously transfixed and anachronistically unseated, and, therefore, unnerving, in the summary process reducing *Great Expectations* to a treatment.[22] There is also, in this comparison, an anticipation of Norma Desmond herself, who, like Miss Havisham, has been left behind, haunted by her other selves, who, via her gestures, her poses, the position of her hands as part of "an exaggeration of the coded gesticulation of the silent cinema,"[23] project through Desmond to disturb Gillis, and to disturb as well the less obviously stylized acting methods of 1950s Hollywood; and, finally, such performative effects return from within the stylized representation of the self, in order to disturb the viewer in disrupting filmic unity. But to return to the house: house and identity are one. Moreover, as if to emphasize further the gothic nature of Norma Desmond's house, and to bring back to us the gothic trace yet again, Gillis also describes the house as "that grim Sunset Castle." (It is perhaps not too fanciful, given the fact that the majority of the film's scenes are shot after dark and in the house, to suggest that "sunset" is itself indicative of a moment of temporal transition, of "translation," if you will, from rational reality to the time of the gothic, even as the name is also suggestive of the twilight of cinema.)

However, it is not only a matter of gothic resemblance and atmosphere with regard to the house. What makes it also uncanny is the spectral persistence of the past within the house. Everything in the house is anachronistic, including the inhabitants, so that the sense is one of constant visitation from somewhere else. It is impossible for the viewer to settle into a domestic, stable relationship with the house, because everything about it forestalls homeliness while emphasizing an uncanny sense of being ill at ease. Furthermore, the past haunts the house's narrative present through the countless photographs of Norma Desmond's younger self. If cinema's greatest illusion is the animation or revivification of the dead through the technology of moving successive still images so as to create a false impression of living, of survival beyond death, this film strains against itself to draw the viewer's gaze to the mortification, the lifeless temporal suspension implicit in the photographic text.

Additionally, the use of still photographs within the film presents the viewer with an uncanny and disjunctive oscillation within the field of the film's representations, and for two reasons. On the one hand, the viewer is looking, not at photographs of Norma Desmond, even though this is what we are asked to accept them as. What we are looking at are endless rows of pictures of Gloria Swanson. Yet these "stills" do not give us access to the actress or her past as such; instead, they figure the singularity of performance, presentation, and representation as so many assumptions of unreal identities. It is not simply that we cannot say that these are photographs of either Gloria Swanson or Norma Desmond (in a certain way, they can only be read, if at all, as both). Rather, the question raised by such images is, more fundamentally, one that calls into doubt any ontological certainty, given that the *punctum* of the still image arrives only to puncture the truth of representation and the grounds of its possibility, through the haunting intimation that any representation is always ghosted by the phantom of a staged and fictive identity. The real and fictive silent screen and era haunt both temporally and diegetically, for these photographs return from outside the film, as projections of those other Hollywoods. At the same time, the viewer is, arguably, disturbed by the presence of still photography, of fixed, "dead" images, within the apparent animation that is cinema, as a countersignature to cinema's ability to perform like Victor Frankenstein. In this use of the photographs there is readable the slightest ghostly echo of *The Picture of Dorian Gray*, both Wilde's novel and the 1945 film version. What troubles about the photographs most radically, however, is not the idea that the photographs might refer unequivocally to some simple, prior presence. Instead, they play on this possibility of locating the knowable and, in doing so double the spectrality of—and from within—representation, its constant haunted status as rem(a)inder, leaving in ruins the promise of ontological guarantee. As Geoffrey Batchen comments on still photography, it "is consistently positioned by its commentators within some sort of play between activity and passivity, presence and absence, time and space, fixity and transiency, observer and observed, real and representation, original and imitation, original and difference."[24] It is precisely such play that is spectral, because it maintains an unstoppable movement between life and death (thereby collapsing the absolute distinctions between such terms), as an expression of spectral *maintenance*, to paraphrase Derrida.[25]

The photographs are not the only manifestation of a ghostly oscillation within differing identities and differing temporalities, with regard to Norma Desmond. Particularly unsettling is the scene in which Desmond has Max run one of her silent films for Gillis. Of course, logic dictates that this is a Gloria Swanson movie that both they and we are witnessing, as Wilder cuts between the projection within the projection and the backlit image of Desmond and Gillis as audience. The movement between shots suggests, to borrow a phrase of Derrida's on spectrality, something "furtive and untimely,"[26] a projection of manifestation of the haunting effect that unsettles time. The time of the narrative is clearly disturbed, but so too is the time of film itself, as one Hollywood is brought to the limit of its expression in being made to confront another. At the height of this uncanny scene, Desmond arises from the couch. Caught in the projected light of the film projector, Desmond silently turns and gestures, in a manner haunted by and recalling her other self, just seen on the screen within the screen. Momentarily, Wilder's film is disrupted internally in an anachronistic overwriting of its own codes, which come together violently while, equally fiercely, resisting resolution into a unified readable image. Instead, film opens itself in an instance of figural and projected alterity, marking the breach of a ghostly aporia, which disrupts and thus speaks, albeit indirectly, to the condition of cinema itself. Clearly the house resonates in the most spectral fashion and, in its and the film's exploration of the condition of Hollywood, projects, albeit ironically, what Robert Stam describes as "Hollywood's collective dread of obsolescence onto the antiquated style embodied in Wilder's vampiric personage [Norma Desmond]".[27]

Everywhere, then, within the narrative and its images apparently gothic motif and motivation appears, as critics have conceded. Indeed, it positively flaunts its necro- and spectro-poetic elements in a manner that is simultaneously ghastly and comic. To recall Richard Corliss, the tennis court is only a ghost of itself, in Joe Gillis's own words, while, on the first night of Gillis's stay in the mansion, he and the audience witness the chimpanzee's burial in the grounds, with Max von Mayerling carrying the coffin in a scene of absurd solemnity and solemn absurdity. And then there is the organ. Not only does the wind blow through its pipes, breathing artificial life into its corpse, as Corliss asserts, but von Mayerling has occasion to play the organ in one of the film's frequent grand guignol moments. This image is reminiscent of *The Phantom of the Opera*, but the question is, which one? Lon Chaney's 1925 film, or the more recent 1943 production, with Claude Rains? Arguably both disturb this singularly gothic instance, as Hollywood returns within its own constructions, both films are caught this undecidable moment.[28] The gothic occasion takes place as the performative event marking the ruin, once again, of representation.

V

As has been remarked previously, Bernard Dick suggests that this is "a film about the living dead." As Corliss's précis points out, the opening image is of a corpse floating in the swimming pool. This scene is, itself, discomforting for the viewer, for the camera is placed in the pool, underneath the floating body, the eyes of which remain open, while the body's disembodied voice begins the narrative, forever displaced from the now lifeless corpse. And, as Ed Sikov sums it up, "[t]he effect is spectacularly macabre. A dimly recognizable body floats slowly across the screen as cops look down and flashbulbs fire. The audience is unnerved not only by the ghastliness of the corpse but also by the position we are asked to assume."[29] This is not, however, the original opening sequence. Another was shot, but subsequently cut before general release, as it generated negative responses in the preview audiences in the Midwest. This missing scene, familiar among Wilder's critics but not generally well known otherwise, was shot in the Los Angeles County Morgue.[30] The shot begins with a body being wheeled in on a gurney, covered with the obligatory white sheet. Past rows of other corpses, the camera follows the body until camera movement, body, and gurney come to rest. A voice asks the corpse how it came to be there, in response to which the dead Joe Gillis sits up, and begins to narrate the tale of his life—and his death.[31]

The trace of death and intimations of the gothic are everywhere, as we can see. A studio executive tells Joe Gillis that one of his scripts is "as dead as a door nail." On his arrival at Norma Desmond's mansion, the scriptwriter Gillis is mistaken for an undertaker, as Corliss mentions, and is shown into an exotic room in which a dead chimpanzee rests in state, where Desmond makes clear the specifications for the animal's coffin.[32] In a later discussion of cinema, Norma Desmond says to Gillis that films are "dead, they're finished," while of scriptwriters she makes the following comment: "You've made a rope of words and strangled the business." Moreover, there is, she acknowledges, "a microphone to catch the last gargle, and technicolor to photograph the red, swollen tongue." This remark comes back to haunt Desmond, however. Later visiting De Mille at the Paramount Studio, the actress is disturbed by the "dead" technology of sound cinema in a scene notable for its silence, when a boom microphone hovers, comically and disturbingly, around Norma's head, as if inviting her to speak. Instead, with a fierce stare and a gesture worthy of the silent screen she swats away the boom. However, the comic-gothic aside, if cinema is the art of the living dead, an act of necromancy, it is also a murderous art, indulging grimly, if we accept Desmond's summary, in a gradual process of self-slaughter, where the entire industry reflexively engages in the voyeuristic act of making the ultimate snuff film.

VI

If *Sunset Boulevard* is concerned with the inescapable confrontation with various haunting pasts or the possibility at the very least of glimpsing the indelible trace of such spectrality, as it takes on a momentarily visible form in various aspects of the film, it is also a film interested in the disturbance, within the industry, of the sites and very condition of its production. The film films the place of film—Hollywood—as the site of its own fears and projections, even as Wilder's film is ghosted by numerous citations of Hollywood's others, some of which have already been considered. The title of the film is an exemplary figure for this doubling of citation and site, of trace and place. Wilder's title projects indirectly a certain manifestation of Hollywood, or, let us say, possible manifestations. The title—*Sunset Boulevard*—configures economically, even as it disfigures itself, the signs of drifting. That slippage at work in the title of the film is announced in that, simultaneous to the naming of the film, there is also named that street from which the film takes its name, and that is, furthermore employed as a metonymic or synecdochic figure for Hollywood; or, rather, for two Hollywoods at least: that of the film, the site of the film's production in 1950, and *in* the film, the place in which narrative takes place. Thus, the title also names, even as it enacts, a kind of wayward instability, an effect of haunting or drifting. *Sunset Boulevard:* the inscription is already doubled, and therefore displaced, within itself, in the disinterrance that is at work. The disfiguration or disjunction named in the street name/film title is a manifestation of a disturbing act of screenwriting as an act of ghosting, serving to project simultaneously the apparition of a particularly gothic manifestation of Hollywood presented through the film's narrative, while presenting itself as an exemplary instance of Hollywood gothic.

The film begins with its title, as do most films, singularity haunted by, threatening to dissolve into generic convention. At the same time, its opening image is that of the street name, painted on the curb, a structural, if not an architectural boundary intimating that, spectrally at least, all boundaries and their figural inscriptions are there only to be dissolved and crossed. The film begins then, clearly enough, in an instance of simultaneity, with both street name and film title, with the one as the other, each in the place of the other, and both serving to disturb the other's "proper" function. Of this shot, Bernard Dick has pointed out that the film starts in the gutter, and that this is a fitting opening visual metaphor from which we can read the film's take on Hollywood.[33] Whatever we are looking at, any certainty we invest in the act of reading is momentarily disturbed via a filmed act of writing, or, to put this another way, an act of projection, the projection of writing, that oscillates—between, on the one hand, narrative summarized in the aphorism of the title, and, on the other, topographical reality—in the momentary stillness of the shot, before the camera begins to pull away, taking in the street itself.

The disjunction and redoubling effected by the border transference of the title alerts the viewer to the film's modernist self-awareness. At the same time, the disjunctive play between textual forms and the film's numerous others belongs to a more general deconstructive play within the idea of representation, a collapse *and* disinterrance between stable notions of "inside/outside," or between the real and the fictional, through which, as Derrida argues, "the point of origin becomes ungraspable."[34] If *Sunset Boulevard* is a haunted text or, at least, if it manifests so many aspects of haunting, the uncanny, and the spectral, this is because it makes itself available as only the sum of the movement of its traces, none of which are given precedence over any others. All is projection and return without center, presence, or origin. To borrow from Derrida again, there is "an infinite reference" between images; there "is no longer a simple origin. For what is reflected is split *in itself* and not only as an addition to itself or its image. The reflection, the image, the double, splits what it doubles."[35] This is not only the case with Wilder's working of the title. It can also be seen if we recall the play in the film between the still photographs or film projection in Norma Desmond's house and the film itself, or if we acknowledge to what extent the film is readable as being, in some manner, always about the production of film in general, and not simply, reflexively, about the example of itself. *Sunset Boulevard* is archly reflexive in a manner that unfolds the condition of all cinema—film is always already caught up in projections of alterity, even when it seeks to suppress its others in order to create the illusion of supposedly simple representation.

As one final narrative example of the simultaneity of disjunction *and* doubling by which the film is both articulated and fragmented, let us take the last scene of *Sunset Boulevard*. After the police and the press have arrived (for the second time—nothing in this film takes place just once; such a scenario is impossible), following the shooting of Joe Gillis, still and movie cameras are set up at the foot of Miss Desmond's staircase. Appearing to break the frame, or, at least, to cross and then recross the place where a boundary between diegesis and the real might be discerned, von Mayerling/von Stroheim assumes a directorial position between the cameras, to direct his leading lady's entrance/exit, thereby disturbing once more the boundaries between filmed and filming Hollywood. The lights go up, the cameras roll, and in that, by now, well-known scene, Norma Desmond moves in exaggerated, silent–screen fashion, as the ghost of herself, the ghost of Gloria Swanson making the image waver, as she descends the staircase. The edit switches to a view through a camera, toward which the actress glides, until her face fills the screen, until she *becomes* the screen. In a final excessive moment, the audience has the gaze of the dead turned back upon it in an encapsulating image *and* its projection, a shimmering, soft focus image supremely silent for all the melodrama of the score, as though the ghostly technology of silent cinema had overflowed, into the space and time of sound cinema, saturating invisibly the diegetic space of the talkie but gesturing beyond that also, to the spaces of newsreel and reportage. Everything about these final moments is extravagant and phantastic. Her face the final image we see, it haunts all the more insistently for the ways in which the scene has doubled every aspect of itself, while Norma Desmond/Gloria Swanson returns our collective gaze in a filmic suggestion of infinite reflection and reference, to recall Derrida. Even the question of the scenic descent redoubles and thus divides. For Norma Desmond's descent is zeugmatic, haunted within itself; it is a descent into complete madness and, also, a descent down the stairs, and this, in turn, is both humorous *and* terrifying, a moment of grand guignol, as Ed Sikov suggests.[36] It is, furthermore, yet another example of the ways in which the gestures of the silent screen haunt Wilder's film, even while the staircase is, it might be remarked in passing, possibly reminiscent of that on which Count Dracula welcomes Jonathan Harker in the 1931 film of Bram Stoker's novel.

Ultimately, how we read this scene remains undecidable. It haunts therefore through the very undecidability of its traces, which, while partly comprehensible as the projected remains of other cinematic modes, remain to be read. In this, it is exemplary, a singular moment. And yet, simultaneously—and this is a sign of, on the one hand, its undecidability and, on the other, the figural redoubling in which it partakes so excessively—the stair scene is, in its spectro-rhetorical mode, typical of every other moment in the film, from the disjointing instance of the title as the inaugurating instance of the film's disturbance of, within, itself. Such projections of Hollywood's others are everywhere in *Sunset Boulevard*, as they are everywhere in the house of Norma Desmond; and yet they are nowhere as such, merely the apparitions caught in the flickering of lights and the recesses of penumbra. There are discernible the effects of ghostwriting at work within and across the film, to such an extent that the film's haunted quality dismantles what Laura Oswald describes, echoing Derrida, as the "logic of the single image."[37] While, as Oswald puts it, films conventionally "produce messages by means of codes governing the organization of point of view,

continuity, and rhetorical associations between elements of film discourse,"[38] as suggested earlier, *Sunset Boulevard* makes apparent its
uncanny and haunted condition through its ghostly play of various cinematic modes of production, and its spectral dalliance with differing
codes and rhetorical associations, so as to unsettle the viewer even as it
haunts its own projected space from within. This, we would conclude, is
even the case with the film's gothic frames of reference. For not only
are there several gothic modes with which the film toys, but the gothic
as that which serves to shape the narrative is also challenged. In this
there is readable the haunting work of modernism.

VII

If the emphasis in matters of genre has thus far been on the gothic, it
is also important that we do not forget that *Sunset Boulevard* doubles
and haunts itself with a contemporary genre—film noir. Even the films
associated with Hollywood gothic in a narrow sense, such as the various
Frankenstein films, *Dracula* or *The Mummy,* were giving way to noir,
and to disturbances of a more immediately comprehensible kind. The
audience no longer had to be transported to Europe to find the
mythopoetic figures of alterity; they could, instead, turn to homegrown
fears, in the shape of gangsters and murders. Wilder acknowledges this
in *Sunset Boulevard,* a film that, according to Axel Madsen, "brought
the American *film noir* to its paroxysm."[39] Indeed, at yet another of the
film's self-reflexive moments, Gillis leaves Desmond's haunted house
for a film industry New Year's party. On his arrival at that party he is introduced by an assistant director/friend as a suspect in the notorious
Black Dahlia case.[40] Here, Wilder interjects a contemporary (and, to this
day, unsolved) Hollywood murder case, as a possible reference to audience interest in both the case itself and to the ascendance of *film noir* as
a genre. The reference is both chilling and yet another example of
Wilder's gallows humor, for, like so many of the young women at the
New Year's party, the victim in the Black Dahlia case, Betty Short, was
an aspiring starlet. This haunting allusion to the Dahlia at once invokes
Hollywood mythology, or what has been described, with reference to
the murder in somewhat paroxysmal prose, as "an almost mythical
symbol of unfathomable *Hollywood Babylon*/film noir glamour-cum-

sordidness,"[41] while bringing back through the fictive framework an eerie, if fleeting apparition.

There are many other aspects of *Sunset Boulevard* that draw on noir, however. From that insistent voice-over of the dead author that punctuates almost the entire film (only to give way to Desmond's final descent), to the sirens of police cars; from the Los Angeles setting with its palm trees and unreal rain storms (recall any Raymond Chandler screen adaptation), to the parody of the film noir plot,[42] where the "crime" becomes the failure of Joe Gillis to keep up his car payments, and, so, is subsequently pursued: in all these motifs, there is much about *Sunset Boulevard* invites us to read its indebtedness to noir, including the camera work and lighting (which we have already attributed to gothic filmic technique *and* European Expressionist cinema). Indeed, the signs of noir are as insistently prevalent as are the traces of the gothic. In the face of this, it is arguable that the interanimation of noir and gothic is indicative of a certain modernist aesthetic, where no single narrative mode dominates but, instead, various modes of articulation compete for our attention.[43]

As Neil Larsen suggests, drawing on the work of Ernesto Laclau and Chantal Mouffe, "[i]n the constant joining, severing, and rejoining of 'elements' there subsists . . . not merely the untruth of representation and "fixity" but the possibility of an alternative form of praxis. . . . Modernism itself might thus be grasped as a profound movement of 'disarticulation'."[44] That disarticulation is at work everywhere in and through *Sunset Boulevard* has already been seen, and all the more so in contrast to the attempted "truth" and unity of representation that Joe Gillis's voice-over strives to attain. To the extent that mainstream Hollywood cinema has always already put to work and thereby subsumed modernist aesthetic experimentation into "practical" and "applied" manifestations such as reiterable techniques for the purposes of the apparent unity of representation, we would argue that that which is modernist about a film such as Wilder's is already spectral inasmuch as it returns disruptively from within all attempts at representation on the part of the movie. That the film is readable as spectral acknowledges the extent to which the film foregrounds its joining, disjointing, mixing, and disarticulation of genres, all of which in turn destabilize the stability of representation on which recognizable genres rely. And it is in the noir technique of voice-over that the disarticulation of modernist aesthetic and/as haunting projects itself.

VIII

Before turning to voice-over, a digression: while film is always spectral, it is not necessarily gothic. In such cases, film can become all the more uncanny, for resisting playing to the more obvious gothicization of those narratives that concern ghosts conventionally understood. Indeed, it is arguably part of the appeal of *Sunset Boulevard* that it mixes genres to the extent that it can be read as doing. Of course, filmmakers have remained enthralled by the ghostly and the gothic, as well as the ghostly that is not conventionally gothic, as a number of films released over the summer and autumn of 1999 make clear. *Blair Witch Project, Stigmata,* and *The Haunting* are the three most obvious examples; following these there is also Tim Burton's *Sleepy Hollow;* but more interesting than these have been *The Sixth Sense, American Beauty, Bringing Out the Dead,* and, subsequently, *The Others* and *The Devil's Backbone,* over which films it is perhaps worth pausing momentarily.

The first, *The Sixth Sense,* toys with the gothic elements of the Hollywood horror genre, though, interestingly, it ultimately rejects these in favor of another kind of storytelling, involving a principal character who is dead throughout the film, and who therefore, in a sense, returns to haunt the movie from the very first, even though, like the principal female character of *The Others,* he never realizes he is dead until near to the end of the film. Such a moment of reflexive revelation is not tied simply to the narrative trajectory, but is indicative in a particularly stark fashion of an uncanny temporal chiasmus implicit in any filmic occasion. Like *Sunset Boulevard, American Beauty* is marked by an interest in acts of filming (this time in the form of video), their temporal interruptions and traces, and is also narrated by a dead narrator, who has to be dead before the film begins in order to narrate from some invisible location, thereby suspending any simple temporal frame, but whose death is not made explicit until the close of the narrative. Voice-over thus serves as a process of bearing-witness, in this example to one's self as an other. Scorcese's *Bringing Out the Dead* also employs a sporadic voice-over, the direct diegetic function of which is never established, thereby remaining all the more haunting for the disjunction this creates in the film, even as it serves in the filmic address to interrelated questions of memory and mourning or, as Nicholas Cage's paramedic character (whose voice is also that of the voice-over) makes clear, bearing witness to, and thereby bringing out the dead. In a certain fashion, this expresses another haunting aspect of the function of cinema—to bear witness, to recall, and to allow for the projection of the other, the *revenant*. Such witnessing and re-membering is worked out through the ghostly apparition of a murdered child in *The Devil's Backbone,* a film that works directly with all the technological devices of cinema in conjunction with the gothic motifs of narrative, in order to offer singular testimony in response to the history of the Spanish Civil War. The effects of such spectral tracing disrupt any straightforward temporality in the film, as already remarked. This is the case whether one considers most immediately those *revenants* that return from cinema's past, a past—perhaps innumerable pasts—projected, for example, by *Sunset Boulevard* onto itself, or whether one considers the technological-spectral *revenance* of the technique of voice-over.

There is clearly a tension, a doubling and disjunction, in *Sunset Boulevard* between a cinema reliant on sound and an other cinema of silent, yet expressive, images. It is therefore part of the highly entertaining ironic displacement that this film effects that the voice-over, while being a cinematic technique belonging to filmic representation, nonetheless remains at the same time resolutely hidden, off-screen *and* of the film, at its margins, so to speak, as we have already indicated. To recall earlier remarks, the voice-over operates between living and dead, real and fictional. And, as if to double the irony and to widen the disjunctive aporia of *Sunset Boulevard* even further, the voice is, as we know, that of a dead man. As Joan Copjec puts it of noir, "the noncorporealized voice . . . issues from a space other than that of the screen, an unrepresented, [and, we would argue, unrepresentable] undetermined space."[45] Furthermore, and in the context of film noir, "speech . . . is the death of the thing . . . and nothing has seemed more obvious in the criticism of film noir than this association of death with speech, for the voice-over is regularly attached to a dead narrator."[46] Inasmuch as the voice is that of a dead man, a man whose "living" had been in the trade of dead words and writing, the voice is also not simply an origin, nor does it come from any identifiable place, as Copjec implies. Its articulation is undeniably the manifestation of the ghost, a form of spectral and technological *revenance*, endlessly iterable—and, therefore, a form of writing rather than voice—through the medium of cinema, and thus always already separated from the subject. Understanding this, we comprehend how, in film in general, but in *Sunset Boulevard* in particular, "image and sound introduce a rupture at the heart of enunciation that mobilises both of them simultaneously; or more precisely, they reveal within enunciation a breach."[47] In film noir, the breach becomes even more pronounced, in the voice's arrival as the projection of the other, in that, to cite Copjec once more, the "noir hero's voice-over narration simply diverges from the *truth* of the image."[48] The spectral voice maintains the hauntedness by returning to reinscribe all the effects of disjointing and doubling by which the film disturbs and is disturbed, by which it is remarked as profoundly uncanny, and by which we, as viewers, are both fascinated and made uneasy. Voice-over thus returns the graphic trace as the reminder of the impossibility of presence, of the present. Voice-over is that ghostly manifestation, an intensification of the phantasmatic, everywhere in the time of the film, yet coming from the film's future, and never present as such. The voice projects itself from the place of an invisible gaze, and the gaze is that of the spectre, watching us watching. There is thus a certain haunting vigilance in film constantly in operation, where acts of memory—memories of and from the past, and the future memory of *Sunset Boulevard*'s present, slipping into narrated past from the dead voice of the screenwriter—conjoin, only to disjoin the times of projection and the times of narration.[49]

Yet the voice is not, obviously, the same as a gaze. Voice-over, this disembodied, incorporeal remainder of that which has never been embodied, is wholly uncanny, more so than any other aspect of the film text. Of the intensification effected by the technological graphics of the voice, Derrida has remarked: "If one holds the voice to be an auto-affective medium . . . an element of absolute presence, then the fact of being able to keep the voice of someone who is dead or radically absent, of being able to record, I mean reproduce and transmit, the voice of the dead or of the absent living, is an unheard-of possibility, unique and without precedent."[50] Given *Sunset Boulevard*'s insistence on the radical discontinuity between silent and sound film, the joke of the dead man's voice-over all the more insistently urges on us the uncanny power of this "unheard-of possibility." With regard to the effects of voice-over, Derrida's commentary on the recorded voice is worth quoting at some length: "Whatever comes to us through the voice thus reproduced in its originary production is marked by a seal of authenticity and of presence that no image could ever equal."[51] Joe Gillis's voice intends precisely to impress itself as imprimatur on the audience, and as countersignature to anything that might merely be seen. Derrida continues:

> The power of television [and, by extension, cinema] is vocal, at least as much as radio . . . a voice sill arouses suspicion much less easily, less

spontaneously, than an image. This is related to the value of real presence imparted by the spectrality of a reproduced voice—to a degree and according to a structure that visual virtuality will never reach. . . . The recording of a voice reproduces a production. The vocal "image" is the image of a living production and not of an object as spectacle. In this sense it is not even an image any longer, but the reproduction . . . of production itself . . . the production is archived as the source, not as an image. It is an image, but an image that effaces itself as image, a re-representation that offers itself as pure presentation. . . . I can also be touched, *presently,* by the recorded speech of someone who is dead. I can, *here and now,* be affected by a voice from beyond the grave. All that is needed is to hear, *here and now,* what was, in the restored present of a self-affection, the listening-to-oneself-speaking or the listening-to-onself-saying of the other dead: as another living present.

But I can also, through a telecommunicative machine capable of reproduction, address myself, speak, respond to the other, thus *represented in its presence* (henceforth dead or alive, from here on it makes little difference).[52]

Here and now, always, and every time. And every time, singularly, with the illusion of an authority that only a technology of iteration, which is also a technology of the phantom, can ensure. The other touches us. Representation transforms itself, in its process, into the staging of the spectre, appearing without appearing in those unbridgeable spaces, between the living and the dead, between memory and event. The ghostly voice-over escapes the medium of delimited visual representation, and, with that, any purely pictorial paradigm with its perpetuation of "one-time-once" (now matter how often repeated, rescreened). In doing so, and in returning in defiance of the logic of "one-time-once," the voice-over turns "sensible thought back on itself."[53] The technique—and technology—of voice-over confirms in an uncanny way what Derrida has identified as Rousseau's suspicions concerning writing as "a technique, a sort of artificial and artful ruse to make speech present when it is actually absent."[54] The authority of the voice is not dispelled by the fact that the speaker is dead, as Derrida suggests, such is the power of auto-affection. Always reproducing itself, in an always-now that is neither an "only-once" nor a "once-upon-a-time" but is, endlessly, an iterable production, the recorded voice "adds only to replace";[55] in being this supplement, it does nothing other than situate an ineluctable process of bringing out, if not the dead exactly, then the other, as phantom rem(a)inder. Gillis's voice is, then, just such a phantom–rem(a)inder; not the enunciation of some absent unified subject, but as, on the one hand, the trace of a writing, and on the other, the haunting effect within that constantly iterable, yet paradoxically singular mark.

IX

Of film noir Slavoj Žižek *asks:*

> What, precisely, is so fascinating about this genre? It is clear that we no longer identify with it . . . what fascinates us is precisely a certain gaze, the gaze of the "other," of the hypothetical, mythic spectator of the '40s who was supposedly able to identify immediately with the universe of *film noir.* What we really see, when we watch a *film noir,* is the gaze of the other. . . . For that reason, our relation to a *film noir* is always divided, split between fascination and ironic distance: ironic distance towards its diegetic reality, fascination with the gaze.[56]

If this is the case, then *Sunset Boulevard* occupies a distinctly eccentric, and yet central place, not only in the genre of noir, but also, significantly, in a number of other locations. It disturbs the gothic and our relation to that, while it disturbs our relationship as viewers of Hollywood in ways in which even those analyses that acknowledge the film's self–awareness do not fully comprehend. As already argued, it displaces itself in and from itself. It disrupts and yet addresses directly the very question of film as modernist—and haunted—text.

The question of the gaze that Žižek brings before us is doubled and opened by this film, and our possibility of watching, or even reading it. For, if there is both fascination *and* ironic distance for us, as modern viewers, always in the *here and now*, of a fifty-year-old film, that condition is always already replicated in the relation of the characters in the film toward silent cinema, whether European or North American. This is the case whether we are speaking of the younger generation of characters, represented by Joe Gillis, or of the older generation, who are both fascinated with, and yet distanced from themselves, as they were, as their own others, who appeared in, or who made, silent movies. And, in conclusion, this is taken further. For not only is there the doubling and chiasmatic opening between "us" and the film, between the film's characters and an earlier, mute Hollywood or German Expressionist cinema, which haunts the film, and the street, of Sunset Boulevard/*Sunset Boulevard*, there is also that equally chiasmatic, if not abyssal, opening figured in the double remove between ourselves and silent film. Ironically, it is Gillis's voice-over, in his alterity from himself (invisible dead narrator, narrating his live, yet dead, narrated other self), that recalls such opening in returning, as narration and trace, as technical inscription without location and always at a remove from the articulation of the image, a constant rem(a)inder of the haunted nature of cinema. *Sunset Boulevard* thus configures itself in clearly graphic, yet immaterial ways. It writes itself as so many figures of ghost-writing announced in the knowledge of technological reproducibility, and a knowing comprehension, to paraphrase Friedrich Kittler, that memories and dreams, the dead and ghosts, have become technically reproducible, as so many layers of spectres, spectres upon spectres.[57] For with *Sunset Boulevard* Billy Wilder acknowledges what is implicit in all forms of electronic media as so many manifestations, mediations, and technical prostheses of graphic phantasmagoria; his text bears witness, inviting us to do the same, that: "[t]he realm of the dead is as extensive as the storage and transmission capabilities of a given culture."[58]

Chapter 3

BIOGRAPHY'S RUINS:
THE AFTERLIFE OF
MARY SHELLEY

When the very *first* perception of an image is linked to a structure of reproduction, then we are dealing with the realm of phantoms.

Jacques Derrida

But it did not occur to one of those spirited and in various ways intelligent people round Berto's table that a complete mutation of our means of nourishment had already come into being . . . such a sea-change in the nature of reality as could not have been envisaged by Karl Marx or Sigmund Freud.

Muriel Spark, *The Takeover*

To think life as the already dead, as if now surviving, as if a still life of all that can be objectified. . . .

Robert Smith

Cette perpétuelle erreur, qui est précisément, la "vie". . . .

Marcel Proust

I

Will an event have taken place in the texts bearing the signature of Muriel Spark? Will an event have arrived that suspends the reception of such texts in relation to questions of delimitable periodization or context? How can we know, how might we be sure, other than, possibly, through the chance of a belated reading that still remains to come, and, through this, the recognition of a disjointing untimeliness? What takes place, if anything, between the proper names of Mary Shelley and Muriel Spark?

Strange effects can take place in the most seemingly ordinary, familiar, or accessible places, as has been seen in the previous chapter, in its attention to the work of the gothic, the uncanny, and those related tropes belonging to phantomatic structures of doubling, reiteration, and the ruination of identities. The gothic—along with those other, possibly "cognate" effects just mentioned—considered not as a genre but as a motif, a singular trace belonging to the irreducible motion of writing, or as that which motivates a particular structure of reproduction, might be read as having arrived in the texts of Muriel Spark so as to trouble, and make tremble, form, ontology, system, and the coherence of any supposedly coherent structure, concept, or determination. Of course, like those ghosts inhabiting *The Hothouse by the East River*, we will not have known this, except as the experience of an après-coup, except through the recognition of a certain act of memory, and a certain "mode of attention."[1]

However, whatever may have taken place, whatever might come to take place, and, moreover, whatever we might believe we recognize—all this will have had to do with the occasions of writing. All of these concerns will have less to do with any discernible or ostensible, simply visible trace, even though it is on such marks that the present chapter will focus, than with an understanding, through the registration of a transformative inheritance after the event, of the possibility that writing, any writing, "as a disseminating operation," to cite Derrida,[2] is always haunting *and* haunted. Moreover, as is well known, writing has the power to disturb on any occasion, to the extent that, in always being in principle separated and separable from any presence or a present, from any author or authority, or any historical moment, it does not exist, even though it may communicate or otherwise produce material effects, "according to all its modifications."[3] All writing aiming to represent life, or *a* life as in the form of a biography, is of less interest for what is conventionally

called either its "object" or its "subject," than for the ways in which, in relation to this strange thing called "life," inscription unfolds itself as being
indelibly deranged by the very phantasmatic operations by which it gets
under way. In the light of this recognition, so-called biography is available as the intensification of writing's spectral condition, if for no other
reason than that, in being a work of what Hubert Damisch calls "projective" memory,[4] it produces, from its very first word, the memory of a life
always haunted by its ghostly double, its afterlife. When that afterlife insists in writing in explicit relation to the motifs of the gothic, biography
gives up the ghost and is left in the ruins that it already is: "ruin is that
which happens to the image from the moment of the first gaze. . . . Ruin
is . . . what *remains* or *returns* as a specter."[5]

II

Of Muriel Spark's writing, Norman Page has observed that the writer's realism is "superficial."[6] Speaking of one of her early novels, *The Ballad of
Peckham Rye* (1960), Page comments that Spark is "less interested in
'pure' realism or 'pure' fantasy . . . than in the intersection or blending of
the two . . . *realistic elements reveal their instability and threaten to dissolve*" (emphases added).[7] Elsewhere, of a later novel, *The Hothouse by
the East River* (1973), Peter Kemp remarks that "several types of literature have been torn apart and their components, clichés and conventions
[have been] cunningly reworked into a collage."[8] Whether collage or, indeed, reworking, are the appropriate figures for what takes place in the
text of Muriel Spark is of less importance than to recognize that there is
a registration clearly of something at work in Spark's writing that disturbs the contours of particular forms and exceeds ontological limits
even as it blurs the delineation of particular narrative structures.

Such disruption of form intimates certain aspects of the spectral and
haunting. Moreover, it draws attention to the very condition of writing itself, and to narrative's disruptive ability to double itself and thereby suspend its own projections of veracity and transparency in the service of any
subject. Certainly (to take one example), at a somewhat mundane level
the very notion of a ballad, to which we are alerted in the earlier of the
two novels just mentioned, is suggestive of an anonymous form of the
narrative relation of history that returns and persists from age to age,

becoming anachronistically disjunctive in its iterability, precisely, perhaps, because its arrival goes unrecognized. Indeed, there is something
strangely, uncannily, interruptive, and disturbing in the mere fact that
one genre is haunted by another. In this case, the act of naming a novel as
a ballad destabilizes not only genre or form but also the presumed authority of the author, and her relation to the text as signaled through her
proper name on the cover, which is undermined by the very reference to
a form more usually associated with the absence of any locatable author.
Throughout *The Ballad of Peckham Rye* there is the infrequent suggestion that a location maintains a spectral persistence that comes to bear
on the present. *Hothouse* is a novel explicitly peopled by ghosts who inhabit a modern-day purgatorial Manhattan, and who, in coming to realize that they died at the end of the Second World War, implicitly ask the
reader to bear witness to the history of the twentieth century through
their spectral revenance. Of this novel, Cairns Craig has remarked that it
is haunted by "ghosts of an unrealized past," brought into focus by "endless repetition" where "modern reality is nothing more than the ghost of
the history that had been promised by the slaughter of war."[9] *Ballad* features Nelly Malone, who "serves as a ghostly chorus" yelling "messages
from the spiritual world,"[10] and the ambiguous angel-devil character,
Dougal Douglas/Douglas Dougal, a "somewhat supernatural being,"[11]
who appears to have certain gothic affiliations, while also being an uncanny instance of a disruptive doubling. He is, as Joseph Hynes puts it,
"double, complex, mysterious."[12] Doubling takes place disturbingly in
The Hothouse by the East River: "everywhere in the novel we encounter
doubles, reflections, and the difficulty if not the impossibility of separating analogues from opposites."[13] Both novels, and others by Spark, address the limits of "material time" and the possibilities of narrative to
cross such limits imaginatively while remaining in an apparently single
time (and often location), while *Hothouse* is an "imaginative exploration
of the passing from this life to the afterlife,"[14] concerning itself as it does
with that most liminal of locations, purgatory, and its effective suspension between states of being.

All such effects and interests are, it may be argued, fair game for the
novel in the twentieth century, or indeed all apparently fictional narrative forms. The supernatural, the gothic, processes of doubling and ambiguity or indeterminacy, disturbances of the temporal: from Virginia
Woolf and J. B. Priestley to Peter Ackroyd and Iain Sinclair, such devices
and the uncanny sensations they can produce are commonplace enough

in the English novel in the twentieth century, that we may pass over them as being simply rhetorical or dramatic devices, tricks of the pen rather than as so many signs of spectrality. However, what takes place when the spectral and the gothic come to be remarked in the form of biography? To what extent do spectrality and haunting make biography possible in the first place? In this chapter we will consider Muriel Spark's biography of Mary Shelley in the light of these questions, and, implicitly, in the light also of the persistent concerns of Spark's fiction noticed by critics such as those cited earlier. As we shall come to see, that which returns, that which persists and disrupts from some other place within a recognizable form, has been an unwavering interest of Muriel Spark's text.

III

Among Muriel Spark's first publications was a biographical and critical study of Mary Shelley, a work that has subsequently received little critical attention from commentators on Spark.[15] Published in 1951, entitled *Child of Light: A Reassessment of Mary Shelley,* it appeared at a time when many of Mary Shelley's own publications were unavailable. In retrospect, it can be said that Spark's biography served significantly in bringing into the light an author who was known at the time chiefly for being the wife of Percy Bysshe Shelley and for her novel *Frankenstein.*[16] Arguably, even the novel was known only in a secondhand fashion to many, through James Whale's film adaptations in the 1930s (particularly his *Frankenstein* and *Bride of Frankenstein*). *Child of Light* included an abridged version of Shelley's *The Last Man,* as that novel was out of print at the time the biography was published, and had been for some time. Thus, already, what has come to be read by critics as Spark's dissatisfaction with any supposed purity or homogeneity of literary form is manifestly evident in the study of Shelley, in which, conventionally understood, biographical, critical, and editorial identities commingle. The significance of this biography is best attested to, perhaps, by the fact that, although it was published in Great Britain it did not have an "official" publisher in the United States. Despite this, a pirated edition found its way into print in North America, as Muriel Spark recounts in her preface to her revised edition,[17] retitled *Mary Shelley: A Biography,* which was published in 1987. Spark republished the biography, as she remarks, in large part because of the existence of the photocopied edition being sold in the United States. Taking into account much of the scholarship on Mary Shelley that had appeared in the three decades since the initial publication, Spark revised the work extensively, dropping the abridged version of *The Last Man*.[18]

Mary Shelley: A Biography is, however, still not simply a biography, divided as it is into two distinct sections, the first—*"Biographical"*—having ten chapters,[19] the second —*"Critical"*—being composed of six.[20] This apparently reductive schematic structure is readable perhaps as a recognition on Spark's part that what is called a life is, in reality, irreducible, after the fact, to the simple or straightforward representation of any individual period of existence, however short or long. A "life," so-called, is only comprehended in its apparently autonomous totality after the event, by and through the response of others as the manifestation of a somewhat spectral survival. Moreover, this "afterlife" of the identity in question, in this case what is conventionally known as the subject of a biography is only ever comprehended through writing. The subject survives not intact but as the production of, in, writing, and only legible or visible as such a production or projection of heterogeneous marks subject to translation. This is the subject's chance, if you will, that it lives on beyond life by virtue of the elements of representation. An identity thus returns, but only in dismembered fragments that are inscribed, iterable, and, therefore, always incommensurable with any attempted gathering of the traces into some ontological whole. Spark's gesture, that of dividing, and thereby doubling her "subject" into distinct parts—biographical and critical—produces, even as it implies or appears to comment at a distance, a signature already redoubled. What is significant in the figure "Mary Shelley," receivable here as only ever living on, and having this chance as a concatenation of a series of signatures, motifs, ideologemes, and so on (belonging equally to 1951 as to any present reading or any instance discernible as coincident with affixable dates in the eighteenth and nineteenth centuries), is always already produced, projected. In a sense, of course, this is true of anything that we call a "life." But what Spark's interest makes explicit, I would argue, is that the work of biography is revealed as being as "fictional" or "fictive," as "literary," as any novel, romance, or history. The projection of a life in its afterlife, re-presented as both central and marginal is, at once, both an intensification (as already remarked) and a mystification of the processes of writing. Working on the tropes and motifs of the gothic, itself already a hyperbolic and dismembered genre, Spark disrupts any straightforward historical or temporal relationship between biography and subject, for the subject returns, if it does so at all, in pieces and never as itself. "Mary Shelley" is thus remarkable only to the extent that what we call the biographical subject is revealed through Spark's insistence on the relation to the gothic as comprising so many "marks or traces of retentions and protensions,"[21] projective memories as the "figures of dictation in the asymmetrical experience of the other that commands a certain writing, perhaps all writing."[22] Biography, according to this understanding, is just this process, this "technique for calling up the phantom."[23]

The biographical chapters of Spark's text delineate not only Mary's life, but explain, in some detail, the lives of her parents, William Godwin and Mary Wollstonecraft, as a means of providing the reader with an understanding of the psychological traits of Mary's character, which Spark interprets in the biography as Mary Shelley's "inheritance" from her somewhat famous parents. Though hardly used, if at all, other than in the case of this particular instance, "inheritance" is a key word in Spark's text, announcing the intimate threading of textual relationships, for it announces itself, as Robert Smith has suggested with regard to autobiography, as both simulacrum and "writing apparatus."[24] Abandoning the possibility of assigning absolute origin while decentering the figure of the subject, "inheritance" announces fraying, asymmetrical filiation and, along with this, the recurrence of broken threads that insinuate themselves into the biographical form as both its necessity and that which it cannot control or dominate, thereby attesting to its own impurity, its own ruin.

The critical chapters address the form, influences, and aesthetic merits of Mary's principal publications, *Frankenstein*, *The Last Man*, *Perkin Warbeck*,[25] as well as her activities as a critic and a poet. In particular and interestingly, Spark is at pains to distance Shelley's writing from gothic fiction, especially *Frankenstein*. As she argues, calling the novel gothic is, at best, a "loose definition."[26] While it may be taken as "both the apex and the last of gothic fiction,"[27] it should be read rather as "the first of a new and hybrid fictional species,"[28] a phrase that should equally be read as self-reflexively performative on Spark's part, being suitably axiomatic for the work of Spark's text throughout her writing career. Such a hybrid, suggests Spark, is one that combines scientific and philosophical knowledge with an eye for realist detail. This, in turn, Spark argues, is quite distinct

from the narrative and descriptive conventions of gothic fiction. The author's disavowal should draw our attention for its effort to make the gothic
invisible as a way of convincing the reader to take Mary Shelley seriously.
However, what interests us is that the attempted distancing from and erasure of the notion of the gothic serves another function: that of opening
the form of biography to its haunting by the traces of gothic detail.
Frankenstein may well be a "new and hybrid fictional species," but, to
make this point again, so also is Muriel Spark's biography of Mary Shelley,
as we shall see if we attend to its gothic traces, the fragments and apparitional details that manifest themselves alongside historical and biographical fact. The very question of the haunting work of detail in Spark's
biography is thus itself important, and will be returned to later.

This resistance on Spark's part to the gothic label is mentioned here
because it goes against the grain of much of the detail of the biographical part of the book, which, as we shall go on to explore, is troubled repeatedly by instances of gothic detail as the marks of a phantom or
uncanny countersignature—or, perhaps, even a "counterphantom"[29]—
situated against the prosaic demands of biography. What in life may seem
merely tragic or terrifying moments can become transformed into gothic
events in writing, especially if the tendency is, in the writing of a life, to
emphasize those events as a network of punctuating instances, or a certain rhythmic pulse. Such moments of iterative punctuation provide
Spark with a spectral framework for the figuring of a life as a life disfigured. More properly speaking, there is projected a resonant afterlife, so to
speak, that, in producing its subject as merely the apparition of so many
effects, serves to effect a double haunting. We are thus placed in a relation
to Spark's text, similar to that between the biography and the figure of
Mary Shelley, from which we are forced to ask: "[h]ave we then a choice
only between phantoms, or between the simulacra of phantoms?"[30] On
the one hand, the signs of the gothic arrive to disturb the realist conventions of biography in the twentieth century (as already implied). On the
other hand, such signs are read in the process of haunting Shelley herself, as though her life were the focal point of a narrative from a gothic
novel, and who is thus returned through the now-haunted medium of biography to the reader as a strangely liminal figure, uncanny in her marginal relation to what is supposedly comprehended as her own life, to
what is proper to a life. We might go as far as suggesting that Mary Shelley inhabits a life to which she has no relation and that she cannot comprehend because it is precisely a phantom afterlife of Muriel Spark's

making. This is, as already suggested, deranged biography, entailing, to quote Rod Mengham on Spark's novel, *The Takeover*, "a loss of co-ordinates . . . an inability to map one's position."[31] If Mary reads, according to certain conventions, as being the victim of powers she cannot hope to comprehend, much less realize, this is because she is herself haunted by the writing apparatus that is signed in the name of Muriel Spark. Thus, Mary Shelley is ghostwritten; in relation to such a writing, as a figure taking dictation from some future phantom who writes Shelley's life *both in* and *as the afterlife to come*, Mary Shelley cannot possibly "identify its causes [or] foresee its effects. . . .[her] relationship to history becomes a case of . . . capitulation to the irresistible, of imprisonment within a circular pattern."[32] "Mary Shelley" is the figure of all "subjects" produced by writing, in which "history" or "biography" are those haunted places where "something repeats itself so that one is simply taken over by the role one is given to play."[33] The appearance of gothic detail must be read therefore as so many iterative instances of a certain, constantly revenant troping, simultaneously returning from a literary-historical past to disturb the complacent certainties of biography, and also being written in Spark's text as that which, returning from the future, haunts and shapes the structuring of Mary Shelley's existence, often tragically. To put this another way, that which narrative makes appear is precisely a certain spectral "superoscillation" between two singularities, gathered by all that oscillates in each of the two signatures, "Mary Shelley" and "Muriel Spark."

For these reasons, the focus here therefore is on the biographical and its modality, rather than the critical part of *Mary Shelley: A Biography*, that location where dislocation, displacement, and disruption as the hauntological emerges from within, and as the sign of, the counterphantom to the ontological boundaries of biography. In particular, this chapter addresses two aspects of Muriel Spark's hybrid biography, with its "double exclusion (*neither/nor*) and . . . participation (*both this and that*)"[34]: part life, part tale of terror, neither one nor the other and yet both this and that, hovering between and exceeding both, blurring the boundaries of each. These are, first and as just mentioned, the liminal, marginal, or seemingly often subservient positions the figure of Mary Shelley occupies in relation to those around her during her life and the subsequent marginality of that life in relation to its own telling, as the life is written by Spark. The second aspect of the biography that concerns us here is what may either be described as the already advertised gothic element of Mary Shelley's life or, otherwise, the gothic modality that disturbs realistic representation, through and in response to which Spark writes that life, already mentioned. There is, then, haunting this biography the displacement of the function of mimesis as mere copy by mimesis as production. The "life" considered as a totality or whole reflected *in* writing is dispersed by a writing-apparatus, a *tekhne* of making-visible incommensurate with that reflective purpose, which produces, and keeps producing life-in-ruins, a life as the ruins of the self in excess of any two aspects of this production—the liminal and the gothic—are mutually interdependent and thereby blur absolute distinctions between either while straining at the limits of both. The text thus suspends itself, even as it exceeds the modes and conventions of different genres, and, in this, enacts its own liminal location. Such a performative effect spectralizes biography while foregrounding the extent to which the act of biographical inscription is dependent on the more or less hidden signs of haunting.

The revenance of the gothic clearly facilitates such spectralization of form. Mary Shelley's apparent marginality in her own lifetime and the role she is made to play in the subsequent retelling of it are inescapably informed by gothic details, as the biographer emphasizes these. Reciprocally, and no less importantly, the incidents in Mary Shelley's life that are either gothic, or made to appear as gothic in condition belong to the sense given by Muriel Spark, that Mary Shelley led a life at the border of other more self-promoting or otherwise public lives, particularly those of her father, William Godwin, her husband, Percy Bysshe Shelley, and Lord Byron. What we can read, along with so many things, from Spark's *Mary Shelley: A Biography* is that a liminal life is one led among, and projected from, penumbra, often cast by figures who shine brightly by comparison. Such shadows are, inescapably, the places from which the gothic phantom can also appear. The story Muriel Spark's text produces of Mary Shelley is of someone who is, while the supposed subject of the biography, nonetheless and perhaps paradoxically, always hovering in the wings, rather than appearing center stage.

A ghostly doubling effect exists in this biography, and one tending in two directions simultaneously. This double effect, one, as already remarked of writing, *in writing,* is registered furthermore in this chapter, in the previous paragraph, as I attempt to situate my own writing in response to Muriel Spark's biography. I note, for example, that the gothic is either that mode—or one discernible apparitional occasion of that mode—of representation chosen by Spark or that it is an expression of

Mary Shelley's life: the gothic doubles itself, in the text that we call a life, and in the life that is configured by the text through which we come to apprehend that life. This is not really an either/or dilemma, however, for it is important that we acknowledge how both aspects of the gothic are inseparable, and that they may be said to be mutually overdetermined by one another. Similarly—and this is, once more, a double figure—I suggest that the biography both marks and remarks on the liminality of Shelley's existence, even as it seeks to narrate her as its principal subject. Put somewhat baldly, Mary Shelley occupies a shadowy and marginal place in relation to others throughout her life, and this particular narrative thread becomes retraced in the act of seeking to emphasize her singular significance. Thus, the text of Muriel Spark weaves the border patterns it appears merely to observe, reiterating through life-writing the *parergonal* as the place-between—between what is often expressed as "life and work" of a particular biographical subject, but also between life and death—from which Mary Shelley can be made to return as both a haunted and haunting figure, and, equally, from which she writes, writing herself the shadowy existences of Victor Frankenstein, the Last Man, and Perkin Warbeck.

IV

To restate and thereby to proceed. That which is called a "life" is clearly spectral. As text, it always exceeds and escapes biography, even, or perhaps especially, when the biography appears in the most conventional form, for enfolded in that form is the assumption of the life surviving beyond death, and, indeed, of thinking life as the already dead, to paraphrase Robert Smith.[35] Writing a life necessarily entails processes of selection, of inclusion and exclusion simultaneously, that occur in the configuration of any narrative subject. In writing a life the biographer is constrained by writing a life, one possible life as a narrative thread pursued, retold, or traced among a number of possible, potential lives. As such, the biography is that act of writing in which the intertext, composed, as Roland Barthes suggests, in terms reminiscent of the condition of spectrality, of *interventions, fictions,* "splinters, fragments . . . overlappings, returns, affinities,"[36] stitches the corpse together into an apparently seamless subject, which then appears reanimated. As has been remarked, biographical inscription is therefore the double act of writing while appearing to hide or make invisible that which writing effects; or, to put it another way, the writing effect that announces *this therefore will not have been writing*. As a textual paradigm, the subject is thus gathered *and* dispersed, phantomized, as Barthes makes clear (143). This double and seemingly contradictory movement is most readable in Spark's repeated return to the intertext fashioned from the overlapping of, and affinities between, fragments of the life-narrative and the gothic mode. Despite its original title, *Child of Light, Mary Shelley: A Biography* is a narrative clearly organized according to some of the darker effects available to literary inscription. These effects of rhetoric and fiction ineluctably take hold, dispersing the so-called life they serve to assemble, across—even as they are deflected by—the constellated fragments of the gothic, which fragments announce from the very first page as the impurity of nonidentity haunting identity.

The first chapter of *Mary Shelley* provides an exemplary moment of liminal and gothic interanimation in a narrative fashion that it is hard to dissociate from the more deliberately stage-managed effects of what we call fiction and its means of representation. It deals almost exclusively with Mary Shelley's famous parents, their personalities, and their circle. They are presented by Spark as interpellated and overdetermined textual figures, subjects of an age of intellectual and ideological transition,[37] marked by political fervor, popular agitation, the debate over human rights, and radical rationality. (But, then again, in any selective reading, what historical moment might not be delineated thus?) We are told that Godwin's personality is marked by "intellectual stoicism," while Wollstonecraft's is one of "passionate pessimism."[38] These psychological traits discerned by Spark, or otherwise overlaid in her act of purposeful reading, are singular and strong enough to warrant a reading of the biographer's assignation of type rather than identity, where bold, gendered delineation may serve as the mold from which the character of the biography's principal character may spring. Spark's identification of the cardinal qualities of Mary's parents functions economically to foreshadow the writing and mediate the reading of Mary Shelley's life throughout the rest of the biographical narrative. It is important that we keep in sight these determining and, for Muriel Spark, incisive *traits* as literary figures, as much as we should regard them as the markers of psychological verisimilitude culled simply from the study of the past. Spark may be read, then, as in the process of determining the parameters for her biographical subject in a manner that owes as much to certain fictional conventions of the late eighteenth century as it does to any historically verifiable record of the lives of Wollstonecraft and Godwin.[39] Indeed, in marking out the limits of Mary's identity in so forceful and simple a fashion, Muriel Spark could easily be forgiven had she titled her first chapter "Sense and Sensibility."

There is, then, clearly a sense on Spark's part of self-conscious determination of the outline of the subject "Mary Shelley" in so "literary" or figural a manner. What is equally obvious in this is that there is only relation, no beginning as such. Like a character in a novel, Mary Shelley will arrive with a ready-made moral personality, to paraphrase Mark Currie, that exhibits not the subject herself so much as what Currie describes as the "technical control" over the narrative of a life, the narrator's point of view, and the reader's response.[40] The extent to which she may go, and no further, is acknowledged throughout this opening chapter by the fairly frequent use of conditional clauses married to collective pronouns, in phrases such as "if we . . ." or "should we. . . ." In no other chapter do such phrases appear so frequently, and there is readable here a teasingly tentative exploration of the speculative limits permitted the biographer. The rhythm of reading dictated by such remarks suggests a constant tension or oscillation as an effect of trying those limits or margins. The arrival *and* return of "Mary Shelley" is thus remarkable for its being a projection produced by the text of Muriel Spark, composed of otherwise invisible traits, figural and phantasmatic apparitions brought into focus through the construction of an identity, which constitution we recognize as "what one calls life . . . the fantasm of the thing, or object."[41]

But to reiterate: we are not concerned here principally or simply with exploring the limits to which biography as a genre or form may be taken, even though this is potentially fascinating and even while what will have emerged is a transformation of the biographical, a transformation we find already installed in its very possibility. Rather, what we are interested in are those suppositions concerning a life written, in certain margins, at the borders of others' lives and the limits of those lives. To pursue the formal limits of biography might seem to be an unjustified—and unjustifiable—strong reading of *Mary Shelley,* given that, on a first or even second reading, Spark's study appears a wholly conventionally shaped, albeit interesting, narrative. There is little about it that is obviously "experimental," in the sense that *Roland Barthes by Roland Barthes* or *Jacques Derrida* by Geoffrey Bennington and Jacques Derrida both play with the limits they refuse to assign to the *biographical mode,* even as they overflow them. Nor is there anything obviously playful or transgressive in the form of Spark's account as there is in Peter Ackroyd's *Dickens,* which is by turns seemingly Edwardian in its certainty over its subject and then self-consciously "postmodern" in its dalliance with identities. However, and to return to an earlier point, in a chapter concerned with liminality and, by extension, with apparently minor narrative detail, it is perhaps the little, marginal—and marginalized—details that should claim our attention, despite the ostensible conventionality of the narrative's broader gestures.

One such detail is, quite literally, marginal and haunting. It concerns also the limits, seen from either side of the edge, of a life, of two lives, the ending of one involving and intimately connected with the beginning of another. It is precisely the type of formal device considered as a writing effect that should draw our attention for being at once so apparently "natural" in terms both of the event being narrated and its use as a means for concluding a chapter, presaging the start of another, and being equally the mark of a double writing. At the conclusion of the first chapter there occurs Mary's birth. This moment, which from certain perspectives might be read as something of an afterthought, is introduced as the chapter comes to a close. The subject of biography is brought in at the very margin of the first chapter. Yet if on the one hand the birth seems inauspicious, on the other its narrative location may also be read as portentous. With Mary's birth comes the other narrative instance of the limit—Mary Wollstonecraft's death at the instance of giving birth, which tragic moment threatens to overshadow momentarily the birth of Mary Godwin.

It is a well-known assumption of critical-historical discourse that it was, of course, quite common for women either to die in childbirth or as its result in the eighteenth and nineteenth centuries, as any reader of novels from the time will confirm, and as particular histories of the late eighteenth and nineteenth centuries acknowledge.[42] It was also, doubtless, reasonably common practice for children to be named after their parents. However, such commonplace occurrences when transformed into narrative can be read as having been spirited away from their factual, historical grounding. Narrative is marked by just this effectivity: the singular ability to transform what might otherwise be understood as the everyday into something strange and estranged precisely because the otherwise unremarkable *is* remarked. The commonplace instances of lives function in a wholly different and, in the instance of this singular biography, uncanny fashion, especially when their placement suspends narrative so dramatically, and when that suspension is formally reinforced through so artificial a hiatus as the close of a chapter.

What we are calling a hiatus might, with more accuracy, be termed an epoch, in the strictest sense: a temporal suspension or moment of arrest in time (historical or narrative). Such suspension is clearly double—one of a series of such discernible gestures throughout Spark's writing, and defined by Brian Cheyette as the author's "abiding doubleness"[43]—in that the suspensive modality is echoed by the formal halting of the narrative at the structural limit of the chapter. Thus, Spark's text—a "life death of the writing crypt"[44]—remarks, even as it suspends and ruptures, its progress in commenting on the violent double event that returns, desisting from itself in the performative violence of the narrative form, in a rhetorical manner akin to that described by J. Hillis Miller as *anacoluthon*:[45] a doubling or duplicity, whereby narrative gives the lie to biography's innocent truthfulness, breaching that "truth" status as it is conventionally understood in all its monological identity. As Miller remarks, anacoluthon undermines "the illusory coherence of any narrative."[46] It has occasion to do so through the disjointing, ghostly work of narrative details at odds with the illusory unity and ontology of the narratorial authority acknowledged in the name of biography. The gothic detail returns as phantasmic detail, the grafting of a phantom "limb" as ghastly illustration and overheated embellishment on the assumed ground of the supposedly objective constative narration of a life. In being noticed, the violent feature causes a more casual reading to go off the rails, as close reading, that which, according to Miller is "essential to reading narrative,"[47] demands of the reader that she put on the breaks, in the face of what comes into view startlingly.

What results? Here, as elsewhere, we have occasion to observe the work of gothic traces, as "*anacolytic* figure[s]," designating "an interruption in the sequence [of a life] itself, within a grammatical syntax or in an order in general."[48] Thus, such doubling, such divisive duplicity, works itself out, as Derrida remarks with regard to another anacoluthonic narrative moment, between *analyst* and *anacoluthon*: between biographical narrative, in the suspensive instance, and as the analysis of, the ruptural beginning and ending of "life," and in the fictional narrative detail by which that narrative has the occasion or chance to proceed while being remarked by an "interruptive dissociation."[49] As the singular-doubling instance of birth–death makes apparent, structural articulation is made possible precisely by what disarticulates so forcefully. And what is it that moves between these two singularities, the analytical biographical commentary belonging ostensibly to the twentieth century and the gothic narrative fragment belonging to the eighteenth? Nothing other than the work of the spectral, as that which opens up (in) any work, beyond the merely rhetorical, to a future witness. "Told in the past tense," as Hélène Cixous comments of Spark's novel *Memento Mori*, "the story is continually interrupted and commented in advance from the vantage of a future which the author knows but the concerned parties do not."[50]

The haunting effect of the scene with all its doubling resonances is thereby heightened, made to seem an even greater tragedy in the literary sense, and given a literary and rhetorical oscillation that remains in ghostly effect into the silence of the space beyond the chapter. Mary's death and Mary's birth are at once the most natural and the most artificial, estranging, and uncanny events in the world. Such a resounding climax is also a *crisis*, a decision-making that determines violently and strongly the reading and writing of a life. The climax is clearly both an end *and* a beginning. Here is written a suspension between life and death, the limit of one life and/as the limit of another, the unrepresentability of which is given a material manifestation in the physical limit of the chapter's end previously mentioned. Moreover, its placement seduces with the promise of the gothic portent. Spark's decision to close the chapter with a double inscription, both death and life in writing, resonates beyond its merely factual and historical instances, which life-writing overflows, and to which it cannot be reduced. The death–life/life–death written of in the doubled Mary affirms a statement of Hélène Cixous: "To begin (writing, living) we must have death."[51] Thus, the biography, having begun before it begins, begins only in beginning again. We are thus witness to the irreversible figuring of what Cixous calls "the birth scene of writing."[52] And then again, the death of Mary Wollstonecraft might even, in a strong reading, be comprehended as a possibly gothic moment wherein may be anticipated a troubled and tragic life for the as-yet unconscious heroine.

Whether this is too strong a reading of so liminal a moment is open to debate. However, I would suggest that we are entreated to subject the moment to the force of such a reading *because* it is figured in so marginal and, seemingly, so "throwaway" a fashion. Given what we call the literary context in which Mary Shelley's most famous publication, *Frankenstein*, and, by extension, Shelley herself, has been placed critically, it may be all too easy to read Mary Shelley's life as simply a gothic life or to read Spark's translation of that life as merely gothic because appropriate to its subject. The risk is there, doubtless, a risk that is seen to be at work in both the writing of the biography and any subsequent commentary on it, or in the reading of its details.[53] But because the gothic is not merely itself, the reading of Spark's text cannot stop here. Certainly, as suggested before, Muriel Spark is scrupulous in her efforts in the second part of the biography to dissociate Shelley's publications from any simple understanding or reading of them as gothic narratives, even though she acknowledges in passing the apparently stable literary contexts and genres that they, in turn, acknowledge to greater or lesser degrees. Yet, despite this, and despite the separation of "life" and "work," the text that the life becomes remains significantly punctuated by events that are narrated in a decidedly "gothic" manner as if, as with Mr. Dick's trouble over King Charles's head, Muriel Spark just cannot keep the gothic out. Yet, as we hope we have made clear so far, the element of the gothic is irreducible to some genre pastiche. Significantly, the gothic reappears, but it returns not as itself, as an example of a genre, but through the spectral traces of itself that exceed any grammar, form, or purely formal concern. Whether the signs of the return of the repressed or the anxiety of influence are those that mark this biography, the gothic elements that recur in the telling of Mary's life do nothing to stabilize the identity of this text. Perhaps "telling" is not the most apposite word at this juncture. Given my conjecture that the biography is punctuated, and perhaps distorted, by so many narrative details and conventions discernible initially as gothic, it might be more appropriate to speak of the biography as a reading haunted by particular literary and rhetorical rhythms of the late eighteenth and early nineteenth centuries. In this reading, Spark's text gives herself over to what Paul de Man (in terms readable as implicitly announcing the spectral) has described as the "intuitive presence of the moment," appearing passively to fuse "past and present."[54] Such a spectral fusion unveils for us the uncanny condition and effect of Spark's writing, described by Hélène Cixous in the following manner: "the contrast between the plainness and false innocence of tone and the savagery of a world the concrete presence of which admirably simulates realist art." The reading of such a contrast, between the realism on which biographical continuity is dependent and the eruption of the traces of gothic narrative that draws attention its multiple figural effects, reveals that "reality is nothing but a mask of death . . . under the cover of insignificant words lurks a great, infernal supernaturalness." Cixoux continues: "Spark makes use of the imagery of hell and all its attributes . . . and yet she pretends to take them as literary references while hell gapes beneath her transparent language. The play of evil is comically modern. . . . Everything is heavy with the weight of destiny, and not of daily life."[55]

IV

If, as Roland Barthes, George Orwell, and Naomi Schor assert in different ways,[56] a characteristic feature of realist writing is its attention to superfluous detail, what may be said of Spark's biography, in which gothic detail is, seemingly, superfluous *and* necessary? The details are superfluous in that they are written as textual apparitions deployed, in conventional terms, to "set the scene" or "mood," to provide, provoke, or, perhaps, perform a frisson. They are necessary in that, together, they make available a counterrhythm or countersignature of reading, marking the text through a series of rhetorical sutures in the act of re-membering the life-in-writing, the life as afterlife, in short, a text. If as Schor suggests in reading Freud's reading of detail,[57] that an excess of detail guarantees truth—or, in the case of a biography, verisimilitude—we would argue, following this, that it is the very excess of gothic detail, its heightened sensibility, that is itself excessive, properly speaking, as well as being fragmentary. The gothic mode is, as we know, both excessive and fragmentary in its discursive and narrative patterns; these are among its defining features. Yet, while Spark would draw our attention to the "facts" of Shelley's life in order apparently to read truthfully the life of Mary Shelley, she does so in so markedly "exaggerated" a manner that we are made to read in two directions at once, confronted by the writerly tension between the desire for transparency in verisimilitude and the occlusion, to which, paradoxically, our attention is drawn, of stylized feature or figure. What we might suggest, in keeping with the Barthesian sense of the work of detail, contrary to any manifest will, intention, or articulated desire, is that gothic detail in its double service, appearing pointedly and repeatedly at the margins of the central narrative, takes on the role of the ghostly *punctum,* as defined in *Camera Lucida.* Against the conscious will of the photographer, a detail appears and draws the attention. It "occurs" writes Barthes, "in the field of the photographed thing like a supplement that is at once inevitable and delightful."[58] The gothic detail is definable in this fashion, or otherwise as a detail *within* or *of* a detail, to borrow from Naomi Schor's discussion of Barthes.[59] It is that chance trace that, despite the attention to the understated in *Mary Shelley* as a sign of its realist-biographical credentials, draws our attention as it participates, while overflowing, in the "economy of meaning."[60]

The first moment of, or, more accurately perhaps, interruption in, Mary's life after her birth that draws the reader's focus occurs when she is seventeen. Prior to this, there is the narrative of Mary's stay with friends in Scotland, in the setting of the north bank of the River Tay adjacent to Dundee. Arguably, this narrative moment and its setting might be considered to create a gloomy atmosphere, but is not in itself necessarily gothic. It does provide, however, what Spark describes as the background for Mary's "creative gestation."[61] Why this should be remains unexplored but, at the same time, there seems an obvious contextualization at work as though the narrative of adolescent transition makes possible for Mary the invention of a grammar of a narrative modality by which she will come to be read, after the event. However, this remains open to speculation. When she is seventeen, Mary's life takes what appears a decidedly gothic turn: she begins meeting secretly and regularly with Percy Bysshe Shelley, we are informed, at Mary's mother's grave in "St. Pancras Churchyard."[62] This strangeness of this moment is, arguably, in excess of its biographical or historical function and suspends, once again, narrative continuity and coherence. The cemetery figures as one of several limit-sites; it offers, to paraphrase Cixous on the necessity of the cemetery, a primitive and theatrical scene that unnerves, and yet by which writing is made possible.[63] This gothic detail of the meeting, with its mention of the grave and graveyard, fulfill the requirements of the Barthesian *punctum* of being both "inevitable and delightful," introducing to the mundanity of courtship the spectral oscillation, the purpose of which is, in turn, to disturb and thereby haunt the structure of biography through the revenance of the ghostly-gothic trope. Spark's text solicits a thrill even as it attempts to convey or unearth the thrilling, if somewhat morbid, element in her subject's life, as Mary and Shelley hover around the limits of, and between both, the living world and the crypts of the dead. The graveyard scene suitably punctuates a moment of transition in Mary Shelley's life; rhetorically it serves to mark the limit between her earlier and later lives. If, up to this point, Mary's life had been unremarkable (Spark's narrative dwells almost as much on the second Mrs Godwin in the first part of chapter two as it does on its supposedly principal subject), she had at least been more or less central, albeit subserviently, to her own biography. (If it remains possible to say this; what is so haunting about this biography, if one can even call it this, properly speaking, is the liminal, shadowy status of its subject.) It is as though more life, more than life is made possible from the scene of death: a new figure "Mary Shelley" is born from this grave-yard, from her mother, the other Mary's, tomb. When the biography in-troduces Shelley on the stage, like a somewhat camp vampire among the gravestones of North London, Mary becomes transformed, produced as a supplementary figure in her own narrative, at least until the poet's death some six chapters later.[64] This is a position that, seemingly, she is either unable or unwilling to escape, as though, again like some gothic heroine, she were held in thrall to the genius of her partner, and his demonic cir-cle.[65] The meeting place of Mary and Shelley is, again, only one of a num-ber of events and details haunted by the gothic sensibility in Mary's life with Shelley.

The poet, interestingly, is nearly always referred to by Spark solely by his surname, as though he were the product of fictional narrative himself, some Byronic hero-villain. The surname survives precisely as a fragment, a signature and trace for an implied narrative, always hov-ering close at hand. Shelley's appearance is, then, also a "return," an act of revenance throughout Spark's biography of Mary Shelley because it is his figure that comes to haunt the reader's and the biographer's imagination. There is a punctuating rhythm to the recurrent appari-tions of the poet, whose rhetorical purpose in the biography is to "make gothic" the narrative and biographical form. Shelley figures as a limi-nal other, a trope of otherness in excess of the parameters of genre, and it is worth enumerating some of the gothic interruptions that the poet brings about. It is certainly Percy Bysshe Shelley—about whom "'frightful tales'" circulate, and who tells terrible stories of himself for the amusement of his company[66]—who brings the gothic to the rela-tionship, scaring Claire Clairmont, for example, into convulsions with his tales[67] and describing to his publisher the production of *Epipsy-chidion* as containing a "'portion of me already dead'."[68] Shelley's pres-ence thus occasions serial interruptions through the appearance of already extreme narrative fragments, which are interruptive and dis-ruptive, which are in excess in their force and effect of any principal narrative strand. Furthermore, the poet is not merely the bearer of gothic tales and rhetoric; he also involves himself in plots typical of gothic narrative. At a one point in his marriage, Shelley becomes enamored of Emilia Viviani, a friend of the Shelleys who is imprisoned by her mother in a convent. Spark interprets Shelley's interest in the following way: "But the fact that her convent prison rendered her unattainable and suggested untold mysteries which in reality Emilia did not possess, sent the poet into high raptures."[69] Unattainable, untold mysteries, high raptures: a performative scene of writing haunts the biographer's apparently plain description. Spark's narrative is clearly as much responsible for projecting the gothic as it is for merely reporting it, once again investing the narrative with the double, destabilizing writing of the necessary and the delightful. Picking up on, bearing witness to the various traces, the textual machine weaves a skein of writing effects, such as the problems caused by vindictive and untrustworthy foreign servants,[70] so that the biography pulses with the anacoluthonic traces of the gothic, so many small, yet monstrous instances of liminal rupture. At another moment, Spark cites a letter from Shelley to Leigh Hunt, in which the poet describes William Godwin's demands on his daughter: "'he heaps on her misery, still misery'."[71] There is a play at work here between carefully chosen citations from the past, which come back to haunt this biography, and the rhetorical and grammatical cadences of the biography itself. Even Shelley's debts are given a somewhat gothic, parenthetical, if not marginal turn: "(The theme of debt throughout the nineteenth century is a social study by itself: debt was the equivalent of fraud; debt had its own prisons, its own police. Debt was a psychosis and by its dangerous nature positively mesmerized its victims.)"[72] From social study and criminality, policing and the carceral, to psychosis and mesmerism: the parenthetical statement, disrupting narrative through its internalized commentary, its momentary shift to present tense, its doubling of debt at the social and psychological levels; this interior statement accommodates even as it enacts instability and insecurity, threat and fear, both externally and phantasmically, debt doubly remarked as the phantomatic figure oscillating between locations. To the reader of latter half of the twentieth century and at the beginning of the twenty-first, there is perhaps something vaguely Foucauldian in this pathology of debt. Extending the discourse beyond the personal instance, the statement at once constructs a psychocultural identity for debt, capable of acts of seduction and hypnosis, reminiscent of the powers of Dracula or Svengali. At the same time, however, the gothic genealogy of the discourse of debt sketched here is placed in a markedly marginal position to the narrative, secured firmly between those parentheses: interruption as exaggeration. It would not be going too far, we suggest, to see or certainly to read in this gesture of Spark's, whether consciously or not, a performative, liminal, and gothic detail, a manifestation of the *punctum* beyond the individual subject, which focuses the reader's attention in a highly economic fashion on one particular impulse behind the writing of the biography. At once material and spectral, the spectre of economic hardship appears to haunt both the Shelleys in particular and the nineteenth century in general. And, in conclusion, at the same time there is, of course, a certain overflow within the sentence itself, an excess of irreducibly heterogeneous discourses.

Hard-hearted fathers, malevolent Italians, and the pressing nature of debt aside, Spark also chooses to emphasize the gothic narrative of the lives of Mary and Shelley together in other ways. On their first journey together through Europe, described in chapter three, detail is provided from their jointly kept journal of a Cossack raid and the report of rats crawling over Claire's face in her sleep. In chapter four, relatives die violently: Fanny takes her own life in Swansea, through an overdose of laudanum,[73] while Harriet Shelley drowns herself in the Serpentine.[74] Subsequently, there are the deaths of the Shelleys' children, Clara and William.[75] Juxtaposed to the deaths of Fanny and Harriet in the fourth chapter is the residence in Switzerland, with Byron and Polidori, where the tale of *Frankenstein* is first conceived, where, it might be said, it undergoes a period of "creative gestation." Later on Mary will write of Byron to Claire, describing him in explicitly gothic terms,[76] while her descriptions of her illness, in a letter to Leigh Hunt, are also suitably gothic in their choice of metaphor: "'I wish I could break my chains and leave this dungeon'."[77] Even Byron gets in on the act, imprisoning his own daughter (by Claire) in a convent, while Claire devises a kidnapping plan.[78] Claire's child will also die, however, plunging Mary "once more into that abysmal gloom" engendered by the death of her own children.[79] Everywhere, the everyday is overdetermined by the haunting inscription of the gothic, so that events are never themselves but always much more, always arriving from some other place to disturb and displace the identity of the biography. And the work of displacement is doubled, inasmuch as Spark not only mobilizes all the metaphors and other figures of gothic narrative, but also cites those places in texts of the early nineteenth century where such figures are already under way, to particularly dramatic effect. Such doubling disjoints the time of writing as the shadowy phantasms of the gothic overflow into the ontology of biography, returning from the past but, significantly, making themselves manifest in the present of the biographical act.

Chapters six and seven give details of the Shelleys' lives in Pisa and Liguria. As Shelley's circle widens, so Mary's importance appears to dwindle further, her role being as a supporting character for the most part. At the same time, yet again, the family we are told had become "inured to [the] *ever-present daemons of fortune*" (emphasis added).[80] Furthermore, Spark's narrative suggests in describing the growth of the Shelley circle, "[i]t was as if, in response to some dramatic law, the actors were assembling on a stage, each a unit of suspense in attendance on the tragic dénouement."[81] This is, perhaps, the most pronounced moment of deliberate artifice in reconstruction. Again, exceeding any purely biographical, historical, or constative function, the narrative becomes excessive, dislocated by the work of analogy inscribed by the *as if*. Indeed, there seems a simultaneous attempt to maintain and to break with analogy articulated by this phrase, which opens the merely historical report onto a strange scene setting, in turn a scene itself. A certain "spectral structure is the law here, both of the possible and the impossible, and of their strange intertwining."[82] The *as if* names an otherwise "ungraspable modality,"[83] a certain invention of an impossible scene, itself governed, *perhaps*, by the invisible, *some dramatic law*. But how will we ever know? It is precisely this impossibility that is so disturbing here—the possibility of the impossible being itself the example of a "unit of suspense." Having set the scene in so exaggerated a fashion, having recounted the arrival of Trelawny to the party and the telling of terrible tales, the beginning of chapter seven provides a frame for the events to follow:

> Mary was always conscious of the transience of things. Experience had endorsed this awareness, and in every appearance of tranquillity she saw, and saw correctly so far as her own life was concerned, an approaching turmoil. It often seems that such people invite the Furies by their own apprehension, that misfortune gains confidence, as a fierce animal will at the sense of a stranger's fear.
>
> It was not long before Mary's "prognostications of evil" took shape.[84]

Constructing the biography in this manner, Spark brings into play that certain sense of evil, which she is able to attribute as Mary's own words.

Mary is imbued with hallucinatory or telepathic abilities, a certain uncanny prescience; she is read as being haunted by phantasms from the future, which, in the retrospect of the narrative, arrive all too unsettlingly. The suspensive modality of citation, crucial to the structuring of representation in the last line above, effects a retreat of the author before the words of the subject, bringing the subject on stage, as it were, speaking from some liminal afterlife. The division in the opening paragraph of the chapter makes a strong impression, moving as it does from the representation of Mary's own feelings, drawn from her letters and journals, to the more speculative, emotionally heightened consideration of a quasi-classical tragedy waiting to occur. While this is not directly gothic in its expression, it is perhaps gothic in register. As an opening passage, it nonetheless relies heavily for its effect on its placement and the general air of mystery and foreboding that it desires to evoke in its rhetorical slippage from the personal to the universal.

Such "gothicization" continues through chapter seven, in the description of the residence of the Shelleys and their guests Edward and Jane Williams: "They were isolated in a small, and at that time quite savage fishing community on the Ligurian coast. On the night of 22nd June, 1822 Mary was awakened by Shelley's scream."[85] Once more, the dramatic interval takes place in a border location, this time the coast. The isolation and savagery are readable as purely gothic effects, and what is all the more disturbing in this brief moment of scene setting is that double effect once more, where the narrative strains between its factual element— the precision of the report of the date—and the sudden disturbance of sleep. Shelley has screamed, we learn, because of a dream in which the bodies of Jane and Edward Williams are seen with torn and bloodstained skin.[86] Moreover, and as if to add to the overall effect of this one incident, we are informed that both the Williams and the Shelleys allegedly experienced hallucinations and visions. And, of course, all of this is to lead up to the sailing accident, and the deaths of Percy Bysshe Shelley and Edward Williams, the news of which is given by that teller of horrific tales, Trelawny, who brings the "*ghastly* information" to Mary and Jane (emphasis added).[87] Thus, the tragic events of the summer of 1822 become reshaped, reinvented, to become punctuated by gothic detail, where the detail halts the reader's attention. Yet even this is not quite the end of the gothic, for there is the moment with which Spark chooses to begin chapter eight, at Shelley's funeral pyre when the dead poet's heart is snatched from the burning body by Trelawny.[88]

V

Was there life after Shelley for Mary? From chapter two on, until his death, Percy Bysshe Shelley occupies a central role, both in the life of Mary and in her biography. Arriving like some Byronic figure, occupying both Mary's life and her biography, haunting her after his death and so foreshadowing an afterlife that all but consumes the writing of another's biography, his effect on writing and on those whose lives he comes into contact with is inevitable and inescapable. His phantom figure transforms narrative. The necessary and unavoidable inclusion of the poet in *Mary Shelley* transforms the biography as much as he transformed his wife's life, a central significance that Mary acknowledges in her journal, and Muriel Spark dutifully reports in her biography.[89] If Mary had come to occupy a less than central role during her time with Shelley, the strange and the uncanny undoubtedly punctuated her life, at least in Spark's version. And even though Shelley was dead, he continued to haunt Mary's life, not merely through the "dark mood [which] had overtaken her,"[90] but also through the tolerance and condescension shown Mary by many of Shelley's friends, as Spark makes quite plain. Mary assumes a marginal role even after Shelley's death, seeking patronage from her father-in-law, editing her late husband's poems, and finding herself ostracized by Shelley's circle.[91] The poet thus circulates, after death, a phantastic figure and fiction in an afterlife of his own, as the subject of so many relays that de-center and displace Mary, both in her own life time and from her own "life," the afterlife of biographical narrative.

Appearances notwithstanding, *Mary Shelley: A Life* is imprinted throughout by the trace of the gothic. Narrative event and historical detail are contaminated by the constant return of the other, which is all the more haunting because it is disguised, as the ghost of the gothic in all its dismembered traces appears in the guise of biography. Such contamination by the traces of the gothic makes explicit that biography understood as a "singular instance" is always "this singularity of the untimely, of non-self-contemporaneity."[92] In foregrounding the singularity of the singular existence in this fashion, situating what is called a life through the play of iterable traces, the text oscillates between, disorganizing in the process, any idea of past and present as absolutely discreet indentities. Or, rather, it can be said that the text allows the gothic past to return through, and in the guise of, the present biography. It receives a call, and, answering that, is translated; it is carried off, it gets carried away, in the transport of the figural. The return occurs most frequently from the margins of the text, and from the margins of a life, across various thresholds, and made more liminal in its recreation. The narrative of Mary Shelley may not be a life she would necessarily recognize. It is, though, perhaps a narrative she may have written, we like to imagine, in other words. Indeed, in one sense this text becomes, by the strange logic of the spectral, a text signed by "Mary Shelley." In the overflow of fragments, traces, and details from one genre to another, Muriel Spark's writing draws to our attention to particular gothic affinities and affiliations, to the ghostly bond between singularities. In disturbing the life of biography with the signs of the gothic afterlife, Muriel Spark's narrative enacts a ghostwriting, as if its liminal subject had returned invisibly, to countersign her own somewhat spectral and liminal manifestation. In receiving the call of the haunting other, biography's identity is left in ruins, but these are the ruins of all biography, its spectral necessity the otherwise unspoken condition by which it has its possibility. The spectres of Muriel Spark—the trace of the gothic and the shade of Mary Shelley—return in order to reveal, as Karl Malkoff puts it, with regard to Spark's writing in general, "the bizarre underpinnings of the superficially conventional."[93] If, as one critic has argued, "the making of fiction serves as Spark's banishment of devils,"[94] in another manner it is also the making clear that phantoms are always with us, and it is to these that we must, once again, bear witness.

Chapter 4

BETWEEN: SPECULATIONS

When I write "what interests me," I am designating not only an *object* of interest, but the place that *I am in the middle of.*

Jacques Derrida

Between is not. Or: between "is" nothing. It "is"—above all—nothing, of which one could talk without it not already participating, and participating in this way, it would pull all talk inside itself, and its nothingness. . . . This nothing of our imaginations, of our names, concepts and our language—this between that cannot be grasped—plays around and surrounds everything we can possibly imagine, name or comprehend.

Werner Hamacher

For we are insufficient to ourselves and become ourselves in interplay with the other; and we do appropriate the other to ourselves; the love of the other returns to the self, and the other is very often, perhaps most often, sought for this return to the self.

William Desmond

I

What is the place or, perhaps more precisely, what is the "taking place," that the notion or motif of *between* designates? Hardly a concept, more a figure for a motion without form, *between,* if it is anything at all, is among the most ambiguous and inaccurate of terms.

A "syncategorem," between re-marks a "semantic quasi-emptiness," even
though "*[o]ne* "between" does not exist."[1] It names, even as it traces, an
unmappable space, a spacing whose crossing implicates a temporality
without measure. It articulates the possibility that something unseen,
some manifestation of the other, has arrived by which it gets going, without necessarily having arrived itself at any destination. Preceding in principle any subject or object, it nonetheless is constituted through an
uncanny motion, uncanny precisely because not only is this *between,*
every *between* without proper home, but also its interval and traversal is
comprehended or recognized after the fact, as the *retrait* of some *après-
coup.* What performative staging or phantom event, then, might this fig-
ureless figure of *between* acknowledge, for example in any act of writing,
so that, in reflecting on this disquieting motif the subject finds him- or
herself, positioned relationally, momentarily, and in an instance that is
both unique and iterable? Can we legitimately talk of *between* when no
place as such exists to which one might apply this improper name, other
than as the necessary and provisional correspondence *between* identities
(which space exists as the taking place of identity), which are themselves
given by the passage and spacing, the interval, of *between*?

II

And why, to risk a speculative assumption and shift ground somewhat
abruptly, might *love* name otherwise the nonplace that is the taking-
place of *between,* not in some abstract fashion, but in the event of every
singular taking place? A *between,* the trace of a difference, will have already taken place when I address my love: for, in recognizing my love, the
other will have addressed me, placing me in relation to an other, to
whom I then address my love, which is an address, as Peggy Kamuf puts
it, "without home, without the property of a subject from which it is sent
and to which it returns."[2] Moreover, the disturbance of which we are
speaking here is registered by the fact, in Alain Finkielkraut's words, that
the "'you' of 'I love you' is never precisely my equal or my contemporary,
and 'love' is the frantic investigation of this anachronism."[3] Love is thus
comprehended, like the motif of *between,* after the fact; it leaves its mark
after it has retreated into the invisible. Love announces and performs
this haunting performativity in its passage across that nonplace, between

self and other, disturbing in its crossing the sense of self, of home: "love always brushes up against the uncanny, the *unheimlich*, the un-home-like. Love brings with it the unhomelike because it is the experience of the sudden or not-so-sudden arrival of the other who *expropriates* address, which is to say *appropriates* it, *exappropriates* it: When I say 'I love . . . ,' it is always the declaration of the other at my address."[4] Thus, I am haunted by this apparition—*between*—that installs a radical instability at the heart of any identity, and which appears most forcefully in the name of love.

III

There are certain interwoven, though obliquely situated, interests in this chapter, as these find themselves caught up in the figure of *between*, a figure of translation and transport, but without either orientation or determination as such. A formless figure, it comes and goes. This ghostly motif announces the difference by which identities and ontologies come to be constituted, and without which they cannot be articulated. Particularly, this is approached through the staging of an imagined "taking place," a hypothetical scenario between one of the *envois* from *The Post Card* and George Eliot's last novel, *Daniel Deronda*. This interest is exemplified through the figure and naming of Daniel Deronda, and through Eliot's own interest in the question of what can be known of the relation between notions of self and other. *Daniel Deronda* challenges the very idea of source and origin through an open-ended narrative concerning identity. It seeks to work through the problem of *between* directly and indirectly, in a series of narrative strands that weave between one another, in terms of personal, ideological, racial, cultural, and ethnic identity; and it does so in a fashion that opens out the enigma of identity and knowledge concerning one's identity as a constant taking place between fictions of stable identity, with which fictions one supposedly identifies. Deronda's identity as an Englishman is destabilized; he finds himself haunted by the address of the other and the call of love. Love is that which, in being sent, in arriving, in being named, undoes any promise of a stable identity, and is thus, as already suggested, one possible signature for what takes place (in) *between*. To quote Peggy Kamuf again, "a loving movement is the indispensable key to what deconstruction does,"[5] and what unveils itself in

deconstruction in George Eliot's last novel is the illusion of national identity as pure, homogeneous, undifferentiated. Love, "as affirmation that
deconstructs . . . opposition . . . love . . . like deconstruction, takes place
along the divided, ruined border,"[6] and it takes place every time as the experience of the singular occasion, moving between one location, one
identity, and the other.

IV

What frustrates any illusion of an autonomous self and auto-identifica-
tion is, it can be suggested, to be read in the play with identity, between
self and other, between interiority and exteriority, that is set in motion by
the proper name and the "figure" of love, and by the event of love's arrival, which figure or event is, as Nicholas Royle suggests, a "condition of
any deconstructive reading."[7] Before we go any further, it is perhaps best
to say that that which is "between" Derrida and Deronda in this chapter
is, arguably, nothing other than "love." What takes place in their names is
just this motivation. Derrida has expressed this in the following terms: "I
love very much everything that I deconstruct in my own manner; the
texts I want to read from the deconstructive point of view are texts I love,
with that impulse of identification which is indispensable for reading."[8] If
love, situated in this chapter provisionally provisionally as one nonsynonymous figure of *between* (and, reciprocally yet, without closing the circle, *between* might be said to figure an event of love, if such an event
takes place), is what amounts to a condition of any deconstructive reading, the occasions of deconstructive reading are, inevitably, very much a
matter of registering the occasion of an affair between identities that remains in play and is untranslatable. Such singular, idiomatic occasions,
furthermore, leave in play their *traits* in any translation, as the sign of
love between one identity and another, that uncanny address between and
within French and English for example, or, in the example of *Deronda,*
one might apprehend this between the so-called English and Jewish parts
of the story. Love, to cite Jean-Luc Nancy, "does not stop coming and
going, never being simply present . . . it is always put into play farther
off than everything that would have to qualify it." Such play, in turn, sets
off resonances, dissonances, oscillations both percussive and repercus-
sive; in short, nothing less than aural apparitions, phantasms of the other.

I shall attempt to signal these reverberative spectres throughout as they play in the nonplace of the in-between, between, let's say for now, Derrida and Deronda.

V

Love. Between. Such motifs neither name nor identify a subject. A subject cannot be located. "I" am not the source, "I" have become the medium for a ghostwriter. "I" becomes this mark *between,* that which is the re-marking of an unstable in-between, between the sender and the addressee. "I" names the unmappable in medias res[9] of apparent locations, locations that are themselves undecidable because always relational and dependent on what takes place between a self and an other. "I," in this case, is always already traced, not as a unified identity but as the phantom figure of a be-tween that abides endlessly, but which is homeless, and cannot be located as *such.* As Derrida suggests, "the 'I' constitutes the very form of resis-tance. Each time this identity announces itself, each time a belonging *cir-cumscribes* me . . . someone or something cries: Look out for the trap, you're caught. . . . One ought to be able to formalize the law of this insur-mountable gap. This is a little what I am always doing. Identification is a difference to itself, a difference with/of itself. Thus *with, without,* and *ex-cept* itself."[10] "I" is thus both incisive and ex-cited, simultaneously the enunciation of relation and non-relation; it re-marks a certain cut or wound, while being also the gift of articulation from the other, the origin of which is undecidable. It announces and enacts a double location that is both interior and exterior, passing silently between these situations. "My" identity, what I call "my identity," is subject to events of resonant trans-ference from incomprehensible addresses to unknowable destinations that leave their trace or mark on "identity," and which determine the structur-ing of identity, while revealing that no identity is ever simply *there* but is always manifestly unstable and contingent on alterity. This very difficulty concerning the knowability or locatability of identity is enacted by Der-rida's texts, between those texts that are signed in his name, and those texts on which his writing operates. As J. Hillis Miller reminds us, "[t]he chief obstacle to a complete cartography of Derrida's topographies . . . is not the extent and complexity of the terrain but the presence within any place on his map . . . that cannot be mapped."[11] So, to reiterate this point:

between takes place but has no place that is proper to itself. A nonplace, it *takes place* as the chance or event *between* different identities, and as the affirmative difference of identities.

VI

Nicholas Royle has stated that "[t]he 'Envois' in *The Post Card* constitute perhaps Derrida's most provocative 'self portrait' and most obvious affront to the conventional requirements and expectations of philosophical discourse. This is philosophy in fragments, on post cards."[12] If these do, in fact, constitute a "self-portrait" the sender is not giving himself away. The post cards might, then, be said to have been sent—are still being sent, having yet to arrive, *finally*—from one of those unmappable places spoken of by J. Hillis Miller. If their senders are some of the possible Jacques Derridas who you might think you could pin down, then it is worth bearing in mind another scene concerning "Jacques Derrida," a scene involving the question of where Jacques Derrida comes from, who he is, what constitutes his identity. A detour then, a circumscription or perhaps, in Derrida's terms, a circumfession, concerning the re-marking of identity, its difference and resistance.

VII

In the interview, "There is No *One* Narcissism (Autobiophotographies),"[13] which deals with, among other things, identities, addresses, destinations, Jacques Derrida makes the following remark concerning his writing and teaching. Of these activities, he has said, "I have this feeling I am doing it from another place that I do not know: an exteriority based on a place that I do not inhabit in a certain way, or that I do not identify."[14] Derrida acknowledges the unknowable other of identity; he is responding to a question aimed at finding cultural and intellectual determinants for the signature and proper name "Jacques Derrida" and what "Jacques Derrida" does,[15] being and doing momentarily conflated in the question. Uncertain yet noticing the spectre of the "between," the interviewer has the feeling that Derrida's "intellectual and cultural heritage is Greek and German" but asks whether there might not also be "a sort of Judaic intrusion, difficult to define."[16] This "Judaic intrusion," itself calling on the other here, might come along, suggests the interviewer, to undo the line of traditional or conventionally constituted division between German and Greek, referring also to this deconstruction as an inscription.[17] Thus, the question involves a certain mark, a trace that is also a cut, a one-time incision to be reiterated over and over, a circumcision, if you will, that signs the name "Jacques Derrida." So, circumcision as signature, an irrevocable event taking place in the moment of inscription. This is confessed elsewhere, in response to a question concerning *Circumfession* (and what that text turns around), that internal margin written by Jacques Derrida for *Jacques Derrida:*

> Under the name circumcision, I am often asking myself . . . whether there is a "real" event that I can attempt, not to remember of course, but to re-elaborate, to reactivate in a sort of memory without representation—or whether this is a lure, a simulacrum . . . a screen destined for the figural projection of so many other events of the same type. . . . Circumcision means, among other things, a certain mark that, coming from others and submitted to in absolute passivity, remains on the body, visible and no doubt indissociable from the proper name which is likewise received from the other. It is also the moment of the signature (the other's as well as one's own) by which one lets oneself be inscribed in a community or in an ineffaceable alliance: birth of the subject . . . rather than "biological" birth. Every time there is this mark and this name . . . the *figure* at least of a circumcision is imposed on me.[18]

Circumcision, the moment of the double signature: the arrival, the address, and the mark of the other, as well as the naming of the self by the other and the communication between the two or, at least, the announcement of a possible *between*; nothing less than the application of the name, public and private. Circumcision is then a figure of the *partage*, the simultaneous mark or trace of the sharing and dividing of identity. The other applies to identity. Circumcision is administered, brought to bear. Perhaps, even, we can say that circumcision is, in a certain way, an *envoi* from an unknown location—the gift of the other—whose arrival promises each time to determine the identity of the self as the place between, in-between the other and an "ineffaceable

alliance." For example, there is the birth of the subject "Jacques Derrida;" "Jacques Derrida,", this proper name, is applied. Circumcision is
an act of giving; "Jacques Derrida," is given. This much is confessed: "I"
announce that which is given, that which is grafted or written on me by
an other.

VIII

But what is confessed and what takes place in this instance *between*?
What does *confession* admit, which is not already spoken in the suffix of
the word, mostly Latin, though originating possibly in Greek, and today
read as *-fession*? What is not already whispered, almost, as it were, in silence, and which, in giving itself, itself becomes silenced? What is there
to be heard in the silent other that the prefix *con-*, conjoined, or just simply joined, does not, always already intensify, amplify, and drown out?
Speaking and not speaking, not quite, Consider the *OED:* "f. *con-* intensive + *fateri, fass-* to utter, declare, disclose, manifest, avow, acknowledge,
prob. from the same root as *fari* to speak, utter; . . . L. *fatus* spoken, *fatum*
utterance, *fatri* (freq.) to speak much."

Disclosure, then, utterance and avowal, acknowledgment. This is what
gets the utterance going, marking not only motion but also displacement,
transition, and translation within the same language, as though something were coming out, coming into the open, coming into view. We are
already under way in the motion and transport of metaphor's drifting and
dispersal. There is a movement here, a rhythm, given the programming of
the confessional act, given also the program of the confessional as put in
place prior to any utterance, as an utterance of the law concerning the
modality of articulation as response before the law. It is almost as though,
in speaking, in aspiration, one gives up the ghost. And there is—is there
not?—something vaguely spectral, something hovering liminally around
the very idea of confession, certainly within and yet as other to those notions of disclosure, avowal, *manifestation*, acknowledgment. Each of these
words, whispering within and yet silenced by confession, also speaks—
albeit with that "roar that lies the other side of silence," to borrow from
George Eliot—not only of this haunting traversal but also of response.
For, there is to be read here perhaps, and this is no doubt the risk one has
to take in every act of reading, responding to, the spectral, where one is

not sure what one sees or does not see (what one "sees fit," as Bennington translates himself: *il a cru bon*[19] [lit. he had well believed]—to believe in any act of reading); there is to be read then, to be glimpsed in the passage, in what passes and what comes to pass, what arrives, what happens or takes place, if it happens or takes place at all, in confession, the response and, of course, responsibility. I respond to the other in my utterance, and, in doing so, I admit my responsibility, I answer yes, yes—for this is a double yes; how could it be anything else at this point?—being both a response, an acknowledgment in reply on the occasion of the call, the injunction of the other, and, at the same time, or nearly the same time, the acknowledgment to myself and to the other of that which I call my responsibility and yet that which exceeds merely polite acknowledgment or the simple calculation involved in the economy of an ethics.

IX

Yet this is only to move around, to circumscribe *-fession,* around that which has always already got going, and what will have gotten under way, to employ the future anterior so as to acknowledge, or, yet again, confess, what will have come to pass, whether or not I notice it, whether or not it is read. (Reading is thus, simultaneously, late, too late, already in ruins, disjointed, out of time, and yet it remains to come; this is well known, it is acknowledged; confession has already taken place.) In the name of love, perhaps, from one tongue to another, within the same tongue, "one's tongue in the mouth of another," to cite John Leavey, "such is translation."[20] Or to put this another way, the other's tongue wrapped around, circumscribing one's own. This is only to circumscribe what is always already ceaselessly under way. All of which is rendered mute, as though the tongue itself were circumcised, the sheath removed to leave the soft flesh exposed as Hélène Cixous remembers in "The Names of Oran,"[21] through that violent inscription, inscription qua intensification, in the imposition of the prefix, *con-*. The sense of this prefix, the *OED* informs us is "together, together with, in combination or union," also "altogether, completely," and hence *intensive*. It occurs in combinations actually formed in Latin, their derivatives, and analogical extensions.

The intensification is suggestive of amplification, a gathering up of all voices in one (and with that a muting of the multiplicity of tongues, silenced by an imposed univocity), while the other meanings indicate, if not a unity, then at least a community of voicings. But what it seems that *con* wants, in such concert, such a concerted effort, a coming together, is, yet again, as already suggested, an erasure of alterity, the non-indifference irreducible on the one hand to any simple selfhood or, on the other, to the other, dialectically thought. Hence, the necessity, the urgency, of cutting through, decisively, this gathering, to circumcise the word, to cut off the tip, to put it crudely, to leave the tongue exposed and vulnerable so that what is already said can be said again, and again, without circumscription. How is this to be achieved, supposing, for the moment, that it is even possible? Perhaps one has to learn to speak, to utter, and acknowledge, to make manifest oneself as an other, where "I" is an other from within circumscription, within the place where systemization is attempted and where it seeks to program writing according to all its laws concerning what is proper. And this would be an articulation, and also a response, not yet heard, remaining to be read, which does not act in any crudely dialectical fashion, but rather circles around its subject, which speaks apophatically, in a mode of indirection or analogical apperception; a writing that is, in short, so many periphrases: a circumfession. Such a writing would not so much cut off or remove anything, as it would cut into the discourse of the law, of the system, inhabiting and disrupting it in a certain way, having a certain relationship to it, a kind of affiliation or relation in nonrelation, occasionally surfacing, as so many partially visible and partially unaccountable apparitions, traces of what cannot be defined as such or reduced to determination. This, then, is where we will have begun, not from any starting point, but within that which the system, the program, the institution demands as its *incipit*, as its decisive, and incisive, cut: the very idea of a beginning, a starting point that gives, confers identity, and yet is never admitted as such: scandalous ~~con~~fession indeed.

X

But one has to start somewhere; there has to be the first step—or not—on the ladder, even if this requires a certain stepping back. We might take a detour here, via the example of *H,* as something that is *between* Cixous and Derrida; another hypothetical scenario. What is at stake in the figure *H* and what might this letter give us to understand about what takes place *between*? It is perhaps a question, again, of tongues, of translation-effects to put it, doubtless, too crudely, as that articulation that separates, that articulates the circumcision, naming singularity, and yet admits, in the (always-already quasi-presence) of a ghostly revenant—to which we give the name iterability—of the discontinuous name of the ontological: "I" (and "I"). *Between* I and I, between the one and the other or, possibly the other of the other here, a "sexuality of translation" or "the intromission of another tongue."[22] To come back to the phantasm or simulcrum of the subject, it has to be asked: what remains to be read, what is avowed, confessed, whenever I say "I"? and what difference does it make, what does difference "make happen," if I place "I" under arrest, in quotation marks like a pair of shackles placed on the supposedly sovereign subject? So, we begin, in this instance, with the letter "H," for Hélène, and for Hegel also, as Derrida reminds us at the beginning of *Glas.* In this text the language of the prepuce, of circumcision and circumfession, of what enfolds and takes place between the left- and the right-hand column, gets under way:

> [t]wo unequal columns . . . each of which—envelop(e) (s) or sheath(es), incalculably reverses, turns inside out, replaces, remarks, overlaps *[recoupe]* the other. The incalculable of *what remained* calculates itself, elaborates all the *coups* . . . twists or scaffolds them in silence . . . each column rises with an impassive self-sufficiency, and yet the element of contagion, the infinite circulation of general equivalence relates . . . each stump of writing . . . to each other, within each column and from one column to the other of *what remained* infinitely calculable.[23]

H arrives also as performative double writing and translation on the first page of Cixous' *Three Steps on the Ladder of Writing,* as the ladder of writing, but also, in its encrypted form, as a semi-paraph, a signature or siglum of sorts, signing itself and countersigning the first page, beginning then with the self, with the "I" that is also (doubled in) *"H,"* one part of that letter, or two parts, more precisely. And Cixous "begins" by acknowledging what takes place between: "I one language, I another language, and *between the two,* the line that makes them vibrate; writing forms a passageway between two shores"[24] (emphases added). Translation, passage, the trait that divides, remarks, and makes a connective thread as the passage of writing. "I" speaks of a singularity, a singularity that has its singular chance only by virtue of the fact that it is endlessly iterable (by you, and you, and you, and you, and, then again, by me; though, if you read "I" when "I" write, are you hearing me or yourself? Whose "I" is this? Can we tell?). Thus, "I" begins only in an enunciation that is also already a graphic re-mark, and never for the first time. There is no first time for "I." Even if I say "I" for the first time in my life, this is not is a beginning, a moment of origin absolutely: I say "I" and thus have already shuttled between "I" and "I," with a movement remarked by Cixous in "-," another incision perhaps, confession of a circumcision, of being marked, and that which simultaneously connects and also marks a boundary, a dividing line. Which brings us to the simulacrum of the phallic column, supposed guarantor of presence, which, as *H* shows us, is precisely never that because always already disinterred, a haunted tomb, as well as being haunted from within by its others, the tongues of the others giving and confessing; those others which countersign, which exceed and overflow sovereignty. In writing "*H*" there arrives a gift therefore, whose coming ruins performatively the very principle of an architectonics of self-sufficient, auto-affective identity, of any architectonics, with which it seems to resonate. For, to be fanciful for a moment, does it not bear a passing resemblance graphically to a house—"even though it is no longer the law in its own house"[25]—to a place without place, that *between* of dwelling, abidingly, to that which "I" inhabits in an uncanny fashion, to habitation qua the being of beings perhaps? "I" dwell(s), therefore "I" is haunted. Thus, any "autobiographical" gesture, like any confession, is already ruined in advance, for in beginning autobiography, however fragmented with this auto-avowal, auto-confession, we have already fallen into and been taken up by the system, the program of the autobiographical. Which is why, if avowal or confession have any chance, they must proceed in secret, by signs, through writing and therefore death; and, of course, every time I write, even if I never write "I," death is announced, in the very fact of iterability that is always beyond my control and which *H* signals, in its own singular fashion.

XI

We're not getting very far, even though I have anticipated a confession on the final page of Cixous's "The School of the Dead": "Writing is the delicate, difficult, and dangerous means of succeeding in avowing the unavowable."[26] Indeed, to admit as much, this is where we began before we began in directing questions toward the figures *between* and *love*, confessing as it were to the aporia of confession whereby any writing is always this go-between situating the subject as a relational response to an other who calls and yet who is neither simply there nor not there. Writing "embodies," if it can be put like this, this immaterial and uncanny motion, and is found in the exemplary condition of *H*, the *gramme* that is also the always encrypted paraph and which, without admitting anything at all, might be said to announce its work and the work of writing in general in the scandalous name of "circumfession." Writing, as Cixous puts it, "is this effort not to obliterate the picture, not to forget."[27] But it is also to remember in a different way, to remember one's self as an other, as other than that other that "I" am. (And *tout autre est tout autre* / every other is wholly other, to risk an impossible translation—note, even if you don't read French, how in the writing of this phrase, everything folds back on itself and yet moves forward: is this not the motion Hélène Cixous is describing in writing and assigning *H*?) How, then, not to forget (which is different from remembering)? With the avowal of love perhaps, in Cixous's case, love—"the writers I love are *descenders,* explorers of the lowest and deepest"—for Bernhard, Tsvetaeva, Lispector.[28] (At this juncture, in response to what Cixous calls a "mysterious affinity,"[29] we might also recall that Augustine suggests that it is love that is encrypted within the system or program of confession: when I confess to God what God already knows about me, and when I confess according to the program of the Church, the secret avowal of my love, my response to the call of the other, is that which resides within and in excess of any rote recitation of sins; I respond to the call, and, in doing so, perform love, whereby "I" is constituted through the mysterious affinity, the uncanny passage *between*.) Each is loved in their singularity and *love* thus names singularity, in other words, as well as naming what passes between as a result of "obey[ing] the call of certain texts."[30] Every time I speak my love, I avow, I testify to singularity. There is no generalizable or systematizable concept of love, for saying *I love you*— always a response to the call and the gift of the other—"creates the event it names."[31] Every love differs from every other love and can only be defined in its exemplarity and, moreover, in the exemplary motion of its ghostly motif between its locations: I *love* you. This event is only possible through the untimely response to the other that thereby constitutes "I" through passage, translation, and transference, all of which are remarked in the singular performativity of *love,* which is what touches both *you* and *I*. Thus love, like justice, or responsibility (and, again, each in their own singular fashion), remains incalculable, undeconstructable; its articulation unveils a between that had already anticipated the possibility of the utterance.

XII

But this is still to proceed too rapidly; stop, rewind, step back. Following the opening strategy on Cixous's part in *Three Steps on the Ladder of Writing* and its accompanying, secreted avowal of the autobi*ogrammy,* there takes place what seems the opening onto admission, confession once more, of love, for writers, and, from this, to the conventions of "autobiography," starting with childhood. Except, we must note, that the childhood, though singular, is shared; it is a writing that reiterates the gesture of the loved ones—a gesture at once singular and shared by analogy with the Derrida of "Circumfession," in his autobiogrammatical response to St. Augustine. Cixous (re)turns to writers who begin (with writing, with living) as the inaugural gambit, so that autobiography finds itself haunted by autobiogrammy. "Autobiography" is staged, placed on stage in a structural auto-displacement whereby "self" becomes enacted through the ruse of citation. Autobiography as confession, as avowal, can never escape the dishonesty of systematization, it always already finds itself enclosed. Therefore, it must open itself to this other writing of the self, semi-encrypted, through the acknowledgment of the iterability of citation—a gesture we will find shared by Daniel Deronda in a statement concerning identity—and the citation inscribed as the necessary performative articulation of iterability. Which, of course, has already taken place, in that opening reading of the letter *H.* So Cixous begins, before she begins, writing being the arche-origin of self, and the self unveiled as that singular place of dwelling haunted by and placed between the inscriptions of the other(s). Thus, there takes place—and it *takes place* precisely because this writing is performative, excessively so, beyond the control or mastery of any constative or mimetic force that the program of autobiography might believe it has— an avowal, a circumfession of the unavowable, in writing. This is the merest chance of the invention of "I" within the system's "confession" of "autobiography" that makes possible what is for Cixous writing's greatest secret: *truth.*

XIII

In admitting the matter of the autobiographical we have to return to a previous remark. Nicholas Royle, as I have already pointed out, identifies the *envois* from *The Post Card* as Derrida's "most provocative 'self-portrait'," a remark itself provocative inasmuch as it could equally apply to "Circumfession." Yet, whether we are talking of either *The Post Card* or "Circumfession" (or, for that matter, a number of texts by Derrida), how sure can we be that what we read is indeed self-portraiture? None of the fragments are signed in the "proper place" and the possible names of the addressees, the potential receivers, are never present; or they are, at the very least, not obviously where one might believe they should be. Peggy Kamuf has pointed out that these names are "censored or cut out."[32] Even as the figure of circumcision marks or re-marks the proper name, the signature, it can also be said to hide identity by cutting it away. On the one hand, as I inscribe the name "Jacques Derrida" I apply it, I make it into a work, I make it work, transforming the name into a thing, an application.[33] Yet, on the other hand, there is that in the name, the other in the identity that is located in the giving of the name, which resists both monumentalization and equipmentality. The other in the name applies the breaks. This is complicated further because names are spectral, they are neither simply there nor not there. As Derrida remarks in an interview from 1983, "all the names of the family are encrypted, along with a few others, in *The Post Card*, sometimes unreadable even for those who bear these names; often they are not capitalized."[34] So, while the professional reader goes off in search of such monuments and the family (en)crypt(ion), the amateur or amatory reader confronts a moment when he or she must bear witness to the fact that the structure of identity is inhabited in a certain way by nonknowing.[35] This nonknowing, I want to suggest, is marked by the "absolute aphorism" of the proper name that comes between identity and being, and between knowing and nonknowing as the signature of *between*. And all that I have suggested so far is exemplified in a certain moment in George Eliot's last novel, *Daniel Deronda* and in its eponymous protagonist whose name offers a particular figuration of *between,* between the knowable and the unknowable, between knowledge and ignorance, between a certain fiction of Englishness and, equally, a certain fiction of Jewishness. Deronda's proper name and the problematic of identities between which it resonates acknowledges how "the subject of writing is a *system* of relations between strata. . . .

Within that scene, on that stage, the punctual simplicity of the classical subject is not to be found. In order to describe the structure it is not enough to recall that one always writes for someone."[36]

XIV

In one of the *envois* Jacques Derrida mentions Daniel Deronda/*Daniel Deronda*. It is important to insist on the necessity of doubling the proper name here because this name is marked by equivocation and enigma, double reading no less, both within itself, *among itselves,* and in the post card/*The Post Card*.[37] Two proper names, two titles: Jacques Derrida/ *Jacques Derrida,* Daniel Deronda/*Daniel Deronda,* all being written into fictions concerning ontology and totalization. Both texts attest, as J. Hillis Miller has put it, of what happens when you let the proper name do your thinking for you. The titles and names all express a concern with identities, cultural, national, inherited, personal, public, and private; they all bear the marks of circumfession and circumcision; they situate themselves as the signatures of the motif and troping of *between;* and all scintillate and ring with undecidability, resounding with the repercussions of the desire "to know" the truth of identity. Even the family names bear a fortuitous resemblance: Derrida/Deronda. If we are to believe, as Derrida tells us, that the family names are encrypted in *The Post Card*[38]—it being a given, we might suggest, that Derrida plays on his name and initials elsewhere: *J'accepte, déjà, derrière le rideau, débris de*—why, in a moment of fanciful speculation, might we not read the inscription of "Deronda" as one of those encryptions? Of course we might, but this will tell us little or nothing about Derrida's identity, anymore than it will give us to understand Deronda's. We thus find ourselves ensnared in affirmative, resistant meshes, in what is described elsewhere as "this net of the first name and family name."[39] This long post card, dated 6 June 1977, speaks, among other things, of what cannot be dispatched; also about couriers, returns, detours, giving, and the memory of a failed delivery concerning *La différance*. Just over halfway through the following remark a parenthesis appears (a note within a post card): "While we walk, she tells me about her work projects (18th century correspondence and libertine literature, Sade, a whole plot of writings that I cannot summarize, and then Daniel Deronda, by G. Eliot, a story of circumcision and of double reading) and we turn into the labyrinth between the colleges."[40] The "she" is Cynthia Chase, as is known, the work on *Deronda* being referred to being an essay first published in 1978, and entitled "The Decomposition of the Elephants: Double-Reading Daniel Deronda."[41] Cynthia Chase's argument is drawn in part from, and as a response to, Steven Marcus's discussion of *Daniel Deronda*.[42] Her reading of the narrative is premised on Daniel's apparent ignorance of his Jewishness, particularly his being circumcised, and the fact that he never seems to "look down." She argues further that *Daniel Deronda* presents itself "to be read in two conflicting ways."[43] Chase suggests that the novel's narrative is at odds with itself, its identity divided, due to the tension between its realist and idealist trajectories; furthermore, this tension is never acknowledged, and this absence of acknowledgment is indicated by the absence of any apparent reference to circumcision in general or Daniel's circumcised phallus in particular. Although using what is conventionally recognized by many today as "deconstructive" discourse to interpret the tensions and the absence, Chase is indebted—as she acknowledges—to critics such as F. R. Leavis, Barbara Hardy, and David Kaufmann, who have traditionally divided *Deronda* into two parts, the "English" and the "Jewish." Chase argues that the narrative insistence on the hero's identity as, specifically, a Jewish identity, disrupts the narrative's coherence and that this reference to identity leads "relentlessly" to the "hero's phallus, which must have been circumcised. . . . Deronda must have known, but he did not: otherwise there could be no story. The plot can function only if *la chose,* Deronda's circumcised penis is disregarded; yet the novel's realism and referentiality function precisely to draw attention to it."[44] The "hero's circumcised phallus [is] proof of origin and identity."[45] The circumcised penis is both the "unacknowledged mark" of Jewishness and, simultaneously, the "exemplary signifier."[46] Chase's argument that circumcision is synonymous solely with Jewish identity is countered significantly by a historico-medical reading by K. M. Newton who challenges Chase's assertions concerning identity and circumcision on the grounds of her "use of historical discourse and her implicit assumptions about the author's intentions."[47] He pursues a reading of the historical and cultural contexts of circumcision and the medical conditions that would lead to circumcision of non-Jews as a form of hygienic precaution, or as a cure for phimosis.[48] Newton's fascinating counter does more than merely offer a historicist riposte, however, for he turns the tables on Chase, employing the various documentary and medical sources to explore and ultimately "deconstruct" Chase's essay, arguing that circumcision may well be "part of the theme of the ambiguity of signs."[49] Newton

moves from this cautious, conditional remark, to the idea that circumcision "becomes a sign of difference;"[50] he concludes with a commentary—
no more than an allusion really—on the highly allusive and indirect nature
of Eliot's imagination.[51] This, for me, remains too centered on the author,
but the movement of Newton's thought can lead to a more general movement away from the idea of authorial intentionality—that Eliot's text encrypted circumcision as an ambiguous or equivocal allusive mark—to the
possibility that we may be able to glimpse in *Daniel Deronda* the trace of
the other coming to Eliot, coming to us, on the way to arriving, but not
having yet been received.[52]

XV

I'm not concerned to engage further in the debate on this matter of a literal circumcision. I do, however, want to pick up on a thread in Chase's
text, in relation to Derrida's post card and the "themes" of identity, undecidability, circumcision, and love. This seems to dictate the return of the
detour, the circumscription. Chase writes that Daniel's "circumcized phallus, proof of origin and identity, is more than exemplary metonymy,
though it is certainly that. It is distinctively significant, not as a rhetorical
structure but as a referent. . . . The scandal of the referent calls attention
to the scandal . . . of rhetoricity."[53] Chase goes on to call the circumcised
phallus the "exemplary signifier."[54] It appears then that Chase, in limiting
the "appearance" of circumcision to the instance of Deronda's absent circumcised penis, and in seeing it as a referent, an exemplary signifier, is, in
fact, rhetorically constructing a desired presence, rather than finding the
signs of it. If we step back from the obsession with the phallus to inquire
after the mark of circumcision as "exemplary metonymy" of identity's con-
tingency, a mark, then, that is traced on the body of the text in other
words, we find in Eliot's circumscription the trace of circumcision powerfully remarked—to borrow a remark cited earlier, the *figure* at least of a
circumcision is imposed. The figure is not nothing of course, but it is also
irreducible to the literal. Neither one thing nor the other, and yet touching on both, the figure, figurality in general, haunts all that which takes
place in-between. As a trait or wound, something strange takes place in
the figural, "a kind of work takes place, mysterious, that will reassemble
the edges of the wound. A marvelous thing also: that will nonetheless leave

a trace."[55] The order of identification and location is thus breached and re-configured by the phantasm of the figural as that which always already returns to and within any ontology. Such revenance is exemplified in the relationship between Derrida's passing remark on a post card and the matter of the figural as circumcision in Eliot's text, in a particular line uttered by Daniel Deronda, in *Daniel Deronda*.

XVI

The line, employing the proper name and the equivocacy of identity, is itself an aphoristic post card, a fragment providing a redoubled double reading of the novel.[56] It names Daniel's secret and his being between identities and cultures. It is spoken by Deronda, and has a quite startling importance for the questions I have raised. The line occurs in chapter 42,[57] when Daniel is taken by Mordecai to a public house, The Hand and Banner, to be introduced to a small club of working men, who call themselves "The Philosophers." When introduced by Mordecai, and asked whether he is anonymous, Daniel replies: "My name is Daniel Deronda. I am unknown."[58] In this response to a call for identity, Deronda marks himself as being, to borrow a phrase from "Tympan," "*[b]etween* the proper of the other and the other of the proper" (emphasis mine).[59] Daniel's response is governed by a referential pun on the part of one of the group to Shelley's "Prometheus Unbound" and the "Great Unknown." The affirmation of identity is doubled and divided between the presentation of the name, as though the name could say everything, and the fragment of a citation, which in and of itself does double work, re-wounding, re-marking Daniel as other than himself and having an auto-biogrammatological mark arriving as the other's text, as the self is unveiled as nothing more than citational haunting, force and possibility. More than this occurs here; the statement is marked by the excess that it already enacts. The remark also takes on the status of an aphorism in the context of the novel and its double narrative—conventionally referred to as the English and Jewish parts—which redoubles the numerous oscillations across and between the text between these so-called parts, at the limits of both, and which refuses to be settled in either one. Daniel's aphorism strikes a chord. The line marks the text; it is the intrusion or incision, the circumcision, the giving and determining of *Daniel*

Deronda/Daniel Deronda, in what is perhaps a sign of love arriving between the one and the other. Such a speculation might appear hyperbolic but is warranted by Hélène Cixous's comments concerning the
passage of love and its relation to "the renouncement of the affirmation
of an identity," which involves opening "oneself": "one must make room
for the other."[60] On the one hand, Daniel names himself, announces
himself publicly, giving out his name and the undecidability that that
entails in response to the query concerning anonymity and the great unknown. In doing so he makes himself less than himself, exceeding ontology by re-marking himself as lack, marking himself as other, his
identity as something other than itself and so is written by that ghostly
inscription from the other that named him at the time of his circumcision. He redoubles the public and private name, that which is simultaneously in full view and yet encrypted. In doing so his commentary is
opened as performative in that, to borrow from Cixous, he makes room
for the other part of himself "who is other, who can only exist, of course,
if I am there to receive. In other words: becoming a receiver, withdraw-
ing, putting oneself way in the back. . . . Perhaps this brings us back to
love. That is: to love the other more than oneself."[61]

XVII

Deronda admits to the unknowable in his identity, that which is other
than the proper name, and beyond naming, at the very limit of the
nameable and thus announces what Giorgio Agamben describes as the
idea of love, which is: "to live in intimacy with a stranger, not in order
to draw him closer, or to make him known, but rather to keep him
strange, remote: unapparent—so unapparent that his name contains
him entirely. And, even in discomfort, to be nothing else, day after day,
than the ever open place, the unwaning light in which that one being,
that thing, remains forever exposed and sealed off."[62] Here is Deronda's
staging and withdrawal of himself, articulated in the uncanny utterance
to which we are alluding. He speaks from either side of the thresholds,
crossing and re-crossing, arriving only to retreat. This aphoristic fragment, announcing within itself the absolute aphorism of the proper
name, marks the birth of the subject "Daniel Deronda" as other than he
was. And this is precisely a circumfessional remark, a circumcisive ut-

terance, because the words are a "mark of belonging and exclusion."[63] It is the circumcisive act on Daniel's part—an act he does not wholly control, the other coming to address the "philosophers" through him—that cuts him from his English identity, and "grants access," to quote "Shibboleth," on the circumcised word, "to the community, to the covenant or alliance."[64] Daniel's self-naming simultaneously cuts and traces the location of identity between fixed locations. Entering the philosopher's circle, he incisively marks the meeting and himself; if I may be allowed, indulged in, a certain play here: his last name echoes with/in another language, French, with both the idea of the circle and a circumcisive cut, *ronde* meaning both circle and slice. Deronda cuts himself from himself in an act of Jewish inscription, albeit nonknowingly, for he has this feeling—does he not?—that he is doing it from another place that he does not know: his identity is determined by exteriority based on a place that he does not inhabit in a certain way, or that he does not, cannot, identify. Daniel's name, this double name of first and family name, the known and the nonknown—Daniel does not know his "family," he knows neither his parental nor his cultural identity, the identity called the "Jewish family" by Derrida in *Glas*[65]—acts as a key and an intercession. His second remark re-marks the name and Daniel's identity, the in medias res between Englishness and Jewishness, as the in-between, even as he is between, between two cultures, two identities, "at once both readable and secret."[66] And it is from this moment of naming, of marking his identity as other, that Daniel moves toward an identity, Jewish identity, at which neither he nor the novel ever arrives, but are always being sent toward, toward which they are directed, posted, destined. As Barbara Hardy puts it, Daniel is left "poised on the edge of a future," left in an act of departure, and open to the unknown to come.[67] Deronda, having been addressed by the other, finds himself sent, directed, but never delivered finally; as Hans Meyrick observes of Deronda, "*when* exactly the end may be I can't predict."[68] Also, of course, the novel has no closure, strictly speaking. There can never be a final identity, no final, self-sufficient or auto-affective determination. This is the chance the novel takes. It is the chance that love names, and which loves the dissonant within identity. Circumcision is thus written onto the body, the body of the subject Daniel Deronda, and the body of the text *Daniel Deronda,* leaving it open. Daniel's cutting remark thus marks the un/remarkable connection to his unknown father, his family, his nation, all of whom he desires to know, with a certain amatory passion.

XVIII

Cynthia Chase is right to suggest that there is that in the text that undermines "the authority of the notion of identity" and that the "deconstruction of this identity has radical implications for the concept of the subject in general,"[69] if, by identity, she can be read as suggesting "stable" or "fixed" identity. But, in turning the absent circumcised phallus into a transcendental signifier of metaphysical proportions, Chase misses the very mark of circumcision, the mark of affirmative resistance, on the body that comes from the other to mark both subject and text, and to mark identity as always inhabited by the other, never fixed. If Daniel Deronda is unknown, he is also, to a degree, unknowable. It might even be said of Daniel Deronda that he only ever has one name, but that name is not his own. And what is at stake in George Eliot's text is, like the work of Jacques Derrida, the effort to show how any "system must remain essentially open."[70] This is what is often missed in both Jacques Derrida and *Daniel Deronda*, the latter's Jewish plot found by critics such as F. R. Leavis to be a failure. It is important to observe that "Daniel Deronda" is, like "Jacques Derrida," what has been called "a half-fluid name."[71]

XIX

But what of love?

XX

Love is missed, it escapes identification; love is the figure for the in-between, a figure that is not to be captured. Love is also a mark on identity, a trace or cut that determines the self as never wholly itself. Indeed, Derrida's reading of Hegel in *Glas* connects at a certain point circumcision and love.[72] As Jean-Luc Nancy suggests, love is such that "one is shared and traversed by that which does not fix itself in any subject or signification. . . . Whatever my love is it cuts across my identity."[73] Furthermore, love is always arriving, Nancy informs us, love always arrives, it is the arrival of the other, so much *other*, in fact, "that it is never *made* (one makes love, because it is never *made*) and so much other that it is never *my* love (if I say to the other 'my love,' it is of the other, precisely that I speak, and nothing is 'mine')."[74] Love, like Daniel's quest for Jewish identity, is never completed, never finished, never done with. Daniel is marked by love; we are informed of his "eagerness to confess his love."[75] Deronda comes to trace a trajectory in the space of the between precisely because his desire to know his identity, his obsession with identity, comes to coincide with his desire to know and love the other, to know and love Mirah. However, it is no doubt easy to suppress love, deny it, ignore it, to imagine a scenario that would appropriate Deronda for a Jewish identity in some way opposed to the tyranny of English identity, even as there are those who desire to appropriate Derrida for similar purposes, in relation to other identities. After all, this is what the professional reader paradoxically desires, attempts, and fears; hence, in the case of *Daniel Deronda,* the dismissal of the Jewish plot as inferior, it being read as the debased, exteriorized other to the "proper" English plot and identity. Yet Mirah's effect upon Deronda cannot be explained away by reference to the two plots.[76] From their first encounter,[77] Daniel is enamored, his desire to know Mirah interwoven with his musings on his (then) unknown mother and the obscured origins of his own identity. What passes between them, an initial glance "but a couple of moments . . . a long while for two people to look straight at each other,"[78] announces what will become a correspondence between the two.[79] Daniel and Mirah address one another with the exchange between their eyes, and it is through this, and the inability to capture the other, that Deronda becomes haunted. Love arrives to inform Daniel that he is not himself; it comes to haunt his identity, and he finds himself obligated, to respond to an opening in himself brought about by the arrival of the other, and to that which takes place in the non-location between identities.

XXI

As Jean-Luc Nancy reminds us, love "consists as much in taking as in giving."[80] However, we are involved, between us, in a paradox, if we bear in mind that commentary on love by Jacques Lacan, of which Derrida recalls to mind, in a note from *Given Time.*[81] We do not have love, love is not ours to give; nor does the other possess love. Love is not yours, not mine. Not Jacques Derrida's, not Nicholas Royle's, as he admits.[82] And, furthermore, "Love," writes Nancy, "is addressed to one alone singularly and infinitely . . . it always flies to pieces as soon as it is sent."[83] This is, it would appear, acknowledged implicitly throughout *The Post Card*, with its numerous sendings, dispatches, fragments even in the perplexity over the question of how love should be addressed. Yet love appears, in different guises, throughout. Love appears again, throughout "Aphorism Countertime." I've no intention of pursuing a "reading" of such appearances, such apparitions, except to note, along with Nicholas Royle, that love is ghostly;[84] it is, noting as we must what has already been said, nothing other than that; it is "traced by the radically other (by death, in short)."[85] Returning to or sending the proper name, let us ask, in the name of love or the name of the other: who, or what, might come to speak in the name of love, yet wholly otherwise? Do we hear a voice, a name; do we believe we glimpse trace of love, one instance of a series of singular reiterations or multiple singularities? Can we help but acknowledge our responsibility to such a ghostly figure, each time it comes, returns, or is sent to us, each time the first and the last? What might we hear?

XXII

There can be no certainty concerning identity here; and, as Derrida tells us, we must fall back on the voice, since we cannot identify any speaker in all certainty.[86] We feel ourselves addressed, called in the name of love, and obliged to respond, to confess. There is *there,* occurring, both in and through the words, and exceeding the words, being more, *other,* than the words, what a certain Derrida might call the "spectral errancy of words. The spectral return does not befall words by accident. . . . The spectral return is partaken of by *all* words."[87] Such errancy traverses and traces every incalculable between. But why do I write of ghosts and love, and the ghost of a love in language? Every trace of love, every note or aphorism, every post card, reverberates, with someone, someone wholly other. Names are put on the line so that it can be seen how love marks, and is marked by, the other of/in identity. Love is traced—and traces—in the space between identities. Identity is never self-identical. This is a given.

XXIII

A "responsible reading," Timothy Clark remarks, "is one attuned to affirm whatever in a text exceeds the closures of representation."[88] Whatever: that which exceeds, that which opens to a certain crossing, that which is always responsible, and cannot be pinned down, cannot be named as some identity or in the name of an identity. Love calls on us to be responsible in coming to map the unmappable, to be open to the possibility of the impossible, and the possibility of this impossible experience is that, in short, which is between us and which remains: to come. Love is always just this exemplary passage between tongues, in what is foreign, other in the language one calls one's own. Note the movement: *between*.

> I wanted to write you, otherwise, but always with the same foreign language . . . (they don't know how much a language is foreign) . . . and when I write you you continue, you transfigure everything (the transformation comes from behind the words, it operates in silence, simultaneously subtle and incalculable, you substitute yourself for me and right up to my tongue you "send" it to yourself and then I remember those moments when you called me without warning, you came at night at the bottom of my throat, you came to touch my name with the tip of your tongue. Beneath the surface, it took place beneath the surface of the tongue, softly, slowly, an unheard-of trembling, and I was sure that at that second that it was not coming back, a convulsion of the entire body in two tongues at once, the foreign one and the other one. On the surface, nothing, a patient, applied pressure leaving everything in place, forcing no movement of the tongue: and then the tongue is all you hear, and we are alone I believe in receiving its silence. It never says a thing. Because we know how to love it, after our passage, without anything having changed in its appearance, it accepts no longer knowing who it is. It no longer recognizes its own, proper traits, it is no longer the law of its own house, it even has no more words.[89]

Part Three

APPARITIONING

Chapter 5

ETERNITY AND A DAY OR, AN "ENDLESS FOREWORD": *TOUT DIRE*

So there was a movement of nostalgic, mournful lyricism to reserve, perhaps encode, in short to render both *accessible and inaccessible*. And deep down this is still my most naïve desire. . . . The discursive forms we have available to us, the resources in terms of objectivizing archivation, are so much poorer than what happens (or fails to happen, whence the excesses of hyper-totalization). This desire for everything + n—

Jacques Derrida

All historical narratives contain an irreducible and inexpungeable element of interpretation. The historian has to interpret his materials in order to construct the moving pattern of images in which the form of the historical process is to be mirrored. And this because the historical record is both too full and too sparse.

Hayden White

I

The chapter that follows is an amended version of a paper originally "given" at the University of Staffordshire's "Deconstruction Reading Politics" conference, in July 1999.

I put the term "given" in quotes because I was unable to present the paper myself, which duty was performed by the conference organizer,

Martin McQuillan, to whom I am grateful for, quite literally, standing in for me, and allowing me to "speak" through him—an act of ventrilo-quism, mimicry, and haunting—by which means I managed a momen-tarily spectral manifestation. What follows provides the beginnings of a reading—a reading that will never be completed—of the conference title, its strange structure and logic, as a way of addressing the fraught rela-tionship that the terms of the title open to view. In extending the original paper, which, in its shorter version had already oriented itself around a particular scene from Theo Angelopoulos's *Eternity and a Day*, I have sought to bring to the fore in a more explicit manner the question of spectrality that was already implicit. Haunting—spectral persistence—imposes an impossible necessity on us: we have to be attentive to ghosts, as the work of Jacques Derrida reminds us on several occasions, and there can be no final word, no coming to rest or closure, whether one is speak-ing of literature or politics, narrowly conceived. Indeed, to take one of the two examples just given, inasmuch as "there is no essence or substance of literature," and given that "literature is not," that "it does not exist" and that its experience "rests on the very thing that no ontology could essen-tialize,"[1] literature can only ever be received as hauntological in that, lacking and resisting all determination strictly speaking, "it" exceeds and overflows ontology. The reason for this is that there is always something other within any structure that disturbs that identity from within, and which, in excess of the structure, enjoins, *entitles*, us to continue in our attentiveness, to listen, to seek to read, and to respond. This "excess," this opening of structure within, onto, and beyond itself—an *it-self*—so as to initiate a move elsewhere is caught both in the impossible phrase *an end-less foreword*, and in the impossible registration of *tout dire*: that, on the one hand, one can say everything, while, on the other, that one can say anything, without constraint. And this, perhaps, is what is given to be heard in the occasion of the title *deconstruction reading politics*.

II

The question here, then, the one with which we begin at least, has to do with titles, of what they entitle us to address. The question of titles and their entitlement concerns the ways in which they determine and demand our response. Who is entitled? To what are we entitled? And what are we entitled to say in response to a conference title such as *deconstruction reading politics*? Perhaps it is the case that part of our entitlement is uneven and unpredictable: it is that which we may lay claim to but, conversely, it is also that which is demanded of us by virtue of the fact that a title designates us as its subjects. It represents its readers as being the agents or subjects of a particular effect, action, or condition. Reading the work of the title, before addressing its specific terminology, the title qualifies and assigns apparent possession. It furnishes us, in principle at least, with a rightful claim, as well in an obscure sense with the entitlement to write under particular titles or headings, even though we cannot be sure of the direction of that heading until after the event. Perhaps that to which we are, or believe ourselves to be, entitled is nothing as such but, merely, various modalities of access made possible through titles that, far from being apparent, are, in fact and in practice, counterintuitive, despite any obvious entitlement. Such a complication demands that we ask what, therefore, titles impose upon us, what mark they leave on us, and what such unreasonable aphorisms as they are give us to think (when we think, if we think of them at all), to attempt to read, even as they may be said to haunt every footstep of our consideration.

It is, of course, all too easy to overlook the title. For it is very small. Like its cognate form, *tittle*, it arrives haunted by its earliest grammatological usages: as a small stroke or point in writing and printing, a diacritical mark or accent on a letter. At the same time, it should be acknowledged that titles appear to embody something paradoxical: intimating aphoristically an apparent proximity to their subjects, they nonetheless maintain a distance: a topographical coordinate always "there" in relation to the perpetual "being here," "being at this moment" that the reader–text relationship constantly unfolds. The title stands between reader and subject certainly, between the "inside" of a text and what, supposedly, lies beyond that immediate text. But, more generally, titles express in their liminal presentation or appresentation (for they represent nothing as such) a suspension, a separation, something that from the start is, in the words of Samuel Weber, "marked by an irreducible element."[2] Titles aspire to the condition of the auratic, as *aura* is understood by Walter Benjamin.[3] Like *aura*, they appear in some haunted fashion to "name the undepictable *de-piction* of distancing and separation"; they return "as the appearance or apparition of an irreducible separation."[4] Moreover, titles thus mark the text in some ostensibly minimal fashion, while bringing to bear an impossible weight.

So, a title or two. *Eternity and a Day*. No, this does not name the
feeling some have occasionally when attending conferences (and, I hasten
to add, I am not including *Deconstruction Reading Politics* in this description). In a certain way, for me, this phrase, *eternity and a day*, identifies, though only in the most provisional manner, something akin to a
structure. I choose this term, only if it can be acknowledged that, by this
word, "structure," it is possible to allow the idea of a form that is never
completely closed upon itself. In being somehow open, ongoing, constituted by a promise, there is the chance that "structure" always exceeds itself. *Eternity and a day* defines the possibility of imagining an in*fin*ite
structuration, where the un*fin*ished condition is always extended. It thus
also names, or possibly entitles, a simultaneity: that of structure and the
impossibility of structure, comprehended as closed, completed.

Clearly, there is some disturbance at work here, a doubling of the
idea of form by that which haunts and therefore also divides it. There is a
ghost in the machine, if you will, a phantasmic or spectral persistence.
The uncanniness, the estranging disquietude, of this persistence is that
its return urges and entitles us to think differently in those very places
where we have become most habituated, where it might even be said we
are so habituated, so at home, that we no longer think, of, for example,
the question of politics. That we have to negotiate the difficulty of the
phantom, of the ghostly other within the safe home, the regular or habitual structure of thought, means that a certain spirit survives, despite
the deadening effects of convention, and that we are, in effect, engaged to
respond to a spectral respiration transgressing the limits of any identity,
or what Giorgio Agamben names, in *Stanzas, pneumo-phantasmology*.[5]
The "structure" thus is haunted by that which makes it possible for it to
survive itself, always overflowing itself. This "excess," if one can call the
effect of spirit or ghostly breath by this name, is named twice, at least: not
only in the word *eternity*, which names duration without limit, but also,
and especially, in the remainder of the phrase—and a day. It is almost as
if, in expiring, the final breath carries the spirit beyond structure. The *remains of the day*, it is tempting to add. But what I wish to identify in that
extension of *eternity* is a kind of superaddition or oscillation, as though
eternity named something and yet not everything; as though, in short,
the naming of a totality acknowledged an ungovernable excess beyond totalization. Adding *a day* implies a limit to thinking *eternity*, as though
that which names the illimitable or incalculable were somehow limited.
It is as though this statement were, on the one hand, in some measure

always inhabited and, equally, already disrupted internally from any habitual thinking of structure, structure as the *habitus* as already implied (where I live, there[fore] I do not think), by what Jacques Lacan defines vaguely in relation to woman's *jouissance* as that which is *"en plus,"* something more (as though "something more" defined, with greater precision, something that *something* did not; as though it somehow stabilized the trembling of that uncanny *something* rather than causing it to supplement its own haunted oscillation);[6] while, on the other hand this title is haunted by a ghostly equivalence, recalling a phrase of Jacques Derrida's: *everything—and all the rest.*[7]

Why choose this expression, *eternity and a day*, as the title and starting point of a chapter, originally presented at a conference entitled *Deconstruction Reading Politics* (along with all that this other title expresses)? This title, the one I'm employing for this chapter, might have been recognized already not as my own but having arrived from somewhere else, as the title of a film by Theo Angelopoulos, winner of the Palme d'or at Cannes in 1998. I will return to the film in a moment. For now, however, what I would like to suggest, as a possibly quite indefensible hypothesis—but, after all, we have to begin somewhere—is that, in a certain way, this title, in naming an open structure, or, to be more precise, an "open-structure-plus (*en plus*)," can be understood as providing a sketch of a reading (if not the ghost of one), or a "foreword" of sorts, of what the words in the conference title already name. *Deconstruction. Reading. Politics.* Each word articulates and is articulated by this "open-structure-plus." There is, in looking at these words, a sense that, to paraphrase Benjamin (citing Karl Kraus), the closer one looks, the more one is aware of a distance. In experiencing this title, one experiences a spectral oscillation between what is close at hand, and what is impossibly, irreducibly distant. Without seeking to read the conference title as a sentence, or otherwise defining possible relationships between the three terms in question (at least not for the moment; other speakers will have attempted to do so in the course of the conference, and do so far more convincingly than I could), all I wish to say, for now, is that, for me, *eternity and a day* speaks indirectly of the promise of, in turn, deconstruction, reading, and politics. It articulates the idea of deconstructions-to-come, of reading-to-come, of a politics-to-come.

Each of these three phrases, which I have presented as "supplementary interpretive addition[s]"[8] to the terms of the conference title, do nothing of course other than to express what is already articulated by each of these

words, *deconstruction, reading, politics*. I am not adding to the title as
though its terms were somehow inadequate. They are not, of course; if anything, they remain excessive, waiting to be read, or to be received. To paraphrase Geoffrey Bennington, I'm really not saying anything more than
deconstruction reading politics when I say "deconstructions-to-come,"
"reading-to-come," "politics-to-come."[9] I merely offer these supplements as
examples of the explicit and somewhat crude expression of the "open-structure-plus" of the structure of reading, defined by Werner Hamacher as "not
yet what it already is," or the "not yet [of] the immanent movement . . .
which it already is."[10] In doing so, I am seeking to acknowledge a necessary
delay *and* anticipation. This is also a means of beginning with certain remnants, so as to remain in a mode of address described by Hamacher as an
"endless foreword," even though this chapter is not located in the place of
a foreword, obviously.[11] This is acknowledged if only to signal a resistance
to definition, which the conference title, indeed, any title, might appear to
demand or entitle. None of these phrases—*deconstruction reading politics*—names a point at which we will arrive. They are each to-come, to borrow from Nicholas Royle, "not as an act or event that might one day
become present, but rather in the structural sense of a promise, a promise
which is—in its affirmation and nonfulfilment—a double–bind."[12] Enough
of prefatory excuses, however. Let's begin (again) by returning to the film,
Eternity and a Day as a preface, of sorts.

III

I am not going to present a reading of the film here, at least not much of
one, though I will doubtless be tempted to sketch in brief a few of its gestures, its tropes or motifs. I do, however, wish to draw on it for the purpose of illustration or possibly illumination, and to borrow from the film
as the occasion for this chapter, as a means of recognizing the inescapable
and necessary work of continuing to negotiate the endless foreword as
the response entailed by acts of revenance. A brief précis of the film's narrative then, or fragments of it, if you'll forgive this representation of a
representation. I simply wish to avoid the assumption that everyone has
seen Angelopoulos's film.

Taking place over twenty-four hours, and yet also most of a life,
through those forms of reading and writing known as flashback, *Eternity*

and a Day follows the wanderings of a dying writer, Alexander, around his Greek hometown, Thessaloniki, on the day before he is due to enter a sanatorium. His wandering takes on a zeugmatic condition. It assumes a haunted, double structure, being, in its aleatory navigation, both tropological and topographical or, at the risk of a neologism, t(r)opographic (a graphic simultaneity *and* supplementarity which is absolutely unavailable to voicing). Alexander wanders through the town and the time and space of one day, even as in memory he drifts through the historical past of Greece, where poetics and national identity come to touch intimately upon one another. He wanders through his memories also, as he seeks to come to terms with the identity that is his, that is written for him by the enigmas of familial, historical, and poetic legacies. The film is thus motivated by the haunting revenance of anamnesis, so many phantasmic projections momentarily brought to light in the place of a singular identity, not itself the terminus for such textual returns, but, instead, a place of witness and relay, a momentary locus from where the overflow of memory exceeds all ontological determination. Alexander's drifting remarks an irreversible movement, for he can never take back or return what he has traced (or what he in turn is traced by); furthermore, *who* he is can never erase the filmic images of memory that "write" this figure for us, a writing in excess of Alexander's identity in the film's present. His movement is t(r)opographic in that, as it maps the town, so it writes the writer, even as, reciprocally, that writer's random motions write both his identity for the viewer and, more broadly, for the film itself. His movements serve as acts of inscription, every image, every cut and edit, the troping of the cinematic configuration of what is called a life. Alexander's motion is then also a motif and a screen. He figures himself through acts of testamentary memory, while being a medium through which arrive other's narratives to which we, in turn, must bear witness.

The purpose of motion, a kind of endless circulation, thus belongs to response and responsibility. Alexander has abandoned his own writing, in order to finish an uncompleted work by nineteenth-century poet Dionysios Solomos, author of the Greek national hymn. In Angelopoulos's own words, "Alexander is trying to finish an uncompleted poem from the nineteenth century with words he gathers himself: like the original poet, he buys them."[13] Yet Alexander, on the verge of departing, has not finished this project. Indeed, there are no signs that he will. In this light, and in its relation to the figure and the hope of a national identity, it is perhaps significant that the poem, that literature, is figured as always incomplete; as the remains, the traces of another's voice given only in brief phrases the poem remains open to a future, always to come. And this is the point, perhaps: literature is always without an identity, without a home of its own; being nothing, it is always already adrift. This, we can read, is figured through Alexander himself, in the fact of his giving up his house, in becoming itinerant. Casting himself from his home, Alexander takes on, at one and the same time, the role of exile while figuring that inescapably uncanny condition of being, addressed by Heidegger. Alexander "no longer feels at home in his most familiar environment . . . being-in-the-world is totally transformed into a 'not at home' purely and simply."[14] Haunted by what Angelopoulos calls "scraps of memory," whether these memories belong to the poet or to the experience of a larger Greek national identity, incarnated in the figure of Solomos, who returns to Alexander's sight and through the cinematic gaze, Alexander thus assumes the role of the exile or stranger searching for home, for the idea of home, in the place that has always been his home but which is nonetheless inescapably haunted. He thus becomes marked in the film's exploration of the spectral experience of that which is both inexpressibly close and irreducibly distant. This is articulated through one of the words he collects: *xenitis*—a stranger, who is a stranger everywhere, even to himself, as Angelopoulos explains in the interview already cited. There is not a simple correlation, however, between word and figure. As Angelopoulos implies, *xenitis*, an old, all but forgotten word, returns as the haunting trace of a spectral and spiritual evocation of an identity, which hovers in the word between the visible and invisible, which returns from a past and announces the opening of identity to itself in the uncanny figuring of identity as being that which, always already haunted, is still to come. Thus, there is expressed through this word, as through every frame of the film, the experience of the auratic as the experience of spectres and a responsibility to the spectral which opens the self to its own incompletion, its own unhomeliness. And this is registered, moreover, everywhere in *Eternity and a Day*, in figures of incompletion, from the references to unfinished poems, to the images of building sites, and to the haunting allusions to the histories of the Balkans—which narratives inform in a different manner another of Angelopoulos' films, *Ulysses' Gaze*.

Travelling, apparently aimlessly, around town, Alexander encounters, and subsequently befriends a boy, an Albanian refugee, who makes a precarious living cleaning car windshields at stop lights. For a while, they travel throughout the town and just outside it. At one point, toward the end of the day, Alexander and the boy board a bus. During the bus journey, the poet Dionysios Solomos, joins them, as do three music students, who set up their instruments and begin to play. Angelopoulos cuts from the musicians to the writer and the refugee. The soundtrack alters, so that, while the music remains the same, it is no longer the same. From being a recording of the musicians' performance, the soundtrack becomes an orchestrated version of the same music that frames what we see. All other sound is faded out, so that there is no traffic, no rain, nothing remains from the world of the narrative. Of the film but no longer in the film, the music consumes its audience, Alexander and the boy, and us also.

All the while this happens—and the duration of the shot is impossible to recall—the image of the boy and the dying man remains the same; not static or frozen, merely still. Sitting on separate seats, on either side of the bus, the two look toward where we understand the musicians to be, though not exactly in the same direction. If we imagine ourselves in the audience, and our gaze constitutes a single, central focal point, the two passengers look outward, over our shoulders and above our heads. They stay in this position, perhaps faintly smiling, perhaps transfixed. What *we* see is that they appear to comprehend—to see, to hear, *and* something else—something beyond our vision, perhaps beyond the narrative, beyond what remains of the day. It is impossible to tell. All we can do is witness this moment, and acknowledge that we can say nothing with any certainty about what we see.

This appears to be a moment of both *ecstasis* and *ectasis*. There is the appearance of being enraptured, of utter absorption, along with, simultaneously, a momentary sense of displacement—both suspension and extension—of the narrative. The scene appears readable as performative: it figures contemplation and suspension, a phantomatic and phantasmatic figuration of being outside itself, as a condition of exalted transport. The shot seems to place itself outside its diegetic purpose in some entirely other relationship to the film. In addition, there is also a feeling of something being stretched, extended beyond itself: duration without duration, as it were, the figuring of that open-structure-plus, as if the grammar of the image lengthens and suspends. How to read this? The only thing I can say about this moment of ecstatic dislocation is that it recalls a similar moment in *Ulysses' Gaze*. In this, a filmmaker, who has been searching for two lost reels of film, supposedly the first film ever shot in Greece—the "first gaze" the filmmaker calls it—sits watching these reels. His gaze is in a similar direction to that of the writer, Alexander. As the audience, we see only

his face, his emotional response, apparent recognition of something otherwise incomprehensible, and the flickering light of the projector, above and
behind him. This is the moment at which diegesis remains strategically,
structurally incomplete and undecidable. Nothing comes to a close, as we
witness a moment of passive suffering in response to the unseen.

What are we being asked to witness here? What do the writer, the
refugee, the filmmaker see? What becomes available for them that we can
never comprehend as such? Is there a question here of a radical praxis in
the relation between narration and bearing witness? Is there a displacement of the image by a gesture? Moreover, what do these brief, yet endless images have to do with *deconstruction reading politics*?

IV

The scene from *Eternity and a Day* just described can be understood as
functioning with a degree of independence. While it is a part of the narrative sequence, it appears to disjoint that sequence, and to indicate,
though not in any direct manner, another space, a period that has nothing to do with narrative. Certainly, it does not appear to modify what
comes after in the narrative. We watch, we listen, and we perhaps attempt
to read the faces of the Albanian boy and Alexander, even though what we
can only read is, as I have already implied, what Peggy Kamuf calls the
"very limit of the reading act."[15] We may read that the film's characters
appear to be reading, to be in the process of coming to terms with an incalculable temporality, an "always-yet-to-come," to cite Kamuf once
more.[16] Yet we have to confess that there is that in the moment, in which
"reading is part of what is read," the acknowledgment that "one has to
read and at the same time that . . . one cannot read."[17] This is our impossible entitlement. Reading this moment, this one shot, would take forever, and, even then, we would never be done with it.

The same can be said for the title of this conference, and for each of
its three terms. "Deconstruction reading politics." When first thinking
about this title, it occurred to me that I was reminded of that moment on
the TV game show *University Challenge* (called *College Bowl* in the
United States) where teams of students compete in the name of their college, when a student, introducing her/himself, says "Jo(e) Smith reading
politics." (Or English, or history, or whatever the student's major may

be.) The statement operates meaningfully and apparently independently of whatever may follow. However, I want to try out a small experiment—one I know is doomed to failure already—by taking the words of the title and, particularly, their sequence at face value. Having said that I had no wish to read the conference title as a sentence, I'm now going to go back on that statement, albeit in a far too hurried fashion.

By the logic of the game show introduction, the title of the conference will hereafter be understood to define an object of investigation or research—politics—and an identity of sorts, a shadowy figure exceeding and escaping identification—deconstruction—in the name of which the inquiry is pursued. Deconstruction reads politics, it promises to add that "supplementary interpretive addition" to the text of politics, presumably because politics, traditionally conceived and organized, is incapable of reading itself. *Reading*, as, for now, the apparently operative term, names a form of opening to which, as Geoffrey Bennington has suggested, certain traditions are resistant.[18] Indeed, and to recall another essay of Bennington's, *"Inter,"* the tradition in political discourse has been resistant to opening itself to what is vacuously or nebulously termed "theory," on the grounds that it—whatever "it" is, might be, or is assumed to be—is not political, never political enough.[19]

However, to return to the conference title: as soon as the title is read as if it were a sentence of sorts, things begin to go awry. If "reading" is the name of this opening, isn't that already named, already at work, in the word "deconstruction"? What does "deconstruction reading" as a somewhat awkward phrase (which at least has the advantage of resisting slipping into the institutionalized coziness of "deconstructive reading" or "deconstructionism") say that "deconstruction" does not? As you can see, the experiment has broken down. There is a breaking point to the reading, and we have to deal with fragments; the possibility for their reassembly is slim. There is a way in which we can comprehend the fragments conditionally, although this too is fraught. I don't wish to advance this as a reading: I am merely seeking here the appropriate figure in the work of the "endless foreword." What I want to suggest is that the scene from Angelopoulos's film, the title of that film that has become the title of this chapter, and those three troublesome words that Martin McQuillan has imposed upon us in this unbearable order, as though forcing us either to determine for them an interesting, if violent, sequence, or, otherwise to read there a kind of *anacoluthonic* openness, can be understood in the way in which they work, as *absolute constructions*.

"In its grammatical usage, an absolute construction is so called because it is independent of its grammatical surroundings."[20] This is Thomas Pepper's definition, and he clarifies further, in identifying the absolute construction with the ablative in Latin and the genitive in Greek, by suggesting that it has "something of the unconditioned condition about it."[21] The title, *eternity and a day*, operates, as does the scene on the bus, as do *deconstruction* or *reading*, as though each had this "unconditioned condition." The absolute construction is only that if what follows is not modified by it or if what follows does not modify the "clause" in question. The absolute construction causes a form of disjunction within the "grammatical" structure. It interrupts and causes sequential logic to desist. It is, we might say, a form of figuration that is also, at the same time, disfiguration. Yet, as Pepper points out, after Paul de Man, to state that a clause or statement is absolute is not, itself, absolute, it is positional: "Its absoluteness, its independence is dependent on what follows or precedes."[22]

Thus, in identifying the figure or clause, phrase, or image, in this manner we are forced to concede that at the same time, even as we believe we can identify anything at all, we cannot close the circle. What the film scene, the various phrases or words, return to us is the knowledge that we have to decide on the undecidable, where, as Peggy Kamuf puts it, "all calculations are opened onto the incalculable, that is, onto a certain future."[23] Reading the absolute construction, reading its position as apparently independent of purely logical forms or grammatical structures, we come to see that the absolute construction opens itself in another direction, perhaps in the direction of the other, if I can put it this way. In response to this, we must therefore continue to pursue the endless foreword that seeks to deal not only with the purely mechanical or systematic but also what is called by Werner Hamacher the "metaphoricity of the text and the phantasmatic dimension,"[24] or what Paul de Man has described as "the rhetorical or tropological dimension" whereby "grammatical cognition is undone, at all times, by its rhetorical displacement."[25]

The question is one of possible relation, of location and/as dislocation (in short, haunting), and the tension that arises as a result of the "unconditioned condition" or the independence that is, could be, possibly, contingent. Or not. It is not an either/or matter, and it may have been misleading of me to have insinuated that, in the conference title, there is either, *on the one hand*, an interesting, if violent, sequence, or, *on the other hand*, what I have just described as 'a kind of *anacoluthonic* openness.' Rather, there are both at work, as the effect of an ungovernable doubling. So, to reiterate:

we are faced with what I am calling absolute constructions: the scene from the film, the phrase *eternity and a day*, the conference title *deconstruction reading politics*, and each of these words—*deconstruction reading politics*, whether or not they are entitled by any form of punctuation or diacritical mark. At the same time though, despite the apparent condition of being readable as absolute constructions, each, in situating itself so independently, wants to lead us somewhere else.

V

If I were foolhardy enough to seek to explore the title of this conference further—to recall a remark of Nicholas Royle's, I feel like a somnambulist in a minefield[26]—I might wish to observe a fundamental asymmetrical relationship. Well, I am, and I will. While it is no doubt true to a certain extent, and we could show this, that deconstruction reads politics, politics in the form of specific political orientations, discourses, politicised manifestations of reading toward a limit, and within limits, cannot by and large be said to have read deconstruction. There are, I hasten to add, notable exceptions.

I am aware that I am not saying anything new, of course. I'm doing nothing here other than rehearsing a number of well-known arguments. Nevertheless, this, it seems to me, is, in one sense, the necessary obligation involved in engaging with the process of an "endless foreword." It is, perhaps, even urgent, in the face of the absolute construction that, instead of being attended to patiently, is all too easily glossed over, and consigned to the not-read, often in advance of any attempt to read. It is often the case that this has been the fortune of "deconstruction." Not read carefully enough, never read carefully enough, "deconstruction" is assumed, subjected to suppositions and judgments that instrumentalize in a more or less pragmatic fashion, or in the name of some supposedly political praxis. The narrowly "political" response to "deconstruction" takes on the form of an "absolute knowing" (as will be discussed later in other chapters of the present volume).[27] This is not unusual. Institutionally, conventionally, traditionally, "within" or "beyond" the illusion of the university the discourse of politics, particularly as it manifests itself in literary studies, all too often has to do, as others have shown, with placing a limit on reading (especially reading itself, whatever the especial features of its politics) and a limit toward which limited reading should be directed. This proscriptive tendency, whether in the name of political exigency or moral imperative, has been recently described by James R. Kincaid (in an as-yet unpublished essay), as "strong theory," where reading is abandoned in the favor of assertion. Bennington also provides an example of this practice for us when he speaks of reading toward socialism, reading for socialism.[28] Can such reading, such an operation that involves the erection of barricades, be said to be reading? Assuming, as Bennington suggests, a journalistic haste, reading is eschewed, in favor of judgment or, more precisely, prejudgment. From this perspective, what is called "theory" is judged "not political, or at any rate, never political enough."

From lacking political commitment to willful retreat from the political, that's the next step. Elizabeth Grosz makes a point related to Bennington's, though here the "problem" is with "Derrida," not "Theory" (there is a difference, even if it is often not recognized). Grosz states: "It has been commonplace to claim that Derrida . . . represents a mode of depoliticization and deflection of feminist, class and post-colonial struggles, [although] Derrida has never written on anything other than politics and violence, even if . . . he does not write *only* on politics and violence."[29]

A number of readers no doubt will recognize this to be the case. Although Grosz is referring immediately to the work of Seyla Benhabib, Nancy Fraser, Linda Nicholson, Jürgen Habermas, and Thomas McCarthy, whose criticism of Derrida is that, unlike some apothecary, he offers "no suggestion of remedies,"[30] one could all too easily supplant these proper names and supply others. In passing, and in contradiction to such a remark, it would be all too easy to show how Derrida, in his continued attentiveness to the saying, the calling, of the other (and even though he does not write only on this calling), has never written on anything except this calling, as if his writings were a formulation without formula of the apothecary's response in *Romeo and Juliet*, who asks, "Who calls so loud?"

In the remarks of Bennington and Grosz, the concern has not been with "deconstruction"; instead, it has been a matter, first, of "theory" and, subsequently "Derrida." It would however be relatively little trouble to rethink these commentaries in relation to the question of "deconstruction." Let me offer one more example, provided this time by Peggy Kamuf. From the state of not or never being political enough, to the condition of depoliticizing, we can move to the situation of being, on the one hand, too political, and, on the other, not political at all:

> Woodward and other journalists . . . see deconstruction as responsible
> for a vast array of institutional realignments, most of which, of course,
> they deplore. Despite [journalism's] hopelessly misinformed account,
> one may be tempted to find it closer to some truth than an opposing ac-
> count of deconstruction's . . . lack of effect because it is . . . "too theo-
> retical," "not political." The fact that deconstruction can be positioned
> as at once too political and not political at all . . . signals that the terms
> in which the political is posed in this debate are inadequate to account
> for all the effects being produced.[31]

It is ironic, to say the least, that Kamuf's account finds some greater fidelity in journalism's distorted accounts of deconstruction than there is
to be found in the quasi-journalistic fervor of political criticism's rendering within the university, discussed by Bennington. And it is because
of the ironic mode that it is possible to return to that asymmetry of
which I spoke earlier. *Deconstruction reading politics* but not *politics
reading deconstruction.*

VI

There appears, however obliquely, to be a certain question of praxis presenting itself here; or at least certain kinds of praxis that might or might
not take place in the strange work of title. This has to do with opening at
the very place where the title appears to have closed off, to have named
everything in a particular manner. It is also a matter of being open to a
call, while also issuing a call. A conference title names the possibility that
an event will take place, without being able to predict or control that possibility. Praxis therefore announces itself in the act of opening and remaining open and, in the space of this opening, signalling the potential
for the arrival of a transformative, irreversible moment. Here is Derrida
on the event:

> It is not enough that something *may* happen for it to happen, of course;
> hence an analysis of what *makes* an event *possible*—however indis-
> pensable it may continue to be . . .—will never tell us anything about
> the event itself. . . . That which occurs, and thereby occurs only once,
> for the first and last time, is always something more or less than its

possibility. One can talk endlessly about its possibility without ever
coming close to the thing itself in its coming. It may be, then, that the
order is other . . . and that only the coming of the event allows, after the
event *[après coup]*, perhaps, what it will previously have made possible
to be thought. . . . Among the immense consequences of this strong logical necessity, we must reckon with those concerning nothing less than
revelation, truth and the event.[32]

Praxis as gesture then, as a gesture in thought or writing that does not
present an image but stages, without ever assuming or appropriating to
itself some mimetic re-representation, the possibility of the *perhaps,*
which imagines rather than represents the possibility of the impossible.
This might, to some at least, sound more like a description of *poiêsis*, of
production that has an end other than itself, rather than the action that
is an end in itself, and is called by Aristotle *praxis*.[33] What I am seeking to
suggest, however, is that the occasion of, or perhaps more accurately, *for*
thinking that the occasion of a conference title or a film title entitles us
to is the singular occasion of a radical praxis, which distinguishes an
other thinking: a thinking open to the future, open to the other, as distinct from a morality, a politics, a philosophy, all of which can be said to
fall into habits of repetitive action founded on the appropriate constitution of an image, representation, or ontological model.

To engage the three motifs of the conference title, this might be understood if I stage a sketched reading concerning the conventional positioning of deconstruction on the one hand and politics on the other. One
of the hypothetical accusations levelled at so-called deconstruction—and
in this generalization here I can no doubt be accused of parodying, but
this is unavoidable—is that it doesn't *do* anything. No change is effected,
no event takes place that resembles political action, activism, activity, or
radical praxis. But the question arises, or at least it should: what would a
radical praxis look like? How would we know it, except perhaps for the
chance of a recognition as an *après coup*? What takes place, what happens,
what arrives, what comes to pass, if anything, between an *aperçu* and the
après coup? And is this a matter of praxis? Is this its incalculable chance?

On reflection, all such questions would seem to deny the very possibility of praxis. They deny its possibility for a couple of reasons at least. To
begin, each of the queries I have thus far situated operate more or less as
responses, reflections, recognitions. They come to be articulated, so it
seems, after the fact, after the event. There is a certain recapitulatory

quality involved. Then, each of these queries functions, if they function at all, according to the force of *contretemps*, of a counter- or contratemporal untimeliness intimating in the most scandalous fashion that a praxis is a thing of the past. If we are still talking about the possibility of a praxis to come, then we are also talking about what is already untimely, and to which, therefore, we need to remain open, not simply in the sense of anticipation but also through the practice of a thinking without limits, a thinking not governed by any economic model of discourse. Third, there is a sense in which speaking of a praxis indicates a fallback, a relapse, into theory, into the planning stages of a propaedeutic on the way to the praxis, as its very possibility and yet incommensurate with the action, the event that praxis appears to name. There is thus the constant act of recapitulation, if not an actual capitulation, a giving-in as it were, to the necessity of theorizing, of programming, of stalling and idling, in the name of praxis that is not yet praxis itself or as such. This leads to a further question: can speech, discussion, debate, communication, the occasion of a conference or merely a conference title, and so on—without even beginning to mention writing—ever be praxis, or is it always a question of untimely, not to say anachronistic, commentary? To speak, or to write, of the possibility of praxis is not the same as praxis. Those who can, act, those who can't. . . .

Without having gotten very far, we already seem to be caught in the most seemingly "academic" of quandaries: how to distinguish between a constative and a performative speech act. Or perhaps not even that far. Because, having intimated the hope for a gesture beyond the confines of the programmatic thought emerging from within, and yet as other than that thought, everything I have subsequently said supposes that there is the speech act concerning praxis, and then there is praxis itself. According to the most classical notions, there is a clear divide, the one already announced, between commenting and doing, between speaking "in theory" and taking action. At the risk of repeating myself, if I am speaking about something, something such as radical praxis—supposing for the moment that I believe I know what that is or might be—then, clearly, I'm not "doing it." Yet, and here we feel a slight trembling as though the spectre of a paradox were about to appear, if I am put in a position of having to speak about what constitutes the language of a revolutionary or radical praxis, I am already obliged to turn back upon the very process about which I am expected to expatiate. Thus, returned to the point where I am supposed to begin, I am, after having started, forced to acknowledge the return of the very point before starting, thereby having to double, redouble, and yet again, divide the position of utterance. Revolutionary; radical. Both, it has to be acknowledged, name or announce a possibly circular, circulatory, perhaps economic, and, once again, a recapitulatory gesture. Having removed the head from the body, we now have to place it squarely back on the shoulders, and so give in to the inevitable. That any radical gesture must always, and in a fashion that is too late, re-member what it is that we are seeking to dismember and which, in fact, has yet to be anatomized.

Between the *aperçu* and the *après coup*, this is where we are therefore poised, like insects in amber. To address the question of the possibility of a radical praxis is to articulate an outline or summary, to offer perhaps a revealing glimpse or insight into the possibility of transformation, of change. Proceeding by the numbers, I can always sketch out what I take to be the conditions of that possibility, what I foresee might take place—without, of course, in anyway being able to govern the outcome. Whether such an outcome will have occurred, whether the one I desire or the one that will have proved the absolute and abject failure of my planning—the failure of my program being as much the outcome of a program as any proposed success—I will only know after the ax has fallen, after something, if anything, has taken place. The logic is as terrible, as tyrannical, as it is inescapable, apparently.

This leads me back to the figure of praxis. On the one hand, the term indicates the practical application of a skill, as opposed to its theory: This has already been announced, and we find ourselves wondering once more about the supposed distinction between types of speech act. There is, however, another meaning for praxis: an established custom or habitual practice. Proceeding as usual, we do nothing other than talk, thinking all the while we're paving the way for change, while remaining where we are and going around in circles which, however apparently radical, are nonetheless circles for all that. We find ourselves suspended in the act of demystification, our commentaries concerning a revelation having to do with the condition of things. Instead of an event, we have an epoch in its most literal sense. We can unfold, unveil, all we wish, but, as long as there is procedure by established custom or habitual practice, we are caught in a perpetual gambits of what might be called *epoch-alypse now* . . . and now . . . and now . . . and so on . . . in an infinitely divisible number of singular instances irreducible to any present, none of which are comprehended as the possible instances of transformation until it is already too late.

Can we escape this? Or am I forced into a constant series of increasingly cynical responses until, like Diogenes, I find myself barking up the wrong tree? Or is it the case that the separation—such as those between *deconstruction* and *politics*, between *poiêsis* and *praxis*, between *literature* and *politics* (again)—misrecognizes the possibility that a praxis is already under way, and the problem is installed in the act of reading according to dominant ontological or other representational paradigms. It might just be—if we are to abandon the all-too habitual notion or custom of thinking a *praxis* as ontologically separate and separable from *theory*, as Angelopoulos's films demand of us, and, with that, the equally pernicious habitual practice of separating constative from performative speech acts—that we night come to recognize the chance that something can arrive in an entirely unpredictable manner, that something has already arrived in the form or occasion of a conference title, for example, in an entirely unpredictable manner by which we are called, which arrival remains all the while a secret in full view interrupting and installing a suspensive possibility as the sign of radical praxis. If we turn back to the moment on the bus in *Eternity and a Day*, we might be able to see, as if by analogy, this very possibility. I had commented earlier that the suspension in the scene on the bus leaves us having to decide on the undecidable. What I want to propose now is that it is not a question of the scene—and that which "ends" *Ulysses' Gaze*—as image, but as gesture. Giorgio Agamben explains the distinction in the following manner: "what characterizes gesture is that nothing is being produced or acted, but rather something is being endured and supported. The gesture, in other words, opens the sphere of *ethos* as the more proper sphere of that which is human . . . . if producing [theory, *poiêsis*] is a means in view of an end and praxis is an end without means, the gesture then breaks with false alternative between ends and means that paralyses morality."[34] It is for this reason that Agamben can remark that *"because cinema has its center in the gesture and not in the image, it belongs essentially to the realm of ethics and politics (and not simply to that of aesthetics)."*[35] Angelopoulos suspends and exceeds narrative and diegetic coherence, thereby liberating gesture from within image, rather than staging some dialectical opposition. In doing so, he opens the structure to the possibility of comprehending what Agamben terms the "pure praxis,"[36] deconstructing any separation between the singular and the universal. Like the conference title, the scene in question qua gesture demands that we witness, if we witness anything at all, just "this experience of the event of language"

as *"the exhibition of a mediality . . . the act of making a means visible as
such . . . a pure mediality without end intended as the field of human action and of human thought,"*[37] irreducible to separable dialectical terms.

In light of this, I want to put forward a somewhat scandalous propo-
sition. In order to call a halt to the established custom of thinking—if, indeed, you can call it this—that praxis names something applied, put to
work, what the title *deconstruction reading politics* entitles is a pure mediality *and* a radical praxis: not only a call to produce acts of making a
means visible, it is also a performative act itself, a radically incoherent
open-ended praxis recalling us, via its gesture, to the responsibility that
we need to engage in, in a praxis of scholarship, of close reading. We need,
for example, to come to terms with the fact that what appears in the guise
of a constative utterance, a statement on an historical or material condition, can in reality be read as performative, to the extent that it puts to
work particular tropes that, once fully comprehended in their work, effect
an irreversible transformation from within the place of their location.
Such scholarship, such close reading cannot of course be programmed.
One cannot propose a methodology of good reading practice; one can
only hope to read patiently, faithfully, with all due attention, rigor, and responsibility. One can only open oneself to the possibility of receiving and
witnessing, as we see in the suspensive gesture remarked by Angelopoulos. And whether one has practiced reading in this fashion will not be
known, and cannot be predicted in advance. This is the chance we take;
this is the incalculable risk of reading qua praxis.

VII

What might have been seen here in oblique reflection from the example
of praxis is that politics, in its most narrowly, conventionally defined
forms, and in its relapse into a formalism that decides against reading,
resists reading through the ploy of accusation, denying the necessity of
reading through the assumption of culpability *somewhere else*. However, this *somewhere else* is, I would suggest, where reading—or "deconstruction"—might begin to take us, where politics might be taken.
Somewhere else resists the specific definition of a politics closed off from
reading, from reading itself. It gives no particular heading, such as
reading-toward-socialism. Instead, it opens onto the incalculable, which

is always already immanent. Which is, perhaps, another way of saying reading. Or *deconstruction.*

Each of the terms of the conference title is notable in different and differing contexts for its ability to produce anxiety or even hostility, all the moreso when it is in the vicinity of something called "literature." You don't need me to tell you this, and those I've cited have all put it better. (But then, as we know, often the work of the foreword, whether endless or otherwise, is not to lay out directions so much as it is to recap in advance what comes after, and that which is to come, however untimely that may have been.) Each of the words produces overreaction. Admittedly, "reading" appears to be the least troublesome, the least confrontational. Unless it is, of course, a matter of how one reads. Deconstruction, misunderstood as a reading methodology, has been accused of all manner of offenses to reading, and it is often in the name of "reading" that deconstruction and politics—or "deconstructionists" and "politicized critics"—have been attacked; an ontology is always, most readily, available to those who read the least, and for whom reading is merely regulated habit. At one level, the anxiety is the manifestation simply of not reading. As Nicholas Royle puts it with regard to what he calls the Cambridge farce concerning Derrida's honorary degree, "texts have effects without being read."[38] But, then, reading takes time, it involves risks, and, in the words of Avital Ronell, learning to read "remains elusive and blinding as it remains the promise of future illumination. But it is a future that will never have completed its task in the present."[39] One reads too much or not enough, never enough. It is *perhaps*, and here is the *hope* to which we are entitled, and which every conference title names, as Geoffrey Bennington remarks, the possibility of a praxis radically open to its own performative incompletion. Allow me to conclude by illustrating this with one more moment from *Eternity and a Day*.

At the end of the film, the writer returns to his home, the house in which he had lived since his birth, in which he and his wife and family had lived, in which all family gatherings, celebrations, and anniversaries had taken place. Now the house is empty and, of course, haunted. All that remains are the writer's memories and ghosts. Standing, facing the Aegean, Alexander is visited by the ghost of his wife even as, throughout the movie, he has been haunted by both personal and political spectres: both his own and those of Greece, as well as those of the Balkans. They speak, and, as she is about to depart, he asks her to repeat something she had once said, but that he has subsequently forgotten. She whispers the words of the film's title. Not quite catching her comment, he asks her to repeat the words as she retreats. Her reiteration, its mere act, implies that "something more," the open-structure-plus that is also the opening of structure to itself, the *en plus,* which is, we would say, that rhythm of the spirit's breathing, coming toward the end and yet stretching itself beyond closure. From off-screen, her voice comes back, barely audible: *eternity and a day.*

All at once, this is too much, and never enough. In being spoken, the words seem banal. They arrive late, too hurriedly, hardly more than a breath, and are too obvious. But the writer doesn't hear them. Everything comes down to this phrase, and yet it is not everything; it is hardly anything at all. In the moment that it is spoken and reiterated, everything—and all the rest—slips away, and remains to be spoken of. Has an event taken place? Will one have been comprehended? At the same time as the phrase is remarked, there is an iterable counterpoint, the recurring susurration of the sea against the shore, the scene being marked, multiplied, by various thresholds, liminal situations. The sea had indeed marked the beginning of the film, and so signifies a series of revenant instances. We are always at a threshold, paused in a gap. Pure interval. Circulation and return, an opening takes place if it takes place at all as a call, figured in the repetition of the name "Alexander"—a name returning in a haunting fashion across time, through narrative motion, and of course over the winedark sea, awaiting response and announcing the interwoven relationship between poetics and politics, between literature and identity. This intimacy is announced indirectly in the phrase *eternity and a day,* the encrypted intimacy of haunting archival traces. There is a double and contradictory relation here. And it is this we need to address: something happens, something is shown, or shows itself, in the spacing that takes place between those two utterances of "eternity and a day," as the phrase is marked by its own iterable division, tempting to read, and unreadable. The question is: how are we to receive this without appropriation? This is the question put to us by the impossible topography of the conference title: *deconstruction reading politics.* Rather than seeking to gather these words up, like Angelopoulos's poet, we should learn to attend to words, attending to the auratic and the spectral; we should learn also to attend to the auratic in the name of politics, attending also to all that is said in the name of this title, that which entitles us and to, *by,* which we are entitled, but which the title does not articulate directly, that which is both so close and yet so distant, that which hovers *between,* between a number of betweens. To borrow a response of Derrida's to a remark already put to him, in words not his own, which he returns: "— Let's listen."[40]

Chapter 6

CITATION'S HAUNT:

SPECTRES OF DERRIDA

The occasions for this chapter's "original" appearances led to two different versions, in two languages, and its subsequent shaping has had to do materially with the response to these situations, in relation to the question of citation and the institution of scholarship. First commissioned for a collection of essays on the subject of citation to be published in German, the essay's title was "Der Spuk das Zitate": . . . eine Serie von Kontiguuitäten. . . . .[1] The other version, "Citation's Haunt: Spectres of Derrida," appeared in *Mosaic*.[2] However, for various reasons, the German version, to all intents and purposes the "original," appeared subsequent to the version in *Mosaic*. In a number of places, in revising the present chapter, I have let the German text invisibly return, transforming words and phrases on occasion.

The German-language text appears without any direct citation of phrases, passages, sentences, or parenthetical reference alluding to texts whatsoever. That version appearing in *Mosaic* comes with parenthetical reference and a "works cited" list. (This version could itself be read as an extended citation, inasmuch as it proceeds, with regard to the absence of citation, in a manner that "cites" indirectly, as it were, the form of Geoffrey Bennington's "Derridabase" in which exposition rather than quotation is taken as the norm.) In both the German and English-language versions of "Citation's Haunt," as in its presentation in the present chapter, where its arguments have been expanded, citations appear without appearing, being presented without quotation marks, and thus disturbing the systematic coherence implied in the relation between argument and authority, priority and supplement; citations are thus made manifest in their visible-invisible relationship to any text. They arrive, if they arrive at all, if their return remains intact, occasionally in their own words, so to speak, sometimes being paraphrased or alluded to, or otherwise only indirectly acknowledged (as is remarked upon in the body of the chapter).

As a complication of the question of citation, its haunting effects, and its institutional identity, I have in the present version provided notes for each citation, giving the citation in question and the conventional bibliographical details. The appearance of the quotations in notes is not intended to assert or allude to authority. In fact, it will be found to be the case that, often, the quotation arrives from a wholly different discussion, a wholly different context, than those by which it is provisionally framed here. The annotated, fragmentary purpose of the quotations presented is to remark the insistence of dislocation in a system, such as an argument, essay, or chapter, that makes identity or totalization impossible. The displacement of the citations in the notes suggests the possibility of another reading, other contexts, always open, and therefore always to come. And, of course, the quotations are only the most immediate, the most visible, traces. Arguably, to each could be appended possibly innumerable other texts.

I

Mecum eras, et tecum non eram.

Augustine

What we have, then, is an enormous research programme, in which the received—and receivable—categories of academic scholarship must not be trusted.

Jacques Derrida

Writing without citation is impossible.

This chapter is deranged from the start, undone from and by the occasion that is called scholarship. It addresses, and seeks to act out, the relationship between spectrality, citation, and the ghostwriting that takes place in the name, the authority, and institution of scholarship. Responding to, and following, a few particular threads (even though these threaten to get out of hand in the annotations), where Jacques Derrida implicitly or explicitly connects quotation and haunting, the chapter considers the extent to which academic or critical writing is always haunted in the very act by which authority and identity is claimed. It thus traces particular hypothetical folds of a certain institutional scene of writing as the manifestations of a "spectropoetics." Citation, far from being the remark of absolute authority, constitutes and affirms a force of dislocation, a certain incapacity to close the system. While making the work of reading possible, citation renders any ontological coherence impossible through a certain phantom dysfunction or disadjustment.[3] However, as is implied, the question of citation is not merely a formal matter, even though the place of citation in any act of scholarly writing is the immediate, the most visible interest. Instead, the figure of citation serves as a singular example, on the one hand, for the obligation one has to the other and, on the other hand, for that which ruins any identity or totality, any auto-affection. The relationship between any single essay, chapter, book, and their citations is always double, therefore, having to do with strife and economy; but one can neither control nor limit the motions or traces of the phantomatic or the spectral.

II

> For all the difficulties we are dealing with here are related to the limit, the problematic limit between an inside and an outside that is always threatened by graft and by parasite. . . . Simultaneously external and internal laws include everything that denotes or connotes both the origin and the destination of annotations, the signature and silhouette of the audience or of the readership with all the marks the signatory and the addressee may leave inside the two texts, the annotated and the annotating.
>
> Jacques Derrida

Why stress spectrality here?[4] To begin with the title: there is a graphic disturbance in the title of this chapter. The disturbance, signaled by the possessive apostrophe, demands that you read the title in a particular fashion: that a place is implied, the place where citation takes place, where it returns habitually, and where, as critical readers, we believe we are habituated in finding citation—in the place, perhaps the scene, of criticism. This is where citation is anticipated, where we assume, even

ahead of its arrival, its inevitable manifestation. Citation haunts criticism
and, more generally, it haunts all reading and writing. Good writing is
always haunted by bad writing.[5]

But haunting this phrase, "Citation's Haunt," is another remark,
without the possessive inscription by which citation assumes to itself its
habitual right to habitation-as-haunting: citations haunt. There is more
than one citation here. Indeed, they may be innumerable, and with them
comes an insistence on the spectral persistence of citations. Citations will
haunt, it can be read, and the haunt of citations is here. And here. *Hic et
ubique.* Thus, this title haunts this chapter, announcing its concerns, interests, and orientations. It gets ahead of itself, even as it remains at, and
as, a border. Thus, the limit always moves within the corpus.[6] In doing so,
it admits (to) disorder: that of the time of citation, *as if*[7] a future perfect
is wrapped up in the past.[8]

In addition to these issues is the manifestation of another haunting
or phantom effect: that of those "spectres of Derrida," to which my title
also refers. Not quite a double genitive, on the one hand this phrase, *citation's haunt*, names the processes of "ghostwriting" that arrives,
though never for a first time, through the work of so many more or less
invisible citations arriving from Derrida's essays and indicated only indirectly or tangentially throughout this chapter. The effect of such ghosting or what, in another place is described, with reference to what is given
to be seen as *apparitioning*,[9] takes place beyond these obvious locations,
however; overflowing, even to the point of excess in what might be called,
mistakenly identified, as style or imitation of style. Even my use of the
phrase *on the one hand* might be assumed to be the sign of an apparition,
an imitation or citation, or both, the former as the imprecise representation of the latter: mimesis as ontological Xerox machine. (Interestingly,
to risk a digression this early in the chapter, although obviously Derrida
does not originate or invent the formula *on the one hand/on the other
hand*, this figure manifests itself frequently enough in his arguments that
any subsequent use transforms the formula in a quite spectral and citational fashion, particularly when its appearances take place in essays concerning Derrida's work.)[10] On the other hand, the phrase, *spectres of
Derrida*, announces those places in Derrida's writing where the question
of citation disturbs Derrida, coming ceaselessly—arriving and returning—to haunt his consideration in different ways.

In recognizing this, it cannot be said that there is an argument here
as such. I am not proposing anything that has not already been said by

Derrida, and often, it could be argued, more elegantly by him than by me. What might take place in this chapter is merely a certain registration, recognition, or admission of the work of haunting within any textual form, as that work comes to disturb the identity or identification of, or distinction between, the forms of imitation or mimicry (the shaping of an apparently original argument in the more or less discernible lineaments of another) and the function of citation itself as a somewhat spectral authority. Citation haunts precisely because—conventionally at least, according to the spectral authority by which quotation is understood to be ordained rather than simply given—it arrives from some other place as an authority, the authority of the other, which intrusion of the guest is paradoxically conjured so as to assert the very idea of originality in argument or research. So, to begin again.

III

> *Excitation.* This term, in so far as it could be described as such (it would be no more a *term* than "the unnameable" or "deconstruction"), is pronounced so as to conceal as best it can the heterophonic pun it nevertheless harbours, like a foreign body. Excitation, that is to say, cannot be read without a logic of ex-citation, of that which dispossesses, ex-propriates or para-cites ever citation. Excitation would have to do, among other things, with an absence of quotation marks. Be alert to these invisible quotation marks, even within a word: excitation.
>
> Nicholas Royle

Writing without citation is impossible.

Es ist unmöglich, ohne Zitat zu schreiben.

Writing without citation is impossible; it is impossible, to write without citation

As obvious, as manifestly self-evident, as these observations will have appeared, they bear reiterating. They bear in and with them reiteration. If I had never written them, their interruptive principle would still be at work. This principle would have returned and retreated in every word here, in every line. Indeed, that which moves this doubling statement has the force of inevitability, coming as it does from somewhere else and bearing the signs of some disassimilating other, the traces of a borderless context.[11] Beginning by acknowledging interruption, the principle announced, announcing itself in a spirit of nontotalizing, nontotalizable participation, attests to a matter of (always ghostly) disjunction or dislocation,[12] of intimate proximity and yet, also, immeasurable distance. This is not merely a spatial matter, however. At the same time or, more accurately, not quite the same time but, instead, signaling a temporal displacement, the idea of beginning begins only by being interrupted, and responding to that interruption. Any beginning is seen to have got under way late; it can only ever "begin" late. Interruption is only recognized, if one has taken account of it at all, in a moment heterogeneous to that which has come to pass. As so many precarious, disembodied figures, then, citation phantomizes the text. The concern is therefore with something haunting (*unheimlich*) within the place of the habitual (*heimlich*), the apparition, and the voice, of an other, which is neither simply real nor not real and yet which, in being neither being nor not being, yet in not being nothing, has always already exceeded all ontological determination or definition,[13] beyond all that is delimitable.[14] Less a question of habitation than of haunting,[15] even though the one always implies, implicates, the other,[16] the spectrality of citation arrives as a summons calling us to respond, to acknowledge it.[17] Despite all vigilance, despite all attempts to maintain a professional wariness, and to proliferate the marks of domestication, order, and the economy of the system, citation will have been coming and going, unseen and unforeseen. Such a silent disturbance in the field of forces is precisely what obligates, even though we could never have seen it coming.

Even though there are no quotation marks here, in reading this opening gambit, citation, pseudo-citation, or, at the very least, the simulacrum of citation may well have been, or come to be, read by some. This is a question of frequency, of interruption, or even cadence, as is known.[18] And then again, such a frequency can and has taken place, there in that qualifying remark disturbing the purity, for want of a better word, of the inscription, and doing so repeatedly. And, if not citation, pseudo-citation or the simulacrum of a citation—which without citation marks is nonetheless a more or less direct citation concerning citation, pseudo-citation, or the simulacrum of citation—then, perhaps, let us put it this way, there appears to be discernible a semi- or quasi-citational atmosphere or, equally, ambience.

A question arises or presents itself in passing, an apparent digression as engagement otherwise considered: is it ever possible (or indeed inescapable) to cite resonance, atmosphere, or, more crudely, tone, style? Or is the perception of this citational character or impression (*mimeto-* or *mnemocitationality*) more a question of reading crudely? Is it a question of interpretation or translation where the question hides itself in an act of supposed identification or determination? Imagine this citation, for example, arriving from a number of places at once, both past and future: "There, there is citation." (By the way, even though this citation is invented, allegedly, a simulacrum of a citation so to speak, this "phantom quotation" is nonetheless a citation for all that; the quotation marks signal this condition.)[19] You can just hear the voice, can't you? Where is citation? Nowhere, as such, yet, in the tone, bearing or, let's call it a family atmosphere or resemblance, despite any claims to the contrary.[20] If we pause here, something might have been observed to have returned. This statement amounts to "quasi-quotation" again in a double manner: for, *on the one hand*, the remark might be understood to resonate with an unacknowledged quotation whether observed or not, while, *on the other hand*, any recognition of a resemblance is suggestive of a certain haunting citational force in which intertextuality is read in a genealogical fashion. Or, then again, perhaps what appears to be glimpsed is a matter of pastiche or parody, as, doubtless, the bad reader would hasten to suggest—and, in this assumption of resemblance, there is to be read an attempt to ignore difference, non-identity, singularity—so as to indict (citation, the question of the law) with the evidence of the ghost of a citation, which is nowhere in sight yet simultaneously everywhere. This would be the verdict, unwilling or unable to acknowledge its own com*pli*city, its being already folded, woven into a skein of inextricable threads. Imagine this haunted and haunting figure: the incited reader, lacking insight and in a hurry to find the citation, which is nowhere present as such (once again), and all the while misreading across the text-as-site the general, diffused stench of the citational, and calling this, that, or the other, parody or pastiche.

—Will he?

Yes, but of course, again, and again, every single time. It is also, very much, a question of the image, of believing one has recognized this, and, invisibly, against such apparent composition, the tremor or disturbance that causes a departure from absolute resemblance. One should not always trust the image.[21] This is, in some sense, simply the will to read without reading. On the one hand, it might be said that texts can have effects without having been read.[22] This is acknowledged: we are still speaking of a haunting effect. On the other hand, a text may be said to arrive without ever having been received, caught up as it will have been within a filter of commentary.[23] There is announced in this strange process a desire to proceed by that most conventional or predictable of literary-critical methods. Supposedly academic language arrives at agreement with a certain journalistic procedure having to do perception: that of similarity or homo- rather than hetero-allusiveness (a dissociative recognition of singularity and iterability) at the expense of difference, *as if* this guaranteed what might be called a kind of proleptic auto-immunization, an inoculation against the very ghost by which all text gets under way, and without which spectral figure, no survival would be possible.[24]

This is no mere hypothesis being presented here. I am indirectly citing, citing without citing as it were, or otherwise alluding. (But then it has to be asked, what is allusion if not a form of citation that because of its indirection already announces its condition of being traced or otherwise returning to its audience an other text?) Without wishing to sound coy, I could establish a series, one that is already immanent but one that, always open and opening itself to, through its own movement, always looping back on itself, leads elsewhere, indicating the impossibility of the closure of any system or any systematic coherence.[25] It would be possible to trace a hitherto invisible network of citations for two incommensurate purposes. On the one hand, it would doubtless be possible to dismiss the hypothetical taint of that to which I have just alluded, and this might be expected or required in the name of institutional norms. Citations could be found that would give authority to my comments on the incited reader. On the other hand, however, proceeding in this fashion would support what is readable immediately above as the parodic mimicry of an argument wielded against essays such as the present one. (Note that "such as": it announces in yet another fashion indirect reference.) Were I to follow this argument through, I might do this in order to show how such an argument or accusation is not merely a misreading. Simply and with all the simplicity of an evangelical fervor, the so-called reader has not read, even though such a polemic may well have cited numerous "sources" in support of its own weary and wearying argument. Everything is exhausted. I refrain from citation though.

It is necessary to abandon this lengthy digression. Is it really this, however? Arguably, it has only the appearance of digression, addressing the matter of citationality or its illusion all the while and being through by an invisible citational force. It could be said that, despite appearances to the contrary, the matter of citation haunts the experience of this passage, of both writing and reading it as the structural and yet disjointing necessity of its possibility—and, by extension, that of every act of writing, every statement or articulation. One possible point is that writing and, more generally, inscription, without citation is impossible, whether directly or indirectly. Writing could not take place without the trace of some other text already under way and which survives. Writing would not be possible without the manifestation or the *revenance* that is named, on occasion, iterability, that very effect or force of citation that opens any system beyond itself. Writing is thus haunted, and in being so maintains the haunting effect. Citation haunts. It can come from any past or any future as I have already implied in what might be called a gesture designed to incite. Writing is just this: the haunt of citation, a haunted house disturbed at its very foundations.

So, to return to where this chapter began, to acknowledge, after the fact, what has already been announced and what is already under way: in order to open this spectral condition to the beginning of a reading, and in order to begin (again, and again) to discern the traces of the phantomatic or phantasmic materiality of writing, I wish to orient this chapter around the more apparent of the apparitions, limiting myself to remarks—extended citations—taken from certain texts by Jacques Derrida as exemplary instances of haunting's implication in the scene of writing generally, as well as in the motion, the phantasmic motif,[26] of citation specifically. These citations will haunt this chapter even though they are nowhere quoted as such. They appear in "Shibboleth for Paul Celan," *Politics of Friendship, Dissemination, Archive Fever, Ulysses Gramophone,* and "At this Very Moment in this Work Here I Am." Allusion will (have) be(en) made also to various other texts that address citation, such as "The Law of Genre," "Signature Event Context," "Psyché: Inventions of the Other," as well as to those that speak of haunting and spectrality, not least *Spectres de Marx, The Truth in Painting, Échographies, Adieu: To Emmanuel Levinas,* and, most recently, *Sur parole: instantanés philosophiques.* Indeed, these and others are already here as ghosts in the machine ghostwriting this chapter. And although I try to hold citations at bay, even this act of naming texts, letting their names return, constitutes citation whether with or without quotation marks. For the most part, however, I will remain in the general vicinity of the passages already acknowledged.

IV

Of course—as is always the case as soon as there is a law, *the* law—all deceptions, transgressions, and subversions are possible, and have been so since long before what is called modernity, even postmodernity.

Jacques Derrida

The implication of a relationship between the spectral and citation is well known. Certainly the argument can be put with some justification that those who are most familiar with Derrida are already familiar with this perhaps most persistent of Derrida's interests. However, what I wish to explore is the peculiar intimacy between the one and the other, between spectrality and citation. If the one is not reducible to the other—and I would argue that the relationship between citation and spectrality could not be less certain—then, at least, what is of interest in opening this consideration is the possibility of beginning to read how one comes to take place in the place of the other, destabilizing the identification of either and thus returning again and again the matter of spectral disturbance, as that which haunts—and is, too, *the haunt of*—all scholarly habit, all that is habitual, and within the most familiar locations inhabited in the name of scholarship. That the citation is spectral, that it partakes of the spectral condition of "literary" writing, and that what appears is not simply some prior text (in the narrow sense of that word—indeed, as Derrida has demonstrated amply in various places the conventional meaning of "text" is always already haunted from within by an illimitable excess and that the notion of text is irreducible to discourse)[27] now being quoted may be comprehended if one acknowledges that the spectral is not merely what returns from a past, or from some anterior location. It is also that which is also to come: the disfiguring figure *l'avenir/l'à-venir*[28] makes this *apparitioning* apparent. It disrupts univocal meaning through that articulation of the other that haunts the simple figure of the future, disjointing in the process the time of reading. Indeed, it is not even necessary to resort to French. For, having just written *now being quoted*, we should pause to consider the interruption, the suspensive modality of this—or that—*now* (but which one?), which is itself, every time, indicative or performative of a certain citational iterability irreducible to any present or presence. This is more than familiar, but no less disturbing or disruptive for all that. In appearing in this manner, this figure operates on and thereby countersigns the text and the experience of the text in a particularly uncanny fashion. Acknowledging this, in the wake not only of Jacques Derrida but also Geoffrey Bennington, Peggy Kamuf, Werner Hamacher, and Nicholas Royle among others, each in his or her own singular approach, it has to be admitted in a recognition of the anachrony discernibly at work that that which is not yet, already is.[29] (Even though I am citing through the function of the proper name, I refrain again from citation, on the one hand to keep the ghosts at bay while, on the other, to allow their resonances full play without attempting to control the phantomatic effect through the process of citation, which in extracting fragments from the body of the text seeks to inter and to fix in place.) In this, the experience of the impossible time of reading, there is acknowledged the fact that reading remains to come, and that we will never have done with it. (Once again this is well known, this is not an "original" observation. In acknowledging this, I only admit to the ghostly power of citational force, all the more resonant for never having been cited as such.)

Citation or quotation disturbs the remarking of the present from within itself. It undermines the articulation of the present moment, especially in the resonance of the present tense of the citation, which is clearly the return of another "present," though never the present as such.[30] All presence, all presentation of the present is internally disturbed, though—and here I find it necessary to make a qualification—such internality is not simply some discernible figure, one half of a polar pairing marking off and thereby stabilizing a spatial or anterior location or locution. This is the condition of text and of writing, the more so when inscription feigns the presence of the subject—first-person singular—in relation to the temporal instantaneity of utterance. It would appear to be this simulacrum of a presence, this supposedly authoritative "I," guaranteeing and gathering to itself, that which is supposedly immanent in its appearance: all possible authority, all possible intimation of a presence or origin. But, of course, nothing could be less certain: for the movement of "I" to take place, it has to be capable of being detached from any source, any authoritative appearance. "I" thus remarks the uncanny force of citationality and, with that, the citation of a phantom effect. Even those inscriptions that are not assumed to have a voice in any "human" sense, and yet are read conventionally as singular or unique, dates, for example, are available for reiteration. Indeed, the force of the date's singularity is only guaranteed by the possibility of its being reinscribed outside of the supposed authenticity of its apparently proper occurrence. Thus, while the date for Derrida can never return *in stricto sensu*, it nonetheless can find itself remarked in a spectral fashion. Moreover, this *revenance* of the date is also a *revenance*, a phantomatic oscillation, that always already haunts the structure and the possibility of dating.[31] There is remarked, therefore, the apparition of the trace of what could never return as such, encoded in both the iterability of the date and the memory of the nonreturn of another date that is the same but not the same.

Of course, the question does not come down only to a matter of dates or, to invoke another well-known instance, the articulation of saying "I." Neither of these singular examples guarantees the singularity or absolute centring that they appear to promise. Neither the date nor the "I" maintains any singularity except by the chance of its being spirited away, reiterated, or cited as is well known. What is not fully acknowledged, however, is that the iterability that guarantees singularity is itself the experience of haunting that is all the more uncanny, all the more spectral in that it admits to the unassignability of any absolutely discernible or traceable originary location, as just remarked. Thus, in both cases the date and the "I" are marked by a certain citational *revenance at or as the origin*, and as the affirmation of the impossibility of origin from the very start, as it were. In this, acts of dating or articulations of the "I" betray a citational relationship to writing in general, despite the fact that the reader habitually or conventionally reads them as inscriptions belonging to a different order of signification such as that accorded signatures or proper names, which also supposedly operate according to laws quite different from other inscribed apparitions and yet are shown to behave as typical modes of inscription.[32] The phantasmatic or spectral condition is not only what comes to haunt citation and all acts of quotation in certain specific situations, particular expressions and their rhetorical deployment, or simply in certain "forms" of writing. All writing may be said to be spectral, though spectrality is equally another name or one possible substitution for the endlessly citational structures that are called or otherwise invoked in the name of writing. (Borrowing a model based on the double logic articulated by Derrida elsewhere, it is tempting to suggest that writing partakes of the doubling work of "conjuring," especially when writing relies on citation for its authoritative force.) There appears to be a certain destabilizing, chiasmatic force at work between the figures of writing and haunting, a force that it is impossible to calm down. Is writing haunted? Does it haunt? Is haunting, along with all its nonsynonymous substitutions and quasi-cognates—spectrality, the ghost, phantasm, the phantom—a formless form, writing itself? The experience of the literary is also the experience of the spectral, though the term "literary" does not refer merely to either a restricted range of texts or an equally restricted—and restrictive—definition of certain texts. Spectrality is what allows citation to take place as displacement, as doubling and haunting. The spectral, neither simply there nor not there, disrupts pure singularity and thus manifests its performative effect in the mark, the trace, and those places where one "begins" with iterability, with what returns; and this is to say nothing other than inscription. As Derrida makes clear the idea of the mark that is not iterable, which cannot be cited or recited, is unthinkable.[33] Every sign, in order to function as a sign, must have given up the ghost.

In addition, the definition and practice of citation are irreducible to simply determined mechanical processes of extraction and repetition from one place to another, obeying all the while the laws and conventions of citation through the proper use of quotation marks, annotations, the various conventions by which acts of citation are bound, and so forth, because what makes citation possible is also what renders its law impossible.[34] The law of citation, and the counterlaw, its ghostly double, will have been returned to in this chapter; or, to put this another way, it is that which will return to us. In the sense that the law always returns or, more accurately, is always already in the act of returning via the event of the citation and every citation, this concern with the law governing citation is readable as having announced itself from at least the beginning of this chapter, at least as that which haunts any consideration of what constitutes a "proper" citation and whether the re-marking of citation itself constitutes a question of property, properly or improperly transplanted or appropriated. For, whether one speaks of the law of citation or whether one speaks of the doubling and division that takes place within, as the sign of the undecidability of the single word haunted from its "first" appearance, the spectral has always already returned and retreated within the supposedly stable site, leaving the merest, yet undeniably most powerful, if not violent of traces. We are witness here to a spectral logic and its abyssal effects, exceeding all binary or dialectical models and forms:[35] *revenance* as/in resonance, the other within, composition and/as annihilation. *Haunting takes place*. Haunting—*heimsuchung*, the search for home—takes place as an uncanny dislocation of location itself, from within the very place where one seeks the safety of authority.

The effects of haunting are discernible even in the genealogical or *genealogico-phantomatic drift*, for want of a better expression, within both the word and concept of citation. (Another parenthetical detour: in the awkward coinage offered here, it may be suggested—may it not?—that the motif of genealogy is always that in which is traced the phantom effect, the ghostwriting, of an improper and disinterred citationality.) One could go so far as to suggest that every time one cites, speaks of citation, or otherwise encounters the manifestation of citation within another's text—the manifestation of the other within the other—one encounters such a drift in both the very propriety that is enacted and in the most precisely observed re-marking of the laws of citation also. Why should this be the case? What authority can there be for such a remark? Arguably, authority resides or is indirectly cited in the promise or asserts itself in the act of citation. Turning from Derrida for the moment to the *Oxford English Dictionary*, the dictionary entry notes that the very idea of citation, its possibility and what authorizes it, is juridical in condition. Citation names the act of summoning to a court, while naming also the summons, the written document itself that cites the court and bears through that citation the authority in the name of which that inscription comes to be presented. At this point the *OED* defers its own authority to that of the *Law Dictionary*. It thereby presents within its definition a citation and with that the process and law of citation, that of issuing an inscription that causes action, referring in the process specifically to process in the spiritual or ecclesiastical court. Authority thus halts and displaces itself, backing itself up by reference to a higher authority. Authority does not reside in a statement without citation. The sign of another must arrive in order to prove authority, in order to authorize from some other place the authority that a definitive statement simultaneously seeks to make manifest and yet which it manifestly lacks. In this process there is to be discerned the ghostly shimmering of an abyssal supplementarity.

Consider the strange phrase *tout autre est tout autre*,[36] a remark disquieting in its legible simplicity. There is a pattern here, of apparent reiteration *and* return, of com*pli*ance and departure, haunted by a singularity irreconcilable with or irreducible to a simple meaning or identity.

Disordered from the beginning, everything hinges on unhinged, semantic, grammatical, and ontological formations. The phrase is marked by a
rhythm, which, in seeming to turn back upon itself, initiates and is part
of a movement, already under way and yet, initially, invisible. This motion
is double, at least. For there appears an apparent equivalence, gesturing
seemingly or ostensibly toward unity and closure, while being also, paradoxically, that which maintains a poiêsis of the citational fragment and
the rupture that is put in effect by any quotation, in ruins, resistant to
any univocity. *Tout Auture. Tout. Autre.* Two times, twice gathered in the
round and marked by equation or calculation through what is at once a
conjugation and a conjuration of being, and the related ontological assumption that the other is simply another name, an identity like any
other. However, everything comes back as the citation of itself, even
though it was there from the start anyway, and even though this citation
of the self is an other citation, a ghostly manifestation. The double work
of, *in*, this figure, interrupts, even as it motivates, discernible structure
and the articulation of that structure. The phrase is marked by, and remarks, both spatial and temporal transition and transference, as the very
manifestation of the work that is any citation's phantom oscillation,
though, of course, we only come to apprehend this in the *après coup* of
response. Without ever knowing how to "translate" this phrase, even
within what is ostensibly one language, that is, French, we nonetheless
read the implication of a motion and a disturbance from one place, one
event, one condition, state of being or emotion to another, to risk a repetition, to fold back on ourselves; which motif, though, strictly speaking,
nothing in itself, performs that haunting, disruptive alterity, that excess
that causes the phrase to tremble in what might be called both its so-
called first citing and first sighting. There, though nowhere as such, the
trait of the spectre is seen, having already retreated. This reaches us late,
as a sign that the time of a reading is in disarray, and as the result of citation. If it reaches us at all, it is with the delay of any quotation, already
caught up in the chains of what can best be described as a quoted quotation.[37] The doubling of the phrases completes and simultaneously leaves
in disarray the single phrase by a kind of figural palindrome, so that the
motion appears to recirculate, to return to its beginning point, to disrupt
and thus paradoxically reduplicate, iterate, itself in its own process. This
returns to us a troping wherein is figured the same, but not the same.

The phrase *tout autre est tout autre* only makes the apparition that
takes place, that comes to pass in the principle and possibility of citation,

all the more apparent. It calls forth and announces that which is to come, that which is always coming as the ghostly effect of quotation, and yet which is of course already under way within the single, singular phrase *tout autre*, as we see or, rather, as we come to see after the fact, as has been remarked already. We have a model here of a radical replacement and re-presentation, that interminable work of deferral, relay, and reiteration. Analogical displacement and replacement figuring the disjuncture between, within, like and like, and what is enacted is the formal taking place of an opening oneself to a revelation of what is always already installed. The phrase (re)cites itself before it has cited itself, in an attempt to think the other, the other thought of the other, from within. Analogy maintains the opening, through the various replacements and displacements signalled in the syntax of the formula. Each figure of *tout autre* is thus invested with the possibility of a reading which is still not yet what it already is: the apparent hermeneutic circle implied in the patterning of the phrase seemingly offering to represent a connection of *arché* with *telos*, while also, always already, opening itself out while touching on itself and in itself as other than this *it-self*, disjointing its own completion. This formula is performative in that it exceeds itself, the *it-self*, as it reiterates, thereby resisting unity and coherence in the singular affirmation that alterity makes possible. Furthermore, because the terms by which the transitional motion is mapped are the same and yet not the same, in a kind of palindromic mapping as we have already suggested, precisely what increment or transformation can be said or read to take place is undecidable. Clearly there is the question of difference at work, however displaced, and this appears focussed through citation as a minimal repetition. Formally, therefore, the reiteration constitutes a pre-phenomenal marking, a material remarking of the text's and language's materiality as a haunted materiality. The materiality of reiteration effects ghostly possession *and* effacement in the motion of an irreversible performative, which, once perceived in its immaterial or spectral efficacity, is comprehended precisely as that which cannot close itself off from the other that haunts it from the start, as it were.

To cite is thus to call, and to recall, anamnesis and response. It is to set in motion what, invisibly, is always already under way, and which does not wait for any perception, any consciousness to set it in motion. What I might call *my* reading is only ever this act of response. If I have insisted on the absence of any originality in this chapter, this is not from any modesty, but rather is an acknowledgment and registration of the fact that nothing begins for the first time in writing, nothing gets going for what we call a first time. The call of citation and the displaced writing that remarks the act of citation (which is citation also) comes from some other place, as has just been suggested. It doubles and divides itself, as can be witnessed. Citation both is and is not citation. It disrupts the authority of identity and of origin, being always already in motion. Destabilizing itself both internally and from the location or locution of the other, citation thereby engages or tropes itself as other than itself in the transport from and as a condition of the command, the injunction, the order: *remember me* says the ghost of Hamlet's father; *do not forget*, the words of Arthur Clennam's father in Dickens's *Little Dorrit*, the words returning as the merest trace, *D.N.F.*, embroidered and secreted inside a pocket watch. A citation may thus return as the gift, the giving, of the other, in which the command enjoins one to inescapable response and responsibility. (By the way, this phrase, *the gift of the other*, doubles itself: on the one hand, that the gift of the other which the other gives, whether this is recognized or not; on the other hand, in remarking *the gift of the other*, one says nothing other than that the other *just is* this gift, this endless giving that can only be known, if it is known at all, after the event. At the same time, there is a gesture of giving that defines citation. In English one may cite, in an essay, for example, but one can also legally *give* a citation, as the buried etymology reveals. Such an act of giving causes citation to remark itself as not simply itself, and thereby in the process operating as the division and the dislocation of itself both from and within itself as performative transport. Citation's haunted and haunting structure operates through a simultaneous and yet anachronistic motion of returning and arriving. There in the ghost of a chance one can begin to read the phantom-performative of citation.

Arriving at this comprehension places us in a closer relation to the condition of citation. We find ourselves involved in a process that has no beginning. At the same time however, what is also observable is that all we can do is begin repeatedly, if only so as to get to the point of beginning *and* departure. The principle of citation is therefore readable as citing, indirectly, not simply some anterior, originary source. Instead, citation in principle and in effect acts as any number of spectral threads or traces—*un des fils conducteurs*: one of innumerable conductors and clews/clues, the signs of a genealogical, if not genetic, imprint hinting at frayed inheritance and heritage, at once generative and generational,[38] and yet also discontinuous and coming apart at the edges, so many threads acting *as if* they were bookmarks. The father's message, the trace of his phantom, returns to haunt the son. This thread attests to a vast and complex network, a *mnemotechnic*. It announces and enacts the impersonal making and marking of an archive and an archiving of memory, all the more uncanny for being irreducible to any human origin, presence, identity or location, being neither simply there nor not there as such. It is, therefore, resistant to an anthropomorphizing, domesticating reading—epistemo-political *habit* as the attempted exorcism of the ghost from the house, the *habitus* and *oikos*—of citation. And of course, as Derrida has insisted in addressing Yerushalmi's encounter with Freud's phantom, the archive, its structuration, is spectral through and through.[39] Returning from the archive, the ghost of and in citation turns our attention toward its own repressed truth: which is that it appears as or in the guise of an indirect manifestation of some other spectre, the spectre of the other, which in turn, internally, as the other of citation haunts the humanist-ideological reading of citation as the voice of authoritative origin even as it resists that reading. The truth of the spectral comes to be unveiled through the phantomatic-technicity of citational transport and return while reciprocally the spectral truth of citation is opened to us.

There is here therefore (though *where*, exactly?), once again, a doubling effect, doubling being the uncanny manifestation of the iterable,[40] where division and constitution take place simultaneously as the possibility of, and also within, the site of citation. Such doubling is made possible by the movement of difference, and the readability of division and doubling reflects the performative work of the ghostly simulacrum. In reading the split within a term such as *pharmakon,* for example, the reader neither has the authority to suggest, nor can he or she locate any originary locus for such authority from which to argue that one half of the double or division has a greater primacy than the other. Both figures within the effect of doubling mimic or mirror one another without either the hope for anterior reference or allusion to the real. Hence, the fleeting sense of the uncanny that arrives or arises in the resistance within structure to any ontological or semantic resolution. What is all the more haunting in such a structure is that the spectral oscillation is there ahead and independent of any consciousness that may or may not read such a disjointing. Derrida speaks of this in discussing the doubled *yes.* One affirmation cites the other Derrida claims, though it is not a matter of one being original and the other being secondary, supplementary, or otherwise a mimetically faithful copy of the first. No, it is not a question of the one and the other but, instead, the other and the other, other of the other, yes, yes, opening themselves in a phantom reciprocity.[41] (One might also consider Kurtz's utterance "the horror, the horror" in Conrad's *Heart of Darkness* in a similar fashion, the horror perhaps being Kurtz's recognition of the anthropomorphic fallacy behind the very idea of the human that the colonialists bring with them and which haunts their brutality toward the Africans.) Rather, one is the ghost of the other; or, to put this another way so as to avoid the misunderstanding of placement and priority by which the vertiginous and abyssal vibration between and in the two might be calmed, each disfigures itself in figuring as part of a doubling matrix, a machinery of spectral projection and oscillation as the ghost *of* and *in* the other. No simple reflection; instead, two haunting traces. No closure, therefore. The double-yes haunts through the inscription of memory and affirmation and the undecidability, which such citation makes plain. Moreover, haunting takes place through the spectral effect of a doubling beyond any simple opposition. Indeed, this is not quite accurate. For the spectral is not simply an *effect* of doubling. It is, instead just this doubling motion, a doubling irreducible to any apparently balanced pair or opposition, and that can return at any moment.

Mimicry, mirroring, and citational specularity are observed in passing here, but this is only fitting given the virtual rapidity of apparition, the briefest of instantaneities hinting at a furtiveness or indecipherability—the encryption—of purpose. (It might be proposed here, en passant, that such encryption of citation could be termed *cryptocitation*: This figures yet another architectural, archival and labyrinthine structure as the dwelling place, the haunt, of ghosts. Or it might be said that this very notion is comprehensible as that which structures and disturbs the idea of the subject constituted by, and as, the encrypted lodging place of the spectral, the phantasmatic other, and of so many haunting citations[42] that is misrecognized and misread as the self, as "I" "here" and gathered together in this simulacrum of unity, uncannily so.) And what could be more furtive, more the registration of a certain haste than the end- or footnote, a manifestation of citation, especially when that footnote concerns itself once again and in passing with the simulacrum of a citation, with haunting and mimicry?

Establishing or, rather, writing itself out of an already woven network or labyrinth of citations and their variations into which it places itself even as it displaces textual organization, Derrida's footnote recites as it cites an archival structure of responses within the various editions of the texts of Mallarmé, themselves responding to and re-citing the encounter with a text, the pantomime booklet, *Pierrot Murderer of his Wife*, all of which variants belong to the text of *Mimique* and all of which are, suggests Derrida, caught up in the complex textile weave concerning anonymous origins, omissions, textual fragments, reflections of variations, and the simulacrum of citation. Citation mirrors or mimes citation, as absolute priority is forestalled and displaced. Nothing other than citation is possible, even while the very act of citation is itself called into question in the process of citation by Derrida, whose dense annotated network transforms itself from speaking of the troping of citation, to enacting the disturbing performative condition of citation itself. And what is more, in some kind of parody of authority, (panto)miming let us say the authority of scholarship, Derrida marshals the citations concerning the Pierrot, that silent figure of mimicry who "cites" in parody the very idea of the human via a series of material gestures, the materiality of which is so counterintuitive that all phenomenal adequation is called into question. Derrida does so furthermore, by pointing out—and this is still a condition of that performative pantomimicry of scholarly reading, a gesture not Derrida's own but haunted by the ghost of the Mallarméan text—that no such citation is to be found anywhere.[43] The citation returns certainly, but only ever in some ghostly fashion, mirroring and citing its other selves, without source, without origin.

In coming back and in being projected from some other place the provenance of which is undecidable, the citations, far from gathering themselves into a determinable set or act, separate themselves from themselves and from within themselves. Instead, like two shoes—as is known their relationship as a pair is undecidable[44]—the spectral possibility opens (onto itself) a spectrum of possibilities as, we are tempted to suggest, the truth in haunting, irreducible once more to all epistemologies, ideologies, and anthropomorphic mimeticisms reliant on the prior or anterior location. And indeed (to return momentarily to that note on Mallarmé) the word "phantom" does not simply arrive in the note on the variations to *Mimique*, the Mallarméan text, whether by that word *phantom* one suggests some so-called literal apparition or the work of metaphor. (But how would we decide on one or the other? In the face of apparition, would this ever be possible?) Ahead of definition the phantom exceeds all such possibility, disabling the reading by pushing at the very limit of interpretability. This is a case of a radical, reflective mimicry, recalling, and calling to, those oscillations, those numbers of yeses. The mime does not have a referent, even though elsewhere the Pierrot bears apparently some filial relation to the recurrent ghosts of Hamlet that trouble the text of Mallarmé.[45] The reference is not to what is real but to another ghost, and thus one is witness to the play of difference, the doubling vibration between two mirrors belonging to what is termed a differential structure of mimicry. The ghost is the ghost of a ghost, trace of a trace. Haunting takes place both in the place *of* and *as* citation. The event of *revenance* taking place otherwise in citation is glimpsed if only because citation promises to make the invisible visible, though never as a presence, never present. In effect, the citational program, what is supposed to take place, is displaced in its very act and in the demand that the act must occur. Thus, the promise, premise, or program of citation is always already haunted within its very structural possibility before a word is written or rewritten.

This promise or unlooked-for gift is inscribed in the citation of a name. It is what takes place, if it takes place at all, in the proper name as the uncanny disturbance within its law and logic. It takes place especially in that moment, during a eulogy, for example, when the name returns, illuminating and making visible the one who is dead and thereby in-citing, ex-citing, the projected spectrum of *revenance* and *survival*, living-on, living beyond death in the citation that apostrophizes the other.[46] We can always anticipate this, and thus cite the spectral return from the future, thereby opening ourselves to it. Again there is readable a strange and awful temporal disorganization. However, this is citation (*l'avenir/l'à venir*). This is what takes place when citation recalls the name. This is the work of citation: to return the voices of countless ghosts from what can all too easily be called the past and, somewhat less easily, the future, as though by the use of such temporal determinations everything could be fixed into place as though one could thereby have done with spectres, with speculation, and with that haunting sensation every time words arrive from somewhere else. What is most haunting is that the movement of *revenance* never comes to a halt, with or without some consciousness to bear witness. It might be said that the spectral is everywhere all the time, yet without a proper time of its own (without an "its own" to which time can properly be said to be appended) and that the protocols surrounding citation are so precise that the laws have multiplied themselves in the name of citation, citing countless examples along the way, if only so as to seek to calm or protect against the haunting vibrations and thereby keep at bay the haunts of citation; which haunts are those very places where citation takes place and to which it appears habituated, in which it finds itself most at home, and yet where it can come to operate the most uncanny effects.

V

> How is it possible for something to continue on, which, in another way, does not seem to exist? I guess that could be taken in a number of ways: it could be the relation of the original to the translation; one wonders which haunts which. Is it that the translation haunts the original, or is it the original that haunts the translation? . . . the question of the haunted and the haunting interchanges in some questions of influence.
>
> John P. Leavey Jr.

Having touched only briefly on so many issues, I have gone too quickly, doubtless, and, perhaps have yet to begin. It is perhaps a matter of touching on the intangible.[47] Throughout this chapter, various texts by Derrida are acknowledged, even though they are not cited *directly*. They are neither invisible nor visible. They are never present as such but translate as much as they are translated. They inform and direct, orient and disorient. It would be more accurate to suggest that, in being cited without being cited, their traces as so many ex-citations, so many ghostly moments of trembling and solicitation, impose themselves without ever having been quoted verbatim. Citations "appear," in other words, in a semitransparent, semi-encrypted fashion, but hovering somewhere between "correct" forms of citation, and the barest possible acknowledgment while remaining tied, as *relics, bits and pieces, remains*,[48] to the protocols and what remains, albeit in ruins, of academic citation.

There is thus a situation, directly in relation to this chapter, its subject, and its writing, that is more or less impossible, and this double bind has to do with hierarchical and other forms of relationship concerning the institutionalization, the normalization of location apropos of the matter of authority. However, and this is very much the point of this chapter, even were I to abandon all pretence toward acknowledgment, however minimal, citation would nonetheless always already have taken place due to the inescapable condition of the spectral errancy of words, an errancy and a return partaken of by all words from the very beginning, as it were. In the beginning was the spectre.[49] Writing without citation will have been, therefore, impossible. In playing on the limits of what acknowledges protocols and the possibility of citation, and, additionally, citation concerning the question of the spectral, I have merely sought to highlight that spectralization which is the interest of any modality that is called citation. Of course, there is the merest possibility that this chapter might be taken merely as engaging in an act of annotation, though hardly authoritative given its citational dysfunction, its brevity and excessiveness, to all the sources that, conventionally understood, might be taken as the various authorities to which we appeal.

Chapter 7

OCCASIONS OF TRAUMA AND TESTIMONY: WITNESSING, MEMORY, AND RESPONSIBILITY

For history to be a history of trauma means that it is referential precisely to the extent that it is not fully perceived as it occurs; or to put it somewhat differently, that a history can be grasped only in the very inaccessibility of its occurrence.

Cathy Caruth

In order to cope with a trauma, we symbolize.

Slavoj Žižek

I

Although there is a significant number of critical works addressing the figure and effects of trauma, or what Ulrich Baer calls "unresolved experience,"[1] and the related role of testimony in literature, there is no single school of criticism, no one methodology as such, dealing with these issues. It is not the purpose of this chapter to read this apparent absence as a deficiency. Nor is it my intention here to supply an "introductory" discussion or objective summary of the work so far done, in order to supplement that work and thereby make up for any supposed lack, even though much of what is sketched in this chapter gets under way by certain inaugural gestures, albeit in a manner dictated as a series of responses. On the contrary, it must be admitted from the outset that any gesture in the direction of regulating a response to trauma or establishing a methodology or mode of analysis should be resisted, if one is to do justice to trauma and the work of testimony, for the singularity of the traumatic and the mark that it leaves is one that beyond what Derrida calls any "calculative rationality . . . complicates and entangles all questions of decision and responsibility."[2] As Dominick LaCapra has suggested, "a post-traumatic response . . . . becomes questionable when it is routinized in a methodology or style that enacts compulsive repetition."[3] Equally, it has to be acknowledged that what is being named as an interest in critical studies and what I wish to explore in the present chapter as the possibility of a critical modality could come under the headings of "mourning," "memory work," "acts of bearing witness" (another possible description of testimony) or, more obliquely and generally, "responsibility" in the acts of reading we call criticism. Perhaps that in reading which we will approach here might most appropriately be understood as "a grammar of shock, absorption and loss," to cite Avital Ronell.[4] Therefore, however one orientates oneself, the emphasis must be placed on a careful reading in response to that which marks the text, hence Ronell's apposite use of the term "grammar," rather than any application tout court of paradigmatic procedures or protocols.

To speak of a "grammar" is not to deny the material horror and aftereffects of an historical event such as the Holocaust; nor is such a remark the sign of some formalist retreat into language games and trivializing quibbles over truth claims, into "hyperbolic or speculative acts" as LaCapra argues in *Writing History, Writing Trauma*,[5] against what he perceives to be the occasional linguistic "excesses" of so-called poststructuralist discourse. It is, instead, to acknowledge and observe how "absence is a structural part of witness," as Michael Bernard-Donals and Richard Glejzer put it.[6] As they continue: "the act of witness is only ever available in another place and in another time [than that of the experience of the traumatic event]. . . . Witness can only be accessible to the extent that it is not fully perceived or experienced as it occurs, and it can only be grasped in the very inaccessibility of its occurrence."[7] It is this "grammatical" register that Cathy Caruth also addresses, and to which we will return. However, it has to be said, concerning the figures of "loss" and "absence," that these are not simply which speak "transhistorically to absolute foundations . . . induc[ing] either a metaphysical etherealization, even obfuscation, of historical problems or a historicist, reductive localization of transhistorical, recurrently displaced problems—or perhaps a confusingly hybridised, extremely labile discourse . . . that seems to derive from the deconstruction of metaphysics," in the words of LaCapra.[8] What is "transhistorical" is, in fact, LaCapra's own analysis here. For he reduces and generalizes, in what seems a fairly metaphysical way, the reading of loss and absence, precisely to the extent that he assumes that each figure is conceptualized in an undifferentiated manner, in the theoretical analyses he addresses. What it is important to realize, in any reading of absence or loss as that which necessitates structurally any response to trauma, is that what is absent or lost is singular, particular to the historial instant of the traumatic event and its subsequent reading or writing. As Ulrich Baer suggests, there is an "obligation to recognize another's experience of trauma as irreducibly *other* and irreducible to generalizations;"[9] moreover, to cite Baer again, every text, every other, attesting to the traumatic makes "an uncompromising claim . . . to be read in its own terms. Yet at the same time...each...opens itself to iteration, understanding, and address."[10] There is thus the "necessity of considering the poetic representation of unresolved experience [that is to say, trauma] . . . as absolutely singular."[11]

II

This is, of course, to point to the very difficult ground on which we find ourselves, hence my own caution concerning the questions of terminology and methodological regulation. It is doubtless the case that such terms and phrases as those toward which I express an initial wariness, if not suspicion, might resonate in various ways in relation to particular protocols or programs, certain manifestations of institutionalized analysis more or less obviously. You might believe on the evidence of words such as "trauma" or phrases such as "memory work," for example, that there is a certain "psychoanalytic" register at work in my discourse. This is so, of course, undeniably, as the following discussions of Freud indicate. It has to be said, however, that, while the question of "reading and writing trauma" is indebted in particular ways to psychoanalysis and psychoanalytic literary criticism—or, to be more precise, certain strands within these nominations—there will also be other aspects to the critique in the present chapter that are not directly accounted for in psychoanalysis, and that therefore exceed the institutional, discursive parameters of such work, while also acknowledging other epistemological models and critical discourses.

There is observable, for example, the matter of a reorientation toward reading history, of reading "history" and its representations differently in relation to trauma, as Caruth makes plain in my first epigraph. Whether or not history can be thought as *always* or *only* a history of trauma, it is important to note two aspects of Caruth's complication of the notion of history: first, that there is the matter of referentiality, of the signs, traces, or marks by which we attempt to recover or reconstruct history. History, in this account, is comprehended as textual. This is not, to stress the point once more, to suggest that historical events do not happen. Instead, as Caruth informs us, the materiality of the historical event is *only ever available* through the relay and concomitant deferral that is the condition of the materiality of signifiers. Therefore, what we call history always comes down to a matter of reading and, equally, rereading and rewriting in as responsible a manner as possible, however neutral we seek to be, or (mis)believe we can be. Second, and at the same time, the work of reading history must necessarily take place precisely because the historical occurrence is neither fully perceivable in the event nor subsequently accessible after the fact of its occurrence.

As another particular dimension to the problem of reading, there can be discerned also, and especially in the use of the word *responsibility*, an indebtedness to ethical demands and requirements and the question of ethics in general. This is also true.[12] If, as Shoshana Felman has remarked apropos of trauma and testimony, that there is "a parallel between [a] kind of teaching [and, we would add, reading] (in its reliance on the testimonial process) and psychoanalysis," the former is not reducible to the latter. Despite this, both "are called upon to be *performative* . . . both strive to produce, and to enable, *change*. Both . . . are interested not merely in new information, but, primarily, in the capacity . . . to *transform*."[13] It is precisely in this demand for the performative dimension and the transformation it entails that responsibility is heard. What amounts to an ethical call announces itself as the possibility of exceeding analysis and, indeed, representation. So, to recap: while there are, or may be, parallels between discourses, there is neither a method nor a school. There is only the necessity, and the risk, of enabling reading as transformative critique. This being the case, it is perhaps best to begin approaching the subject in hand by offering the following provisional statement as a means of initial orientation, or, indeed, an affirmation of responsibility: all critical acts should manifest responsibility to texts being read beyond, and in excess of, the calculation of any program of reading (within limits), methodology, or school of thought, but what that responsibility might be cannot be decided ahead of the encounter.

Paradoxically, though, no reading can ever account for everything in a text. Reading, therefore, can never be completed. There will always be (and have been, always already) some trace, some haunting remainder, with which we have to live, that we must admit, and yet for which we cannot account, finally. As Gayatri Spivak has remarked, "One cannot be mindful of a haunting, even if it fills the mind,"[14] and this is chiefly because, with regard to trauma, there is what Baer calls a "twofold *structural* disjunction between an experience and its integration into narrative memory, understanding, and communicability. . . . All such experiences . . . [are] located somewhere outside memory yet within the psyche."[15] That this paradox or impasse exists in no way lets the reader off the hook from assuming responsibility. Rather, reading, considered as precisely the response that recognizes its responsibility in the face of the impossibility that reading also entails, must continue, must respond to the other, all the while accepting and acknowledging that, in bearing witness to the other, one cannot master, control, determine, or domesticate the other through some normative ontological or epistemological process. This is all the more so when it is a question of seeking to represent traumatic events, of seeking the adequate or appropriate mode of representation. As Bernard-Donals and Glejzer make clear throughout *Between Witness and Testimony: The Holocaust and the Limits of Representation*, there is that about the trauma of an event such as the Holocaust beyond representation or narrative adequation, so excessive is its horror. All responsible criticism engages in both a recognition of its own responsibility and the impossibility of such an endless demand, a call to conscience if you will. Reading trauma as a material manifestation of the other in a given text may well be asked to call on the discourses or disciplines of psychoanalysis, history, and ethics (considered narrowly as one "strand" in the discipline of philosophy), but it is irreducible to any disciplinary economy, or the calculation implied by accommodation between programmatic discourses. Reading and writing trauma, always as the response to singularity, effects its transformation, if this happens at all, not in any calculable control of critical position or the representation that any critical or historical modality may believe it can make possible, but in the production of a reiteration of the traumatic excess "which troubles testimony and narrative and forces the reader to confront the horror of the limit."[16]

III

At the risk of repeating myself then, let me reemphasize these issues in other words: the act of criticism as the manifestation of nothing more nor less than good reading in these terms becomes, therefore, a form of testimony, a bearing-witness or being called to witness. This is good reading as such. But the radical otherness, the alterity of that to which we must respond, is understood when it comes to be recognized that testimony, as with responsibility and in order to be responsible, *in order to be testimony and not merely an account generated according to some protocol,* has to be transformative or inventive. It must take that risk. It cannot be dictated according to the prescription of certain rules operative in the same fashion every time reading takes place. On the subject of a responsibility exceeding any program or protocol, Jacques Derrida remarks:

> I will even venture to say that ethics, politics, and responsibility, *if there are any,* will only ever have begun with the experience and experiment of the aporia. When the path is clear and given, when a certain knowledge opens up the way in advance, the decision is already made, it might as well be said that there is none to make: irresponsibly, and in good conscience, one simply applies or implements a program. Perhaps, and this would be the objection, one never escapes the program. In that case, one must acknowledge this and stop talking with authority about moral or political responsibility. The condition of possibility of this thing called responsibility is a certain *experience and experiment of the possibility of the impossible: the testing of the aporia* from which one may invent the only *possible invention, the impossible invention.*[17]

Testimony, therefore, and "testimonial criticism," if such a thing takes place, cannot be prepared or prepared for ahead of the event, the arrival of the other. Testimony, in order to be such, cannot be calculated, for every testimony must respond to the singular specificity of the traumatic experience. If responsibility is understood, then both the alterity and the singularity of the other have to be admitted. If, as Shoshana Felman suggests, we live "in the age of testimony," by which name she indicates "the era of the Holocaust, of Hiroshima, of Vietnam,"[18] and to which it would be necessary to add "September 11, 2001," then it has to be recognized at the same time that what is called an era or an age is marked by the registration of historical events incommensurate either with one another or with that very epochal similitude that the notion of the era or age, in the naming of an identity based on sufficient, that is, calculable, resemblance suggests. Testimony is irreducible to some concept or figure, some genre or species of narrative within historical narrative or literature.

The aporia of responsibility that I have sketched demonstrates this in showing how conceptual thinking operates within limits and with the imagined horizon of some limit, as does Felman's invocation of "age" or "era."[19] To speak of either "trauma" or "testimonial criticism" is both to assume that one knows what both trauma and testimony are, that is, that there are stable concepts appearing in the same form, time after time, and to believe also that such a criticism is, in fact, a delineable or delimitable conceptual form. Yet, as Ulrich Baer cautions, "in addition to historical differences [the very differences that the thinking of an "era" occludes], 'trauma' is not a stable term. An experience registers as . . . traumatic. And this remains fundamentally unresolved, not because of the event's *inherent content*, but because recourse to an external frame of reference is unavailable."[20] To risk a somewhat counterintuitive formula at this juncture therefore, which doubtless says too little and tries to say too much, literature *just is* testimony and it is this that imposes upon the reader and the act of criticism the burden of an incalculable responsibility. (Another way to think this would be to recall Walter Benjamin's well-known comment that all documents of civilization are also documents of barbarity.) Reading is the act of bearing witness to literature's memory work where the reader must respond, must make impossible decisions, in response to the attestation of impersonal memory. To read thus is to admit to a degree of guilt, and to affirm a responsibility with regard to that guilt. And the responsibility entailed herein truly is incalculable, for in every act of witnessing, every response to the other in its singularity, I sacrifice countless others.[21] Yet, it is for this reason that we cannot reproduce reductively through the gesture of generalization. In a very risky gesture, Jacques Derrida identifies the dangers of such thought, precisely around what is taken by many as the name of trauma par excellence, Auschwitz. While, to quote Alexander García Düttman, it is undeniable that the singularity of Auschwitz "is incommensurable: not only because *nothing similar* can be thought or imagined but above all because something unlike anything else compels us to think and act in such a way that *nothing similar* ever happens,"[22] Derrida—as Düttman points out— "warns us against discourses, which, taking Auschwitz as the model"

> are in danger of reconstituting a sort of centrality, a "we" which is certainly not that of speculative dialectics but which is related to the unanimous privilege which we occidental Europeans accord to Auschwitz in the fight or the question which we oppose to speculative dialectics, to a certain type of occidental reason. The danger is that this "we" would take from memory or sideline proper names other than Auschwitz, ones which are just as abominable, names which have names and names which have no name.[23]

It would be a gross misreading to see in this statement some kind of denial of either the historical event or the traumatic significance of Auschwitz. It is, though, crucially, urgently important that we comprehend how Derrida is illustrating the dangers in a certain limit-thinking with regard to certain aspects of normative historical representation and, equally, the dangers of letting the proper name do your thinking for you. In fact, the danger of the proper name is that, in letting it come to assume some privileged position in one's discourse, thinking—and, therefore, responsibility—stops. There is, then, the difficult business of thinking Auschwitz, and, indeed, any traumatic event, in all its inexpressible, irreducible singularity, a difficulty that remains with regard to any narrative of trauma. For what remains, as the trace of the traumatic figuring the articulation of a name such as Auschwitz or the name that has no name, such as September 11, 2001, is what Alexander García Düttman calls "the possibility of survival, of another memory and another promise, [which] depends on a certain unreadability."[24]

The work of criticism that addresses trauma, testimony, and memory must then necessarily explore what Cathy Caruth has described as the "enigma of the otherness" in the revenance and articulation of trauma, which the human agent "cannot fully know."[25] Caruth demonstrates a two-part disruptive or disjunctive structure in the nature of narrative form, of which more, in relation to trauma, appears in the second section of this chapter. This structure allows for the articulation of the subject's act of witnessing and responsibility involved in acts of memory and witnessing through the other's arrival that forces on the subject a knowledge previously withheld. The return of the other opens the subject's complicity to him- or herself, not necessarily as a specific guilt for a specific act, but as the culpability, and the responsibility that *that* entails, as a condition of Being, in which, as beings, we all share, and which has itself to be acknowledged (as Martin Heidegger makes plain in his analysis of *Dasein*, in *Being and Time*).

In exploring this mode of narrative, I am seeking to show how criticism's function is to reiterate, and thereby bear witness itself, to the disarticulating modality already installed in various forms of fiction or "the literary" as so many acts of witnessing and memory. The question of trauma and testimonial criticism becomes one, I will argue, of a patient tracing of that which constitutes the literary text as both a function of memory and responsibility and as a mode of technicity, a making appear, to which, in every act of reading, all readers must bear witness and for which they must take responsibility as a definition of the act of reading itself. There is implied an open series of responses, each opening itself to, and in, a potentially, infinite, disjunctive chain.

Such a model of reading and the understanding of the literary that it invokes has at least two effects, which it will be the function of this chapter to examine and explain: (1) the motion of the return or supplement, the revenance of testimony, implies the call of the other as intrinsic to the act of narration; as such, it inscribes an iterable circulation. In this, we may read a narrative modality that functions against the facts of history and is suggestive of a poetics of witnessing and of the work of trauma as the work of memory irreducible to any historical model. (2) At the same time, such return, and the persistence of witnessing it implies, is suggestive of the fact, once again, that we can never be let off the hook regarding our acts of responsible reading. In short, the function in part of testimonial criticism is to open to the reader through a recognition of the other's articulation, a recognition that what Heidegger calls the "call of conscience" is not simply always already in effect but always remains to come. Thus, we will never have done with reading, and reading remains also that which is to come. The folding and unfolding of structure traced by Caruth thereby is read as the necessary ethical figure of a reading resistant on the one hand to closure and on the other hand to any simple sense of continuity or linearity in narrative motion. As Ulrich Baer puts it, trauma remains open and undecidable because there is no possible immediate recourse to "an external frame of reference." The very idea of narrative itself, or, more generally, textuality, involves, remarks Baer, the "epistemological possibility and the moral necessity of considering the poetic representation of unresolved experience . . . as absolutely *singular*,"[26] and knowable only, paradoxically, in its singularity through the open seriality that narrative makes possible.

In exploring the work of critics such as Baer and Caruth, Derrida and Felman, among others, I am therefore attempting to engage with these particular exemplary interventions by tracing, albeit briefly, the fractured intercessions between and exceeding various discourses, as these concern themselves with matters of memory and subjectivity, guilt and being. The impossibility of a representation in relation to the singularity *and* iteration of trauma ties the question of testimony both to the idea of the secret and the question of the unrepresentability of the instant of the traumatic event, as Derrida has made clear in *Demeure*. However, as I wish to argue, our inability to represent the traumatic instant is neither simply a moment of replaying the silencing of articulation by which the traumatized subject is produced, nor is it, equally simply, an acknowledgment of empathy and, therefore, an undifferentiated identification with the victim of trauma;[27] instead, the work of criticism becomes a matter of addressing the "impossibility and necessity" of bearing witness to the "unexperienced experience,"[28] and it is through the structural gap, in that grammar of absence and loss, that the other comes to be heard.

IV

Trauma, it might be said, is a ghost. Given that "the essential character of traumatism" is best described as a "nonsymbolizable wound,"[29] to read trauma is to register the sign of a secondary experience and recognition of the return of something spectral in the form of a trace or sign signifying, but not representing directly, that something, having occurred, has left its mark, an inscription of sorts on the subject's unconscious, and one that, moreover, can and does return repeatedly, though never as the experience as such. This is not to say that the traumatic event, that factual or historical event that one day took place, never happened or was not real. It is to register, however, that for trauma to be comprehended as trauma, as that which, in appearing, inflicts itself on the subject and thereby causes suffering, is never experienced for the first time *as trauma*. As Dominick LaCapra rightly remarks, "[s]omething of the past always remains, if only as a haunting presence or symptomatic revenant."[30] The traumatic is, therefore, what is phantomatic or phantasmatic. Structural through and through the traumatic phantasm—and, indeed, all phantasms in general—are contradictory, as Louis Althusser suggests. As he puts it, "something occurs . . . but nothing happens . . . everything is immobile."[31] The subject of trauma is rendered immobile, unable to move beyond the haunting effects left by trauma, and can only experience in a damaging, repetitive fashion, the disjunctive spectres, remains of what is "nonsymbolizable." And yet, paradoxically, the phantasm is a symbol; what has to be understood however, is that the symbol is not a mimetic representation, it is not an image of the experience itself. It belongs to the order of apperception rather than perception. As Althusser argues, Freud's notion of the phantasm is analogous with the workings of figural language:

> [w]e are obliged to observe that in the phantasm Freud designates something extremely precise, an existent—though nonmaterial—reality, concerning which no misunderstanding is possible, and a material reality that is the very existence of its object: the unconscious. But we are also obliged to observe that the name Freud gives to that reality . . . is the name of a *metaphor:* phantasm . . . the concept of the phantasm in Freud . . . can . . . be, *for us,* the concept *of the limit*.[32]

While I would revise Althusser's understanding by suggesting that, at least as far as the phantasm of trauma is more of the order of catachresis than metaphor, it is clearly incontestable that the phantasm thus remarks both the otherwise unsymbolizable, and also the grammatical or structural displacement, as the necessary movement in the production of meaning; in doing so, it becomes available—it is only ever available—as the inscription of (and, indeed, *at*) the very limit of representation, rather than being or belonging to representation. The haunting trace not only attests to what is "outside memory yet within the psyche," to recall Ulrich Baer's words, it also reveals an irreversible and therefore structural passage between, in Dianne Sadoff's words, "the material, physiological realm and the correlate mental realm."[33] In coming to terms with this disjunctive passage as intrinsic to the psychic incorporation of trauma, and the subsequent ghostly reiteration by which trauma came to be comprehended, Freud "stumbled," as Sadoff continues, "on the concept of representability. . . . Mnemic symbols, reproduced scenes, and dreams . . . situated images . . . in a pictorial and verbalized spaced, traversed by memories, fears and desires."[34]

Interested by what Cathy Caruth describes as the "peculiar and *uncanny* way in which catastrophic events seem to repeat themselves for those who have passed through them" (emphasis added),[35] Freud sought to explain the experience of trauma through Tasso's story of Tancred and Clorinda. Tancred "unwittingly kills . . . Clorinda . . . when she is disguised in the armour of an enemy knight. After her burial he makes his way into a strange magic forest which strikes the Crusaders' army with terror. He slashes with his sword at a tall tree; but blood streams from the cut and the voice of Clorinda . . . is heard complaining that he has wounded his beloved again."[36] As Tasso's narrative, recounted by Freud, illustrates, the protagonist is lead inadvertently to repeat his initial act, and it is only through the structural repetition, that unconscious reenactment and the resulting haunting traces of Clorinda's fate—the blood, the voice—whereby she "returns," not as herself but as a phantasm of herself, that Tancred receives the forceful shock of understanding the significance of his earlier action. Structurally, the event becomes dislocated, doubled, *and* displaced in reiterative fashion in both Tasso and Freud's accounts, its meaning *for its subject* produced through the spatiotemporal disjunctive inscription that Derrida names différance between the "first" recounting of act, the historical fact, and the subsequent, supplementary textual re-marking in the revenant signs. As Cathy Caruth says, "this understanding of trauma in terms of its indirect relation to reference does not deny or eliminate the possibility of reference but insists, precisely, on the inescapability of its belated impact."[37] And it is for this reason that, in Freud's account, trauma, is "understood as a wound inflicted not upon the body but upon the mind," whereby "knowing and not knowing are entangled in the language of trauma."[38]

Cathy Caruth elucidates further the structural significance of trauma, expanding Freud's insights beyond the already undeniably significant recognition of that which haunts through the traces of its reiteration. What the critic finds powerfully moving in this scene is not only Tancred's illumination. It is also Clorinda's voice: "a voice that is paradoxically released *through the wound*."[39] Caruth explains: "[t]he voice of his beloved addresses him and, in this address, bears witness to the past he has unwittingly repeated. Tancred's story thus represents traumatic experience as double. On the one hand, there is that dimension already acknowledged by Freud, in which trauma is figured and read as "the enigma of the human agent's repeated and unknowing acts." On the other hand, the story admits for Cathy Caruth the "enigma of the otherness of a human voice . . . that witnesses a truth"[40] not completely comprehended by the subject. It is thus a matter of giving acknowledgment to the other, of bearing witness to that alterity. In learning how to read and write in response to trauma one must therefore acknowledge the crucial problem "of listening, of knowing, and of representing."[41] Critical readings and literary or filmic texts concerned with such issues are obligated to bear witness by asking "what it means to transmit and to theorize around a crisis that is marked, not by a simple knowledge [by which one might suggest a knowledge available to adequate representation, if such exists], but by the ways it simultaneously defies and demands our witness."[42]

Such is the "'technical' difficulty," to use a phrase of Avital Ronell's, regarding any critical or literary act concerning trauma and testimony.[43] I believe that Ronell employs the word "technical," simultaneously marking it off through the cautionary use of quotation marks, to emphasize the fundamental condition of technicity, that is, as remarked earlier, an act of making something appear. How does one verbalize or visualize where there is nothing present as such, and yet where there is a nonmaterial reality and its material effects? The difficulty, Ronell suggests, "consists in the fact that trauma can be experienced in at least two ways . . . as a memory that one cannot integrate into one's own experience, and as a catastrophic knowledge that one cannot communicate to others."[44] Slavoj Žižek puts the problem another way:

> There is an inherent link between the notions of trauma and repetition, signalled in Freud's well-known motto that what one is not able to remember, one is condemned to repeat: a trauma is by definition something one is not able to remember, i.e. to recollect by way of making it part of one's symbolic narrative; as such, it repeats itself indefinitely, returning to haunt the subject—more precisely, what repeats itself is the very failure, impossibility even to repeat/recollect the trauma properly.[45]

The difficulty explained by Žižek and Ronell is that of some impassable point in thinking, where what comes to be revealed, even though we cannot say what it is, is the acknowledgment of a radically discontinuous structure between self and other. As Derrida remarks, "one needs the other to be determined, in order to relate to history, to memory, to what is kept as a nameable or nameless secret. There is some sealed memory, kept as a crypt or as an unconscious, which is encrypted here."[46]

V

Acknowledging that the aporia of trauma is impassable, to the extent that the experience cannot either be integrated into memory or remembered in such a fashion that one can "overcome" trauma through a kind of mimetic reassembly of the absent experience, perhaps it remains the case that one's response and responsibility has to assume different forms, different modalities, different readings. Such possibilities, in acknowledging the limit of representation, open themselves to other articulations, might make it possible to "begin again" in such a way that the traces of the traumatic are comprehended in their irrecoverable condition so as to allow for what architect Daniel Libeskind describes as a "hopeful future."[47] Clearly, it would seem that the question of how one responds is not so much a matter of *mimesis* as it is of *poiêsis*.

Libeskind has, himself, confronted just such a problem as an architect asked to respond in the appropriate manner to the Holocaust, and to the relation between the violence of forgetting imposed by trauma and what he describes as the "invisible matrix or anamnesis of connections in relationship . . . between figures of Germans and Jews"[48] on several projects. One such project is the Jewish Museum, Berlin, in which the architect has sought to address the memory of the relation between Jewish culture and tradition and German culture, not simply in dialectical terms but, instead, through the material reality offered by the memory and history of the city of Berlin, as one space wherein traumatic erasure and silencing took place. Libeskind's project was thus to be able to speak of the invisible within the visible, the unspeakable within the articulated, thereby symbolizing indirectly the unsymbolizable of the traumatic event. To this end, the museum could not be merely a memorial, imposing itself as another form of silencing by gathering so many "representations" of absence as though these were somehow representative of all the facts that were the case of the Holocaust, and thereby allowing for the possibility of the necessary act of witnessing to slide into some form of empathic voyeurism. Instead, Libeskind chose to rethink the very space of the museum, and passage through it, in order that every "participant," as he puts it, will experience [the museum] as his or her own absent present";[49] in order that every visitor's "role," as it were, is not defined solely as objective or constative—as a visitor, I do simply not observe and reflect on represented events to which I believe I have little or no relationship, as is the case in conventional museums—but is, also, inescapably, participatory and performative (and therefore transformative, auto-transformative)—in the act of passage I experience and thus am asked to remember, to symbolize, the invisible, the silenced, the erased, of Berlin *within* the visible, present, articulated structure of the museum, which both belongs to Berlin and yet also traces Berlin's alterity. This is achieved by Libeskind through the very nature of the spatial and architectural experience rather than because of any single item in the museum's collection, each of which is always in danger of functioning as synecdoche for the trauma of the *Shoah* as a whole, and thereby falling into mimetic representation inappropriate to the "anamnesis of connections in relationship." Specifically, Libeskind has sought to rethink the museum in performative terms through the incorporation of "roads" and "voids" between the galleries, and between the previously existing Berlin Museum and the Jewish Museum designed by Libeskind. Libeskind's comments from his website are worth quoting at length:

In specific terms the building measures more than 15,000 square meters. The entrance is through the Baroque Kollegienhaus and then into a dramatic entry Void by a stair which descends under the existing building foundations, crisscrosses underground and materializes itself as an independent building on the outside. The existing building is tied to the extension underground, preserving the contradictory autonomy of both the old building and the new building on the surface, while binding the two together in the depth of time and space.

There are three underground "roads" which programmatically have three separate stories. The first and longest "road," leads to the main stair, to the continuation of Berlin's history, to the exhibition spaces in the Jewish Museum. The second road leads outdoors to the E.T.A. Hoffmann Garden and represents the exile and emigration of Jews from Germany. The third axis leads to the dead end—the Holocaust Void.

Cutting through the form of the Jewish Museum is a Void, a straight line whose impenetrability forms the central focus around which the exhibitions are organized. In order to cross from one space of the Museum to the other, the visitors traverse sixty bridges which open into the Void space; the embodiment of absence.

The work is conceived as a museum for all Berliners, for all citizens. Not only those of the present, but those of the future who might find their heritage and hope in this particular place. With its special emphasis on the Jewish dimension of Berlin's history, this building gives voice to a common fate—to the contradictions of the ordered and disordered, the chosen and not chosen, the vocal and silent.

I believe that this project joins Architecture to questions that are now relevant to all humanity. To this end, I have sought to create a new Architecture for a time which would reflect an understanding of history, a new understanding of Museums and a new realization of the relationship between program and architectural space. Therefore this Museum is not only a response to a particular program, but an emblem of Hope.[50]

Libeskind's architecture responds to the singularity of historic catastrophe and its material effects. His work does this, moreover, in taking into account the urgent need, the responsibility once again, to make possible an event that can exceed the programming of institutional representation, and the calculability, the economy, of witnessing and memory within any mimetic paradigm. As his commentary makes clear, we can only attest to what is absent, not bring that which cannot be symbolized back. In bearing witness however, there is always a question of a poetics of witnessing that is affirmative in that it is open, and opens itself, in radical ways in relation to an understanding to come, incommensurable with any knowledge conventionally conceived.

On another occasion, Libeskind was asked to design an urban project for the site belonging to the SS surrounding Sachsenhausen concentration camp. The initial suggestion that the site could be used for housing, thereby effectively "domesticating" and forgetting the experience that haunted the location, was rejected by the architect, as being inadequate to, and incommensurate with, any project of "mental rehabilitation"[51] necessary in Germany. As Libeskind describes it, "the paradoxical challenge of the work is to retain a strong memory for generations to come and at the same time to formulate a response which provides new possibilities, new activities."[52] One of the ways in which this was achieved was through decentralizing the site of the concentration camp, originally to have been the "monumental central" location of the proposed housing development; deregulating the order of the site provided for Libeskind a way of displacing the camp from its axial prominence, which would simply have repeated without transforming what was represented. Another transformation proposed was to use the land in such a way as to effect "ecological intervention and invention,"[53] allied to the economic needs of the city of Oranienberg. Libeskind saw the necessity of providing training facilities for the unemployed, as well as other public services such as "physical and mental health clinics," "a library, archive, museum," and the accommodation of small companies, specifically those "connected to cultural production, such as instrument makers, furniture restorers or ceramicists."[54] Libeskind's responses to the Sachsenhausen location suggests an affirmation of responsibility in the face of one singular instance of trauma, a responsibility that manifests itself in the resistance to a predictable programming of redevelopment and therefore situates its own affirmative singularity. Yet, while retaining the singularity of both trauma and response as the work of an act of "reading" (in the broad sense) as previously discussed, Libeskind also acknowledges a more theoretically broad comprehension of the task engendered after trauma, without reducing that to a method in itself. He writes: "The task of urbanizing the territories formerly connected with the Sachsenhausen concentration camp raises the most fundamental political, cultural and spiritual issues of the 20th century. What must be faced in any endeavour to recreate and redevelop such an area is the need to mourn an *irretrievable* destiny, in the hope that this mourning will *affect* the connection between the political program, the area's topography and its social use"[55] (emphases added).

Libeskind's language gives full recognition to the condition of trauma, but also demonstrates how the possibility of thinking transformatively according to a poetics of mourning and memory irreducible to any simple act of representation can bring about the translation from "mourning" to "morning." A new start that does not forget and yet moves forward is signified precisely in Libeskind's erasure of the "u," yet leaving both the letter and the erasure to remain, in order that the necessity for mourning is not abandoned, while also indicating that it not become a form of passive identification with the victims of the camp, thereby forestalling any hope of political or spiritual change.

VI

Trauma effects an incision in the self, so that one effectively becomes two,[56] by a process of what Nicolas Abraham and Maria Torok have called an "internal psychic splitting."[57] These two selves are the one who experiences and the one who survives.[58] This is the case, whether by "self" one indicates a single subject, an individual subjected to a catastrophic experience, or a national, communal or cultural subject, such as a nation or race.

Yet this splitting, this division and doubling that produces the discontinuous subject, doomed to be haunted by the repetitive return of the spectres of trauma, is not only a form of forgetting brought on by the extremity of some original experience; it is also, as Freud's narrative example makes clear, a manifestation of incorporation. The subject incorporates into him- or herself the signs of the traumatic, thereafter being unable to comprehend them. What distinguishes such incorporation as traumatic, however, is that the signs do not become assimilated in that psychic process termed "introjection," whereby the subject grows in "continual process of self-fashioning . . . introjection represents our ability to survive shock, trauma, or loss."[59] As Abraham and Torok put it, "*incorporation results from those losses that for some reason cannot be acknowledged as such.*"

> There can be no thought of speaking to someone else about our grief under these circumstances. The words that cannot be uttered, the scenes that cannot be recalled, the tears that cannot be shed—everything will be swallowed along with the trauma that led to the loss. Swallowed and preserved. Inexpressible mourning erects a secret tomb inside the subject. . . . Sometimes . . . the ghost of the crypt comes back to haunt the cemetery guard, giving him strange and incomprehensible signals, making him perform bizarre acts, or subjecting him to unexpected sensations.[60]

Where the phantasm had been for Althusser a metaphor, for Abraham and Torok, the spectre of trauma, in its incorporation, is *antimetaphor*, as they term it, because it effectively blocks all access to figurative contiguity or correlation, and therefore to any proper or appropriate narrative or symbolic reassembly. Hence, my suggestion that we would do well to understand the trace of trauma, in its resistance to any naturalization or domestication, as a figure of catachresis, the absolutely monstrous trope without discernible or otherwise accessible relation to its source or origin.

The figural paradox of incorporation and that amnesiac mechanism belonging to trauma may be comprehended if, in following Slavoj Žižek's reading of Primo Levi on the Holocaust,[61] we make the distinction between understanding and knowledge, which, in other terms, is also the distinction already alluded to between representation as *poiêsis* and as *mimesis*. While, rationally, we may know or be able to have access to all the historical facts (or as many of the facts as can be discovered) concerning a particular traumatic historical event, neither historical facts nor statistics, nor any historical account aiming to represent faithfully the past solely through the narrative ordering of such factual details, will ever wholly help either those witnesses who survive or those who after the event bear witness to what took place *understand*. There is always already opening, once again, that incommensurate gap, and with it, the fateful repetition. Understanding does not belong to the rational, the logical, the mimetic; it arrives, if it arrives at all, through articulating a certain relationship to that of which the facts cannot speak, and, whereof they must, therefore, keep silent. Understanding is only possible—and this is not some guarantee or promise—if one begins by comprehending the process of a certain "translation" already discussed—where the corporeal registration of shock and horror is effectively *decorporealized* and simultaneously *incorporated*.

Thus, if, as I have already claimed, literature just names, or is understood as the name of, *for*, the work of witnessing and memory, and if it does bear witness and remember, moreover, through the symbolization of what remains unsymbolizable and unrepresentable, it has to be appreciated and grasped that reading literature, in order to be responsible, cannot merely content itself with a reading of character motivation, of plot summary, or, indeed, with an analysis the epistemological grounding for which is to be located in an assumption of literature as conforming to realist criteria of representation. Rather, as one possible hypothesis, narrative takes place through the assembly of signifying fragments moving through various flows, whose intersections gather in moments of intensity so as to project phantasmatic symbolizations of what otherwise cannot be articulated. In such terms, narrative or, perhaps, even literature itself is the indirect articulation of what Maurice Blanchot has described as "a speech unheard, inexpressible, nevertheless unceasing, silently affirming that where all relation is lacking there yet subsists, there already begins, the human relation in its primacy."[62]

We might take, for example, the narrative of Mary Shelley's *Frankenstein, or the Modern Prometheus*. The story of a man, Victor Frankenstein, who assembles something almost human but not quite—something other than human that, in its uncanny resemblance to the human animal, constantly reminds its maker of a disturbing otherness within any notion of self or being—is, in one sense, clearly fantastic, impossible. The narrative thus represents what is, strictly speaking, unrepresentable, even though Mary Shelley is at pains to point out that there are those in the scientific community who have suggested that her narrative represents a not "impossible occurrence." The author goes on to remark, in a form of qualification, that "however impossible as a physical fact, [the narrative event of the construction of a human being] affords a point of view to the imagination for the delineating of human passions more comprehensive and commanding than any which the ordinary relations of existing events can yield."[63] At pains to point out that *Frankenstein* is not merely some supernatural tale of spectres, Shelley clearly wishes it to be understood that the story concerns the articulation of a certain imaginative, psychological understanding—a poetics, in short—incommensurable with any strictly realistic representation or adequate knowledge.

Thus, we find ourselves witness to a particular, singular narrative responding to that process of transition between physical and mental realms and, at the same time, that narrative's inability to verbalize or bear witness to epistemological crisis. Historically, *Frankenstein* is available to us as being both caught in and traversing the space between the external and internal, symbolizing, we might say, the registration of a cultural experience of trauma in the face of the epistemological shock to the self of then "new" sciences. It moves between differing modalities of comprehension concerning self and other, or the two halves of the split self, which it remarks materially through the characters of Victor Frankenstein and his creature. The novel is suspended in its traversal between external physical world and internal psychic states, however, in that—and this is a sign of the materiality, the historiality of the narrative's attempt to respond to the traumatic reception of new knowledge, and out of which comes the narrative's imaginative understanding—it still finds it necessary to apprehend its concerns through the ostensible depiction of creator and creature as essentially separate, and yet inseparable, characters.

Yet, what is really fascinating in Shelley's narrative, despite the corporeal externalization—and thus as a manifestation of anthropomorphic representation signaling the inability to move beyond the otherwise inaccessible, inexpressible experience of trauma—is the movement of structural repetition. Victor Frankenstein's creation pursues his creator relentlessly, returning and haunting both Victor and the narrative itself. Significantly, apropos of the question of traumatic revenance, we should read such returns and reiterations not as the arrival of a significant character, so much as we should comprehend how the narrative is itself marked and interrupted, traumatized, by this iterable interruption. And while Victor Frankenstein may have scientific knowledge, he has no understanding of what he has done; its meaning is inaccessible to him, and so he is pursued by this monstrous phantasm of his own making. Similarly, the narrative can only function through its various doublings and repetitions, and its material, uncloseable fissure between externality and internality, its constant reminders of the divisions of the subject announcing, in a quite singular manner, the trauma of modernity. The reciprocal shuttling of its various "voices" renders the text as a weaving machine; the sovereign narrator is dismembered through a technology of witnessing. And the reader is confronted, perhaps traumatized, by an image of a possibly traumatized creator unable to take responsibility for the other, a figure of abjection, trauma, and alterity, not-quite-human enough and yet all-too-human in a particularly modern sense: technologically reproduced, grafted, re-marked, commodified, and made monstrous. And yet, to conclude this brief sketch by reiterating what is, for me, the key issue here, this is not only to describe Frankenstein's creature, or even Victor Frankenstein's nonrecognition; it is also to say something, albeit indirectly, about *Frankenstein*, the text:[64] for, arguably, it bears all the hallmarks of traumatic narrative unable to escape its own condition, doomed to fold onto itself that otherness that haunts it throughout.

It might be said that it took less than a hundred years for literature to respond to the processes of internalization that trauma simultaneously names and encrypts.[65] That wholesale internalization finds itself re-marked in Joseph Conrad's *Heart of Darkness*. While *Frankenstein*'s registration of the traumatic is fundamentally epistemological in nature, Conrad's narrative strives to address the trauma of the colonial enterprise, and to bear witness to that. Were we simply interested in reading characters as traumatized, we could, doubtless, focus on Kurtz. (And, indeed, I do wish to turn, if not to Kurtz entirely, then, at least, to his final words.) However, I want to stress that *Heart of Darkness* records trauma at its most basic lexical levels, through the very choice of words by which the attempt at representation takes place. (Again, given that Conrad's novel offers its readers a first-person narrative, it would be easy enough to domesticate the reading of trauma by seeing its articulation as, simply, only, the articulation of the narrator, Marlowe's, psychological condition.) The narratorial voice (which, it has to be stressed, cannot be equated simply with Marlowe's, if only because Marlowe's account is both marked by the voices of others, as well as being a response to, and therefore framed by, an anonymous, invisible narrator who begins *Heart of Darkness*) is traced by a poetics of the limit, a materiality of the letter attesting to both the limit and inadequacy of representation in the face of catastrophe and horror, and the importance of bearing witness to the fact, and in the face of, the inexpressible.

This "limit-language" occurs throughout the novel through the use of several hundred words, all sharing prefixes the work of which is either to say that determinate knowledge or representation cannot take place or that knowledge and representation are only this admission that one cannot know, one cannot represent trauma. These are words such as *interminable, immensity, imperceptible, untitled, unknown, inscrutable, incomprehensible, inconclusive, uncanny, unknown, insoluble, impossible, unfamiliar, incredible, impenetrable, unspeakable, inconceivable, inexorable, unforeseen, invisible, indistinct*. Their frequency simultaneously maintains the narrative and yet interrupts or suspends, disabling narrative at every point and leaving it in shocked disarray and being possibly performative, inasmuch as they remark the failure, the inadequacy, of any act of representation. Such words speak to the obligation to read and to the impossibility of a reading.

Thus, one aspect of Conrad's writing situates the responsible act *in* the materiality of the letter in order to respond *to* the materiality of history, and in order to acknowledge how, on the one hand, it is impossible to record historical events in any direct representation, while, on the other, to show indirectly how any such mimetic act is inadequate to the intensity, the immensity, of traumatism. Rather, Conrad's poetics of indirection attest to history as a history of trauma, to recall Cathy Caruth's words. In its deployment of a limit-language, Conrad's novel attests to the technical difficulty concerning trauma spoken of by Avital Ronell, for it undeniably inscribes the trauma of colonialism as (in Ronell's words) "a memory that one cannot integrate into one's own experience, and as a catastrophic knowledge that one cannot communicate to others." What such language also gives us to understand is how "repetition [is] at the heart of catastrophe."[66] Nowhere is this, along with Ronell's traumatic double bind, articulated more clearly, than in Kurtz's final moments: "Did he live his life again in every detail of desire, temptation, and surrender during that supreme moment of complete knowledge? He cried in a whisper at some image, some vision,—he cried out twice, a cry that was no more than a breath—'the horror, the horror!'"[67]

If repetition is at the heart of catastrophe as interval and fault, it is also at the heart of darkness, a darkness naming the absolute inaccessibility of the traumatic event. Kurtz's words clearly repeat themselves in the rhythm of trauma's return and which iteration "splits the mark [in this example, Kurtz's doubling, dividing articulation] into a past that can never be fully rendered present and a future which is always about to arrive."[68] Structurally, what has to be acknowledged here is that not only is Kurtz not experiencing the traumatic as such but only responding to its inaccessibility and expressing the mark it has indelibly inscribed upon him; also, his articulation—one that, in its reiteration, has the possibility of echoing and remarking itself endlessly—is itself doubled by Marlowe's memory of it (a memory that haunts Marlowe, and which returns on Marlowe's visit to Kurtz's fiancée).[69] It is to be noticed that Marlowe cannot say for certain what Kurtz is witness to; he can only pose an unanswerable question. Furthermore, that repetition is worked out in Marlowe's own words. He says twice of Kurtz that "he cried," "he cried out twice," and that, whatever Kurtz bears witness to, it is both an image and a vision. There is a splitting and duplication at work here, once again, both of which are the signs of traumatic incorporation; these effects do not merely "belonging" to a particular character's psyche, but are inscribed at the heart of the language. Moreover, the extent to which trauma is both witnessed and replayed is to be comprehended in the way in which, in the iterable movement of Marlowe's response, constative description appears to fall into performative speech act. What this suggests, *what it imposes*, is an open structure of witnessing. Marlowe does not know how to assimilate Kurtz's words, but bears witness to them and to the trauma they appear to signal, thereby enacting otherwise, transformatively, the act of attestation, and, in the process, opening an ethical relay. The structure of *Heart of Darkness* is thus mobilized by what J. Hillis Miller has called a "proliferating relay of witnesses. . . . The relay of witness behind witness behind witness, voice behind voice behind voice."[70] That we as readers comprehend this means that we are only the latest, not the last, in the relay of witnesses to the unspeakable in every singular traumatic event. This is the impossible responsibility we bear. For, to recall the words of Maurice Blanchot, what is encrypted in those words, "the horror, the horror," and in the relay they interrupt and maintain, is "a speech unheard, inexpressible, nevertheless unceasing, silently affirming that where all relation is lacking there yet subsists, there already begins, the human relation in its primacy." And what is important, as Blanchot reminds us, and as we come to understand from *Heart of Darkness*, "is not to tell, but to tell once again, and, in the retelling, to tell again each time a first time."[71]

A question might heard here: how do we come to tell, to take part in that "relay of witnesses"? Perhaps by taking responsibility for listening to the contours of this telling, and so beginning again—*each time a first time*—a process of bearing witness to the phantom traces of trauma, and thereby opening ourselves to the ineluctable transport of witnessing.

VII

Perhaps, in conclusion, it is necessary to shift our ground, as does Hamlet when faced with the invisible ubiquity of the ghost and its traumatic imposition. Nowhere as such, and yet everywhere; and yet everywhere different. Attuning ourselves to the possibility of a spectral analysis, as the necessary responsibility enjoined by the belated recognition of the traumatic wound; forcing ourselves to confront the *nothing-and-yet-not-nothing* and the *neither-nowhere-nor-not-nowhere* that nonetheless leaves a trace in passing and has such a material effect—and what, after all, is trauma except the experience of this invisible, incalculable *nothing*—we may perhaps discern a trembling of sorts. If we seek to address ghosts, haunting, spectrality, along with other textual apparitions, then we need to acknowledge that we are responding to what has already come and gone—and has returned again, as Freud's consideration of the traumatic demonstrates so clearly. As this chapter has already asserted, it is thus a matter of reading as response, response as responsibility, and responsibility as witnessing. The experience of the spectral is, in being both responsive and responsible, the experience of being touched through reading by that which is other, that which is prosopopoeic: "a voice or a face of the absent," as J. Hillis Miller has it, "the inanimate, or the dead."[72] Seeking to read the spectral condition of trauma is thus an effort to bear witness to this voice or face, and this witnessing is, moreover, not the presentation of proof on the part of the witness. As Derrida has commented recently, "[w]hoever bears witness does not bring a proof; he is someone whose experience, in principle singular and irreplaceable . . . comes to attest, precisely, that some 'thing' has been present to him." Expounding implicitly on the virtual, spectral condition of witnessing, Derrida continues: "[t]his 'thing' is no longer present to him, of course, in the mode of perception at the moment when the attestation happens; but it is present to him, if he alleges this presence, as *re-presented* in the present in memory."[73]

Derrida's remark, ever attentive to the virtual trace of the spectral by marking off with great caution the question of the nonpresent "presence" of what returns "in memory" through the quotation marks that surround the "thing," complicates our comprehension of witnessing, of reception and response. The experience of witnessing assumes an uncanny dimension through its temporal disruption and the revenance, which is here invoked. In the present context, we can expand on this definition of witnessing to remark that what is being described is the condition of reading and of the text: That which we witness in any text, through any act of reading, is no longer present except as it is *re-presented*. Yet this "representation" cannot be named this, properly speaking, for there is an indirection in the very idea of revenance forestalling the desire for mimetic, anthropomorphic, or logocentric relapse. As the question of witnessing implies, there is, once again, an ethical dimension beyond any programmatic ethical response to the matter of reading the spectral, traumatic trace, in responding to the revenance of the absent, the other. To paraphrase J. Hillis Miller, the dead continue to live on, to survive beyond life, in the afterlife that we call reading. And reading, as Miller informs us, "is one major form of the responsibility the living have to the dead."[74] We see this in *Hamlet,* of course, in Hamlet's so-called vacillation in his efforts to read his father's ghost and the ethical dimensions of that ghostly return. In the last pages of this chapter, let me turn, undoubtedly too hastily, to two writers who address in different ways the matter of return and witnessing: W. B. Yeats and Paul Celan.

In 1939, the year of his death, Yeats wrote *Purgatory*, his penultimate drama. An old, unnamed man stands with his son in the ruins of a house, the old man's parents' house, and the place of his conception. Though never presented as characters in the play, the man's parents return to him (the boy never sees them) as ghosts, coming back as they were on the night of the old man's conception. He witnesses as "present in memory" the "invisible" events leading up to his conception: his father's drinking, the sound of his father's horse's hooves as it approaches the house, and his mother's anticipation.[75] What also returns through the haunting return of the parents is the revelation of the father's murder by his son, the old man. The old man subsequently kills his own son,[76] only to hear the endless reiteration of the hoofbeats, which in its ghostly iteration (as with the ghosts of the parents, we neither see nor hear the horse or the sound it makes) evokes the endless revenance of the mother: "And she must animate that dead night/Not once but many times."[77]

What is most startling about the play's revelation of the return of traumatic encounter, witnessing, and subsequent uncanny revenance is not that the phantoms of the past will return and that, inescapably, it is our responsibility to encounter them. Instead, the most haunting aspect, if you will, appears in Yeats's understanding of the ineluctable endlessness of the spectral, the phantomatic, the revenant condition of the traumatic. Furthermore, *Purgatory*'s structure, like the ruined house in which it takes place, is of the order of the phantasm—we are compelled to witness the spectralization of space as the encounter of the haunting that takes place. It is not simply that the house or the old man are haunted; rather, the play takes place as the possibility of haunting, and as the various manifestations of reiteration make plain, haunting is not located as originating in any one place, person, or act. For what we witness, in seeing the old man's response to the dead and his misreading of the situation, is his own bearing witness to the hauntedness of the mother's phantom. Even as her ghost "must animate the dead night . . . many times," so there is nothing other than "the impression upon my mother's mind."[78] A phantom herself, her mind is always already haunted, her "soul" unable to be released from its "dream."[79] It is the memory of her memory of the invisible, the absent, the other, which is *re-presented*, the implication being that the old man is merely the latest, and not the last, in this ghostly series. And that the old man is, himself, *re-presented* as being the momentary locus, the mark, trace or, if you will, *gesture* (as that figure is employed apropos of cinematic representation in chapter six) of memorial apparition and projection, intimates that it is to the memory of memory that we must be responsible. The old man is not the origin of events, as both the mother's dream and her spectral "animation" make apparent, even though she is never witnessed as such but is only relayed, projected through her son's mind onto our imagination. She is in effect a figure for the trace of the spectral, her son the screen on which haunting comes to be projected momentarily.

There is thus played out by *Purgatory* the poetics of an experience of "self-referential self-presentation"[80] as being inescapably haunted, as marked immanently by the spectral to come, a marking of one's self always already displaced, haunted by one's other, as we have already considered. Coming face to face with this phantom other is refigured in another manner that is equally haunting by Paul Celan. Much, if not all, of Celan's poetry takes on the form of encrypted testimony, memory, of bearing witness, and addresses in complex, often labyrinthine fashion, the responsibility the living have to the dead, particularly in relation to the Holocaust. This is not the place, nor is there the space, to develop an analysis of Celan, much less a reading.[81] However, I do wish to consider, briefly and in conclusion, one poem, "Ich kann dich noch sehn":[82]

> I can see you yet: an echo,
> palpable with feel-
> words, at the farewell-
> ridge.
>
> Your face shies faintly
> when all at once
> becoming lamplike bright
> in me, at the passage
> where one says the most painful never

"Ich kann dich noch sehn" appears to address a figure that, already having departed, nonetheless projects traces of itself, certain ghostly resonances to which the speaker is obligated to respond, and which the poem, as a reading of these apparitional marks, provides testimony. That "yet" (translation of *noch*, which is also translatable as "still" or, in some contexts "only just" or "one day") speaks of what is barely visible, is retained, and that remains on the edge, the limit of memory. "Seeing" thus sees nothing as such, the verb being the displacement in language for memory, which further becomes "translated" from itself in the invisible, yet resonant figure of the echo. The line seeks to reiterate that to which it responds, that which is invisible and leaves its mark. This projection of the ghostly other emerges like a light "in me," an illumination of the phantom as phantom, as nothing other than the phantasm to which the opening of the poem addresses itself, to which it responds and which returns even as the poem seeks to turn toward the figure of the other with its "feel-words" (*Fühl* is also translatable as "antenna," the translation used by Michael Hamburger, thereby translating the poem into an insect responding to various otherwise imperceptible, invisible stimuli). That point of lamplike brightness, that illumination as enlightenment whereby the speaker of the poem recognizes the spectral nature of the other, comes at the point, place, or passage (*Stelle*) where the phantom, having returned, retreats. This passage is also a passing, a passing away, and Celan's poem records this motion in its own rhythmic fluctuations.

The passage of the other takes place, coming and going, continuously in the text, and as the motion of the text, the two stanzas figuring this pulse, this breath. And what we come to read, between the lines as it were, from the first line to the last, is that the figure of the revenant haunts all the more powerfully for having always already passed beyond that farewell- or parting-ridge, which is, itself, nothing other than the very limit of *re-pre-sentation*, the limit to which Celan's language goes.

However, this sketch of the poem's work is only provisional, in the face of the *way* it addresses us, moving as it does beyond its textual place or passage. In its performative operation, the ways in which the text enacts the condition of passage and limit, the illusion of a voice is merely that: one more phantom or phantasm returning to illuminate our comprehension and to enlighten us—as does the old man of Yeats's play in his own fashion—as to the responsibility that haunting imposes, that responsibility that the living have to the dead. As experience of witnessing, the poem testifies not only to that ghostly face or echo that has already returned and retreated; it also testifies before us, before each of its readers (as Derrida describes in speaking of the disjointing and haunting structure of testimony).[83] In operating in this manner, Celan's poem is spectralized, responding in its ethical obligation to the other, by returning as the apparitional address, testifying, as Derrida puts it, "for someone who becomes the addressee of the testimony."[84] We are translated, in effect, becoming the "you" to whom the poem is addressed, haunted by its spectral, testimonial structure, and thus trauma is remembered, borne beyond the irreducible singularity of its event.

As Derrida says of another poem by Celan, what the poem means or says is ultimately of less importance than our experience of it, this experience of haunting, its uncanny power, and the experience also of the "strange limit between what can and cannot be determined" about the experience of witnessing.[85] The poem bears witness to an act of impossible witnessing and to witnessing as the marking of a limit between the possible and impossible, the visible and invisible. This question of witnessing, of the response and the responsibility that reading imposes on the living, is thus intimately implicated in every aspect of the poem before and beyond any consideration of content. This is what we name spectral persistence, and which comes to be figured through our acts of reading the singularity and alterity of trauma.

Part Four

AFFIRMATIVE RESISTANCES

Chapter 8

ORIGINS OF DECONSTRUCTION?
DECONSTRUCTION, THAT WHICH
ARRIVES (IF IT ARRIVES AT ALL)

A (metaphysical) thought, which begins by searching for origins or foundations and proceeds to a reconstruction in order, infallibly finds that things have not happened as they ought. . . . The more naïve believe in a paradise lost, the more cunning restore order by claiming to think, in order, the absence or loss of order. For Derrida, as for Heidegger...one is constructing things on an unquestioned value: *presence*.

Geoffrey Bennington

. . . (but what is more problematic than this concept of an original base for a fictional work?) . . .

J. Hillis Miller

Men can do nothing without the make-believe of a beginning. Even science, the strict measurer, is obliged to start with a make-believe unit, and must fix a point in the stars' unceasing journey when his sidereal clock shall pretend that time is set at Nought. His less accurate grandmother Poetry has always understood to start in the middle; but on reflection it appears that her proceeding is not very different from his; since Science, too, reckons backwards as well as forwards, divides his unit into billions, and with his clock-finger at Nought really sets off *in medias res*. No retrospect will take us to the true beginning.

George Eliot

This chapter had its "origins" as a paper presented at the annual conference of the IAPL (International Association of Philosophy and Literature), at one of two panels entitled "Origins of Deconstruction," terms that this chapter, clearly, takes as its title.

I

What does this phrase, *origins of deconstruction,* imply, name, or state? What do those who make such an impossible demand wish to identify, or otherwise believe they can locate? In whose interests is such a remark? What, in the articulation of this strange phrase, remains either silenced and unread or otherwise remains to be said? Does it give us to read a disabling and impossible temporality in the same place as the desire for an identity? Who is interested in pursuing "the origins of deconstruction"? What haunts the structure of this expression? Does it amount to an idiom or axiom? Of what order are the motifs of this phrase? What "concepts" does anyone believe to be mobilized in whatever this phrase stages or puts on stage? What is going on *between* "origins" and "deconstruction"?

—Everything takes place between. (Everything, that is, and all the rest.)

II

To hypothesize about or otherwise to inquire into the "origins of deconstruction" is to repeat, whether intentionally or otherwise, the age-old metaphysical demand or desire for foundation, for Logos and, from such a location, to reiterate the desire for discernible order or progression as the historicity of that founding originary site or concept. Accompanying such an inquiry for an ideality, at once "supratemporal and omnitemporal,"[1] would be the assumption of or search for an absent presence or identity, which, in itself, is comprehended as complete, undifferentiated, homogeneous, full, simple, and self-sufficient. Yet, as Michel Foucault has it, in a "response" from 1968 to the Paris Epistemology Circle, such activity is always fraught from the very start by its own premises and practices because any such "analysis of discourse [is always] . . . a quest for and repetition of an origin that escapes all determination of origin."[2] Still, one behaves as though there were both beginnings *and* a traceable continuity between those beginnings and the point at which any such inquiry begins with the injunction to turn back, as though one could offer, in Jacques Derrida's words, the reconstitution of "the pure tradition of a primordial Logos toward a polar Telos."[3] Indeed, as Foucault in the article already cited points out, such behavior is, if not a manifestation of institutional power, then the institution, the singular *inauguration,* of a power whose purpose is to effect a kind of self-reflective, self-interested discursive maintenance of that very continuity. It is, in turn, the function of the metaphysical demand to delineate that continuity, thereby maintaining the very same continuity. Such a gesture "function[s] to guarantee the infinite continuity of discourse and its secret presence to itself in the action of an absence that is always one stage further back."[4] As Foucault's remarks make plain, the processes in question are, of course, not restricted either to the immediate or previous interests in a supposed "history," "historicity," or "genealogy" of "deconstruction" (which I place in quotation marks in order to suspend the possibility of a ready assumption of meaning, value, or identity for this word), which acknowledgment might serve to orientate, in however occluded a fashion, the various chapters in the present volume according to the motif of the occasional. There is identified, therefore, the work of a certain procedural thinking, as is explicit in Foucault's comments, and as already addressed at the beginning of this paragraph; and, again, before that particular starting point, in the initial epigraph to this chapter.[5] I thus find myself retracing my steps in the very process of seeking to get under way.

As is well known, Jacques Derrida has in a number of places addressed the logic of a search such as the one just sketched, and, equally, its fruitlessness. It is tempting to suggest that this "major concern of Derrida's analysis," as Arkady Plotnitsky sums it up,[6] has been with Derrida from the beginning of his published works in 1962, with the "Introduction to *The Origin of Geometry.*" "The Time before First" offers another example.[7] While the motif of "origin" or "origins" (and the plural, at least, initially, does nothing in any drastic manner to "origin-singular," at least not unless we call into question the concept and thinking of "origin") as starting points appear to promise a beginning in being called to our attention, such a gesture only "'begins' by following a certain vestige. *I.e.* a certain repetition or text."[8] In "Qual Quelle,"[9] the impossibility of assigning either origin or source is also considered, as Derrida responds to these motifs in relation to questions of identity and consciousness in the text of Paul Valéry. The source, we read, "cannot be reassembled into its originary unity."[10] In addition, we learn it is the philosopher, as exemplary representative of the laws of the institutional search previously outlined, who (according to Valéry), always in search of the origin, of an originary voice or presence, voice as the guarantee of presence, reproduces what Derrida calls the "crisis of the origin"[11] (a crisis acknowledged in Bennington's earlier remarks) in the very act of writing on such a theme, whereby there is to be perceived "[d]iscontinuity, delay, heterogeneity, and alterity . . . a system of differential traces"[12] that get both the idea and the motif of the origin going. It is, we might propose, the very errancy of the motif as performative trope that haunts and motivates the very search or, more accurately, re-search, the always too-late recovery, for the always already *retrait* of origin.

The procedures by which the search for origin get under way and by which crisis comes to be reproduced take place repeatedly around the name of "deconstruction" also. Whether within the limits of an institutionalized program of analysis, proceeding by all the protocols that such a program prescribes or, more generally, in posing the ontological question that concerns itself with determining "deconstruction" and, specifically, "origins of deconstruction," as though the terms and the concepts they appear to name are taken as understood; in such gestures, it must be admitted that nothing will have been comprehended concerning what has been said, for example, by Derrida and others with regard to the figure of "deconstruction." As Derrida has remarked,

> [d]econstruction, in the singular, is not "inherently" anything at all . . . the logic of essence . . . is precisely what all deconstruction has *from the start* called into question. . . . Deconstruction does not exist somewhere, pure, proper, self-identical, outside of its inscriptions in conflictual and differentiated contexts; it "is" only what it does and what is done with it, there where *it takes place* [emphases added].[13]

That "deconstruction" only "is"—without being anything as such—that it only has some momentary, provisional figuration (if this can be said) where and whenever it takes place, if it takes place as that which announces both singularity and iterability, suggests that it is impossible to speak of "deconstruction" "in the singular." This is well known. This also suggests, furthermore, that because "deconstruction" can only be discerned where "it" takes place—without assuming an *ipseity* for deconstruction—and because every instance will necessarily be perceived as differing from every other in the various "conflictual and differentiated contexts," "deconstruction-in-the-singular" cannot be assigned origins other than the "origin," if we can use this term in this fashion, of its taking place on every occasion. Moreover, that "it" can only be reflected on "in the singular" as an event both inappropriate to and unappropriable for any "univocal definition"[14] or totalizing determination signals that fact of "its" instability, as announced in the destabilizing motif of *différance*, and, therefore, "its" undecidability, the undecidability of any "it" for deconstruction. Certainly, in the light of this, it would be an act of misrecognition or misappropriation to attempt to gather together the work of various deconstructions, if in such a gathering there took place the erasure of differences between them (regardless, for the moment, of the "system of differential traces" making up any "deconstruction") in order to produce the "univocal definition."

Several contiguous remarks need to be made: (1) whatever goes by the name "deconstruction" simultaneously *exceeds* and *lacks* any ontological or metaphysical determination; (2) "deconstruction" is irreducible to any statement or formula beginning "deconstruction is . . ." or "deconstruction is not . . ." (i.e., any modality producing identification as stabilization, whether of an ontological or negative theological condition); (3) deconstruction (and here I will abandon the quotation marks), if it *is* anything, is that which necessarily *takes place* within any manifestation of structure *as* necessary to and yet radically incommensurable with or irreducible to that structure's identity or meaning, or indeed the horizon of any such possibility. As Derrida remarks of deconstruction, it is "*firstly* this destabilization on the move in, if one could speak thus, 'the things themselves'; but it is not negative" (emphasis added).[15] It is thus provisionally figurable as the non-identity *of* and *within* yet also other than any identity, where "non-identity" is comprehended not as negation or dialectical opposite, but as the sign of *différance*. Deconstruction thus provides a provisional "name" for the trace of an alterity by which the perception of identity is made possible even as otherness remains invisible, unacknowledged. If it is anything at all, it does not in fact require or await a subject's cognition or consciousness (as Derrida remarks in "Letter to a Japanese Friend")[16] to determine what is called deconstruction by assigning an undifferentiated or universal meaning to, or identity for, a "singular event," for want of a better phrase.

One of the problems surrounding the misunderstanding and misappropriation of deconstruction, so-called, is ontological specifically, as well as being more generally metaphysical. If we turn to Martin Heidegger briefly, on the problem of determining Being, the procedures by which deconstruction as an institutionally domesticated term is made to operate in some quarters, or otherwise to dwell unproblematically in analytical or critical discourse, comes into focus. To recall a point just made, it appears as if deconstruction functions as a name, yet what it names is not this precarious trait but something determinate and delimitable; it is, therefore, a name used to identify a "certain sameness in differentiation." The phrase is Heidegger's, and he employs it to determine particular ontological approaches to the apprehension of Being: "we understand being . . . in such a way that it expresses a certain sameness in differentiation, even though we are unable to grasp it."[17] From this awareness, Heidegger concludes that, with regard to Being, "there is no genus in itself."[18] The same can—or *must*, of necessity—of course, be said of deconstruction.[19] This is insufficient, however. The definition of genus must, necessarily, be raised. Heidegger asks (and answers) thus: "What is a genus? That which is universal and common to the many and can be differentiated and organized into species by the addition of specific differences. Genus is inherently related to species. Genus is inherently related to species and thus to species-constituting differentiation."[20]

It is instructive to watch Heidegger construct an apparently circular logic here. In admitting to differentiation, he determines genus according to a range of species comprising differences that are relational rather than of the order of radical, heterogeneous difference. Being relational, such differences are also subordinate, appurtenances in the order of the self-same, in accordance, and of a piece, with the notion of genus. Thus, the analysis of genus, proceeding by the acknowledgment of differentiation according to which the architectonic is delineated, makes a gesture by which it can fold back on itself, whereby "species-constituting differentiation" is the connective fiber that allows us to know or assume genus. Such "species-constituting differentiation" is only that belonging to the order of the same: that which constitutes the species and, from that gesture of folding back, to the implicitly circular reconstitution of the genus as an identity comprising so many genus-constituting species. In turn, the genus then becomes of the order of the self-same called the universal:

"[t]he universal, comprehended and defined as species-enabling genus, is usually called 'concept.'"[21] However, "If being is not a genus, then it cannot be comprehended as a concept, nor can it be conceptualized. . . . If the delimitation of a concept . . . is called definition, then this means that all definitional determinations of being must on principle fail."[22]

Quite simply—though I do have the feeling that this is all far from being simple—all misunderstanding concerning deconstruction has little to do with any "deconstruction." Rather what takes place around the name deconstruction and the impossibility of assigning it an essence is the exposure of a crisis in thought that remains to be read fully. Such misrecognition arises from an ontological imperative, as it were, a will toward a particular manifestation, time and again, of a certain kind of seamless, undifferentiated conceptualization. Being is not available to ontological inquiry, it is not a category or entity like others, and can only be known, as Heidegger makes clear in *Being and Time*, through beings and through a recognition of the irreducible difference *between* beings, which in turn allows for the thinking of being to arise as an *après coup*. Similarly, deconstruction. Irreducible to either concept or origin (whether singular or multiple), deconstruction can only be known, if it can be known at all, as that which is already under way, already at work and within, ontological inquiry and conceptualization as that which disorders, from the beginning, all such investigation.

In the face of these statements concerning this peculiar name "deconstruction" and the potential itineraries for reading that they might be imagined as generating, it has to be said that there are no *"origins of deconstruction"* as such.

Such a response must give the reader pause, however. For, even though this statement situates itself in relation to the question or demand concerning origins-of-deconstruction and it does so, moreover, by pointing out the ways in which such a question might be construed as being articulated within and by wholly conventional parameters, its articulation is made possible only by those same conventions. It is given according to the very program identified as the limit of the question itself. Responses, therefore apparently in opposition, announce a role already assigned in the structure of identification described as speculative dialectics. Situated in opposition to and subordinated by the instituting violence of the demand, the assumption in this response is that the question (or demand) with reference to origins-of-deconstruction is to be read in an entirely predictable way, and that this is the only reading available for that which calls this and other essays into being, a title that is not posed as a question as such but, instead, is simply stated: origins of deconstruction. The banal conventionality of the retort is clearly apparent in its resistance to the assumptions seeming to motivate the phrase in question. Furthermore, the reply—and this clearly is a reply, even if no question or statement were present, given a reading of the conventions of its various remarks—is markedly unoriginal, in all senses of that word. For not only does it say nothing that has not been said before, many times in a number of different ways, it presents nothing "original," it has nothing of an "origin" about it. It belongs to the predictable academic gesture—or genre, the response or remark or, rather, re-mark, this being the re-statement, the re-situation of more or less established, if not canonical, positions or locations within some manifestation of that dialectical structure, repeated again and again, without the adequate or necessary consideration of the concepts, motifs, tropes or terms herein employed.

—It seems we're caught in the middle, without being able to locate where we are. So, let's begin again.

II

Supposing the impossible. This is what is called for in the issuing of a request or command to write on "the origins of deconstruction": a speculation on the possibility of the impossible, specifically in the guise of mapping or determining so-called origins. At the same time what is required in at least one reading of the injunction that causes this chapter to be written is a gradual delimitation of the proper, of what is or might be proper allegedly to so-called deconstruction "in the humanities," "in the university, today," "in the history of Western thought." What is demanded, in effect, is a response involving the work of cartography. It is necessary to recognize though that such labor would have to proceed in the face of the unmappable, as though the inscription of every topographical coordinate invoked or implied countless others, in a constellation that, far from being exhaustible, would moreover enervate in the face of its own generative powers. Before—such a fantasy!—the location of any origin as such there would take place inevitably and inescapably multiplicity and multiplication, a fraying even as one seeks to tie together loose ends. One has, therefore, to turn back, to define the starting place of this chapter not as a starting point at all, but instead as a necessary response, a reaction, to the impossible injunction and the impossibility that the injunction addresses and comes to proliferate. Doubtless, there is more to say about this imaginary scenario.

The impossible attempt to consider the concept of origins, the origin, the very idea of an origin or origins *for* or *of* the notion of the origin (*an* origin, *some* origin) or, in fact, considering origins in all their impossibility, clearly becomes even more impossible when the question concerning the location of origins is linked to this strange word, deconstruction. It appears then that I am asked to think with supposition and with speculation, supposing for the moment supposition or speculation to be modalities of thinking rather than the suspension of thought narrowly conceived in favor of some process of projection or conception, and asking for some impossible answer. The answer is impossible, strictly speaking, because the very idea of an answer implicitly assumes a moment of finality. There is implicit, often all the more marked for being so tacit, in the idea of an answer the assumption of speculation, projection, and conception as modalities of thought that are perhaps related to but not wholly consonant with the rigorous thinking of a concept. There is furthermore in the assumption of the speculative project the idea that its problems can come to rest so that, teleologically or hermeneutically, where one ends is the origin itself, unfolded and refolded onto itself, a supplementary doubling of what had been there all along. As though the end were the beginning, as though destination were origin. The logic of circularity and the circularity of logic here inscribed are clearly haunted. And what haunts the effect of closing the circle is this phantom or phantasm of the origin, an origin, from the very elusiveness of which one must start all over again, fulfilling the promise of that Foucauldian assessment to which I had earlier alluded. What disturbs therefore, to return to where I began, is a barely submerged desire, all the more compulsive for being so caught up with the impossible and masquerading as some institutionally authorized archaeological or archival retrospect. Believing one can begin at all reveals in any such inaugural gesture the call of the institution, and the subjection of subjection interpellated by that call. Assuming I can assume any such question automatically leaves me with the impossible task, even or especially if I believe I can engage in a demystification of the premises by which such a call gets under way.

The very idea of the origin is thus that which arises inevitably and the search for the origin or origins belongs to a question or family of questions impossible to answer—*what if? What if* there were origins *for* deconstruction, *what if* there were an origin or origins *of* deconstruction? This is the phantasm of the starting point, the illusion of a beginning, and, it has to be added, *a beginning all over again*. Such a start, such an "origin," begins and can only begin then as a response to a response.[23] Such circularity concerning origin is observed, once again, by Heidegger, in "The Origin of the Work of Art."[24] At the very beginning of the essay, Heidegger, stating that the "question concerning the origin of the work of art asks about the source of its nature," offers the predictable answer—"the usual view"—to that question: the artist.[25] Immediately after, however, the question and answer are folded back on themselves, as Heidegger continues by pointing out that the determination of the artist as artist only arises as a result of the work: "The artist is the origin of the work. The work is the origin of the artist."[26] Thus, "origin here means that from and by which something is what it is and as it is."[27] On this understanding, no absolute origin is either possible or conceivable, given the enfolding and regenerative reciprocity of the structural schema proposed by Heidegger; a schema, I would add, that propels itself in a double act: that of a doubling of any singular locatable place of origin outside or before any event, and also a dismantling, not only of the traditional conceptualization of origin, but also of the stabilizing separatism of the binary calculation: artist/work. Interestingly, Heidegger's gesture also disturbs the temporal priority on which any notion of origin is founded. More than this, however, there is in Heidegger's instituting complication a performative element. Clearly displacing itself as a response to a question arriving from some other place, Heidegger's beginning, in Dennis J. Schmidt's words, "must not be taken as an excuse for an awkward or misfired beginning to the text but as a comment on the character of the beginning as such."[28] However, I would argue for risking a stronger reading than Schmidt's: as just stated, Heidegger's gambit works so startlingly precisely because he does not merely *comment on* his subject, as would the philosopher on the source, issuing what he or she believes to be a constative statement. Rather, the performative dimension has to be insisted on here. It is precisely this performativity that destabilizes logical calculation from within, radicalizing the thinking of origin from the start. And yet, of course, it is not so simple to decide on whether Heidegger's argument or the way in which he states it are simply *either* performative *or* constative. For, similar to the suspensive operation at work in Heidegger's scandalous assertions concerning a disseminative reciprocity between artist and work (or work and artist), so too, before any determination, his own discourse materially suspends the possibility of identification through its redoublings and divisions, especially in the first page, but also, arguably, throughout the entire essay. As J. Hillis Miller remarks apropos this suspension between the constative and performative, "[t]he tension between the two functions means that the performative aspect of the text makes it produce deceptive, illusory knowledge, or the illusion of knowledge."[29]

III

But this is merely an illustration and a detour. If I attempt to imagine an origin or more than one origin, or even no more origins either for or of deconstruction, deconstructions, my response is then not a beginning as such (but this is already announced and is hardly original). I find myself entering into or, perhaps more accurately, locating myself within and in relation to a self-reflexive circularity that disrupts the certainty of the metaphysical demand, while engaging with the possibility that such an encircling "opens up its own conditions." Reflexive engagement clearly identifies itself as a response to the call, the demand, the injunction to speculate. In turn, such an injunction arrives or arises, coming to be seen as not, itself, an instituting formulation but, rather, a response within itself, to the other in itself, to that speculative *what if.* Speculation hides itself and yet returns in, thereby exceeding the violence and logic (the violent logic) of institution and demand. This is where we are.

Imagine though for the moment the impossible; imagine that this is the place to begin: that it is possible start to speak of "origins of deconstruction." One might start, cautiously and conventionally enough, with a quotation. "Necessarily, since it [deconstruction] is neither a philosophy, nor a doctrine, nor a knowledge, nor a method, nor a discipline, not even a determinate concept, only what happens if it happens" [*ce qui arrive si ça arrive*].[30] It is perhaps noticeable that the bracketed French— and it seems that, if there is a history or even an origin, or origins of deconstruction, one is always enjoined, silently, invisibly, or otherwise, to bracket the French, to demarcate some boundary, some location or idiom—appears in other words in my title. As one beginning, I have let go the more normative, more conventional translation (what happens if it happens) in the title, in order to emphasize arrival, a certain unexpected, yet inevitable phantom insistence, a certain idiomatic interruption or eruption of arrival, as though arrival, and, specifically, the *arrival of an origin*, never happened only once, for the first time, but could be spectralized, taking place over and over, and in a manner moreover irreducible to, uncontrollable by, any taxonomy or conceptualization of arrival. Which, of course, takes place already in the name of deconstruction. [A parenthesis: it is not going too far perhaps to suggest another translation, one redolent, inadvertently or not, with what might be called a "biblical" resonance: that which comes to pass (if it comes to pass). Such a phrase appears to acknowledge, to comment on, a simple event— *and it came to pass*. However, it might more appropriately be considered a performative statement the rhythms of which are pertinent to the present consideration. The articulation or inscription of the line, whether in the present, past, or infinitive forms—it comes to pass, it came to pass, to come to pass—delineates a movement, the first part of which, coming toward a location or point of reference (such as the subject) and arriving from a future, the second part, departing from the point of reference, traversing it, and moving into a past. Writing or speaking this phrase traces materially—performs—that on which it is the purpose of the phrase to comment. Such a motion in the materiality of the letter marks and is marked by a disorientation of spatial and temporal assurances, announcing as it does a "destabilization on the move."] The spectral figure of an unanticipatable arrival, the ghostly arrival of such a figure, might be said to figure—possibility of the impossible—origins-of-deconstruction. That which cannot be anticipated concerning the arrival thereby speaks of the undecidability of deconstruction/s, if I can say this, and therefore, perhaps, of "deconstruction's origins" (do deconstructions "originate"? do deconstructions cause origins to arrive, to happen or to come to pass? are deconstructions original?) even as origin takes place, in the chance of deconstructions. How do we do justice to this?

In the face of the experience of the undecidable that the idea of the "origin" names, it has to be recognized and stressed, again and again, that the very idea is enigmatic, *auto-occlusive* perhaps; all the more mystifying even, precisely because these names, *origin, origins*, are all too often deployed as though what was being named were blatant, all too obvious and self-evident, as though nothing could be clearer than the possibility of the origin. And also hieratic and encrypted. For the mere sign of an origin or origins blares the promise, the illusion of a secret. And it is in such illusory certainty, a rhetoric, if not an hegemony, of certainty,[31] that one encounters precisely the obscurity that is situated at the obscure heart of any notion of origin. Take the example and notion of tradition, as Foucault suggests:

> it is intended to give a special temporal status to a group of phenomena that are both successive and identical (or at least similar); it makes it possible to rethink the dispersion of history in the form of the same; it allows *a reduction of the difference proper to every beginning,* in order to pursue without discontinuity the endless search for origin. . . . Then there is the notion of influence, which provides a support . . . which refers to an apparently causal process . . . [in which there is to be seen] the phenomena of resemblance and repetition. . . . There are the notions of development and evolution: they make it possible to . . . link [events] to one and the same organizing principle . . . to discover already at work in each beginning, a principle of coherence and the outline of a future unity, to master time through a perpetually reversible relation *between an origin and a term that are never given,* but which are always at work.[32] (emphases added)

Tradition both authorizes and is authorized by origin. The one-and-only time of origin is what tradition (or racial purity, or the destiny of a nation) both needs and by which it keeps up the game. Influence, identity, succession, causality, resemblance, repetition, development, evolution: in short, the delineation of what amounts to a genetic purity. This is the secret, a secret out in the open, promised by the idea of origin and yet also hidden by that very idea, which obscurity justifies the inquiry into origin, and which deconstruction arrives, if it arrives at all, to interrupt.

IV

So, to return to the question of what happens, what arrives, what comes to pass, what takes place, what passes (if it passes), what arrives (if it arrives at all) *and also* what also cannot pass or come to pass, before which I am immobilized, in the face of the impossible, impossibility itself: the demand, the call of the title, this impossible title, *origins of deconstruction.* This title arrived, as such things often do these days, in e-mail, a demand and a request, an invitation from a friend, at one and the same time, then, both friendly *and* threatening. Its arrival recalled a question concerning arrival, concerning that strange figure of the *arrivant,* asked by Derrida: "What is the *arrivant* that makes the event arrive?"[33] Derrida continues:

> The new *arrivant,* this word can, indeed, mean the neutrality of *that which* arrives, but also the singularity of *who* arrives, he or she who comes, coming to be where s/he was not expected, where one was awaiting him or her without waiting for him or her, without expecting *it [s'y attendre],* without knowing what or whom to expect, what or whom I am waiting for—such is hospitality itself, hospitality toward the event.[34]

Neutrality *and* singularity. Bearing this in mind—and returning to the first citation of Derrida, the one appearing, it should be noted, after the title (both titles, that which arrived via e-mail, unexpectedly, and my own) and yet being one source, though not the only origin, for my title— it is no doubt possible, however reckless, to suggest different titles for this chapter, if only so as to disrupt any sense of priority or origin: *deconstruction, that which arrives or happens (if it arrives or happens at all)*; or *deconstruction, who arrives (if s/he arrives) or happens (if she or he happens at all).* Whatever, or whoever, arrives unexpectedly might just cause an event to happen perhaps; this is the hope; and, in anticipation of this originating arrival, I must wait without expectation concerning the form such an arrival might take; what is wholly, radically, original or, perhaps, ab-original here is that which takes place *between* the *arrivant* and the subject. It is here, if anywhere, smallest of chances, that deconstructions, origins, will, therefore, have occurred. *Origins-of-deconstruction coming to pass in between.*

A note of caution. Everything takes place in "between" (between beings, for example, or between the artist and the work of art). Yet, in the words of Jean-Luc Nancy, "[t]his 'between,' as its name suggests, has neither a consistency nor continuity of its own. It does not lead from one to the other; it constitutes no connective tissue. . . . From one singular to another, there is contiguity but not continuity."[35] It therefore follows that one cannot speak even of an origin (as such) *of* or *for* whatever chances to present itself *in* or *as* the figure of *between,* let alone *of* or *for* whatever one thinks one means when one speaks of *deconstruction. Between,* therefore, a motif without motive, the name of in-difference, intimate proximity *and* unbridgeable spacing—deconstruction, in other words, at the origin (one is tempted to say) of any search for origins or foundations, as Geoffrey Bennington has it.[36]

V

This is still to be too precipitate, however. Forestalling the illusion either of a beginning or any supposedly "original" starting point as the beginnings of a tracing, consider the following consideration of Nancy's on the subject of origins:

> . . . meaning can only be right at *[à même]* existence. . . . It is the indefinite plurality of origins and their coexistence . . . we do not gain access to the origin: access is refused by the origin's concealing itself in its multiplicity. . . . The alterity of the other is its being-origin. Conversely, the originarity of the origin is its being-other, but it is a being-other *than* every being *for* and *in crossing through* [à travers] all being. Thus, the originarity of the origin is not a property that would distinguish a being from all others, because this being would then have to be something other than itself in order to have its origin in its own turn . . . the being-other of the origin is not the alterity of an "other-than-the-world." It is not a question of an Other . . . *than* the world; it is a question of the alterity or alteration *of* the world.[37]

Alterity, inaccessibility. There is inscribed here a response to, as well as in recognition of, the priority and primordiality of alterities, heterogeneous and illimitable, irreducible to a negative theology governing or desiring to determine finally any conceptualization of an other. Such a determination would still imply an origin or source "beyond" or "other than," as the extract makes clear. If origin is an other, to place for the moment Stéphane Mallarmé's tongue in Jean-Luc Nancy's mouth, this is to comprehend origin radically as *différance* rather than source. Origin, therefore, nowhere as such, has always already returned not as itself but as a trace within any being as the non-identity of beings irreducible to any dialectical stability. There is, then, never the possibility either of an hypostasized Origin, or even multiple Origins, if by such a figure (and

"Origins" still is the name of figure-singular, if it is understood as indicating so many "species" belonging to a genus aspiring to the universal concept of "Origin") there is implied merely the polyvalent possibility of several sources for deconstruction. Rather, it is necessary to stress, in order to conclude this "make-believe of a beginning," and following Nancy, that the idea of origin is incorrectly assumed if by this notion one believes one can identify or locate that to which deconstruction can be traced and yet which is separable from deconstruction, and thereby delimitable. At the same time, and to turn back to the beginning of this chapter, it is also incorrect to assume that "deconstruction" is a given, that the meaning of this word has been resolved epistemologically, which the presumption of origins would appear to announce. Indeed, one might risk the proposal that, if origin *is* an other, is every other and wholly other, and is only perceived through the trace of *différance as* that irreducible disjunction and "what makes every identity at once itself and different from itself,"[38] it is also possibly the case that deconstructions, having to do with traces, "with the logic of the 'nonpresent remainder'," as Nicholas Royle puts it,[39] are the crossings-through of that sign the being-other of origin, an origin, origins. Or, to put this in another's words, in other words, "what emerges is in fact the very 'origin' of [deconstructions], the material trace or the material inscription that would be the condition of possibility and the condition of impossibility"[40] of *origins*. Comprehending the materiality and singularity of an inscription or articulation always already taking place, and recognizable only after the event as having taken place in every singular instance, we are forced to acknowledge also the impossibility of determining an essence or being. Any act of naming deconstruction must affirm this differentiation-at-the-origin, as it were, of deconstructions. In conclusion, we might illustrate this through indirection and detour, by citing Philippe Lacoue-Labarthe's anti-essentialist analysis of the relation between language, alterity, and being:

> Existence . . . [is] language, or more precisely, the faculty of language, which, in the being *[étant]* that is man, does not come under the heading of being—so that man "is" not only the being that he is. The faculty of language, the ability to name, is in reality intimacy itself, the intimate differentiation of the being . . . For this reason, language is not, in its essence, purely and simply being *[étant]*; yet there *is* language, or language exists. . . . Language is the other in man; it constitutes him as man

himself. Man does not *have* language . . . man is constituted beginning with language. . . . Thus language can be considered man's origin.[41]

No absolute originary articulation therefore, but radical origination in every utterance. Every time there is language, every time difference and deconstruction take place, every act originates, originating itself as other than itself, and this can and does only take place, repeatedly, *between*.

Chapter 9

HAUNTOLOGY OR THE POLITICAL?
(OR, NO POLITICS, NOT NOW):
ALWAYS ALREADY DECEIVED

This chapter was, in its first version, an invited presentation, given at a conference, "Almost Always Deceived: Revolutionary Praxis and Reinventions of Need" held in Spring 2001 at the University of Florida and organized by the Marxist Reading Group. As with the chapter that follows, the present chapter addresses the motif of spectrality as more than a merely rhetorical figure in political discourse and in the effort to think otherwise within particular strands of marxist critique.

I

Today . . . *we have to re-think* the relations between knowing and acting, between constative speech acts and performative speech acts, between the *invention* that finds what was already there and the one that produces new mechanisms or new spaces. In the undecidable and at the moment of a decision that has no common ground with any other, *we have to reinvent invention or conceive of another "pragmatics."* (emphases added)

Jacques Derrida

... it is essential to educate the educator himself.

Karl Marx

Society, languages, laws, *customs,* the arts, politics . . . every effect
that is unequal to its cause, requires conventions—that is, *relays* or
intermediaries, by the indirect means of which a second reality takes
hold, blends with the perceptible reality of the moment, covers it
over, dominates it. . . . In our desires, our regrets, our quests, in our
emotions and passions, and even in our effort to know ourselves, we
are the puppets of nonexistent things—things that need not even
exist to affect us.

Paul Valéry

I feel I should begin with an apology. Not least, in the context of the
themes of deception and need, I feel the need to apologize for what
might appear to some to be the hubristic rhetoric of my title. Imagine it: a presentation at a conference concerning itself with questions of
the possibility of revolutionary praxis, of reinvention and need, that
sneaks in, parenthetically, the statement, "no politics, not now." The very
idea; how deceitful.

Some might believe, of course, that they can locate a reference, if not
an allegiance, perhaps *even* the semblance of a style in my title: clearly, I
hear someone say, there's a play on that title of Derrida's, "No Apocalypse,
Not Now," and, in fact, I have quoted this essay to which I'm alluding in
the form and place of the epigraph, thereby opportunistically taking the
double occasion—of a conference and a citation—to acknowledge in another's words the urgency that attends matters of reinvention and need.[1]
Although speaking in response to the threat of the nuclear as is known,
Derrida's remarks clearly address (as my emphases intend to highlight) a
political situation in terms of exigency and invention, along with the exigency of reinvention *qua* politics *and* rhetoric, which will be my topics;
hence the appropriation of those comments here. You will note that the
rhetorical reiteration of necessity makes the urgency all the more
marked, and in a particularly performative manner. However, with regard
to my title and that of Derrida's, there is a structural similarity at least, a
certain echo, that might be taken to suggest reflection as relationship.

And then "hauntology"; now there's a Derridean word, a word, moreover, that is highly overdetermined, expressly operative, *and* provocative, the subject of so much misunderstanding as a result of its *first* appearance, in *Specters of Marx* (but is it really the first appearance, as such? And what would qualify such a remark?). So, to anticipate and to recap in an untimely fashion that which is both already exhausted and not yet read, as that which haunts the articulation of my title: the problem comes down to a question, once again, of appearing to have to choose between, on the one hand, deconstruction (so-called) and, on the other hand, Marxism (again, so-called).

This, I imagine to be the strong reading. In subjecting the title to the strong reading some will, therefore, have acted, perhaps to the extent of believing they know, ahead of the event, the position that these comments will have taken. If this is the case—and I, for one, can imagine such a situation—some, therefore, will have already responded to the invisible yet material effects, if not efficacy, of rhetoric, or what might be termed, albeit with a certain caution, *merely* literary language. Indeed, to make a remark all the more rhetorical for having to be abandoned immediately as it is made, the question is very much *the* question of a rhetoric, of one rhetoric in the place of the other, and—to double the question—the question of what takes place when one is asked to choose between two rhetorics or, rather, to be placed in a position of having to decide on that which, strictly speaking, is undecidable. And this response will have arrived, in some cases, supposedly in the name of politics. Yet, as I want to explore in a very limited fashion, the distinction between rhetorical and political effect is not quite so neatly discernible nor as self-demarcating as is occasionally asserted; this is already both shown and articulated in the epigraphs. I want to address this troubling of location in order to open the matter of that which the rest of my title announces: the apparently incommensurate choice between whatever is named as hauntology and, equally, whatever is named as the political. If it is assumed that my title is merely allusive, only a pun, then something has already exceeded the field of vision. With this in mind, Paolo Friere's remarks concerning the work of the word should be borne in mind: "the word," writes Friere, "is more than just an instrument. . . . Within the word we find two dimensions, reflection and action, in such radical interaction that if one is sacrificed—even in part—the other immediately suffers. There is no true word that is not at the same time a praxis."[2]

Friere's reading of the word and what one can do with words (to risk
sounding like J. L. Austin for a second) instantaneously collapses any dialectic founded on principles of the absolute separation of theory and
practice. Refusing the accepted relations between thinking and doing, it
reinvents the work of the word, even as it puts the word to work, in the
name, and perhaps the exigency, of radical or revolutionary praxis. If, as
is claimed, "Die Philosophen haben die Welt nur verschieden *inter-*
pretiert, es kommt drauf an sie zu *veränden*" ["philosophers have only
interpreted the world, in various ways; the point is to *change* it" (emphases in original)][3] perhaps this is because the word, rhetoric, literary
language, what you will, is separated crudely from the world and, gathered as *philosophy, discourse, language, theory*, is ontologized according to a false binarism, which, in the name of political *praxis* (as though
this were not a word), is comprehended only, merely, in propaedeutic
fashion. Talking and thinking are simply stages on the way to praxis, and
not praxes, albeit of very different orders, in and of themselves. Friere
makes this unequivocally explicit, but Marx can be said to anticipate
him. Given the rhetorical amplification that Marx deploys through the
strategic use of italicization, this, the last of the "Theses on Feuerbach,"
highlights in a performative manner, while appearing merely to comment on a certain dialectic structure: deception, we might say, as reinvention, necessity being the mother, perhaps, of praxis. And it is
deceptive, duplicitous even. For, in a particular way, it has to be admitted that interpretation is not only the apparent opposite to change. Interpretation as reinvention is change, or at least has the potential, to be
so inasmuch as it translates and transforms; is this not what Marx's
statement is disturbed by here, within itself? Do we or, rather, *should* we
not glimpse this possibility?

However, to stall for a moment longer around this question of rhetorical device and the occasion of a title: the all too obvious allusion in my
title aside, what I wish to insist on here is that this remark is not meant
to suggest that we abandon politics, or that there is no politics, especially
no politics today, not now, if by *now* there is intimated a fixed point instead of the naming of an open series of instances, infinitely extending, in
which at any moment the political, in all its heterogeneous manifestations, takes place. Rather, I would like to propose something equally obvious, though somewhat counterintuitively so: that the question of the
political, if not politics as such, is always a question of that which exceeds
and is therefore irreducible to any given moment thought of as the

present. The political is that which is never simply or only *just of* the present, as any reflection on the overdetermination of classes, for example, in different cultures and at different historical moments would show.

II

It is necessary at this juncture to take a small digression around the reception and nonreception of "deconstruction." This is done for two reasons: (a) in order to suggest, immediately, that a marked suspicion on the part of certain materialist critics towards "deconstruction," particularly what is perceived as its apparently overly rhetorical or formal interests, is misdirected insofar as such wariness, distrust, or skepticism is often grounded, albeit in mystified ways, in acts of reading that are still governed by rhetorical maneuvers typical of institutionalized reading practices, and are therefore auto-recuperative, despite supposedly radical intentions; and (b) to signal an attempted suspension of such a haste in the name of the political concerning the exemplary rhetoric of the spectral and the hauntological, to which this chapter will turn following this detour.

It has to be said then that, in suggesting that the political is never simply *just of* the present, this is not to impose some "deconstructive" reading; this is not merely the mobilization of an apparently discernible rhetoric. It is not this precisely because, as is—or should be—familiar, deconstruction "does not await the deliberation . . . or organization of some subject or consciousness."[4] It is also the case that, if some believe they have recognized a rhetoric of a piece with what they believe to be a "deconstructive reading," no reading has taken place here but merely a programmed response. Regardless of any ostensible political position assumed on the part of those who respond to what they think of as a "deconstructive gesture," this response is overdetermined by particular institutions and protocols of analysis. To the extent that "deconstruction," so-called, has been transformed or, rather, translated into a "technological and methodological" shibboleth[5] within universities, both in the United States and elsewhere, says more about the ideologies and practices of the institution than it does about "deconstruction," "the work of Jacques Derrida," and so on (as is discussed elsewhere in this volume). And to this extent, the fetish that, on the one hand, "deconstruction" has become, while on the other, that which has become "deconstruction," can be seen to have been commodified and, therefore, refetishized through determinate identification. Such is the discernible effect of an ensemble of structures and motivations operating in a certain way on, and through, the proper name. In short, rhetoric functions in the service of the political. "Deconstruction," so-called, is therefore merely one exemplary production of an ideological drive that can be read in terms of a pragmatism or, even, a praxis in concerted action with a will to incorporation of the non- or a-methodological / a-technological other, in order to keep the wheels of institutional structure turning smoothly. And of course, the processes, the mode of production, by which incorporation takes place in this fashion, do not belong solely to the modality and structure termed the university. They belong typically to the more widespread effects where incorporation-up-to-a-point—the necessary, regulated consumption that maintains the normative functioning of any system—serves to define and mediate particular "corporate," incorporating and incorporeal, ideological-spectral operations.

This is what can be said to take place in the name of deconstruction and in the application of so-called "deconstruction" as a proper name pertaining to a particular pragmatics of institutionalized reading, wholly consonant with the principle of "business-as-usual." Commodified deconstruction is thus readable as that site where, ideologically and economically, the politics of the institution has manifested an extended moment of false consciousness, the work of which is simultaneously to hierarchize and marginalize, to include and exclude, in the otherwise spectral collusion and confusion of ontology with commodification. Indeed, were there time, I would argue that commodification involves the co-option of the ontological in processes of mystified reflection, in order that, whether student, scholar, or consumer, we are almost always deceived, called by an ontological-economic paradigm that interpellates us as (mis)reading subjects, subjected to the idea of well-regulated, efficient, and normative applications of one more theoretical model *comme les autres*. Why such practice, though, on the part of the institution? Perhaps, typically, because such political practice shores up what J. Hillis Miller describes as "'our' most basic ideological assumptions . . . the ones the university most needs to get on with its work."[6] Of course, shoring up ideological assumptions takes place at every point from left to right in the traditional political spectrum, and, as previously remarked, the university is only one privileged site of such activity.

There is, therefore, discernibly at work at least two effects. There is that effect called by Derrida auto-immunization, by which the institution gets going and maintains both its productivity and its modes of production. At the same time there are also to be noted the effects of a double, and interrelated, politics: of mimesis and community, in which the work of auto-immunization serves to play a part. I stress the doubleness—and should also stress perhaps the duplicity—of such a politics here. For the community to function, indeed for any notion of community to be operative, there has to be both an economy as well as a politics of auto-representation, which allows subjects into their community according to the extent to which each subject can be transformed, can transform him- or herself, thereby coming to recognize him- or herself as an individual copy of the community in general, as if he or she were simply one reflective part of an undifferentiated whole. Thus, community manifests itself through processes of inclusion, incorporation, reflection, and resemblance. It makes its subjects appear as so many facets of itself; this is the pragmatics of community. Effectively, therefore, a material effect takes place through a phantasmatic translation: there occurs the haunting of the subject by an ideal image constituted by the rhetorics of resemblance. Such modes of production clearly function, at least in part, via the immaterial structures of overdetermination and interpellation. It is in recognition of the material effects of that which is neither simply there nor not there, strictly speaking, that it is necessary to return to the figure of political untimeliness, in order to comprehend the spectral condition of material constraints.

III

Concerning the matter of political untimeliness and its haunting power: what is called "the political" (without assuming any simple, single ontology here), is always haunting inasmuch as it never simply manifests itself in any present. Having always to do with what takes time, and exceeding any given time, the political, considered as a heterogeneous ensemble of discursive, epistemological, and material traces, leaves its mark, having withdrawn from the immediate and obvious events that go by the name of the political. If time "is nothing other than this repeated inclusion of the other within the same,"[7] then the political is a matter of what is registered elsewhere, invisibly, included in and yet in excess of any given moment. The time of the political is always untimely, because such time is that of "a delay . . . that exceeds the limit within which one is required to do something."[8] How might this be witnessed?

It is possible to comprehend the phantom effect already at work, more or less visible, and according to considerations of rhetoric related to "tone," "register," "timbre," and so on, in a number of Marxist commentators, three of whom must suffice for now: Paolo Friere, Louis Althusser, and Raymond Williams. The commentaries attest to the temporal disorder of the present caused by the return and retreat in excess of any limit on the part of the apparition. Such revenance, far from being merely a rhetorical motif, actively determines the condition of the political in the following remarks. Friere comments on the necessity of comprehending culture "as a superstructure which can maintain 'remnants' of the past alive in the substructure undergoing revolutionary transformation."[9] Learning to discern and respond to ghostly traces, bringing them into view, is, for Friere, part of a revolutionary praxis by which people "will be able to free themselves more rapidly of these specters, which . . . have always constituted a serious problem for every revolution."[10] In this example of the word as radical praxis, the spectre returns to trouble the possibility of revolution, and spectres are thus nothing other—but what a "nothing other"—than the "cultural remnants [of] the oppressor society."[11] All radical cultural action, as both interpretation and change, has therefore "the same objective: to clarify to the oppressed the objective situation which binds them to the oppressors, *visible or not*"[12] (emphasis added). Praxis is readable in this definition as the illumination of the spectral moment we name interpellation; it is the making apparent of the apparition that, in being always already at work invisibly, has maintained its power through the deception it produces invisibly.

The spectre is irreducible equally to any one determination or any single effect, however. While for Friere, that which is spectral is that which returns from some other place to oppress unequivocally in more or less visible ways in any given present moment, for Althusser that which is spectral is more neutral. Althusser acknowledges the spectral in a consideration of Hegel, from *For Marx*. The development of consciousness and the "dialectic of its production" occurs, says Althusser *"through all the echoes of the essence it has previously been, and through the allusive presence* of the corresponding historical forms."[13] The past, available only as "internal essence (in-itself)" of present consciousness, is nothing other than the convergence, if not of "all that is solid [which] melts into air,"[14] then of these echoes defined by Althusser as "phantoms of the historicity of consciousness."[15] Persisting without presence, phantoms inscribe the contours of any supposedly present moment of self-reflection, a constant reverberation that both hails and inhabits awareness and calculation in the present.

The phantomatic traces named remnants and echoes by Althusser and Friere indicate a politics of ruins as well as politics in ruins; the untimely vestige of the political intimate that the very idea of any political ontology is impossible to recuperate. What remains is, to use Raymond Williams's term, residual. While Williams, ever the good materialist, never to my knowledge mentions spectres, ghosts, or phantoms, he does at least echo both Friere and Althusser, alluding to the spectral condition of the political through this figure of the residual. "Any culture," Williams writes "includes available elements of its past. . . . The residual . . . has been effectively formed in the past, but is still active in the cultural process...as an effective element of the present."[16] Recognizing that which is residual ideologically is a necessary activity for Williams in any truly "authentic historical analysis." In such analysis, "it is necessary at every point to recognize the complex interrelations [and] . . . to examine how these relate to the whole cultural process rather than only to the selected and abstracted dominant system."[17] Coming to terms with the residual, learning to be attendant on echoes, tracing the cultural remnants of an oppressor society: all, I would suggest, involve a degree of acknowledging and working with the spectral, understood as the "disadjustment" of any present identity or ontology,[18] from which situation it has to be admitted—no, politics is never merely a question of what is named "now." This "now" or what might be called "our time" is nothing other than "our experience of being 'out of joint'."[19]

To begin to consider the very possibility of conceiving any revolutionary praxis is then *necessarily and inescapably* to confront this impossible anachrony and, therefore, to think with ghosts. Thinking with the phantom means gaining insight through the illumination of, and from, what is both there and not there, the understanding of which sheds light on anything that might be named "the current political situation." It is also to be aware of the distinct modalities of historicity and materiality that inform any given instant. The different manifestations of materiality, which, after Paul de Man we can identify as "the materiality of history, the materiality of inscription, and the materiality of what the eye sees prior to perception and cognition,"[20] and none of which are reducible or alignable to the others, give us to comprehend that which persists, coming and going, between the visible and the invisible. Coming to see this, is also, in effect, having to recognize that there can be no facile separation of, say, theory and practice, word and world, that which is imaginary and that which is real, that which is rhetorical and that which is political. What is called for, in the light of misrecognition is, at least, a reorientation of the notion of praxis. Such a possibility calls always for the necessity of reinvention, to be attentive to that which calls us to the impossibility of reinvention as the possibility of other politics, the other of politics as well as any politics of the other. It is to concede, along with Antonio Gramsci, the necessity always to begin, *again*. For, as Gramsci acknowledges, in a parenthesis: "(one *always* finds that the beginning *always* has another . . . beginning! [emphasis added])."[21] Without delaying too long over this remark, I would draw attention in passing to Gramsci's inscription of the doubling of necessity, those two *always*, where the political and the rhetorical are inescapably intertwined, each supplementing, each haunting, the other. In short, there is to be witnessed in that rhetorical redoubling, which is also a rhetorical duplicity, which effectively performs and performatively effects the gesture of a revolutionary praxis, a turn that is also a return, and, therefore, the situation or occasion of a possible opening onto a politics to come. Beginning again is, we might say, the exigent figure of any radical politics, starting repeatedly from an awareness of that which has always already returned, and which, in imposing itself all the more powerfully for being invisible, inhabits and inhibits both our political choices and the possibility for response.

IV

Moving on, or perhaps beginning again, then, with a provisional comment on the political: the political is, always, and in so many ways, that more or less loose agglomeration or constellation of practices and discourses that, informing what we name the present, as the experience of politics in the present and having material effects *today* (and on every other *today*), nonetheless always arrives from some other place. Never simply or even a program, the economy of the political is an economy of surges and returns, of persistences and resonances that, in having material effects and yet being so often immaterial, occludes the very locations from which the political addresses us. Like so much public opinion by which it comes to be translated and encrypted, politics wanders and, in its wandering, is marked by the "ubiquity of the specter,"[22] while never being present in any space *as such*. To the extent that we fail to recognize this and that our failure arrives from our own sense of political urgency or the desire for some program, or the need to think, to act now, or to think now so as to cause or to bring about a revolutionary praxis in another *now* to come, we are, in the words of the conference title, almost always deceived. Indeed, I would like to take the liberty of reinventing the title of the conference, to suggest that we are *always already deceived*.

To reiterate my opening gambit: some might be forgiven for thinking that everything I've said so far is so much rhetorical avoidance. I return to this because it is typical certainly of the "strong reading" as a gesture of identification put to work by Aijaz Ahmad in his critique of *Specters of Marx* in the name of a supposed "dialogue between . . . Marxism and post-structuralism, specifically deconstruction."[23] That Ahmad conceives the issue in terms of dialogue—and, implicitly, dialectic; he sneakily, perhaps rhetorically, states the one while implying the other—between perceived models or ontologies of thought indicates the extent to which, in misrecognizing "deconstruction" in this manner, he is *always already deceived*, interpellated and situated in a manner typical of institutional neutralization (hence my earlier digression concerning so-called deconstruction's nonreception). It *is* a strong reading inasmuch as, in situating any dialogue so reductively in the name of assumed and undifferentiated identities, it is not a reading at all; it is, however, an act of political identification in the name of politics, and therefore all the more rhetorically coercive. This is borne out by Ahmad's remark that *Specters* offers that which a "Marxist of my kind would find unacceptable in deconstructionist ideas of politics, even when the ideas are at their very best."[24]

That phrase, "of my kind," gives me pause. I appreciate that it is merely rhetoric, but what rhetoric! What haunts this seemingly off-the-cuff gesture quite manifestly—and the fact that it appears to be delivered en passant indicates the seriousness with which we should halt at this, and all such, remarks—is an appropiative "personalism," to borrow Robert Young's word.[25] The logic is that anyone who is a "true" Marxist "would find" (note the suspensive possibility left open by Ahmad) no room, either for disagreement with Ahmad or, conversely, agreement with Derrida. At the same time, the deliberate vagueness of "of my kind" announces a very unscientific unspecificity that abrogates all "true" Marxisms to the name of Ahmad. There is something comically magisterial in this. This is not even to begin to point to misidentification, the violent totalization, that takes place in that other phrase, "deconstructionist ideas of politics." However, leaving aside all the errors of ontology and reading that haunt such rhetorical legerdemain, what is both interesting *and* disturbing in Ahmad's critique as the end of reading in the name of politics is the identification on his part of what he calls "the plenitude of motifs and metaphors, and . . . the centrality of the *form* of rhetoric . . . [given which] one would be inclined to treat it as primarily a *literary* text." *One would be inclined?* Well, to recall a remark of George Eliot's from somewhere, either one is or one isn't, and such rhetorical posturing is merely that. Moreover, and more seriously for Ahmad though, "[t]his literary quality is deeply embedded."[26] Had I the time, I might be inclined to ask whether quality can, in fact, be *embedded*, and what this seemingly geological or archaeological metaphor thinks it's doing in relation to so nebulous a concern as "literary quality." However, I do not have the luxury to address such matters, save to say that Derrida responds to Ahmad, remarking that "one understands nothing about [a] text if one fails to take into account the specificity of its gesture, of its writing, composition, rhetoric and address."[27]

Leaving this specific matter behind, we nonetheless have to acknowledge its exemplary, if obvious, condition, for two reasons at least, and in order to move from the specific to the general, to paraphrase Marx: (1) the assumption of or focus on rhetoric as the excuse for not attending to the political dimension (supposing for the moment that the one excluded the other) is itself the expression, deliberately or not, of a certain relapse into a peculiarly old-fashioned, if not reactionary, formalism. Ironically, this appears to take place in, or to be haunted by, the reversion to a politics of reading in the very name of a supposedly radical politics. As Richard Joines, a Marxist suspicious of Derrida's politics but open to reading up to a point, remarks, "If in Derrida's text form and content are inseparable, and if this combination eludes the traditional reader, we need to become untraditional readers who understand how to read for hints and indications, how to distinguish between the What and the How."[28] (2) The second and associated reason has to do with what has already escaped in the moment that a certain rhetoric is observed from the side that is supposedly political. To the extent that Ahmad, as an example of a Marxist of "his kind" (whatever *that* might indicate), dismisses as predominantly rhetorical Derrida's text through in part a rejection of the spectral as merely tropological work, I would suggest that such a supposedly politicized reading is *not yet* political, *not yet* political enough, inasmuch as it closes its eyes to the possibility of the spectral as being more than simply rhetorical. To the extent that readers of the Ahmad kind put up the blinkers at the first sign of any trembling in the field of vision, the radicality of the hauntological exceeds what can be seen, and one remains with the programmatic assertion of ontological form. Such a reading "renounces . . . the necessity of thinking a certain *impossibility as also possibility*,"[29] which gives a chance to an other political beginning or a return of the political in other words.

V

What appears to appear here is a certain resonance within the ideas or identities of the rhetorical and the political, a resonance disjointing any full or simple identity. What comes into view once again, which was there all along as that hauntological disturbance within any ontological representation, is that there is not simply a question of rhetoric on one side or politics on the other. Indeed, I would argue that we cannot say with any assurance that we know for sure how to identify the political as distinct from the rhetorical, or that either can be said to be discrete or kept separate from the contaminations of the other. With this in mind, I wonder what Marxists of the "Ahmad kind" might make of the rhetoric of Marx's consideration in *Capital* of the mysterious quality or, as Marx himself puts it, the "enigmatic character of the product of labour, as soon as it assumes the form of a commodity," or what he otherwise describes as the "*fantastic* form of a relation between things" (emphasis added).[30] Derrida has, of course, commented at length on the spectralization of the commodity in *Specters of Marx*,[31] but it is nonetheless worth returning to Marx's commentary.

At once trivial *and* mysterious[32] the commodity doubles itself and is thus all the more uncanny for Marx. Indeed, as is admitted, the commodity's queerness is all the more remarked for persisting in, while being irreducible to, its material reality. Moreover, its doubling disturbs precisely because its identity is resistant to ontology as a result of what Marx identifies as its "metaphysical subtleties."[33] Another sign of the doubling and division of, *in*, the phenomenon of the commodity, is the fact that its qualities are "at the same time perceptible and imperceptible by the senses."[34] Simultaneity announces both *this* and *that*, and yet, apparently, *neither* this *nor* that in its supplementary logic. In excess of any purely economic determination, Marx acknowledges a particular haunting effect and the power of that work. Such seemingly impossible simultaneity registers at once the mystified condition of both the reality and the very idea of commodity. Marx's analysis of the condition by which the commodity asserts its strange power mobilizes "la dimension du fantasmatique [the phantasmatic dimension],"[35] (to borrow a remark of Derrida's from an, as yet, untranslated interview, "Du marxisme") that is within and yet irreducible to any politico-economic ontology. As such, Marx's commentary points the way to a mode of critique-as-praxis that "helps us in understanding the structures of real public spaces, the media, the virtualization of [forms of] exchange etc."[36] (Another brief detour: in the light of this, a future reconsideration of Marx's analysis of credit and what he calls "fictitious capital" seems not inappropriate, as part of, belonging to, the anticipation of the virtuality of "virtual" or immaterial capitalism with all its material effects, and the concomitant abstraction accompanying capitalism's own multinational vanishing act.)

However, what particularly interests me in *Capital* is the following troubled, troubling analogy, on which Derrida is strangely silent:

> . . . the light from an object is perceived by us not as the subjective excitation of our optic nerve, but as the objective form of something outside the eye itself. There is a physical relation between physical things. But it is different with commodities. There, the existence of the things *qua* commodities . . . [has] absolutely no connexion with their physical properties and the material relations arising therefrom.[37]

It might be posited that, more than mere rhetoric, more than a simple or simply literary figure for addressing the otherwise incomprehensible—and, in doing so, thereby moving political discourse beyond what might easily have become an impasse as the haunting experience of the aporetic—Marx's phantasmatic perception announces, all the more persuasively for its relocation in the spectral register, the commodity's ineluctably seductive power. In a vertiginous rhetorical coup de grace, Marx does not so much apply a hauntological analysis as, in confronting the aporia of the commodity, allows the spectral, and what he has elsewhere called the *fantastic* to disclose itself. This does not, of course resolve the aporetic in the commodity. Indeed, it can be said that in addressing the undecidable of the commodity Marx allows the aporia and the subject's experience of it to remain. But what is allowed to remain as the remains that are inexplicable within any strict Marxian analysis is, for that reason, and for the reason that the remains ruin the totalization of identification, all the more haunting for that. After all, as Gayatri Spivak has recently commented on the very subject of the aporia and one's encounter, "one cannot be mindful of a haunting, even if it fills the mind . . . the aporia] can only be described as an experience."[38] And this, I would argue, is precisely what Marx is engaged in here, describing the experience of the inexplicable, uncanny encounter with the commodity qua commodity: not simply as something produced, but as being marked by the otherwise inexpressible.

It is this otherwise inexpressible, the "esoteric" (to borrow a much-used word from Richard Joines's discussion of Derrida already cited),[39] which enables *and* haunts all future thinking on the commodity, and which comes to be given exemplary analysis by Jean Baudrillard:

> The whole apparatus of the commodity law of value is absorbed and re-cycled in the larger machinery of the structural law of value . . . political economy is assured a kind of *second life,* in the framework of an apparatus . . . where it retains its efficacy as a referential of simulation. The same goes for the previous apparatus of the natural law of value, which had been taken up as an imaginary referential ('Nature') by the system of political economy and the law of commodity. This was use value, which led a kind of *phantom existence* at the heart of exchange value. . . . And each phase of value integrates into its own apparatus as a *phantom reference,* a puppet or simulation reference. (emphases added)[40]

Baudrillard's remarks clearly belong to that tradition of radical praxis among Marxist and other leftist commentators already acknowledged, in which the ubiquity of the spectral is doubled in being found and being addressed. Especially fascinating here is the way in which Baudrillard responds to the movement of the phantom, rather than merely observing it. For notice how, in moving from the example of commodity law to questions of value, which, themselves are read as fundamentally structural, if not in fact as belonging to or constituent components in a *technics* of economic productivity, the critic acknowledges the persistent "apparitioning" of the phantom from within and, once again, in excess of any structure or framework. Baudrillard's hauntological rhetoric is singularly significant not only for its observation of the phantom but for its insistence on the perpetual coming and going, the existence as he puts it, of the phantomatic trace. There is thus something that attracts our attention because it is constantly in motion and yet irreducible to any ontological determinant that is named "phantom." There is thus an economic doubling at work, rather than a straightforward constative commentary founded on a dialectic of material production/immateriality. The doubling is inscribed in and through the motion, the motif of the phantomatic trace, as the haunting motivation in any commodity, any commodity law, any conceptualization of value. What comes to light is that the mode of production is always already haunted.

VIII

So, another beginning: "When Marx adopted an image of the fantastic [the spectre] to depict a concrete political phenomenon, he was both using dominant discourse as well as deconstructing a cultural metaphor; he was referring to a new attitude in bourgeois culture as well as pointing out the ultimate source of this posture . . . . the imagery of the fantastic was shaped by and gave form to concrete problems."[41] Recognizing this, we understand how Marx is both Baudelaire's and our contemporary, and that there is something *literary* about Marx that exceeds and yet comprehends political economy. What marxism has forgotten has been marked by Derrida's insistence on the spectre and the motif of hauntology, as the signs of the return of modernity's repressed. Marx's exemplary comprehension of the commodity points the way to the possibility of an analytical, possibly literary language, that in the text of Baudrillard and, I would argue, elsewhere, is fully operative. The discourse on the hauntological admits to another possibility, that of a radical praxis of critique in which the singularity of any situation or event is available to a critical intervention without resorting to the strictly economic reproduction of a factory produced—post-Fordist perhaps?—political discourse. What is inexplicable for Marx becomes transformed by a comprehension of modernity that admits to the proliferation of phantoms, specters, ghosts, revenants, while allowing for the registration of the undecidable in any political or economic formation. And the modern is *enchanted,* to employ Etienne Balibar's term, "precisely insofar as it is the world of objects of value and objectified values."[42] Referring to *The German Ideology,* Balibar speaks of the emergence of ideology as a Marxist theory of social consciousness.[43] Such ideological consciousness brings about a *"fantastic* 'world',"[44] immaterial, not immediately present to perception and, yet, paradoxically powerful in material ways. Whether one speaks of words, spectres, echoes, phantoms, consciousness or residual elements, the registration of an invisible persistence with real consequences is highly suggestive, both rhetorically and politically, as Volosinov knew in demonstrating how there are no boundaries between ideology and the psyche, and in arguing how the work of ideology exists "only in the context of my consciousness."[45] While not suggesting that the consideration of the fantastic or phantasmatic is anything other than a small, local political gesture; and without pretending that, reined in within the university, any so-called political discourse always runs the risk of deceiving itself, it is nonetheless necessary to mobilize otherwise invisible, and therefore potentially, disturbing, dissident forms of articulation, especially as these operate as practical, if not performative, strategies from within, and yet exceeding, mainstream discourse, including, of course, so-called Marxism.

This is nothing new, and, clearly, Derrida is neither the first nor the only thinker to pursue this project, even though the benefit of historicized hindsight has recently allowed him to remark in the interview already quoted that "if university work on Marx is always necessary, there is also the risk of domestication, of the neutralization of the revolutionary injunction of Marx."[46] If this is obvious for some and disquieting for others, then, at least, they are only almost always deceived, rather than being simply always deceived. What it is necessary to recognize, however, is that any form of praxis, whether inside the university or beyond, always runs the risk of becoming business as usual and, to that extent, redundant, especially when such praxis articulates itself as teleological, as the means to an end or as means subordinated to an end.[47]

VIII

In conclusion: coming to terms with the work of so-called hauntology is one possible location from which to begin again in order to expose politics as endless praxis that, in turn, is affected by the residual echoes of other historical moments in different ways; such processes announce a necessary responsibility in coming to this understanding. Politics is thus comprehended both as spectral *and* real, immaterial and material. The political is seen, in Giorgio Agamben's words, as *"the exhibition of a mediality; it is the act of making a means visible as such."*[48] Yet still, it has to be acknowledged that the spectral analysis, as it has thus far manifested itself in relation to politics, has remained apparently obdurately silent on the question of class. Is this silence a retreat from class? Does the silence speak a certain complicity with the politics of liberalism and the ethos of free-trade capitalism? Or is it the case that class, to borrow Hegel's formulation, when stripped of specific historicized analyses of class struggles, class relations, and class consciousness, is an empty concept? Reduced to abstraction, is it the case that the idea of class runs the risk of becoming nothing other than a spectre, the sign of an empty rhetoric? As Nicos Poulantzas has argued, the problem of the theoretical status of class in Marx's own works has led more to misunderstanding than to scientific clarification, not least because "Marx's analyses of social classes never refer simply to the economic structure (relations of production) but always to *the ensemble of the structures* of a mode of production and social formation, *and to the relations which are maintained there* by the different levels."[49] Any social class in its cultural overdetermination and historically concrete specificity always "presents itself as the effect of an ensemble of structures."[50] Structures can be institutional, material, economic, imaginary; any given ensemble might incorporate elements from what can be identified provisionally and with all the necessary caution as base or superstructure, or articulate itself from one to the other. The effects by which class position is produced is, for all the material specificity of that position, nonetheless often hidden, if not invisible. Capitalist modes of production, and the cultural modes that collude with capitalism, work *so* successfully because they operate in *so* phantomatic a fashion. It might just be that the silence of spectrality anticipates the necessary work of reinventing the need to think the production of class otherwise. Perhaps we need an other rhetoric in the name of the political if we are not to be almost always deceived. The beginning-again work of reading hauntology as the name for the effect of an ensemble of structures will be necessary in order to make visible as such the political and ideological means and modes of production by which various, otherwise invisible, ensembles and their relations come to be comprehended in their own spectral work of determining and thus materializing class positions and class consciousness.

Chapter 10

LETTER TO MARTIN MCQUILLAN, CONCERNING *"THE NEW INTERNATIONAL"*: THE INDELIBLE MARX OF HAUNTING

Dear Martin,

Thank you, first of all, for inviting me to participate in the edition of *Parallax* addressing the question of "the New International,"[1] as that figure is raised in *Specters of Marx*. I'm writing this letter in lieu of an article or essay because I don't have the time to write something that might be, on the one hand, more formalized, and, on the other, more formulaic, although, doubtless, there's the risk of the formula in the format of the letter also. Concerning *Specters of Marx*, the question of time or, I should say, untimeliness or anachrony, is of great importance, as you well know. In relation to this, there is also a matter of hurriedness. In fact, there has always been a question of hurrying, and of a lack of time, of not taking enough time, not to mention intemperance, with regard to *Specters* and its reception. After the event, in his contribution to *Ghostly Demarcations* even Derrida has admitted of *Specters* that he preferred "to *rush headlong into defeat*."[2] This is part of its "history," as well as the burden it bears, in the guise of the manifestation of the various critical receptions and resistances. Of the lack of time taken as a general avoidance of the impossible time of reading, Derrida remarks that there "is no excuse for contenting oneself with flying through a text . . . the effects of thus skimming . . . on the fly are not limited to the hastily formed impression."[3] We should bear this in mind throughout as a caveat.

Let me then start with a remark concerning an aspect of time with regard to readings—or not-readings—of *Specters of Marx* before I address the question of "the New International" for you. Let me say this at the beginning:

First remark: there has been and will have been a rush. This motif is indissociable from, and is perhaps the motif par excellence apropos of, *Specters* in particular and the political in general. There will have been a rush, today, several months before the deadline for submission of responses to *Parallax* (one sign of which being that this letter finds itself with you six months or so before that submission date) over this matter, and the immateriality, of "the New International." Indeed, there already has been, and that is commented on in the beginning of this letter, in its inaugural remarks. There has also been a rush to interpret, to analyze *Specters of Marx*, to render or translate it into an intelligible commentary, or the failure of such, on the supposed debates between deconstruction, so-called, and Marxism. In their different ways one could refer, if one had the time, or took the time, to those essays by Eagleton, Ahmad, Jameson, and Spivak, all of which can be found in *Ghostly Demarcations*. We won't get into all the ontological and epistemological problems pertaining thereto, in a statement such as "between deconstruction and Marxism." You and I know all of these. As Derrida has said, its exhausted, we're all exhausted,[4] and, anyway, there isn't time, and I'm in—doubtless, too much of—a rush (like Matthew Arnold in response to the notion of *Geist*),[5] to comment on the rush to comment in any other way than that evinced so far.

In any case, there has been a rush to pin down *Specters of Marx* (bearing, in some cases, the signs of a certain commodity fetishization or fetishistic commodification in the guise of a mapping and domestication of figures, themes, interests, etc.). There has been an effort to tease out *Specters'*—and, therefore, by the operations of a logical economy, Derrida's, deconstruction's—allegiances to Marx and Marxism, finally and unequivocally. And, more generally, for Marxists of a certain kind, of a proprietorial or "prioprietorial" kind, as Derrida puts it—he asks of Marxism: "is it still the private preserve or personal property of those who claim or proclaim that they are 'Marxists'?"[6]—there is the always hurried attempt to claim ownership to Marx, to the correct Marx, and to have Derrida spell out his and, by extension, so-called deconstruction's so-called affiliation to Marxism; which, by the way, is not so much an affiliation as the determination of or desire for a hierarchical subservience;

there is discernible the desire for an act of subordination, involving the partial if not complete erasure of difference, in the communal guise of consolidation and conflation.

This rush is not simply the question of speed. Or if it does in fact turn out to be a question of speed, let me just qualify that by saying that the rush is double in itself, and therefore divided, haunted, in the very disarticulation of its articulation. And this, therefore, is also then very much a question of speed announced by the doubling, spectral movement that inhabits our habitual usage of such a term. Indeed, we may suggest that the dependence on speed and on the concomitant rush is the sign of a certain ontology of reading as not/reading in the name of politics in particular quarters. While speed can be a matter of first or preemptive strikes, especially and perhaps *always* in the name of a politics or any political ontology, in the assignment of the name of politics in the justification of speed, there is also a concern here with addiction, as the spectral trace already derailing the question of not-reading (which is very much to the point, concerning *Specters*). While it is impossible to find the right speed, and acknowledging after Pascal that when one reads too fast or too slowly one understands nothing,[7] we nevertheless have to contend with what Derrida calls the aporia of speed,[8] to which one might add, the aporetic of the right time, of the want of time, taking time, the untimeliness of certain projects (and, therefore, the urgency at which such anachrony hints), and so on.

Thus, in the face of this, there has to be admitted that the rush to decide, and the speed attendant on that, bespeaks, in signaling the velocity and acceleration that has accumulated around and toward particular aspects of *Specters of Marx*, all the indelible marks, the tracks and traces, of an addiction.[9] Derrida, in thinking the relation of a toxicomania to the literary in "The Rhetoric of Drugs," comments provocatively on the reading of addiction as a figure of one's being haunted, of the ontological haunting of the self by the other, and the self's addiction to that sense of being haunted, as well as, and concomitantly, suggesting the need to invoke the phantom:

> But first consider the figures of dictation, in the asymmetrical experience of the other (of the being-given-over-to-the-other, of being prey to the other, of quasi-possession) that commands a certain writing, perhaps all writing. . . . These forms of originary alienation, in the most positive, productive and irreducible sense of the word, these figures of *dictation*—are they not drawn into a history in which drugs . . . one day

came to take a place left vacant, or to play the role of an enfeebled phantom? Rather it would be a matter of methodical provocation, of a technique for calling up the phantom: the spirit, the ghost (*Geist*), inspiration, dictation. More precisely, and what makes the matter even more convoluted, we would be dealing here with a methodology of the counter-phantom. What is a counter-phantom? It is the phantom that one plays against another phantom, yet it is also the phantom of the phantom, the alibi phantom, the other phantom. Have we then a choice only between phantoms, or between the simulacra of phantoms?

But let's not act as if we know what a phantom or a phantasm was, and as if it were enough simply to set out the consequences of such a knowledge.[10]

The figure of addiction, of being-addicted, which addresses itself to the ontological condition of Being, is also the figure of the hauntedness of being, that inescapable division of any identity from within by the self's uncanny double or other, its non-identity on which any sense of being is dependent for the act of identification, and yet which the self can never calm down.

But to return to the specific question of Marxism. This addiction manifests itself as an addiction to determination (all the more manifesting the signs of its being-addicted in the necessity to repeat itself), the hurried efforts to construct an identity, and the concomitant rush that comes with such attempts to control the other, to make it conform. So, we can say that the question of speed is, for Marxists of the Anglo-American variety at least, also a question of a classical ontological habit. There is, moreover, an onto-addictive trait in relation to an attempted double inoculation: that of Marxism into so-called deconstruction and that of a perceived strain of deconstruction in Marxism, albeit not those aspects of deconstruction, so-called, that act as an allergen for conventional political modalities and critical discourses. The allergen that is (in) "deconstruction," that setting to work of the other, is that precisely which both causes an allergic reaction, while also being the haunting trace that a certain Marxist tendency seeks, if not to eradicate, then at least to domesticate (not recognizing that the condition of the house is to be haunted), if not, in some cases, actively exorcise. Derrida has remarked of this Marxist tendency: "Their aim is to convince themselves, or to affect to believe, that they are dealing with something familiar, at a juncture in which, no longer finding the usual landmarks, they cannot, after all, claim to be confronting an enemy from the right, a 'class enemy'."[11] In its own onto-theological project, a particular sect of the Church of Marxism cannot tolerate an other messianicity—there is not the room for two holy ghosts, or the manifestations of what Werner Hamacher calls, in his essay from *Ghostly Demarcations*—whereby he describes a developed commodity-analysis capable of examining its own excess as that which haunts it—the "paraphenomenal spirituality and spectrality."[12] Perhaps, as something of a momentary detour, this is something Marx tacitly and proleptically acknowledges in *The Poverty of Philosophy*, when in rebuttal of Proudhon, he speaks of "the *shadow of movement* and the *movement of shadows*, by means of which one could still have created at least a semblance of history."[13] What Marx finds incredible is that, in insisting on material existence in social economy, Proudhon denies the possibility that *"anything can appear."* However, I must move on, as I find myself spending too much time on this. It remains only to say, pertaining to the phantasmatic-addictive situation in which the matters of speed and the rush are caught, that it is, doubtless, the sign of the habit to which I'm referring that there has been such a bad reaction in certain places.

Second remark: Despite various comments on Derrida's part, only one of which I have the time to cite, Marxism of a particular kind demands of so-called deconstruction that "it" show "its" affiliations, not only unequivocally, but also, as you will have gathered from what's been said so far in a particular manner and after a certain fashion according to a particular formula or register. What is being asked of so-called deconstruction is that, before being admitted to the party, it take out its party card, that it registers in the appropriate manner. The issue over which the manner of its registration, and of the register in which Derrida chooses to address the question of Marxism, is the question, already raised, of spectrality. In a radio interview regarding in part *Specters of Marx* published in *Sur parole: instantanés philosophiques*,[14] Derrida has remarked, doubtless to the surprise—or perhaps not, given the tone of Terry Eagleton's "Marxism without Marxism"[15]—of a certain Marxist reading of this text, that

Au fond, ce livre *[Spectres de Marx]* est avant tout une réflexion sur cette catégorie de spectralité qui m'intérese depuis très longtemps, on peut on trouver dans mon travail des prémices très anciennes, le spectre n'état pas seulement le fantome, le revenant, ce qui revient à contretemps nous rappeler un héritage, mais aussi ce qui n'est ni mort ni vivant, ni réel ni iréel, qui réintroduit la dimension du fantasmatique dans le politique, et nous aide aussi à comprendre des structures de l'espace public actuel, les médias, la vir[t]ualisations des échanges, etc. C'est un des motifs principaux de cet essai. Cette catégorie de spectralité peut etre très féconde, et c'est donc un des fils conducteurs de cet essai.[16]

Fundamentally, this book is, above all [before anything] a reflection on this category of spectrality which has interested me for a very long time, one can find it amongst the oldest premises of my work; the spectre was never only the phantom, the *revenant*, that which has returned in an untimely fashion to recall to us a heritage or inheritance, but is also that which is neither dead nor alive, neither real nor unreal, which reintroduces the phantasmatic dimension in politics, and it helps us also in understanding the structures of real public spaces, the media, the virtualisation of [forms of] exchange, etc. This is one of the principal motifs of that essay. This category of the spectral can be very fruitful, and it is thus one of the clews ["conductive fibres" but also a "lead" in a *policier*; furthermore, there is clearly visible, and yet not unequivocally so, the ghost of filiation in the fleeting glimpse of the "son;" we are speaking here of inheritance *and* discontinuty, transference *and* translation] of that book.

As you and I both know—but it *does* bear reiterating for those who either choose to play down or otherwise not acknowledge this—on the one hand, the spectral is always more than just the appearance of the ghost while, on the other hand, the spectral is that uncanny trembling of an excess, if I can put it like this, that troubles the economic restrictions of an identity homogeneous with(in) itself, and which, in its disturbing resonance and radical otherness, is always of a wholly other kind, beyond all economic determinations reliant upon the imposition, for example, of a structure of self and other as in the figure of dialectical opposition (such as "Marxism and deconstruction").

The question of the spectre, has been read, then, if it has been read at all, on the part of certain Marxists, with far too much haste. If everything I am saying here is neither more nor less than a recapitulation, a reiteration of already debated points, then this is nothing else other than an effort, in an equally hurried fashion, to put the brakes on a little. The necessity for reading is both a matter of reading differently and reading difference in the name of the political. As Richard Joines has remarked on this necessity,

Marxist readers whose primary concern is . . . the "real" world ought to be more cautious when approaching a figure like Derrida. . . . If Derrida were merely part of an ensemble of ludic practices . . . he could be dealt with as we are used to dealing with other ideological mystifications . . . why should Marxists have to think differently about such issues? They need not, unless part of the praxis of Marxism includes understanding what a political philosopher such as Derrida does . . . and how his stratagems transform.[17]

Of course, as the essays collected in *Ghostly Demarcations* for the most part show, there are those Marxists who have, undoubtedly, taken up the demand to think differently. Essays, such as those by Warren Montag, Pierre Macherey, and Antonio Negri, engage in a sustained manner with this very question of spectrality and, of course, with the spirit as well as the letter of Marx, in the reading of *Specters of Marx*. The problem is perhaps one of being on the same wavelength, of attuning oneself to the reception of spectres, and, thereby, opening oneself to a different reception and to the difference that is remarked as Derrida's reception of spectres in *Specters of Marx*. When Fredric Jameson remarks that the spectral figure constitutes "the new figurality . . . of a somewhat different type than those that began to proliferate in Derrida's earlier work,"[18] he is not wholly correct. First, the figures of ghosts, phantoms, and the spectral have appeared, as Derrida has just suggested, in some of Derrida's earliest publications. Second, Jameson's differentiation between figures such as "dissemination" and "hymen" (figures from Derrida's "earlier work"), and "the figured concept of the ghost or spectre,"[19] is a reading that assumes a somewhat critical commonplace concerning Derrida's writing that it is discernibly marked by a shift from the earlier, more straightforwardly "philosophical" interest, to a somewhat "literary" interest ("you could just as plausibly argue that Derrida has grown more literary over the years").[20] Such a reading marks a slip into determination rather than reception, and thus gives up the maintenance of reading. However, this is not to suggest that Jameson is lacking in care or attention, but rather to note how the frequency of spectrality is such that it can escape notice altogether. What Jameson and a number of the other commentators in *Ghostly Demarcations* do show are the signs of an effort to take the time over Derrida's text. These are more in evidence than the hurried attempt to write off the matter of spectrality. It can hardly have escaped anyone's notice, that the most strident antispectral dismissal—Eagleton's—is also

the shortest piece in the book. But, presumably, politics is—or can be—
like that: too (self-) important, in too much of a hurry, to waste any time
over other, less significant matters that are left, Eagleton points out, for
discussion in places like Cornell and California, also identified as Ithaca
and Irvine.[21] But despite—or, perhaps, *precisely,* because of—this minor-
ity status, there is nonetheless a sense of the declamatory dismissal ring-
ing with greater volume than the carefully considered response. In this,
as Warren Montag points out in his contribution to *Ghostly Demarcations,* the "anti-deconstruction" cause has brought together certain
Marxists with "their most bitter adversaries in what would appear to be a
quite unprincipled alliance."[22]

    I do not have the time to reassemble the arguments of the antispectral
lobby, and, in a sense, it is neither necessary nor desirable to repeat what
others are only too happy to repeat for themselves and to themselves, as
typical of that "facile consensus,"[23] described by Derrida in the interview
just cited. Let me just remark, however, with reference to Terry Eagleton,
whose position is exemplary *and* symptomatic, singular *and* wholly programmed, that there is a kind of negative-performative at work specifically
in his reiterated jibes directed at Cornell and the University of California in
particular, but also more generally in the question of intellectual engagement with the issues at hand in the North American higher education system. If we give our attention to such material repetitions, treating them
momentarily as a kind of troping effect, is there not readable a sense of so-
called radical thought's already having been domesticated by the university? What is performative here, I think, is that, behind the dismissal of
so-called deconstruction in Ithaca and Irvine, there lurks the nagging,
haunting doubt on Eagleton's part that Marxism, whether in Oxford, or,
for argument's sake, Glasgow, or, indeed, wherever, is itself already domesticated, co-opted, and, further, that it has colluded with its own recuperation—or I may just be reading too much into this (*or,* third possibility,
it may be that, like Aijaz Ahmad, I find myself drawn to motifs and
metaphors, to a certain form of rhetoric, that makes one inclined to treat
Eagleton's essay "primarily as a *literary* text").[24] Yet, as Derrida points out
in *Sur Parole,* "Si un travail universitaire est toujours nécessaire sur Marx,
il y a un risque de domestication, de neutralisation de l'injonction révolu-
tionnaire de Marx" ["if university work on Marx is always necessary, there
is also the risk of domestication, of the neutralisation of the revolutionary
injunction of Marx"].[25] The performative in Eagleton lies in the fact that
the accusation he turns against so-called deconstruction in general and

Specters of Marx in particular can be said to be exemplified by the matter of Marxism in the university today. And this, as Derrida acknowledges, is its risk, and precisely the reason for what might hastily be called the odd timing of *Specters,* as well as the apparent, occasional obliquity of address. Which is, I would suggest, precisely why we need to take the time to acknowledge the question of a spectropoetics or a politics of hauntology, as the, once again, excessive and material trace that itself protests and is resistant to the policing effects of academic neutralization, the hegemony of which is and has been, arguably, more in evidence with regard to Marxism than in relation to any other discourse.

From the vantage point of particular manifestations of Marxism, it is, then, the very notion of spectrality, which has not been understood, in what might be called the broader context of Derrida's work, and specifically with regard to this very question of the New International as a figure of a political hauntology, rather than one of political ontology. It has been misread, or not read at all, as a result of that lack of time that is frequently a constituent element in any politics conventionally conceived. It is thus that very "enigmatic component"[26] that your call for papers identifies, albeit fleetingly. It is that which is enigmatic about the notion of the New International, and for this reason, moreover, Derrida identifies in a reiterative fashion all those apparitions of the "without" in the passage that you cite, and to which we will have to return. When Derrida says, that the figure of spectrality has haunted his work from some of his earliest publications, and when he gives the motif of the New International that phantasmatic turn, suggestive of a psychoanalytic register (as is clear), this should give us pause. This figure without determinate figuration has allowed for an effort to "try to understand what the political is," as Derrida put it (in an instant of disarming litotes) in a talk on *The Politics of Friendship* at the University of Sussex,[27] rather than being merely one possible figure for the proposal of a new politics. As Derrida commented at Sussex, such a misunderstanding is misleading. The concern with the spectral intimates a more general concern in Derrida's texts with that which cannot be theorized, which resists theorization, and which, therefore, overflows the limits of a programmatic theorization or, let us say, *programmed* thinking, which is not necessarily thinking at all. To allude to the Sussex talk again, Derrida remarks that there is no such thing as a deconstructive politics if, by the term *politics* there is implied a *program;* furthermore, *Specters of Marx,* before being about Marx, is what Derrida describes as a "personal, singular commitment."

Thus, to return to this point, again: despite the fleeting appearances, as well as the condition of having always already retreated and thereby re-marking a disarticulating untimeliness, the spectral, which is never sim-ply a single figure, is there in the text of Derrida, though never as such. Two of the most obvious instances of apparition are in the reading of Mal-larmé, in *Disseminations,* in the discussion of the discussions around Van Gogh, in *The Truth in Painting.* There is also the consideration of spirit, of the frequency of *geist* in the text of Heidegger; and there are also many other fleeting, disabling glimpses of the spectral, which there is not the time to enumerate here. Such apparitions are evident in the two pas-sages[28] that have been chosen for discussion in the special edition of *Par-allax,* and it is to those I wish to turn, finally and yet also in too much of a hurry, having the feeling that I will have spent far too much time in get-ting to this point in this letter. In considering the phantasmal figuration at work here, I wish to suggest that spectrality and the hauntological are instances of what Derrida has described as *materiality without matter.*[29] Although this phrase will sound paradoxical, if not nonsensical to some, it nonetheless draws our attention to the trace of spectrality, and the effi-cacity of such a trace in disrupting all sense of programming and domes-ticity by addressing what takes place even though there is nothing materially "there" in the "real" world as such.

Before commenting on these passages, though, let me come back to the question of time. It seems to me necessary to say, in response to the framing of this project, that the matter of time is very much an issue here. In relation to this question of time, and, more precisely, timing, there is in the projection of this project a degree of violence, relating to expropriation, appropriation, excorporation and incorporation, exhuma-tion even (which inevitably prefigures the possibility of yet one more act of interring), if not a violent dismemberment, a forensic anatomization, by which this project gets under way. (Which is not to say I object, nec-essarily; I know that you're aware of the dangers, as you are of the fact that there is, after all, attendant on any project, always the risk of a nec-essary violence in relation to the text of the other.)

The violence is most obviously figured in the disfiguration of *Specters of Marx* through the abrupt, provocative excerption of the two passages in question, which are not in themselves whole. This is espe-cially the case with the first of the two passages, marked by the violent inscription of ellipsis. If there were time, we could usefully examine what has been omitted, especially in relation to the question of the

"New International." For example, cut from the first passage in that first instance of ellipsis and/as erasure are some twenty-one lines. In these there is the call for the extension of international law in a manner akin to the gradual, historical broadening of human rights. The example of the expansion of human rights is what has already taken place. Moreover, It is also that which—implicitly in Derrida's formulation—"takes time" or has taken time (the time of historical expansion). With this, international law has to catch up (as though its time were only just beginning to manifest itself, too late we might say, in the face of the injustices practiced in the name of the State and capital, with which Derrida fleetingly annotates the passage in question), if such law is to "be consistent with the idea of democracy and of human rights it proclaims." Such a gesture, furthermore, should belong to a supplementary expansion of international law "beyond the sovereignty of States and of the 'phantom-States'" mentioned prior to the passage with which we are concerned. Such phantom-States (drug cartels, the Mafia, are the examples given) are materially effective in that they have, according to Derrida, dematerialized themselves within the fabric of modern society and culture and have been able to do so, furthermore, doing it with such effect precisely because they are not anomalous but wholly consonant within, and defined by, the operations of capitalism. (They are also phantomatic in that the economic operation of such shadow organizations, in not being anomalous or aberrant in relation to capitalism, may be read as simulacra of the capitalist mode of production by which the State maintains its identity.) Without understanding the phantomatic materiality of this situation as that which makes it possible, we comprehend little or nothing. While the relation between the drug cartel and capitalism may be widely understood, along with the violent relation between the two, as a faux-dialectic founded on a narcissistic and wholly classical mirroring or co-dependency, what has been left out of this precisely is the extent to which the reciprocal dysfunction or co-addiction within and as a component of capitalism is, simultaneously, haunted and relies on the very manifestation of the spectral effect that it produces. But I'm taking too much time here; allow me to be a little hasty, a little schematic.

First ellipsis, first passage, continued: Derrida then turns to the idea of the possibility of working with, and from within, the idea of the State, the "State apparatus."[30]

But let's pause for a moment over this most fleeting of instances. This phrase appears to be haunted, somewhat suggestively, by the phrase "Ideological State Apparatus," employed by Louis Althusser in his essay, "Ideology and Ideological State Apparatuses."[31] I suggest this only tentatively and, admittedly, fancifully, as the merest ghost of a chance, reading in this possibly uncanny oscillation what might be described as a spectro-rebarbative countersignature to a certain self-reifying Marxist discourse, so material as to be positively moribund. However, as fanciful as this may be, it is important to recall that, in the essay in question, Althusser, in defining ideology summarizes Marx's own discussion and understanding of this concept in *The German Ideology* "as a pure illusion, a pure dream, i.e. as nothingness . . . an imaginary construction whose status is exactly like the theoretical status of the dream among writers before Freud . . . Ideology, then, is for Marx, an imaginary assemblage . . . a pure dream."[32] That which is ideological is therefore of the order of the phantasm, a figural reality without matter that, nonetheless, causes material effects.

While Althusser does not use the term phantasm or phantom in direct relation to the question of ideology and its definition, Marx does. In *The German Ideology*, Marx, in seeking to "demonstrate the development of ideological reflexes and echoes" of "real life-process" (that is to say the lived material conditions and modes of production), describes the ideas that inform the ideological as "phantoms."[33] While a reading of this passage would doubtless seek to neutralize the uncanny resonance by reading the "phantom" as *merely* a metaphor, and a question, therefore, not of politics or logic but of style, we would suggest a comparison of Marx's figure of the phantom in the definition of ideology with Althusser's own discussion of the figure of the phantasm in the text of Freud, as metaphorical through and through, from which tropological reality comes its very power (a power shared in its illusory yet efficacious operation with ideology).[34]

It is of course impossible to say whether Derrida's remak is haunted by the text of Althusser. We cannot tell or decide; this is a possible resonance, all the more uncanny for being impossible to calm, or to decide upon, one way or another, "in given and limited conditions," as part of the working out of the profound transformation provisionally named by the "New International," as the signs of an inspiration brought about by the "spirit" of Marxism. Clearly, there is little within this first elided passage that would make some happy with Derrida's engagement with

Marx from a certain Marxist standpoint. But, if we are to think about the possibilities of a "New International," it is nonetheless necessary to return to the passages in question what is circumvented in the call for papers. Naming provisionally the "New International" serves as an act of polemical provocation to think otherwise within, *against,* the program and the programmed reception of Marxism. And it is a sign of the failure to think otherwise that the reception of *Specters* has also been, in some quarters, a resistance to *Specters.* It could be said that there has been a response of sorts, issued as a demand, that Derrida *get with the program.*

First passage, second ellipsis: another sixteen lines, over which I can spend even less time than the previous twenty-one. Here, Derrida speaks against the smug triumphalism of liberal democracy in the face of the ever greater global instances of "innumerable singular sites of suffering." This passage is strikingly vocal, as Derrida demands the necessity of crying out in the name of starvation and extermination, against the sounds of singing and celebration. Again, doubtless, such a remark is open to interpretation as merely an extension of the liberalism that Derrida criticizes—though the validity of such a critique is specious to say the least, if the criteria by which the critique is made are comprehensible in terms of formulaic and formalist yardsticks of a "one true Marxism" (the "party" comes down— does it not?—to a programming of deafening, and equally progammed, house music). What is to the point, in seeking to open out any dialogue that is not simply the restatement of entrenched positions—and it is this to which a certain political standpoint is deaf (perhaps because of its own insistent and, occasionally, parodic clamor)—is that the necessity of thinking a "New International" would be involved in the effecting of juridical and political changes *contra* the various manifestations of capitalism's effects in the shape of such "crimes."

Second passage, sole ellipsis: eleven lines. What is omitted here is an allusion to the relations between the State and the party or labor union; or, to be more precise, the interdependent correlations or forms of mirroring that determine these relations, whereby the historical modes of party or union production, far from signaling opposition to the State or the possibility of an alternative formation, in fact reproduce reciprocally the structures and modes of a certain organizational model. The union-party-State model figures itself and its component parts in a synecdochic,

metonymic, and supplementary chain, and have done so, as Derrida suggests, for approximately two hundred years. There is here at the same
time a semantic and economic mode of production at work. This is, to
some, perhaps, a scandalous assertion and also, perhaps, the reason for its
excision, so that the passage with which we are asked to contend reads as
a more straightforward critique of the idea of the party, and the concomitant notion that the time of the party is over, or is otherwise coming to an
end. But what particularly intrigues me in the choice of this passage is
not so much this "internal" ellipsis as the "ellipses" that invisibly mark
the "outer limits," for want of a better phrase, of the passage in question:
for this is taken, somewhat starkly, from a sustained discussion at the beginning of chapter four of *Specters,* which addresses the "mode of production of the phantom, itself a phantomatic mode of production" in
direct relation to the *Communist Manifesto* and its spectral traces, as well
as the Communist International as the incarnation and the end of the
spectral. Taking this discussion, it has to be said, as is implied in the call
for papers immediately before the citation of the second passage, that if
we are going to talk of the "New International," we still have to recognize
that we have to deal with ghosts, with a certain spirit, and with the appearances of the phantom. Moreover, what has also to be recognized, all
the moreso as it is precisely this dimension that has been operated on, excised, and rendered to a certain degree invisible, is that in the passages
that are not presented in the call for papers there is manifest the question
of the necessary reconfiguration of certain principles of analysis of capital to which Derrida alludes in the epigraph to this chapter.

What can be said for now, however, is that these acts of citation operate in an intriguing manner. While part of the criticism of Derrida and
Specters of Marx is that there is a somewhat general avoidance at work
and with that, allegedly, a level of generality to the Derridean response to
Marxist discourse, it is interesting that the process of citation in this call
for papers reproduces an act of generalization, in the name of the urgency
of thinking what so far has yet to be thought vis-à-vis *Specters.* Whether
or not Derrida's commentary is general, "too" general, the acts of erasure
serve —albeit inadvertently, because of a sense of speed that is misrecognized as political urgency?—to generalize, if not to universalize, further.
In such a process of extraction there has occurred in the extracts having
been presented an conceptual idealization, if you will, of the idea of the
"New International." Furthermore, this imposed idealization speaks of an
effect of haste. The act of cutting not only speaks violently and of an

inescapable violence, it also concerns the violence of a lack of time and intemperance. There is about the gesture of citation a sense of urgency, of speed, and this is traced not simply in the gesture of citation but also in the pre- and proscription that attends citation, as well as in the discursive programming taking place in a call for papers such as this. Not, of course, that there is anything necessarily sinister in this (although there can be). On the contrary, it is a common, everyday occurrence, which has to do with the framing of identities, with the founding of a community, and with the programmed protocols of certain aspects of academic work. In another context it might be read as having all the hallmarks of the founding gestures of party-formation. Yet—and it is important that, in reading this, we also read that—the matter of violence and its relation to the matter of speed, all of which do imply business as usual, are precisely the very same gestures that aim at the damping down, the neutralization, of spectral effects and an unpredictable, possibly lawless efficacity. And *always in the name of.* There is always violence, there is always the presumption in such a nomination, whether it be self-nomination (claiming to speak for others, as with a single voice) or the nominal identification of the self-same as the conjuration of community.

There is another violence as a sign of the lack of time that is at work, however. Or, to put this another way, there is the violence of tracks left by speed, and this has to do with the framing remarks of the project. It is remarked that, "[w]hile there has been heated debate over the first two terms of the book's sub-title ('the state of the debt', what it means to be a Marxist today; 'the work of mourning', ghosts and spectrality etc.) there has been little written concerning the third enigmatic component 'the new international'." The rush is indicated, almost breathlessly, in the hurried parenthesis, its speedy, attenuated series of remarks, a swift process of summary and an equally hurried operation of punctuation, which trips you up even as it encourages you to fly over this. There is, needless to say (but I'll say it anyway), too much speed, if not facile consensus, in the apparent assumption of equivalence between ghosts *and* spectrality, as though the one were always, simply the other, as though one could reduce, if not deny the difference, thereby promoting a single identity. Perhaps the speed here is deliberate, if not performative: perhaps the telegraphic, if not telecommunicative process that I read at work in this parenthesis, and the sentence in which it is embedded, enacts the lack of time taken on the part of some. Perhaps the rhetorical haste signals in some manner, as a commentary on or critique of, the lack of time taken in response to the questions raised by *Specters*. There is also a more obliquely remarked yet nonetheless forceful effect of speed in that opening, qualifying remark and, indeed, in the structure of the sentence as a whole: "[w]hile there has been heated debate . . . there has been little written. . . ." Is this readable as suggesting that "heated debate" is another name for "enough" or "too much" discussion? Does this imply that we have done with certain aspects, and, for the lack of time, it is now high time to move on, a reading that is possibly supportable if we take the time to return again to the parenthesis and the various modalities of acceleration that are discernibly at work?

Another aspect of the relation between violence of speed is that "etc." Speed, we should recall, in the words of Paul Virilio, *"is not a phenomenon, it is the relationship between phenomena."*[35] While, doubtless, etc. can be read as referring to, operating on, or as a condition of, both a lack of time and the speed of the parenthesis in general, the etc.'s proximity to the expression "ghosts and spectrality" is haunting. I take the liberty of reading the proximity as a sign of relationship (a dangerous reading habit, but necessary) because of the absence of any comma that would mark off the phrase "ghosts and spectrality," thereby assigning it as part of a more or less rapid telecommunicative and virtual series taking place here in lieu of reading. The speed of that etc. suggests an act of running past the graveyard in the dark, of being afraid of the ghosts, or of the merest suggestion of spectrality.

But what troubles me most—and this, by the way, is precisely what troubles the call for papers as a text with its various protocols and strategies, its headings and citations; which is also to say that there is that which haunts and displaces the call for papers from within; there are the signs of spectral traces that return all the more forcefully despite or perhaps because of all the guiding indicators, all the speedy rhythms and motions of this brief text. These phantoms and phantasms have to do, undeniably if obliquely, with the double question of both the timing and the tempo of this call for papers—to reiterate, what troubles me most with regard to the violence of time, and, in this case, of reading too quickly, is that which is marked in the extrication of the term the "New International" from the title. Such acts of extrication announce that, yes, we're in something of a hurry, we need to get on, there's no time to lose. Moreover, in this gesture it is as if we are assured, or can assure ourselves, and others, that the terms *are* indeed and in fact separable, that the title is open to such an easy anatomical scrutiny, to a dismemberment that makes it (and the text that goes by this title) somehow easier to read. What interests me, then, with regard to the framing of this project—and, doubtless, these are the signs of both strategic and, in some sense, pragmatic concerns—is the desire to address what has yet to be addressed in *Specters of Marx* and the tension between a more general sense of what remains to be addressed, to be read, and the belief that we can decide that what remains is just this question of the "New International" as though this term and this notion, in the manner of some violent act of citation, could indeed *be* so easily detached.

To make the point once again, there is in all of this a sense of hurrying and, with that, the sense of intemperance by which speed is haunted. And the fact that you state—if indeed it is a fact and not only a rhetorical or narrative strategy, a kind of troping of suppression and exaggeration—that no one has yet discussed Derrida's suggestive and provocative linking of the "New International" to the decline of the political party (it may be argued that this perceived "decline" could be read as a declension of traditional notions and parameters of politics in terms of the party, or, otherwise, the "deconstruction" of the idea of the party formed along the traditional limits of politics, declension taking place as the disarticulation that occurs as a result of a thinking otherwise, or a thinking [at] the limits of party-political discourse), acknowledges, on the one hand, the signs of the rush while, on the other, an admission of not knowing what should be made of this. Speed *and* perplexity in the face of, and surrounding, Derrida's formulation, "the New International." This is a formulation that, in toying with a formula, appears to tantalize with the possiblity of formalization, of a return to habit. Such seductive possibility is all the addict requires to rush headlong back to the habit that has never been shed. There is in this the trace of a discernible desire to read the haunting figure even while denying the spectre. In calling Derrida to acknowledge an allegiance to a traditional, conventional, or institutional Marxism, the phrase, "New International" is read, ironically, as being *haunted* by that other, previous International. Such a reading of the spectre issues from a community on the Left in a gesture of reading grounded in a broader politico-epistemological analytical mode, which is reliant for the limits of its act of reading on conjuring or configuring an identity that simultaneously recalls the anterior instance while limiting the play between the one and the other, precisely so as to neutralize the efficacity of revenance on which the notion of the "New International" is, in part, reliant. However, the "New International" as name is not limited to its conjuration of an other International, even if this is a provisional starting point. It is an appropriate response to the increasing spectral-ization of modern existence through the proliferation of teletechnologi-cal media. The "New International" is a spectro-political event read by Derrida as a reaction to what traditional politics can no longer address. When Thomas Kemple remarks that "the 'specter' *(Gespenst)* that haunts contemporary society is not something that has flown from the dead remains of proletarian upheavals or political chaos . . . but the frightening projection of our own absence from the technological pro-duction of history,"[36] he provides us with an act of thinking otherwise in terms of the spectral that makes it possible to comprehend why the mat-ter of spectrality as a politics without institutional affiliation, not yet thought programmatically, is so crucial.

Structurally, then, and as the passages in question make plain, the phantomaticity of the "New International" is not simply the product of the trace of an older International, even if this "New International" ap-pears to conjure, or counterconjure, a textual presence in the name of one of the spirits of Marx, if not exactly of a Marxism. The haunting of this figure, "the New International," is already at work, even if it were not for the glimpse of some predecessor, and it is the sense of haunting, of being haunted from within as the trace of non-identity within the apparent ap-peal to the anterior identity of the "International," over which we need to take time.

Time is running out, though, and there is, more than ever, a sense, of urgency that has to do with the limits imposed by the call for papers ("be-tween 500 and 7000 words"). Let me therefore be even more schematic in relation to the passages in question:

First response: in what way does "the New International" name? Does this name identify anything as such? You'll notice that in most cases there is a degree of caution. This phrase, "New International," is written with that caution signaled in the quotation marks around the phrase that are usu-ally ascribed by those in a hurry as just another of the signs of decon-struction. In the face of this, what is important to read here is that there should be a wariness not to take this name as ontologically operative. If it names at all, it names various interventions in the field of politics, as that which is other to politics conventionally thought, and articulated in the places where politics, institutionally, does not think, where the limit of the political is the aporia in conventional political discourse. The "New International" does not name, and is not assigned to, a single identity. Thus, this phrase plays with the very idea of identity that it refuses to assign. It does so, moreover, in order to signal the material efficacity of that which is radically unformalizable, and which, moreover, has "its" chance (for as Derrida's passage makes clear, and as already stated, there is not one "New International"; the question of identity is irreducible to a single identity, even though the material effects concerning international law hurriedly signaled by Derrida are, of and in themselves, singular) only in those events that are the signs of resistance, "inspired by at least one of the spirits of Marx." The phrase "New International" is therefore the sign of what Arkady Plotnitsky has recently described as a "radical formalization."[37] Such a formalization operates nonclassically in relation to the thinking of classical epistemologies and political discourses, whether by this one indicates the thinking that moves (within) the idea of the State, the idea of international law, or the idea of Marxism, as that is configured oppositionally, and yet, as a dialectical manifestation, being susceptible to becoming one more expression of classical epistemological or, as Derrida has put it, canonical thought. (And, in certain readings of *Specters of Marx,* all the signs are that this is, in fact, the case, that Marxism of a certain kind has not thought differently in its acts of reading.) Thus, to cite and paraphrase Plotnitsky once more, while the efficacity of the so-called New International "manifests itself" through various effects such as denouncing in various, different fashions the limits and inadquacies, for example, of "a discourse on human rights," "it"—if the "New International" can even be thought of as an "it;" this is the problem Derrida has presented us, and to which we are obliged to respond—nonetheless "cannot be thought of in terms of an underlying (hidden) governing wholeness. . . . This efficacity is neither single in governing all of its effects (individual and collective), nor multiple so as to allow one to assign an unambiguously separate efficacity to each lawless individual effect . . . this efficacity or the corresponding 'materiality' . . . is inconceivable" in the framework of the classical epistemological discourse, within which various Marxisms articulate their political identities. Thus, the notion of the "New International" is radically suspended in the very moment in which the notion and name are inscribed, every time. Its inscription, always the most provisional, conjures or configures the phantomatic or phantasmatic haunting of "its" identity and structurality from within itself, so-called. The identity of the "New International" is already spirited away from itself and within itself: renewal and radicalization in the guise of a counterconjuration of "the [theoretical and practical] critique of the state of international law, the concepts of State and nation, and so forth," rather than the adherence to operating oppositionally and dialectically within classical epistemological, ontological and political frameworks.

Second response: How is this seen or read by Derrida? How do we acknowledge this? We begin to see it, if we see it at all, in that "profound transformation" already under way. We see it in the hypothesis of an irreversible mutation, which figure speaks to the trope of "New International" not as some metaphor that operates normatively or can be read normatively (and this, in part, indicates the problem of the reception of this disfiguring inscription), but, instead, as an instance of catachresis wholly appropriate to the notion of spectrality. We see "it" in "its" multiple signs ("we have more than one sign of it"), those increasingly numerous apparitions, apparitions of and as transformation or mutation "inspired by at least one of the spirits of Marx." As Derrida reminds us, "there is *more than one.*" It is important at this juncture to recall that this translated phrase, *"more than one,"* is of course the inescapable normalization and neutralization of the haunted French phrase *plus d'un,*[38] the meaning of which in French is radically destabilized, spectralized, within itself and from itself. This phrase, as you're aware, names that which is more than one and, also, to put it somewhat awkwardly, is "no more one." There is nothing to "it," so to speak, and yet "it" is always already multiple, doubled and divided in "its" identity. This phrase attests to the question of the spectrality, of what is "discreet, almost secret"—what, we might say, gets *lost in translation* between so-called deconstruction and Marxism—and yet what is more and more visible, never a single identity, always more and less than this, never a presence, but traced everywhere, in multiple, irreducible ways. Thus, this expression operates economically *and* excessively in so many registers: it names otherwise the work, the performative efficacity, of the phrase, "New International," as well as the spectrality of this phrase, and the spirit in which it is deployed; it speaks discreetly, almost secretly, to the effects of this passage concerning the effects of the "New International" and it highlights or enacts the event of the spectral disarticulation within articulation as at once both spectral *and* material, which takes place, furthermore, not simply as the work of semantic oscillation within the play of a single word or phrase (who would dare accuse Marx of being simply semantically playful in his knowing use of the word *Wesen,* which Derrida only hurriedly, and in an untimely fashion, addresses toward the end of *Specters*),[39] but, significantly, as that semantic effect that addresses the material question of thinking political intervention otherwise. That there is both the effect of *more than one* and *no more one,* that the question is one of registering the "discreet, almost secret" tracing allied performatively to the haunting figures of the "New International" and the *"plus d'un,"* which are "more and more visible," and that this is signaled as the fleeting, untimely, and speedy rush of spectral appearances irreducible to a single or harmonious identity, is readable in that reiterative troping of numerous *withouts,* which simultaneously link *and* displace, ten times tracing the "alliance without institution" that Derrida tentatively names "the New International."

Third response: Why is the observation of such conjuration and the haunting that returns as its result necessary? This takes us to the second passage, and to the question of the party, already anticipated earlier. Alliance without institution names, on the one hand, the maintenance of the hope of the revolutionary injunction, of the hope also of resistance and spirit, in the face of normalization, domestication, and neutralization, which is always the risk of institutional consideration, as Derrida acknowledges. On the other hand, not wholly separate from the previous point, alliance without institution, in keeping with a certain revolutionary injunction or radical spirit, affirms the question of radicalization and renewal, whether theoretical or practical, while at the same time resisting, in multiple ways, the classical politico-epistemological formalization of the institution, as, for example, in the form of the party, where this formalization names those modes of production and modes of representation wholly or partly coterminous with the classical and capitalist formations of the State. In speaking of ghosts, in addressing the figures of spectrality and haunting, in mobilizing a discourse on spectrality that is neither reducible to classical formations, nor available to the formulation of a theory of the spectral (as a generalizable theory along the lines of classical paradigms of the theoretical), there becomes possible the chance of seeing what remains unseen and therefore unread. What haunts the very idea of the party is the ghost of a resemblance to all those hegemonic forms, formulations, formalizations and institutionalizations, against which the idea of the party in oppositional political terms first emerged, in the name of the International. This is something Marx himself had recognized perhaps—and I say this hurriedly—in his mobilization of the term *Wesen,* in its naming of essence or being, which meanings disturb from within *Wesen's* use in terms indicating the institutional collective *(Zeitungswesen, Steuerwesen)* that serves the State in its modes of production and representation. As Derrida says in *Specters,* Marx banks on such spectres and spirits as the word *Wesen* conjures.[40] As Derrida remarks, in the French *Spectres,* parenthetically, almost in too much of a hurry: "là, plus de *Wesen.*"[41]

But, there, I've already spent too much time on mere preliminaries; I've taken up too much time, without having enough time myself, despite the fact that I'd wanted, all along, to reply in a certain spirit. And, of course, if this arrives at all, it will do so in an untimely fashion.

Julian

Part Five

READING TO COME

Chapter 11

GUILTY READING

Usually this taking care of the commentary is just considered to be the necessary condition of something called scholarship, but I invite all to consider the possibility that scholarship can be a more or less polite name for *reading avoidance* (which does not presume that we know what *reading,* without the *avoidance,* is).

Thomas Pepper

Writing has no sooner begun than it inseminates itself with another reading.

Jean-Michel Rabaté

Reading . . . must not claim to reveal hidden meaning, to translate the text into which its proper, literal language of meaning; reading must pose itself as an act which sets the text to work, as a work which deconstructs textual oppositions to testify to figural differences.

Bill Readings

I

What is it to read?

How are we to answer this question? Is it answerable? Will we have done with it at the end of this chapter? The very difficulty of answering lies in the apparent simplicity, the naked transparency of this question. All at once it appears readable and yet, for all that, remains to be read, if not unreadable. We cannot escape this problem.

II

1968 seems like a good year from which to begin, and to which to return, if we are to speak of the question of reading, and to talk about this act of reading, moreover, that does not assume itself to be innocent. Indeed, it appears desirable, if not necessary, as an introductory polemical gesture or opening gambit—as a means of seeking to read reading—to state that guilty reading "began" in the year in which *Reading Capital* was published, even though it has been suggested that a more significant moment of which a kind of reading was the product was not, in fact, this year at all. Rather, another provisional starting point might be the Algerian War of Independence. For example, Robert Young begins *White Mythologies: Writing History and the West* with the following statement: "If so-called 'so-called poststructuralism' is the product of a single historical moment, then that moment is probably not May 1968 but rather the Algerian War of Independence—no doubt itself both a symptom and a product."[1]

That is not true, of course, strictly speaking. It is neither true nor not true. As a statement concerning the beginning of reading, it is at least guilty of a kind of rhetorical manipulation in the interests of reading differently, so to speak. But, then, neither is the statement with which we began true, absolutely. However, these appear to be readings, of sorts, even if they avoid reading or acknowledge, indirectly, that reading is deferred. They might perhaps be "strong readings," if this phrase is read as suggesting that they are not readings at all, but are, instead, statements that are keen to present a position, regardless of reading. If they have any virtue, these two statements at least present the possibility of a spacing of "beginning-to-read." No single origin, therefore.

This is still a guilty act. We have just admitted as much, though not in so many words. And guilt, the admission, and the concomitant question of responsibility implicated in any guilty act, is also an appropriate place from where to start, even if the moment of introduction is both a double gesture, a deferral, and an excuse.

Nevertheless, one has to begin somewhere, perhaps where one always begins, in the folds of a citation. The first clause of the previous sentence offers one possible answer to a question put by Roland Barthes as the title of an essay: "Where to begin?."[2] It also echoes a comment made by Geoffrey Bennington—"We must begin somewhere, but there is no absolutely justified beginning"[3]—which, in beginning the third division of his "Derridabase," is not so much a beginning, not a beginning *as such,* as it is a reiteration, a recapitulation, of remarks made by Jacques Derrida, first in *Of Grammatology:*

> The first gesture of this departure and this deconstruction, although subject to a certain historical necessity, cannot be given methodological or logical intraobitary assurances. . . . The opening of the question, the departure from the closure of a self–evidence, the putting into doubt of a system of oppositions . . . these errant questions are not absolute beginnings in every way, they allow themselves to be effectively reached, on one entire surface, by this description which is also a criticism. We must begin *wherever we are* and the thought of the trace which cannot take the scent into account, has already taught us that it was impossible to justify a point of departure absolutely. *Wherever we are:* in a text where we already believe ourselves to be.[4]

Then in *Margins of Philosophy:*

> For the same reason there is nowhere to *begin* to trace the sheaf or the graphics of *différance.* For what is put into question is precisely the quest for a rightful beginning, an absolute point of departure, a principal responsibility. The problematic of writing is opened by putting into question the value *arkhe.* What I will propose here will not be elaborated simply as a philosophical discourse, operating according to principles, postulates, axioms or definitions, and proceeding along the discursive lines of a linear order of reasons. In the delineation of *différance* everything is strategic and adventurous. Strategic because no transcendent truth present outside the field of writing can govern theologically the totality of the field. Adventurous because this strategy is not a simple strategy in the sense that strategy orients tactics according to a final goal, a *telos* or theme of domination, a mastery and ultimate reappropriation of the development of the field. Finally, a strategy without finality, what might be called blind tactics, or empirical wandering.[5]

These statements, which reject the very possibility of the "absolutely justified beginning," might be read as directing the operation of the present chapter, as well as serving to comment on particular arguments of the first chapter of this volume. Certainly, they gesture toward a strategic excuse for an understanding of response throughout this book, understood as so many interruptions. For, given the impossibility of justifying one beginning over another, It is arguable that one could "begin" almost anywhere in *Occasional Deconstructions,* while getting no further than thinking on the impossibility of beginning, again and again. Furthermore, the second clause of the remark from which this detour began acknowledges another remark of Derrida's concerning citation: "everything 'begins' then, with citation, in the creases *[faux plis]* of a certain veil"[6] There is here a recognition of the impossibility of an absolute beginning or origin, while performing an operation on the text so as to open its inner workings to our view.

Rather then, say, perhaps, that we begin, before beginning, with an interruption (an interruption in the "history" of reading, or reading [as] a history of interruptions?), this being one possible acknowledgment of responsibility in relation to the place with which we have chosen to begin.

Beginning, then, with Louis Althusser, beginning also with the question of guilty reading:

> But as there is no such thing as an innocent reading, we must say what reading we are guilty of.
>
> We were all philosophers. We did not read *Capital* as economists, as historians or as philologists . . . We read *Capital* as philosophers, and therefore posed it a different question . . . we posed it the question of its *relation to its object,* hence both the question of the specificity of its *object,* and the question of the specificity of its *relation* to that object, i.e., the question of the nature of the type of discourse set to work to handle this object, the question of scientific discourse. And since there can never be a definition without a difference, we posed *Capital* the question of the specific difference both of its object and its discourse. . . .
>
> To read *Capital* as philosophers is precisely to question the specific object of a specific discourse, and the specific relationship between this discourse and its object; it is therefore to put to the *discourse–object* unity the question of the epistemological status which distinguishes this particular unity from other forms of discourse–object unity. Only this reading can determine the answer to a question that concerns the place *Capital* occupies in the history of knowledge. . . .

Hence a philosophical reading of *Capital* is quite the opposite of an innocent reading. It is a guilty reading, but not one that absolves its crime on confessing it. On the contrary, it takes the responsibility for its crime as a "justified crime" and defends it by proving its necessity. It is therefore a special reading which exculpates itself as a reading by posing every guilty reading the very question that unmasks its innocence, the mere question of its innocence: *what is it to read?*[7]

We note that Althusser returns to the question of reading Marx, specifically *Capital*, in a particular way, so as to move beyond other ways of reading—as a philosopher. Nothing could be clearer, and yet, at the same time, such a statement of guilt articulates another question: what does it mean to read *as a philosopher*? To read this phrase, *reading as a philosopher,* is at once all too easy and impossible. Indeed, it seems so straightforward that it is not read at all. Thinking we know what it means, we pass over it without question, without reading. Yet, Althusser confesses to engaging in an interested act of reading, and proceeds to explain what exactly such an interest, such a responsibility, entails.

In this act of confession, however, Althusser acknowledges that which cannot be avoided. No one who reads is innocent. In order to comprehend what it means to read as a philosopher, it is therefore necessary, ignoring any institutional definition of what a philosopher is, to suggest what might constitute this "innocent" reading, at least on the evidence presented by Althusser. Reading as a philosopher in this local instance—the guilty reading—is opposed to other readings: those of the economist, the historian, the philologist. Such innocent approaches to the text do not necessarily read at all. That is, their relationship to the text is technical, mechanical even, perhaps exploitative. They mine the text of *Capital* for example, extracting from it what can be used, put to work in a profitable fashion. Meaning thus becomes use-value, the text reduced to the restricted economy of the thematic reading process. In such a process, the reading is, in a curious, violent, and peremptory fashion, concluded before it has got under way. On the history of technical foreclosure on reading, Suhail Malik's comment on technics in general is instructive: "From Aristotle up to—and perhaps including—Heidegger, technics has been taken to be a means to an end . . . technics as a means isn't just a concrete instrument or thing like a weapon or tool. It can be some rules, a procedure or method for conducting an exercise or ourselves . . . or it can be some 'know how', a knowledge or (acquired) skill, which is employed in order to obtain what is required."[8] We might even suggest that, as a commentary on reading, no reading takes place at all, so institutionalised, so mechanical has this procedure become.

On the other hand, to read as a philosopher, we would hesitatingly and provisionally propose, would be to read not so as to extract a use-value or commodity from the text, or to treat the text as a commodity, parts of which can be used up, leaving only waste. Rather, it would be to activate the text within the history of thought, and against certain strands within that history. Such a reading, the guilty act of which Althusser speaks, is, strictly speaking, technological neither in method nor intent. Instead, reading mobilizes the text within a field of forces that are, in part, if not historical, then "historial," and to which the text belongs. Yet the reading is guilty, precisely because it takes responsibility for the very question of historicity, which innocent reading would ignore. Whether or not Althusser achieves this is not the question here. Jacques Derrida has commented on the limit to which Althusser's reading of Marx goes, in an interview with Michael Sprinker. It is worth considering Derrida's response, inasmuch as it is instructive concerning the point at which Althusser's reading breaks off, a point of arrest that is markedly similar, from a certain perspective, to that discerned by Althusser in what he might term "nonphilosophical" or "nonscientific" readings of *Capital*. Derrida's "reading" here might itself be read as extending the act of "reading as a philosopher," the "guilty reading," to the Althusserian reading:

> It seemed to me that according to his reading of Marx, let's say the "good" Marx is the one who emerges beyond neo-Hegelian metaphysics, beyond anthropology, etc., to finally reach a theoretico-scientific problematic. But I believed and I still believe now that one must pose many historical or "historial" questions about the idea of theory, about the idea of objectivity. Where does it come from? How is objectivity's value constituted? How is theory's order or authority constituted? . . . I did not see these genealogical questions, so to speak, on science, objectivity, etc. being posed by the Althusserian discourse, or at least not in a manner that seemed satisfactory to me. From that, it seemed to me that his reading of Marx constituted in dropping a bad text or a pre-Marxist one, let's say, and in constituting the Marxist text . . . as a text that had moved beyond metaphysical suspicion . . . good politics never comes

from a limitation on questioning or on the demand of thought . . . I thought that what he was saying was not wrong . . . but that it was necessary to further question the axiomatic of discourse.[9]

In that moment where necessity for further questioning is raised can be read the question of reading's responsibility, and implicitly in that, a question of the politics of reading, which extends precisely the Althusserian interrogation of what it means to read. However, the question of what Althusser achieves is not at stake because the immediate concern in responding to the Althusserian commentary is not with a reading of Althusser's text. Instead, the interest here, as elsewhere throughout this study, is with *reading*, with questions of reading differently. This is not a reading of Althusser, so much as it is a strategic opening of reading, in itself and to itself, from the other of reading (which is not, of course, not reading). The Althusserian fragment provides the occasion, not the object, of such a procedure. It is enough, as a place from which to begin, to understand how, in positioning this act of "reading as a philosopher" strategically, his gesture opens for us the means to read differently, to interrupt reading from some other place, as a sign of the responsibility that accompanies every act of reading, and yet is overlooked.

Hence a philosophical reading, provisionally defined, is one which, in seeking to begin reading a particular text, makes it possible for the reading to be turned back on itself. In instituting any act of reading, the question *what is it to read?* must always be asked. Reading must ask this of itself in the act of the "philosophical" movement of self-reflection, as Althusser makes apparent. Furthermore, it must engage in this self-questioning endlessly as the admission of complicity and the responsibility that that entails. Innocence clothes reading in the moment when reading comes to a halt. The guilty reading is not that reading that would strip bare its object. It is, on the contrary, that rhythmic event whereby reading is revealed, revealing itself, in its nakedness, and yet not totally so. Reading can never be completely naked, it can never be returned to a state of purity and innocence, back to some original act of innocent reading. For this would be to place ourselves—impossibly—before reading, before the movement of reading that is never done, and in which we find ourselves. Hence, the reading of which we are guilty, which takes responsibility in shedding the illusion of an innocence.

III

For some, however, this is impossible. We are always caught up in the folds of guilt, through acts of reading. Take, for example, the guilty reader presented by Francis Barker, Samuel Pepys, in *The Tremulous Private Body,* the book read, *L'escholle des filles,* the text in which Pepys confesses his guilt, in other words, privately to himself as the writer–confessor of the sinning reader, his diary, specifically February 9, 1668:

> So. An image of a man. A typical man. A bourgeois man. Riven by guilt, silence and textuality. Forbidden to speak and yet incited to discourse, and therefore speaking in another place. Who says sing when he means fuck, who fears sex and calls it smallpox, who enjoys sex and calls it reading, who is fascinated and terrified by texts and so reads them once, but only for information's sake, who is sober and drunk. . . . A representation of a representation, moreover. Behind it all, not even an adulterous act, but an act of reading. A lewd book.[10]

The passage read by Barker is not the only mention made by Pepys of this "lewd book" (Pepys's phrase) and it is instructive to consider the desire to read, which the possibility of reading guiltily engenders, and by which it is propelled. *L'escolle des filles ou La philosophie des dames, divisée en deux dialogues* (att. Michel Millot and Jean L'Ange [1655]), is first mentioned by Pepys on January 13, 1668: "I was ashamed of reading it."[11] He is not so ashamed of reading it, however, that, nearly a month later (February 8), he returns to the bookseller to purchase the book.[12] On the following day comes the passage with which Barker is concerned.[13] There is much that might be commented on between the three entries having to do with reading. Not least noteworthy are the matters of translation, return and reiteration, denial and avoidance, and the parenthetical statement, only partly legible in the manuscript, that climaxes in a kind of comic French, as though English were too proper a language, or otherwise improper, in which to record the response to reading as erotic trembling.

Francis Barker addresses only the last of the three entries, omitting, furthermore, a partially unreadable, parenthetical overflow of the pen concerning overflow (see n.13). What can be read in the first entry, from January, is the passing confession of another act of guilty reading, another *lewd book,* the *putanta errante.* Pepys gives his secret reading pleasures away, even as, through this allusion, he names that text, of which *L'escolle* is, itself a reading. Not that Pepys acknowledges this directly, or that he has read the earlier Italian text. Also traceable across the three diary entries is the spacing and reiteration—the insistence with which Pepys acknowledges the text's lewdness is telling—that generates the very possibility of reading, as well as signing a desire to read, and to continue to do so. Thus, the passages articulate a representation of reading, as a rhythm method building to a climax. Reading is itself the private, secret act, and the private record of the diary returns this event to its writer who reads himself coming back, so to speak, within a narrative of his own making, as simultaneously, subsumed by, and seeking to control, what it means to read.

Barker understands this, and expresses the overflow within (and as a result of) reading, that movement, which, more than reading itself, is always traced by a writing: "[t]he scene of writing and of reading, is, like the grave, a private place. We must explore the contents of this privacy, in relation to what is publicly speakable, and draw the structure of confessions and denials of desire."[14] This double gesture is a figure of representation as representation moreover. Reading re-presents what is not present, the other text, and, in this, Barker's text is no exception, re-presenting that representation of a reading, the text of which is neither simply there, nor not there. For the act of reading, in being a double movement of simulation and dissimulation, concerns itself with the impossibility of presentation, even though it is always concerned with what comes between representation and re-presentation. Reading thus opens that spacing, reading as spacing itself, in the suture of the hyphen of "re-presentation," and between the desire for *representation* and *re-presentation*, in a performative gesture of analogical appresentation.

And this is precisely what we are able to read in Francis Barker's text, wherein reading spaces and thereby performs in other words the articulation of Pepys' text of that already displaced *lewd book.* Barker opens reading as that which is always already remarked in an abyssal reduplication, whereby those two words, *lewd book,* read or, at least, desire to read, Pepys' own diary, as much as they seek to return to us the condition of what Pepys claims to read, "for information's sake." Indeed, in reading this, I do no more than enact the very condition of reading. Herein is the performative aspect of reiterative spacing, of deferral and displacement caught in a "representation of a representation" of a representation, and fuelled in this unveiling by the desire to read. This in turn is inseparable from the analytical engagement.

Thus, while Pepys' diary is a spectacular revelation of the ways in which reading and writing mean to say one thing while saying quite another, or, perhaps, saying the one thing in quite another way, Barker's text reveals how the action of guilty reading—which phrase, "guilty reading," is really to say nothing more than just *reading,* the salient quality of reading being that it is guilty—can never escape its own complicity in the rhythm in question. Such reiterative process is caught everywhere, even as Barker confesses Pepys (who has already confessed himself), but nowhere moreso, perhaps, than in that single word—*Riven.* Defining all the readings, and being a reading itself which says everything and nothing, this term perpetuates the division of the private scene. This works itself out in the subsequent sentence of Barker's text. Notice the insistent reiteration of that *who,* which seeks to pin down the subject, while serving, paradoxically, to trace the desire to read in the very rhythm of reading that those *whos* re-present, without representation.

Despite the obvious attempt to make plain what Pepys' reading is charged with obscuring, displacing, denying, Barker's own reading, in all its clausal divisions, disperses itself in its very performance. This gesture comes, again and again, despite that desire to reveal all, to give names, through the act of reading, to those acts that are themselves not acts but are, instead, revealed as naming-readings. Such a process, of what we might describe as a nominal-analytic, imposes a reading as a halt to reading, as though everything were said, and done with. Nothing other than an attempted act of mastery, Barker's text presents a moment of violent policing dressed up in the guise of re-presenting what reading supposedly cannot say, even though the text succeeds only in representing reading, and that, moreover, as a movement, in which it is caught.

If, as Peter de Bolla suggests, reading is a process whereby the self identifies and thus attempts to stay the interpretation of the self, through a number of claims concerning itself,[15] then Francis Barker's text, in addressing the guilt of Pepys's secret act of reading so forcefully, reveals not only an act of reading, but also a reader. Or, perhaps, two readers, at least, for there is the reader Barker would appear to wish to be. Here is the reader who no longer has to read, who has everything under control. Furthermore, there is the reader who does not read either, but who awaits the arrival of the reading, as though everything that could be said, had been said, as though reading were over and the text had said it all; as though, in Roland Barthes's words "reading is nothing more than a referendum."[16] There is that process that, in the guise of reading, is never reading as such. Instead, such an imposed activity leaves the reader, idle, intransitive. If reading is reduced to nothing other than a process or principle of gathering the signifiers or referents so as to make a political decision, then reading is halted before it can begin. There can be no interest in reading, only in the action of connecting those traces that can be assigned a meaning or value in common, those that carry, bear, or carry back the same. The *fainéant* reader is allowed to seek for nothing other than this return for his or her effort. There is only the choice to accept or not to accept. This is what, as readers governed by particular institutions of reading, we are asked to do: to take it or leave it or, as Barthes puts it, simply "to accept or reject the text,"[17] and to vote on a proposal without reading it. Accepting, acquiescing, we are forced into idleness. Reading idles, it runs, ticking over, getting nowhere. Reading, so-called, is thus figured as an act of violent inscription on the reader, to which the reader can only respond through another binarism, acceptance or rejection, placing the X in the box on the referendum ballot, effectively erasing the self in abandoning the act of reading and, with that, the responsibility that all reading entails. At the same time, however, the possibility of guilty reading opens to us, and allows us to open, the "theoretical" or the "political" in those very places where such acts of reading have been discounted, unless of course such readings can be made to assume the identity of the referendum once again.

IV

If we are to talk of "theory" or "politics," we have to acknowledge that, on the one hand, certain acts of reading can be and have been read as "too theoretical" or "too political." On the other hand, those same readings, or different readings of a similar kind, can be read as "not theoretical" or "not political enough." Often, it is a political decision to decide on the status of "theory" and the kind of reading that "it" supposedly produces. It is nothing other than a political reading, which often amounts to the same thing as a *strong* reading, which is not really a reading in the event, but, rather, the return of the referendum. Whether we situate the fiction of a beginning with regard to reading in 1954, 1966, or 1968, then, and, all the while, between those dates and the present, little really seems to have changed. If there is a change, it is perhaps a changing of the guard and, with that the accommodation of domestication. The literary institution remains exactly that, though what has become institutionalized, and what perhaps no longer reads because of the domestication effected through institutionalization, is a politics (of reading), which wants to (not) read "theory," but to present a "reading" of the strong variety, and so have done with the very kind of activity that would be a necessary countersignature to the enforced passivity sanctioned by the institution, in the name of literature.

What is the name of the prohibition of reading from the other side? In one sense, it has to be given the name of *post-theory*, as Geoffrey Bennington has defined that:

> Post-theory has often become a thinly made-up return to pre-thoeretical habits and a sort of intellectual journalism. . . . "Theory," from this perspective, is (was) not political, or at any rate not political *enough*, never political enough, so it must be politicised. Politicising it means culturalising it . . . culturalising it means historicising it, historicising it means interring it. The logic of this position . . . going something like this: theory shows us that texts have no intrinsic identity in themselves independent of the readings they are given; reading is therefore essentially *free* with respect to the text being read; so the readings we in fact come up with must have motivations that are not prescribed by the text being read; those motivations are, like it or not, essentially political; so it is incumbent upon us, on the Left, to read for socialism, towards socialism. All *other* readings and reading methods are also therefore accountable in political terms, and most importantly, readings or reading methods that do not recognise this intrinsic politics of reading are *ipso facto* reactionary.
>
> The ("theoretical") problem with this argument . . . is that it is caught in a contradiction between the sense that meaning is indeterminate . . . and a sense that it is determinable. . . . Knowing what we want (socialism) means being confident that we know what we mean—but this means that we believe *we* can write our texts—our readings— which are determinate with respect to their meanings, whereas our basic premise is that texts are radically indeterminate with respect to their meanings.[18]

Post-theory, having done with theory, having had enough to do with theory, having claimed to have read quite enough of what it misreads as "theory"—in naming it "theory," in providing an identity that can be described as an "it" in the first place—decides that "theory" was not, never was or is (or by the imposing temporal logic of such an argument, *never will be*), *political enough*. What is *political enough* for those who claim that this is not what "theory" is, was, or shall be, is hardly ever read. The *political enough* remains within the realm of the unthought, except, of course, along institutional lines, which is another way of saying, from a certain perspective, the unread. The *political enough* is precisely what those who have read "theory" as not *political enough* claim to be, though to what extent those who are *political enough* have read carefully what it means to be *political enough* remains unclear. Except that, in the name of no longer reading, those who are *political enough* can always justify their having done with reading, and specifically reading "theory," exactly because they can say that they and their readings, so–called, are *political enough*.[19]

Bennington's analysis provides a clear enough assessment of the accusations leveled at certain kinds of reading. We are still with the guilty reading, therefore. However, what is also clear is that, on the side of (a) politics, not/reading allows for judgments to be made, guilt assigned. Since 1968 (or any other of the dates just now remarked), the movement away from reading on the part of some has been accompanied by the inevitable evasion of the acknowledgment of complicity, which would make the continuance of reading undeniable. Also elided therefore must be the question *what is it to read?* With the act of sentencing—*not political enough, never political enough*—comes the pronouncement that has replaced that question: *we know what it means to read.* As Bennington points out, with guilt comes the death sentence and subsequent burial, which is nothing other than the inevitable outcome of the arrest of reading. *Politicizing: culturalizing: historicizing: interring.* Bennington's reading reveals the extent to which the reading that is politicized within narrow ideological or institutional parameters expresses an attempted mastery over theory, even if this means rejecting it out of hand. With this sought-after mastery, there is expressed a desire to account for what it addresses, whether the meaning of its own texts, or the texts of others, as part of a teleological process, where reading, in a totalizing, utopian translation, means *reading-toward-socialism*.

However, in the face of this movement, Bennington offers a reading in the place of not-reading, which appears in the guise of *reading-*

toward-socialism. Unfolding the logic and movement of the latter, his reading acts as a countersignature to the seemingly inexorable progress. This gesture, tracing first the advance, and then, in turn, stalling it through the activity of a reading that proceeds as the necessary contrapuntal effect from within the place of the nonread of *reading-toward-socialism*, performs the urgent reason for the pursuit of reading. This reading performance on Bennington's part is itself the expression of the—political?—responsibility that every patient reading entails, and which it also addresses in the face of haste or an apparent reading process that is in fact the abandonment of reading in name of the project. Contrary to the project, in this case *socialism*, which would have done with reading, reading becomes all the more obligatory, all the more compelling, as that which still remains to come, if the reader is not to fall into the place of nonreading.

What does *reading-toward-socialism* fail to read? It fails, and in so doing abandons the pressing responsibility, to acknowledge the incommensurable aporia within its own logic, which Bennington's reading of reading brings into focus so tellingly, and which the passage we have cited performs with that ironic proximity necessary in all close reading. In producing a paraphrase of the politicized reading of theory's reading, it is shown at what point the politicized reading arrives at an *impasse*. Politicized reading maintains the precarious balancing trick of "on the one hand, on the other," which is its theoretical problematic, and is that which installs the aporetic *between* the desire for determinate meaning and *the sense that meaning is indeterminate*. Yet, if we can begin to read the aporetic in *reading-toward-socialism* as a dual project that desires arrival and abandons reading as not being political enough, we may, perhaps, begin to understand, that is to say *read*, that the aporetic marks that place where responsibility begins. The aporia does not excuse us from responsibility;[20] it is, rather, responsibility itself, the responsibility to re-formulate the question of politics in the face of the limit of *reading-toward-socialism*, which cannot account for itself, and is, itself, found guilty of that of which it would seek to indict others. Reading, in one sense is always this: the response to the other as responsibility. Bennington's text manifests this responsibility through an act of reading that opens, rather than forecloses, on reading. In doing so, he makes it possible for others to read how political and institutional structures must be opened to a certain reading act, which extends beyond discourses or semantics, although these also remain to be read.

Reading as undifferentiated augmentation or supplement to the truth of political discourse is never reading, clearly. It is, instead, passive reception and the promise of an equally passive future transmission where, in such an act of indifference, reading stops and something is lost in translation: the political itself, we might well suggest, in favor of the narrowly Political, the party line. There can be no reading, therefore, without the chance of the object being turned against itself, from within itself as the alterity of the subject opens the subject to the question, that is, to reading, through the seemingly untheoretical gestures offered by Homi Bhabha, which address the condition of reading otherwise as part of a "commitment to theory": "reading between the lines," "reading . . . against the grain," "progressive reading."[21] None of these can be read as naming a reading program. Nor can they be transformed into a program, a method, or template for a procedure. Throwing a spanner in the works of the narrowly political reading, they disable any possibility of a technics of reading (which would not be reading at all, as we have argued). However, they do suggest a reading activity, which is only similar to itself in being reading, and yet is different in each event, and is marked as different not only from other readings, but also as the difference (of reading) from within the apparent unity of the discursive object. Each phrase appears commonplace enough. So much so, in fact, that we might be tempted to take them for granted, not reading their significance as expressions of the "mask of camouflage," to cite Bhabha. In naming a movement of reading that resists a unity of definition or the *pure teleology of analysis,* such phrases are *camouflage* or *mask* without the suggestion of anything beneath or beyond. Thus, in the very act of reading itself, reading swerves away from the implication that there is a final meaning that can be read, beyond reading and to which reading is subservient. Reading denies the end of reading, that we can have done with reading.

V

Reading continues, therefore. Never the same, reading swerves. It deviates from itself and within itself. This is not simply a dialectical or oppositional movement. It is, rather, the necessary and inevitable movement by which reading proceeds, even if reading becomes, or is always, misreading. This is the mark of a difference that makes possible the rhythm of reading, whereby it becomes the inscription of a countersignature to another text, a translation, in that oscillation between a reading and a writing. This is the case, even if there is that necessary sense of identification between the reader and what is read. Indeed, that deviation of the countersignature, the act of close reading that projects the alterity of the text being read, is itself unavoidably traced—even as it haunts or traces—the question of identification. Reading always takes time, therefore. It proceeds across time, as a matter of multiple temporalities: those of the reader and the narrator, for example. Furthermore, reading takes place, continues to take place, across time. From one reader to another, from one poet to another. At the same time, this suggests, as is well known, that reading remains and, as already intimated, there is reading to come. Reading thus becomes caught in the impossible double bind. Seeking to abolish the distance between that on which it discourses and the manner of its act, it will never entirely take the place of what it attempts to read, even though we take the time to read of that displacement.

Of course, to paraphrase and twist Nicholas Royle just a little, there is reading and then there is reading, even if one, or the other, is, if not *not* reading, then the failure of reading, or, from the other side, the resistance to reading.[22] It is becoming apparent that there are matters of orientation and disorientation with which we should concern ourselves. The situation of reading always dictates this. It is an issue of relationship, of relation between nonrelation perhaps, expressed in the suggestion that we read as philosophers, as opposed, let us say, to reading in a deterministic or technical fashion. There is also the question of how we situate ourselves in relation to a representation of a representation, to the private act, the public discourse, or to the readerly text. There is the matter of orientation in the face of a resistance to theory in the name of reading, a *reading-toward-socialism*, or the matter of learning how to read that accent of deviation that determines the reading of others. There is, furthermore, the situation of reading and its orientation to that which apparently prohibits or proscribes reading, yet which, nonetheless, situates itself as a reading between the lines or against the grain. All of which leaves us with the secret and the confession, offered by Hélène Cixous: "Everything we read: remains."[23] This statement simultaneously keeps its secrets and reveals them, placing them in plain view, in the light of day. Do we know how to read this? Can we begin to orient ourselves? This performative sentence disorganizes ahead and in the event of reading's efforts all reading, simply considered. It disjoints the time of reading as any simple time. Giving everything away at once, Cixous's words speak of attempted readings in the past and the very idea of readings to come. There is no essential unity to this remark. In its disunity the statement is a reading—perhaps even the most *real* of performances, commentary in the guise of reading—of all acts of reading properly considered, at once the most obvious and (because of that) the most repeatedly forgotten, concerning the nature of reading. In forgetting the condition, the disorientation of which Cixous writes, readers seek to raise, explicitly or implicitly, acts of reading to the level of a generality.

What disorganises here? What installs the disunity into the sentence and, therefore, its reading? A very little thing, indeed. Almost nothing. Silent. Inarticulate. The mute sign of a certain passage, a processing, disarticulating the time of reading in the event of reading. The colon, that which is, at one and the same time, the greater part of the large intestine, the guts and the punctuating pause of intermediate length, marking a distinct break in either a sentence or a rhythmical period. More commonly, it is that punctuation that signs the discontinuity of grammatical construction, usually, though not always, indicating antithesis, illustration, quotation, or listing.

This disturbance in continuity and rhythm serves to direct our reading both backwards and forwards, even while what remains toward, as, the end of the sentence—*remains*—might be read as that which is antithetical, illustrative, or the citation of the clause with which the sentence begins. *Remains* thus names everything and nothing as such. It names what we have left behind in our acts of reading, those remains of texts, for example, for which our readings have been unable to account, and which, therefore, remain as yet unread, and still to be read. The remains of reading remain. As such, they remain as the unread, past and future, at the same time, though not the same time at all, in the temporal disorganization of reading. Remains thus names the very undecidability that reading encounters, which close acts of reading open to the reader, and, concomitantly, project the reader toward future readings, as, once again, the responsibility of reading, in the face of the undecidable: (of that which) *remains*. Through Cixous's formulation, we can learn to read this, even as we are put in the position of not knowing quite how to situate ourselves, how to orient our reading of this statement. What we can read, nevertheless, is that Cixous's statement, enacting the condition of reading, inscribes the inescapable circumstance or predicament faced in *every-thing we read*. Everything remains.

Here is one possible reading, another, one of several. It says and does not say the same. It says it without saying it. Without the plural subject, without the community of readers, this phrase, *everything remains*, addresses what reading fails to grasp, what it leaves behind, what it does not read, while, all the while, and as the remainder of the statement, it reminds us that everything remains to be read. The impossible logic of this statement only compounds, condenses, and yet opens out what is to be read in Hélène Cixous's remark. There is no getting around or, for that matter, beyond this. However we seek to read this sentence, we always come back to reading.

Might it be possible to stabilize the statement by recourse to its context? There is that remark already cited, a chance observation, made by Clarice Lispector, and brought back in writing by Cixous, as the reported words of another. But it is still a question of the remains, the remainder, what remains, and, specifically, unread—what Cixous calls "this unknown untorn page"[24]—unknown, untorn, unwritten, not yet written, not yet read, already written, but not yet read. The untorn page, a rem(a)inder, of all that comes before the printed, published word, which Cixous so desires, and yet, also, secret, hidden from view, neither there nor not there; but then, of course, "not everyone carries out the act of reading in the same way"[25] even if the assumption has been, occasionally, that there is only one way to read. Cixous also acknowledges that guilt that is indissociable from reading, which is: "also a clandestine, furtive act. . . . First we must steal the key to the library. . . . Reading is eating the forbidden fruit, making forbidden love."[26] We read guiltily, and therein is its pleasure, that indescribable sensation that can only be obtained through escape, secrecy, and consumption. Reading consumes our worldly identities even as we consume (in) reading: the sensual reciprocity with the other, that pleasure that comes only in giving oneself up to all that is forbidden. The greatest pleasure is in doing it in secret, but right before everyone else, in plain view.[27] But still, *not everyone carries out the act of reading in the same way,* which perhaps may explain in part the pleasure, without getting any closer to the secret. Every act of reading is singular, even—especially—the act of rereading. Reading names escape for Cixous, an escape that is simultaneously a movement into the word and out of the world. In this, reading is comparable to writing, and it is in this comparison that reading is defined here, even though not every act of reading is the same, and *not everyone carries out reading in the same way*. The act of reading imagined by Cixous is traced in that ineluctable slippage, from a reading to a writing that marks all true reading. However, even as we acknowledge this to be the case, we still have to understand to what extent the provisional definition of reading that Cixous provides in *Three Steps on the Ladder of Writing* does not reduce reading to a uniform practice, a shared act that is the same for everyone or the same every time.

Thus, there is read in this oscillation the difficult negotiation between singularity and generality, between what is singular in the act of reading and what is iterable, which iterability makes known paradoxically, the singularity of the act, through its transmissibility. The transition effected in reading/writing is, for Cixous, the passage out, into another world, while being also the escape into the forbidden library. (It is forbidden to the extent that the key *must* be stolen.) In being explained, such secretive, solitary passage nonetheless gives nothing away. It is this perhaps that confuses, as much as the significance of reading. Reading thus escapes, taking flight ahead of all attempted acts of reading, any single definition of what reading might or might not be. Its secret significance lies in the fact that *we don't acknowledge it*, even though, paradoxically again, it appears that reading is only accorded recognition as that which is insignificant. Yet, in assigning this insignificance to reading, a reading—which is also an evasion as well as an identity for reading which allows it to avoid definition—is imposed.

How then does Cixous name reading, without naming it? How does she identify the very situation that reading makes possible, which is itself, and which it gives access to for the reader, without pinning reading down to the act of reading carried out in the same way? What is the silent name readable between the lines as a possible figure for reading? *Hejira*—that departure from home, from family and friends. This departure transforms, translating the reading subject. It makes possible change and freedom. If reading escapes, however, there is always that predicament for the reader that reading departs ahead of the act. The reader can never catch up, nowhere more so than in that very moment when reading slides into writing, into eating, into *forbidden love*. And then again: *a real reader is already on the way to writing*.[28] this describes what it is to read, while accounting for the fact that we have not yet done with reading, and that we cannot keep up with its movement. This marks an encounter with the unreadable, that moment when, far from bringing reading to a crashing

halt, the reader is faced with the compelling evidence that reading must
continue. Reading can occur only at another moment, elsewhere, not
here, not now, not for good. This is read by Cixous in that concession of
what reading changes. Reading remains unreadable to that extent that
reading must begin again.[29] Already on the way to reading, there is, in the
negotiation between what can be said about reading and what is unreadable, the tacit articulation of the remark that has already escaped and that
speaks of reading's flight.

If reading flees, if the text evades absolute definition while providing
a possible means of escape, there are occasions when a certain resemblance of reading, perhaps nothing more than an apparition, will return
to haunt the scene of the crime. There is a ghost here, at work. The
other, that which *presents itself as simultaneously* read, haunts Timothy
Clark's words:

> It is again a question of "the other" . . . this term names the event in
> poetry, meaning and inscription which escapes human control,
> grounding or anticipation. . . . The *other* is engaged in writing in terms
> of an ineluctable secondarity in written meaning—for even in being in-
> scribed the written presents itself as simultaneously *read* through the
> resonance of significations unanticipated in the act of inscription. . . .
> The other names the space "of deferred reciprocity between reading
> and writing."[30]

There is in this remark a deliberate performative operation perhaps, an
improper citation that comes and goes without duration, almost too
quickly. It is a question of speed, the speed at which the other, the spectre
or revenant, returns, and, in returning, will have retreated. The frequency
of telecommunication interrupts the calm surface of the page. Words interrupt the expression of the other within the writing of the citation. A
resonance is established that is irreducible. Clark's writing presents itself
as simultaneously *read,* even as it seeks to read, and, in so doing, to write,
the figure of the other countersigns the act of writing. In this, the signature of the other, that inscription of the unanticipated event within whatever we seek to write as a reading, appears to read our text. As "the other"
names that event, so *event* is a kind of naming. *Event* names not the place
of the other, for this would be to assign, however implicitly, the aura of a
static unity for the other, although this is only dimly apprehended. Instead, it should be understood that *event* names, not the place, to reiter-

ate the point, but what takes place. What takes place in the event, as the taking place of the event that is named by Clark the other, is that act of *unanticipated* reading. Reading, as we have said, takes time, and *event* names the time of reading, even if, such time, escaping human control, is not our time—not my time, not your time. The time of reading, that of the event of secondarity *and* simultaneity, is, thus, untimely, never quite at the same time (even as itself).

However, if the *event* that the other's reading marks is that of a temporal displacement within and against the act of writing, then the other is also comprehended as a spacing. The other at work in our writing, and which makes the writing possible, not only effects a displacement as that necessary temporal possibility of a writing, it also spaces writing and, in doing so, makes it available to another reading. Writing as a reading remains unfinished therefore. Displaced in its own movement and response to the other, writing begins to slide immediately into the place of secondarity, into the place of what remains to be read. This is readable to the extent that the passage remains unreadable, although it strives to read, in part, that other discussion of reading that, in being written about, comes back, presenting Clark's writing as, itself, *simultaneously read*. In this situation, Clark's writing/reading reveals the condition of every text. Always remaining to be read, the text is unreadable, inasmuch as it cannot be decisively determined. As Clark's discussion of Derrida returns to Derrida, and as Derrida returns via Clark, so this act of following the movement of Clark's inscription *and* that countermovement, the back-and-forth within Timothy Clark's text of Derrida's writing—which is also a reading concerning the difficulty of reading conclusively when seeking to negotiate with the other in writing—fails to read in its act the reiteration of those prior texts. Furthermore, this pursuance of textual doubling, in opening this movement, in "opening" a movement that has already undergone a process of unfolding, tacitly acknowledges through the abyssal structure onto which it is entering that it will itself be subject to repetition, displaced through other writings, other readings, as the citation from the text of Timothy Clark both implies and performs.

Derrida's return ghosts through Clark's own prose. In a sporadic, attenuated fashion, his critical negotiation between reading and writing addresses us: *secondarity . . . written meaning presents itself . . . simultaneously read*. This is not a question of a general hauntedness in the passage, so much as the fact that, in the citation, Derrida's words rhythmically interrupt, while simultaneously dictating Clark's writing as the other's resonance. We are witness to the situation of force and signification that inscribes the written, disrupting the reading process, as *the other is engaged in writing in terms of an ineluctable secondarity within meaning.* The signification at work here is not that of one text's simple reference to another, to a prior text. Clark's passage is, in some sense, a paraphrase of and countersignature for Derrida's "Force and Signification," though it does not escape its haunted condition. The emergence of the "prior" text, re-citing itself and prescribing the writing comprises its own signification, at the expense of critical commentary, and enacting in an unanticipated fashion that *power of repetition in alterity.* The *affirmation and nonfulfillment* that entail all acts of reading are, and will continue to be, remarked here. And so too is that guilty acknowledgment of complicity that articulates the oscillation between every reading/writing.

If complete escape is impossible, it is still possible to consider the possibility to come, in or through some im/possible relation. To appear to read schematically, and yet to move elsewhere. To transport reading, in the act of reading, beyond the merely schematic, or otherwise across that boundary established in a reading that seemingly halts in a gesture of closure or finality. To repeat, in order to give *oneself up to textual repetition* and yet, through that very rhythmic recurrence of repetition, that coda in which is traced the structure of a writing, to open within that form the space where reading projects itself as still to come, not as the possible moment of closure in the future, but as the unfulfillable promise of reading's futurity, and, with that, its structural openness.

The availability of alterity is only possible through repetition, through the spacing staged by the reiterative reading of commentary. Reading thus takes place as the event made possible by the spacing of the other, the other's spacing within the self-same that repetition appears to enact. This space or moment of alterity is readable, it might be suggested, in that reading of the first step. Acknowledging that there is never a first step that is not always already a movement of repetition, we read the irreducible interval installed by the very gesture of reading. Moreover, repetition can be said to name certain *rhetorical* or *tropological* structures, along with *figuration*, which remain singular while being readable as repetitious in condition. It is thus part of the very fabric of the text, one aspect of textuality itself. In repeating the structure of the text through reading, it is necessary to read that repetition, even as repetition becomes repeated in the attempt to read carefully and faithfully. It is very much a matter of reading *textually*, as Paul de Man puts it, in relation to the "resistance to theory," which, he argues,

> is a resistance to the rhetorical or tropological dimension of language, a dimension which is perhaps more explicitly in the foreground in literature (broadly conceived) than in other verbal manifestations or—to be somewhat less vague—which can be revealed in any verbal event when it is read textually. Since grammar as well as figuration is an integral part of reading, it follows that reading will be a negative process in which the grammatical cognition is undone, at all times, by its rhetorical displacement.[31]

However, it is precisely in the face of reading *textually* that there has been such resistance. De Man's identification of the *resistance to theory* is, in the rhetorical maneuvering of this passage, also a resistance to acts of reading, where the *act* and *reading* name a certain response to the other ungovernable by any program. Does this then imply that *reading* can be equated with *theory*? Is the former a synonym (of sorts) of the latter? Or do these terms relate to one another only in that manner of a "non-symmetrical and non–totalizable relation?"[32] Is there discernible a certain rhetorical displacement as the effect of reading *the resistance to theory*?

VI

What should be clear by now is that what interests me here, throughout every twist and turn, detour, and return concerning reading is this issue of theory and, implicitly, that which de Man names *the resistance to theory*. If, as we have already seen, that which goes under the name *theory* is/was read from particular perspectives as merely formalist in its orientation, then, from the other side, so to speak, that side that is observed by Paul de Man from where resistance is organized and projected, *theory* might be read as being "too political."[33] As a nontotalizable and heterogeneous ensemble of reading practices or acts, *theory* went, and continues to go, beyond the bounds of what constitutes reading, through the insistence, on different occasions and in different voices, in asking political questions.

Of course, *theory* does have a particular institutional history and identity, peculiar to Anglo-American universities, where it has come to be defined. This is well known and much discussed.[34] The identification of "theory," whether on the part of those who are in favor of "it," or by those who resist, is in some measure an act of reading that has stopped. The resistance to theory, which is still there, is, in so many ways (not least in its institutional acceptance in a process of auto-immunization), and before anything else, a resistance to reading, as de Man makes plain. Moreover, it is, clearly enough, a political resistance, inasmuch as it the gesture of obstruction is constituted through resistance to reading in particular ways. Those whose voices are organized in this manner, whose commentaries stop short of reading, or who read with a kind of journalistic haste, are not only resisting readers (if they are even this). They are, as Shoshana Felman makes clear, "resisting reading for the sake of holding on to our ideologies and preconceptions."[35] Reading is displaced, brought to a violent halt by the assumption that what is termed within the institution *theory* and what Paul de Man calls reading *textually* has been read and, therefore, should not be read, should no longer be read, should never be read again, unless within carefully prescribed parameters.

Such resistance to reading, while no doubt having something of the affirmative, not to say, evangelical aura about its oppositionality, is, nevertheless, if not wholly, then certainly in some measure, an act of surveillance, structured by negativity and prohibition, All of this is familiar, undoubtedly. Yet in the face of not reading, and in the face of the prohibition against reading in various ways that manifests itself in the shape of resistance, naming reading *theory* so as to displace reading with greater economy and efficacy, it bears repetition. Despite the familiarity, the asymmetrical transport between reading/not-reading remains in operation. If you are reading this, you are no doubt situated on the left of the divide. ("Left" in this case refers to a purely spatial relationship, not necessarily to a political determination.) If you are not, in any sense of not-reading, you're not. This is all merely reorientation of course, albeit a necessary process in order that we might return to reading and, in particular, reading *textually* if we are not to be forced into the position of idle, and accused, readers. Found guilty of reading *textually*, we would be sentenced to be plunged into idleness.

De Man's response to the question of resistance is to describe exactly what shifts the ground, and so displaces rhetorically, tropologically, figuratively, all anticipation of definition that it is the operation of resistance to produce. His description requires that we read the displacement at work in the first sentence of the fragment, so that what is resisted is exactly that *rhetorical or tropological dimension that can be revealed in any verbal event when it is read textually.* The sentence is frequently in danger of slipping away altogether, as it modifies and transposes its attention, situating, defining, rejecting definition, pausing parenthetically to prepare for the final statement, where *any verbal event* is in some measure a nonsynonymous substitution[36] for that object of institutionally approved reading, *literature.* In this wayward sentence, the figure of *literature* operates in at least two opposing directions, and is made clear by Philippe Lacoue-Labarthe: "the figure is never *one.* Not only is it the Other, but there is no unity or stability of the figural; the imago has no fixity or proper being. There is no 'proper image' with which to identify totally, no essence of the imaginary." It is precisely the displacement within the term of the totalizing ontology effected through a registration of the excess acknowledged by Lacoue-Labarthe that we need to read, in order to see how, in being the contested ground on which the struggle for reading occurs, the word needs to be read as a figure that disfigures.[37] There is perhaps most immediately available the narrow sense of the word, especially given the context within which reading is being discussed. *Literature* names narrowly forms of writing, whether poetry or prose, fiction or essay, that have been judged to have an established and, perhaps, even unequivocal aesthetic value. It has been read and subsequently judged of being suitable for further reading—though only in a specific custom. Nevertheless, *literature* can also be read as naming the movement of writing in a more general way.

Reading this contest between a more restricted and more open value for the term *literature,* we would suggest that the necessity for reading *textually* could be located here. There is installed the (dis)figuration of displacement that de Man argues for in the face of the *resistance to theory.* It is this displacement that *resisting readings* are incapable of reading, which institutes within the reading that resists, the resistance of reading, the resistance to what remains to be read. Displacement within *literature,* displacement from and within itself as a supposedly univocal identity, offers a glimpse of what reading might effect. It performs the slippage we named earlier the nonsynonymous substitution: from *literature* to *any verbal event.* Which is already a translation, where *any verbal event* is already silently written into *literature,* and which is what slips away, even as we attempt to grasp it. If we are to begin to be "good readers," we must at least acknowledge that which always slips away, in that very moment when we believe reading has taken hold.

To admit to the image of reading as always leaving something behind, of being unable to grasp at everything, will worry some and infuriate others. However, reading entails risk. It is an act that takes risks, which is itself risking everything in the event of reading, because reading opens itself to the other, and to the chance encounter with textuality. This is why reading of a certain kind, whether reading to escape, reading guiltily, reading textually, or reading while acknowledging that there are remains and that no mastery over one's subject is possible, finally, is referred to by Timothy Clark as an act or an event. The act of reading is risky precisely because nothing is decided ahead of the event. Reading should not bring with it a program or method, but should, instead, proceed step by step. In this way, reading not only opens itself, it remains open to the force imposed upon it by the structure of the text, that which causes the reading to swerve. Thus, it might be said, reading must involve itself in, and be constituted by, a politics of openness, as well by a politics of the opening. Such a politics would no doubt be altogether a much more open and, therefore, risky, affair than that reading that is, as we have seen, either the manifestation—or, perhaps, the manifesto—of a resistance to theory, which is, arguably, precisely the opposite of a politics of openness in being so governed by and directed toward an eschato-ideological instance of arrival.

In both the examples just remarked and previously considered, there is, albeit in different ways, the very opposite of either risk or openness (and being open necessitates risking oneself). It is not simply enough to say that the resistance to theory or *reading-toward-socialism* (for example) are simply both examples of not-reading or the limits of reading, although they are, when read from certain perspectives. Rather, both examples, and others like them, are often expressions of the negotiation between reading and not reading, and between reading within limits and toward a limit. Though ostensibly different, and articulating within conventional discursive parameters a politics of an imagined Right and of the Left, both resistance to theory and reading-toward-socialism operate according to an economics of reading, in which reading is organized according to the Law.

Thus, the very risk of taking risks in reading (which itself cannot be programmed), in being open to that which is unreadable ahead of the event or in the very act itself, is that effort in which reading must read its encounter with the limit, which occurs all too often in the name of the limit we know as politics. While politically motivated reading of a revolutionary or oppositional nature has come about historically, as Shoshana Felman argues,[38] because of the desire to confront the limit, this has frequently resulted in the redefinition, the reconstruction, and the reintroduction of limits. Yet the risk that cannot be avoided is the encounter with, and the consequences of, that which "can never be known in advance."[39] There is always the chance of coming face to face with that which, in the event of reading, will disarm all protocols, all programs, all methodologies, all self-circumscribing modes of exegesis. We cannot account for this, nor can we anticipate it, and it is precisely this in/conceivable encounter that we hazard every time we read. Felman gives us to understand the risky double bind in which reading places us, in our relation, as readers, to the text, to textuality in general. While we can conceive the likelihood of "finding in the text something one does not expect,"[40] nevertheless, we cannot conceive what, exactly, it is we will find. We will never be able to resist the unimaginable.

Yet, if reading is proscribed ahead of the act, as a general principle by which a community of readers, so-called, agrees at what point reading is to be resisted, the unexpected, can be, if not avoided, then denied. Felman imagines the "resisting" or politicized reader who can always, in effect, end up resisting reading.[41] We have already seen this at work, and not only in the examples of the *resistance to theory* or *reading-toward-socialism*, which may be read, coincidentally, as offering a dualistic model akin to Felman's own proffered examples of the "chauvinist or feminist."[42] This effect of resisting reading is remarked in other ways: by Althusser in his acknowledgment that reading was not carried out, as "economists, historians, philologists";[43] by Barthes as "the literary institution,"[44] where, as he informs us (as will be recalled), reading is nothing more than a referendum. The resisting reader who, together with other resisting readers come together to offer a *resistance to theory*, demand nothing less than an excuse for reading, what Bhabha describes as "a pure teleology of analysis whereby the prior principle is simply augmented . . . its identity . . . consistently confirmed."[45] The figure of *resisting reading* desires not only constant confirmation but what goes by the name of mastery. And what this comes down to is the question of what it means to read. What we read in Felman's commentary is how the movement of reading, when subsumed by the movement of politics, or, more dangerously, the political movement, comes to a halt. No longer in motion, reading stops.

VII

There would appear to be a certain anxiety concerning reading. This fear, produced in the face of the unreadable and the prospect of reading-to-come, is related to an anxiety concerning identity. The acts of reading that call a halt to reading's motion are either explicitly or implicitly concerned with reading up to a point. That point is the constitution of the subject or the subject's identity, whether by identity we mean the individual reader or a reading community seeking to define itself. Michel Foucault addresses this:

> Seneca stresses the point: the practice of the self involves reading, for one could not draw everything from one's own stock or arm oneself by oneself with the principles of reason that are indispensable for self-conduct. . . . But reading and writing must not be dissociated. . . . If too much writing is exhausting . . . excessive reading has a scattering effect. . . . By going from book to book, without ever stopping . . . one is liable to retain nothing, to spread oneself across different thoughts, and to forget oneself. Writing, as a way of gathering in the reading that was done and of collecting one's thoughts about it, is an exercise of reason that counters the great deficiency of *stultitia,* which endless reading may favour.[46]

Situating or orientating the self involves reading and does so, furthermore, in relation to an act of writing, which is, itself, part of the process of reading he describes. In this process, writing gathers reading, which, according to Seneca, when pursued in too desultory a fashion becomes excessive and scatters or fragments the self. Does this fear of excess not name the fear of endless reading that is encountered in what is named the *resistance to theory*, or in those who are named *resisting* readers, who resist *reading*?

The very idea that one could read too much is itself a construction, or, perhaps, an alibi, for calling a halt to the act. Reading must desist for the good of the self. The idea that reading might prove to be *excessive* suggests the fear of an overflowing of limits. Behind this figure of *excessive reading* is a utilitarian anxiety. What happens to what we have read, if we do not put it to some use? What happens to all that reading, if we fail to perform like the worker bees Foucault imagines, transforming our reading into writing? Reading has to be put to work, has to be translated into a writing, as a means of curbing excess.

Excessive reading is not the only name given to the fear. It is also termed *endless reading. Gathering. Collecting. Taking. Exercise.* These words name the imposition of limits on reading, limits that suggest a form of economism, of self-disciplining, and self-organization. The self has to be placed within, subjected to, a regime wherein reading is curtailed and made to perform for a purpose, the purpose of giving meaning to the self. Otherwise, the self is scattered. The subject is spread *across different thoughts*. Unable to keep everything in mind, incapable of retaining all that is deemed an excess—and thereby speaking indirectly, without definition, of an appropriate amount, the right measure, so to speak—the self will *forget oneself*. Too much reading makes one *forget oneself*. The self is liable to be lost in the textual field, consumed by the other. Seneca's anxious recommendations for self-discipline appear to anticipate the very possibility of *escape*. There is a sense behind the precautionary prohibitions concerning too much reading that what must be avoided at all costs is the risk of the unexpected.

Anticipating excess means to anticipate the effacing of the self's limits, and thereby circumvent this through the *gathering in* that is writing. While this speaks of a certain possible dissolution of a purely psychic subjectivity (the self itself overflows, overflowing itself through the encounter with the textual excess), the metaphors of *gathering, collecting, exercise, taking* figure a predominantly physical activity, with which writing might be aligned. Reading, on the other hand—how might we define that? As a mental process? Certainly. But there is also the encounter between the self and the object that we call the book, which is in part physical. To read is both an act and an action. It already crosses boundaries, and cannot be confined solely by a definition that describes only physical or psychic activity. It involves both aspects of the self and thus, in engaging the self, denies either an isolated meaning free from the other.

The effect of *excessive reading* is to produce in the self not only that scattering, the fragmentation and dispersal of selfhood, but also, and especially, a specific form of the deregulation of the self. Too much reading or reading of the wrong kind makes you lose reason. What excess of reading points to, then, is not simply excess, that is, *too much reading*, but all reading pursued without its eventual subordination to routines of regulated, productive physical activity. It is not that there can be too much reading or something called *excessive reading*, as distinct, say, from reading within limits (even though this is the Senecan scenario as the excuse for the policing of reading). Instead, we must read that *all* reading *is* excessive. However, If the self is revealed as becoming fragmented through the act of reading, this is a formula that may be read either as "if reading reveals the fragmentation of the self or if the self's fragmentation comes about through the act of reading"; on which of these remarks shall we decide? Which is the more immediately readable? It is important to acknowledge the double, contradictory movement of reading, that which is revealed in the event and yet which, it must be admitted, is, after a fashion, always already installed, *textually*, so to speak, and is also *not yet*. Such is the effect and sign of excess, as the disordering of temporality implicit in reading. This is expressed in the following disorientating formula of Werner Hamacher's, which indicates a constant oscillation, perhaps the articulation of an idling effect, between an unspecified proximal past and a future to-come, neither of which can be resolved into a present, or reduced to a stabilizing center: "[r]eading is still not yet what it already is."[47] The temporal and spatial disruption of this phrase makes it (partially readable as) almost unreadable. Structured around the immanence, the glimpse, and the promise of reading, it nonetheless resists becoming that which would be most desired: a calm(ed) and calming supplementary analytical commentary, which would not only have moved beyond the text but would also have assumed a position outside the text prior to reading (as though such a thing were possible).

Reading is not yet what it already is. How to come to terms with the seeming paradox that Werner Hamacher traces, follows, unfolds, and patiently lays out? The passage from which this remark concerning an impossible temporality is taken is worth citing at length:

> For even before the reading reproduces the sense of absolute knowing, whether affirmatively or *ex negativo*, through its supplementary interpretive addition to the text, the reading in question has already entered the circle of the text, already become an immanent moment of its movement. . . . And even before the reading becomes what it already is, even before it enters the dialectical circle of cognition . . . this reading

is still not yet what it already is, still halts before the threshold of its
origin and falls short of its destination, arrives too early—and too late—
for itself and its consciousness, and thereby opens out its hermeneutic–dialectical circle into a parabola. Although the reading does not
approach its text in an external fashion, it is not yet the immanent
movement of self-reproduction which it already is. The reading . . .
must commence from the not yet in the unity of the not yet and the already present: at a remove from that unity of arche and telos which
would constitute the finally successful reading itself as identical with
the system of absolute self-consciousness. For the dialectical logos the
reading remains an endless foreword, one which transforms the logos
into an anticipation of itself and without which that logos could not
exist; a supplementary addition which reveals the final conclusion always already drawn by the system to be open after all. The reading introduces its "self" into the circle of synthesis as a difference that cannot
be synthesized.

This difference, which has both logical and phenomenological,
structural and temporal determinants, is the condition for the reproduction of the text in its reading, and through those traits of delay, of
remainder, of anticipation which it introduces into every act of interpretation, this difference presents the dialectical operation of reading
with an insuperable obstacle at the very entrance to the dialectical circle: an incorrigible deviation from meaning's path and process of meaning towards itself. . . . A reading which wishes to elude the suction of the
dialectical circle as far as possible, in order to put itself in a position to
descry the structure and dynamic of this circle, must begin precisely
from these remnants of its own activity in the text, from that which it is
not yet itself, or which it no longer itself is. It must begin, therefore, not
merely from the logical structure and the systematic implications of
such remnants, but also from the metaphoricity of the text and the
phantasmic dimension which is at work in it, from the as it were literary character.[48]

A number of readers are located here. There is the reader already implied in the immanence of the *already is*. There is Hamacher, the reader
who reads himself moving through the impossible figure of reading.
And there are others. This phrase maps the doubling contours of the
passage we have before us, a passage, which, we might add, is nothing
other than the passage of reading, *in* reading, via *delay, remainder*, and

anticipation. The passage described and enacted by Hamacher is the passage in and through which passage is both summarized and enacted, although this is not yet a reading. The phrase announces the incalculable difficulties encountered in pursuing the very condition of reading. Reading takes time, but it is impossible to find the right time for reading, the appropriate rhythm. Hamacher's phrase, *even before*, names the difficulty and assigns to reading the status of what he calls an "endless foreword." At the risk of being reductive or too schematic, it is worth staying with this remark.

Even before. Here is the location of reading where the act is *still not yet what it already is*, otherwise reiterated as the *immanent movement of self-reproduction that it already is*, and named the *not yet*. Hamacher calls this a unity—*the unity of the not yet and the already present*—though this is, it has to be confessed, a strange unity, traced irreducibly by that double trait, a doubling that is also the division that structures all reading, disjointing ahead of any reading, reading/unreadability, as what remains to be read. *Even before* appears to mark a simple temporality, an a priori location of the dilemma written in the impossible structure of *not yet/already is*, or *not yet/already present*. Location, therefore, as dislocation, past *and* future, though neither as present, as we have already stated. For, if the *even before* seems to be the inscription of the *a priori* in returning to us ahead of the passage, it also displaces the apparently straightforward temporality of its statement in returning that which has yet to be recognized, which is *immanent* and *not yet*. Thus, if I am to admit the force of these two words, I must learn how to read that which is inescapable and, yet, which cannot be read. In doing so, I have to understand how the phrase announces *delay*, *deviation*, and *anticipation*. Such an understanding involves that written engagement *of* and *in* writing/reading, where the necessary and ineluctable trembling and contagion of reading opens the aporetic we name responsibility, and through which, in response, comes the equally necessary and ineluctable movement of repetition.

In attempting to read, we get nowhere, and yet there is movement somewhere else. *Even before* we have got to the end of this citation, which we have anticipated, we have got no further than the paradoxical dis/location of the *even before*, which always names a step backwards, before the idea of the beginning, while inscribing the temporality of an *always-yet-to-come*. Never external to the text, neither the program by which we bring the text under control, nor the meaning rendered by the act of reading, *reading does not approach its text in an external fashion.* An *endless foreword,* reading remains that figure of difference-within, the saying or giving, the apparitioning, of the other, that reading can never synthesize as such. It does not becomes itself. Reading cannot, through in the form of the supplementary addition, complete and thus close the *hermeneutic-dialectical circle.* Nor, through the act of interpretation, can it utilize what remains, finally, as part of a movement of *meaning toward itself.* Reading's wayward movement deconstructs the *dialectical operation even before* the circular enclosure gets under way.

Realizing all the problems, all the impossibilities, Hamacher nonetheless seeks for a reading movement that will find a motion appropriate to reading. Such a re-citation involves the consideration of *remnants, metaphoricity,* and the *phantasmatic.* Reading must begin again, *from the as it were literary character.* This expression, *as it were,* names, as it were, what cannot quite be named. Yet it also signals that which, in its name, indicates through indirection what is proximate to the trace, the remnant, the ruin, fragment or (what) *remains,* as it were. Were we to turn Hamacher's projection of a reading that eludes *the suction of the dialectical circle* toward his own text, we might discern the operation of *metaphoricity,* the *phantasmatic dimension,* the *literary character* in this singular and proximal remark: *as it were.*

This phrase installs movement, yet interrupts the flow, as it were. Through the act of coming close, but in not being, exactly, the expression of *literary character* itself, in intimating that the expression (in this case, *literary character,* which is, itself, already insufficient, inasmuch as it is a nonsynonymous substitution, a supplement, for *the metaphoricity of the text* and *the phantasmatic dimension,* none of which are, themselves, phrases that can govern the play at work in the semantic chain or act as master terms) is not enough, never enough, never that exactly which impels, propels, and compels the act of reading, the phrase, *as it were,* opens that which is already under way, the movement of difference, while re-marking the excessive trace in language.

Consider also, momentarily, the metaphors of the text, several of which are structural or spatial. Circles, parabolas, entrance, obstacle, path. Such figures sketch for reading its own haunted or phantasmatic structure, where reading must navigate an unmappable topography, an impossible architecture or architexture. The circle and path particularly invoke the ghost of Heidegger and a certain structural configuration of the inescapability of the metaphysical. The figure of the path suggests the figure of an eventual return to the house of meaning, despite delays or obstacles, where arrival is always already written into departure. *Not yet what it already is*, reading is both divided and suspended. This is its double bind. However, to read as metaphors, the *as it were literary character*, those very figures that seek to hide their figuration, that is, their metaphoricity, in their appeal to *structure* and the *systematic*, are we not thereby placing ourselves in a certain relationship with the movement of the text, from within its contours? Reading circle, path, obstacle, entrance as the remnants of an inescapable structure, a structure in ruin, where the remains of structure remain to be read—herein is the possibility of acknowledging the to-come of reading, *as it were*. At the same time, however, these figures keep the secret of their figurality by placing themselves in plain view. If their secret is maintained, if they are not read as the remnants or ruins of the literary, then it has to be understood that the difficulty rests in the act of reading. We are taught to read in such a way within a certain discourse, named by Hamacher as the *hermeneutic-dialectical circle*, so as not to read this figurality. Seeing the circle for what it is, reading the *as it were literary character* of the figure rather than its *structural or systematic* truth, we reach the moment at least where we realize the necessity for leaving the path.

This is the chance reading imposes on us, the chance we have to take, and the chance also by which reading might happen, if it happens at all. In the words of Thomas Keenan, "[t]here is no road for reading, no path or method: simply the effort and the fatigue of the difficult chance. As chance, reading and its inability defy calculation in advance, refuse prediction."[49] The element of *chance* in reading should be not only that which we have to acknowledge, along with Keenan. It should also be recognized as a governing factor in the event of reading that disorganizes all institutionalizing and programming efforts. Chance has to be maintained—but how can we do this, without seeking to resort back to some calculation?—if reading is to continue, if the reading act is to be truly a response, and undertaken responsibly. Therefore, despite the persistence of the metaphor of the road or path, it has to be acknowledged, even before reading has the possibility of getting under way, that *there is no road for reading, no path or method*. In spelling this out, Keenan does not so much move beyond Hamacher's commentary as he abandons all pretense of the path as a structure or route on which reading may pursue or from which it deviates. Reading, in this reading, *and its inability*, affirm waywardness, disorientation, and the disjunctive encounter through which occurs transformation—of reading, of the self—as the affirmative resistance to the calculable, and to prejudgments or presuppositions or, indeed, prediction.

If there is a certain sense here of the text folding back upon itself, bringing the probability of reading to a halt in the act of a turn that also resembles a return (whereby we return to earlier issues, even in the doubling gesture of their return through the offices of reading to us), this is inescapably the effect of reading, as well as a sign of what it means to read responsibly. Repetition increases incrementally. It adds to itself in the process of reading, even as it displaces the effects read in earlier articulations. This is part of the inevitable and incalculable *chance* in which we involve ourselves *in* and *by* reading. It explains why, as Keenan puts it, we *return to what is impossible for us*. We seek out the contours of that which we desire to read and, in doing so, countersign those features, those figures in an encounter that both transforms and doubles, lovingly and violently. Reading, which must proceed by chance, must begin by reiteration and, in so doing, disfigure for ever the make-believe, the *fiction*, of a beginning.

After a fashion, then, we could read in the remnant of Keenan's text the reiteration of a number of issues concerning reading already addressed, albeit in different ways, in different contexts. This would create the appearance of gathering together the threads, seeking to weave together disparate strands, so as to give a sense of unity. This in itself is a chance, but also the limitation of chance, where reading sets out (along the path?) to create the family atmosphere, the family resemblance.

These threads can doubtless be picked up, woven together, transformed into what might be called a reading of reading, as though to simplify the task and thereby provide a sense of more or less stable identity. Such apparent simplicity is the *chance* we might give into, in the face of that other chance, *the difficult chance* that is reading without a *path or method*. It is that which Keenan suggests we desire, often in the face of reading's *difficulty*, its frustrations and the *fatigue* that it imposes: "Why must we leave off reading only to return to it? What is its difficulty such that it does not simply frustrate us but instead incites us, regardless of our desire for simplicity, for the simplicity we associate with our selves?"[50] The simplicity we desire is far from simple, concerned as it is with the constitution of the self (as both Hamacher and Foucault make plain). It is complicated by that ambivalence on the part of the reader, who stops and starts, in a shuttling motion, and so returns to reading,

motivated by that *simplicity* that reading, in truth, can never become.
But the paradox is driven by the fact that the simplicity we desire to impose on reading, to put the breaks on so sharply that we come to a breaking point, is the simplicity we assume for our identities; we wish to read
so as to simplify, to ignore the textile weave, to render reading into an undifferentiated totality. Reading-as-simplicity desires the production of an
identity ignorant of alterity, ignorant of the difference that makes it possible, and unenlightened also concerning, to recall Hamacher, *the immanent movement of self-reproduction that it already is.*

   Nevertheless, because there can be no prediction or calculation that
would reduce the chance by which reading proceeds, returns, stops, and
starts, again and again, simplicity in reading can never, simply, impose on
reading an identity that brings all reading to an end. Despite those feelings of frustration and fatigue engendered by the continual unveiling of
the "possibility or impossibility"[51] of reading, it has to be remembered
that "one must be able to stay nimble as one reflects, and stay on the 'surface' whilst reading between the lines":

> . . . there is no reading without interpretation, without commentary—
> *in other words* without a new writing which slightly displaces the
> meaning of the first, pushes the perspective of the aphorism in new di-
> rections and *makes it come into its own.* Every reading gives birth to a
> different text, to the creation of a new form . . . the text, the expression
> of a system of forces, acts on the reader and . . . *in other words again it
> makes him come into his own* . . . we can discover in a text only what
> we ourselves are but were unaware of. So reading transforms the
> reader and the text at the same time. . . . A new reading/writing de-
> stroys the traditional categories of the book as a closed totality con-
> taining a definitive meaning, the author's; in such a way that it
> deconstructs the idea of the author as master of the meaning of the
> work.[52] (emphases added)

As there is no reading *without interpretation, without commentary,* so,
clearly, there can be no reading without writing. Reading is simultaneously disjunctive *and* transformative. Effecting fraying and rupture, it
"becomes" that which it already is, immanently, while also being that
which it is *not yet.* (As we know after Hamacher.) This is the effect *of* and
in reading. It is also what reading makes possible, its performative hope.
We have already comprehended this reduplication and destinerrancy,

though to speak of effect, of what may be effected, traces an act simultaneously in the text, immanently so, and by the text, which takes place in the act of reading. This is noticeable in the definition of text, described by Sarah Kofman as the *expression of a system of forces*. This definition is itself the reading of what reading causes to take place. This *expression* is read as that which *acts on the reader*. This transformative condition, that which de Man describes as reading textually, remarks the self. In doing so, it opens up the self to the division within itself, whereby reading's effect is to unveil the self as never simply itself, never the desired unity of undifferentiated selfhood, but rather as being marked by that reading described as the *expression of a system of forces*.

There is partially readable here a difference between Kofman's consideration and de Man's understanding of text, which we might ascribe to an act of reading between the lines, and which, moreover, concerns a question of *the* "surface." While, for de Man, the rhetorical, tropological, and figurative effects of the text, when read, cause system and structure, logic or "grammar" to be disfigured—"reading will be a negative process in which the grammatical cognition is undone, at all times, by its rhetorical displacement"[53]—the effect is that which is either read or not read. Effect is read by de Man, in this instance at least, as remaining at the level of textual operation, even if reading moves elsewhere.

For Kofman, however, the act of reading transforms the text of the self also, which reciprocally manifests itself in the reading/writing of the text, narrowly conceived, as the book, the printed word, the essay. This is not to say that de Man is not aware, in other places, of the self as text, or that he does not read the self *textually*. However, and as a means of focusing on the doubling (of) effect, it is necessary to observe the extent to which Kofman makes explicit the unstoppable movement of reading as the effect of misprision, which makes reading, finally, so *impossible*, leaves its trace on the reader. This effect is remarked economically, as the figure of supplementary doubling, and in the movement—*of* and *in* reading—between text and reader, in the phrases: *makes it come into its own; makes him come into his own*. These remarks are not simply statements, observations on the function of aphorism in Nietzsche's text; they are already readings, which reduplicate the effect of reading, and which we are given to comprehend through Kofman's reiterated phrase, *in other words, in other words again*. This effect takes place throughout the fragment, at least from the seemingly aphoristic pronouncement that there is no reading without interpretation or commentary. Inasmuch as this defines reading after a fashion, it also comments on, interprets reading. It thus effects even as it disseminates its effect.

The reading effect reiterates and reduplicates itself supplementally, performing its own discontinuous character. Kofman's text is readable as being organized and disorganized by the nature of these commentaries, these readings of what it means to read. Rhythmically punctuating the structure of commentary, they comment contrapuntally, and so counter-sign that discussion of reading of which they are a part. Reading assumes "on the 'surface'," in other words, materially, the act, the performance, already implicitly under way. Each reading simultaneously suspends or arrests, while enacting the promise of the transgression beyond itself, its movement figuring that temporality which is that of an always-to-come. Reading these statements of Kofman's, we learn to read for disjunction, disfiguration, heterogeneity. In reading these, we read the survival of reading, through *chance*, through repetition, and reiteration. This is reading in ruins, reading (as) remains. This chance is dictated in part by the infectious condition of Nietzsche's own ruined, ruinous text, about which Kofman is writing, and which she acknowledges elsewhere. Contamination is inescapable, especially when it comes to reading. As a result, reading or, at least, the desire to read, can become, like laughter, uncontrollable: "[i]nfectious *laughter* is catching, highly contagious and . . . almost impossible to bring under control. Likewise, I suspect, infectious reading."[54] So, David Farrell Krell, also commenting on Nietzsche. The idea that reading might be infectious produces laughter, doesn't it? Infection, derived, the *OED* informs its readers, from the Latin *inficere*, means to dip in, to stain, taint, spoil. The reader might dip in to a book, so to speak, and become infected, contaminated, as something is transmitted. What gets transmitted? The desire to continue reading, perhaps, which is *almost impossible to bring under control*. The very idea that reading is highly contagious, and that a certain strain of reading, all too easily transmissible, can taint: is this not perhaps the fear that is named in that phrase of Paul de Man's, *the resistance to theory*? The first sign of the contamination that reading effects is a somewhat delirious joy, a destabilization in the face of figuration, doubling, motion, all of which produce concomitant effects in the reader. One can imagine the diagnosis: the patient lost all sense of self through reading textually.

Doubtless there is a desire for escape, accompanied by laughter. There is quickly discerned a transmission between physical and physiological symptoms of reading, and from there to moral or mental depravity. This all smacks of pathology and guilt, more than the hint of dissipation, of wasting the self. The self is *spread* as Foucault, in reading Seneca, puts it. Excessive reading exhausts. This is another of its symptoms. And it is no doubt a sign of reading's being excessive that, our resistances lowered, our immunity down, we become infected, and crave to spend ourselves further. But herein is the Catch-22 of reading: the infection drives us on in our craving for the excessive, to be at once secretive, guilty, and yet to flaunt our contaminated, depraved condition. Unable to stop, we *leave off reading only to return to it.* Its infection is such that it *does not simply frustrate us but instead incites us.* Caught up in *infectious reading*, we *return to what is impossible for us.* Reading courses through the body, and there is no cure.

VIII

The uncontrollable in reading might be said to figure what Levinas terms, in another context though in relation to reading, an "inexhaustible surplus."[55] This is neither simply a matter of formal or figural polyvalence, however, nor the pursuance of that in an equally formalized reading gesture. Recognizing the *inexhaustible surplus* in what Levinas calls "all this materiality of saying" does not come down simply to a matter of discerning what is hidden in sentence structures, grammar, "words, phonemes and letters,"[56] as part of a purely semantic or linguistic register, even though it may begin there. Were it only that, reading would have begun a thematization. We would have been guilty in such an act of reading of abandoning the possibility of *guilty reading* in favor of playing what Emmanuel Levinas calls, with some caution, a "sign game."[57] While the text of Levinas starts repeatedly with reading processes and exegesis of some textual form, narrowly conceived as a book, a poem, an essay, or the Talmud, for example, there is, nonetheless, another purpose at work in the process of reading. This is its responsibility, for Levinas. Reading, in its ethical response, unveils a process of Saying incommensurate with, and irreducible to, the form of what is Said. While, specifically, the citations from Levinas' text on reading concern that kind of interpretation called *Midrash*, the acknowledgment of the Saying that exceeds the Said is central to a Levinasian ethics. The ethical moment in reading arrives in the recognition that reading is a response to the Saying of the Other. The chance taken in reading is that, in such a recognition, the Saying can always fall into the Said, and reading will not have taken place in any radically *ex-tensible* manner.

At the same time, however, running the risk of domesticating the Saying, at the very limit of reading, there comes the chance of perceiving through the movement of difference how "it is the Saying that always opens up a passage from the Same to the Other, where there is as yet nothing in common . . . there is both relation and rupture, and thus awakening. . . . An awakening signifying a responsibility or the other."[58] In the chance that reading takes, assuming it to be attentive, patient, trying persistently to find the right speed, the right rhythm, and resisting itself the fall into that purely thematic habituation, there arrives this comprehension of nonsimultaneous relation *and* rupture. Reading opens to itself the already opened minimal dislocation that is termed by Levinas an *incompressible nonsimultaneity*.

Thus, reading proceeds, and is possible, as we know, only via this chance, of undecidability and the irreducibility of difference. The motion of reading as process is remarked structurally by Levinas in the announcement of a *first* movement: "the statement commented on exceeds what it originally wants to say."[59] This commentary, this reading, does not rest here, however. It continues, even as it exceeds and extends itself by announcing "what it is capable of saying goes beyond what it wants to say."[60] There is partially readable, then, the figure of an *incompressible nonsimultaneity*. The second of the two clauses cited reiterates and moves beyond that reading that precedes it. It thus reads the reading, even while the former commentary remarks in anticipation what will come to be remarked in the following clause. Then, the next analysis: it "contains more than it contains."[61] Reading is illustrated in its own action. Reading makes this possible, even as it pushes up against its very limits, and overflowing itself in the process. We read, for example, that there is a statement, "the statement commented on." In commenting on that statement that is elsewhere remarked upon, Levinas reads in this instance not the statement but the act of reading. We read also that the statement says something other than what it wants to say. This something other belongs, not simultaneously but in the disjointing time of reading, to the statement and to the reading. That this something other, this saying, is articulated within the said of the statement, and yet is not fully articulated, is acknowledged in the phrase concerning that capability as the possibility, immanent within the materiality of the remark, as that which exceeds. Irreducible to any constative utterance, inexhaustible surplus is always already under way as the phantom performative haunting Levinas's language, which is, of course, nothing other than reading.

Reading is clearly never finished; it only ever commences as Jean-François Lyotard puts it,[62] and this entails an infinite responsibility, as has already been suggested, and as J. Hillis Miller makes clear, regarding the ethics of reading: "by 'the ethics of reading' . . . I mean that aspect of the act of reading in which there is a response to the text that is both necessitated, in the sense that it is a response to an irresistible demand, and free, in the sense that I must take responsibility for my responsibility and for the further effects . . . of my acts of reading."[63] Miller opens for us a vertiginous structure in this seemingly simple statement. Clearly, the act of reading happens a response to some text. In this, the reader must take responsibility. Responsibility does not end with this response, however. There is not a simple structure, a resolvable teleology of cause and effect, where on one side there is the text, simple and complete, on the other, the reading of that text, equally as simple. The matter of reading does not simply come to a halt, and that the duration, however extended, could one day call a halt to its own act by coming to an end.

For even as the act of reading takes place, it places itself in the position of making itself available to other acts of reading, issuing its own *irresistible demand,* while also being haunted by that demand, issued to which the act of reading is the response, for which it is responsible. There is a doubling, a ghostly disturbance. This is what reading causes to take place. Thus, placing him- or herself in an open, serial relay, the reader must also take responsibility for the effects of reading to come. Reading must be measured then to that extent that responsibility is not only situated in and by the response, but that it must take responsibility for the future conditions of reading's reception that are, strictly speaking, incalculable. Reading's responsibility is, therefore, in attending to the *inexhaustible surplus* that reading not only responds to, but which it also puts into play. Acknowledging that it is capable of maintaining that indefatigability, even while it must seek to negotiate without bringing under control the undecidable, is this not a recognition of how reading sets foot into what Hamacher calls *the circle of the text,* how it has already been anticipated in this gesture? And is not this recognition the first step in a response that, in understanding itself, takes responsibility, as Miller puts it, for its responsibility, or which, in the words of Althusser, "takes the responsibility for its crime as a 'justified' crime?"

IX

But the same goes for all commentary, on any author, on any text whatsoever. In a writer's text, and in a commentator's text (which every text in turn is, more or less), what counts, what thinks (at the very limit of thought, if necessary), is what does not completely lend itself to univocality or, for that matter, to plurivocality, but strains against the burden of meaning and throws it off balance. Bataille never stops exposing this. Alongside all the themes he deals with, through all the questions he debates, "Bataille" is *nothing but* a protest against the signification of his own discourse. If one wishes to read him, and if this reading rebels right away against the commentary that it is and against the *comprehension* that it must be, then one must read in each line the work or the play of a writing *against* meaning.

This has nothing to do with nonsense or with the absurd. . . . It is—paradoxically—a manner of weighing, in the very sentence, in the very words and syntax . . . a manner of weighing on meaning itself, on given and recognizable meaning. . . . And reading in turn must remain weighty, hampered, and, without ceasing to decode, must stay just this side of decoding. Such a reading remains caught in the odd materiality of language. It attunes itself to the singular communication carried on not just by meaning but by language itself, or, rather, to a communication that is only the communication of language itself, without abstracting any meaning, in a fragile, repeated suspension of meaning. True reading advances unknowing, it is always an unjustifiable cut in the supposed continuum of meaning that opens a book. It must lose its way in this breach.

This reading—which is first of all *reading* itself, all reading, inevitably given over to the sudden, flashing, slipping movement of a writing that precedes it and that it will rejoin only by reinscribing it elsewhere and otherwise, by ex-scribing it outside itself—this reading does not yet comment. This is a *beginning* reading, an incipit that is always begun again.[64]

The contours of this commentary should seem familiar by now, though its reiteration is nonetheless necessary for having the appearance of a recapitulation, of sorts. Both statements, the one concerning reading on the part of Jean-Luc Nancy, the other the apology for necessity (which attempts to take responsibility for its "crime"), appear to assume a reiterative condition. Indeed, Nancy's opening remark encourages and even cajoles the reader into heading in this direction. It is perhaps as a means of *beginning reading* that an *incipit* is remarked, as the sign that there is in reading that which *is always begun again*. The semblance of familiarity and of structures of return might appear to take the weight off reading, allowing us to stop listening. This might occur in favor of a more idle gaze, indiscriminate and lacking focus. Moreover, semblance as re-semblance, re-assemblance, also serves to take the weight off both response and responsibility. It is precisely in constituting the likeness that we attempt to close the circle, return to the path, create a frame in which we install the re(as)semblance and, in the process, block our ears.

If we rush to the assumption that Nancy's text is simply a recapitulation, we come face-to-face with two related questions: why does reading have a greater, though more difficult, chance of proceeding in the dark, through the blindness of listening, through the understanding of auditory response as reading? And why does the gaze somehow limit reading or blind us to it? Reading must begin by returning, by turning back, and by proceeding in the dark. As the text of Nancy gives us to understand, this is the ineluctable motion of *all reading*. Significantly, what we are given to read here, in order to begin over again, is the careful negotiation between singularity and generality. This is indicated by Nancy through the reference to Bataille as author and the text signed in the name of "Bataille," and remarked as such through Nancy's use of quotation marks. (Which, of course, mark off the name from its other inscription, directing us to read the difference between those two uses of the proper name.)

Bataille provides for Nancy the singular example, but, at the same time, this name signs a general textuality addressed in passing as *all the themes he deals with . . . all the questions he debates*. The general condition of the exemplary and singular text implied in the name *Bataille*, which at one and the same time countersigns itself, in that it names both a *writer's* and a *commentator's text*, and *does not*, therefore, *lend itself to univocality*, is described as the gesture of an *incipit*. It is this displacement Nancy's text invites us to read. This opening is caught, as is the tension—the spacing between one text and another, between generality and singularity—in both Nancy's commentary on that *all* that Bataille's text addresses and in the insistence that *one must read in each line* that which "Bataille" resists in his own discourse. *All* and *each* thereby figure the movement between generality and singularity that disfigures and thus displaces from within any possibility of univocality. The passage remarks, then, even as it performs its effect through its own passage, the general condition of reading, or, rather, the conditions to which all reading should aspire. This is the case whether one is speaking of the discussion of Bataille, or on the fragment in general. The regulations by which reading takes its chance—and even in this commentary there is the inscription of balance and countermeasure, chance and regulation, the signs of weighing, by which reading is set, or sets itself, in motion—are commented on clearly in three places.

First: it is acknowledged how *any text, every text,* is a *commentator's text,* to greater or lesser extents. Every writer is a commentator, an analyst, a reader, and every reader also writes or analyzes in some measure. The reciprocity at work here is not a sign of simple equivalence, of symmetry, but is, rather, the opening of a necessary and inescapable diachrony—which is also an anachrony—if reading is to take place, to have its chance. This is understood if we understand how every writer is his or her own reader, and how every reader, in beginning the act of reading, engages in a process of writing. Thus, the figure described here is not so much circular, as it is a somewhat risky movement of return, a turning back as well as an effect of revenance, a haunting. In this turn and return, there is also that passage, in reading's taking effect, of *the sudden, flashing, slipping movement of a writing that precedes it and that it will rejoin only by reinscribing it elsewhere and otherwise, by ex-scribing it outside itself.*

Second: however provisional or intimate an act, reading always remains spaced, placed and displaced (displacing itself in being reading) *just this side* of its act of analysis. In maintaining the act of what Nancy terms *decoding,* reading, prior to any abstraction or articulation of meaning—which term names the suspension of reading—strives toward its own limit. However, *all* reading, even that reading that pushes *at the very limit* through its *unjustifiable* incision into the body of the text, is always, inescapably enmeshed in the movement of language. Or, we should say, simply, language, because there can be no comprehension of language, of its motions, its rhythms, without an awareness of articulation—that is, the passage of *communication* (however fraught, exhausting, or impossible this may be).

Third (and here we return to a point made in the first remark concerning the general condition of reading, as well as finding the return of a point made elsewhere): all reading slips into a writing, which has already begun, of course, as the a priori gesture on which reading is predicated, of necessity. This is not simply a moment of absolute origin, however. For reading returns, even as writing returns through reading.

So we read therefore, in the commentary on reading's generality, through attention to the singular effects by which reading proceeds and, indirectly via the detour or singular example of Bataille *contra* "Bataille," how Nancy *sets the text to work.* Erasing any identification of reading and writing as univocal or static oppositions, and resisting falling into the production of a meaning that suspends reading, Nancy *weighs* the means by which reading and its impossibility proceed. Through this, we begin to read the *weight* of responsibility imposed by the general condition of reading, and not only as a general condition but also in every singular act of reading. Reading announces itself as *a manner of weighing* without hurrying to decide on a meaning. The responsibility of this *manner of weighing* serves in turn as a possible counterbalance to the *guilt* of that *unjustifiable cut,* by which reading, *all* reading, must begin. And, as we know, *the same goes for all commentary, on any author, on any text whatsoever.*

X

But every determinate addressee, and thus every act of reading, is affected by the same "death," it therefore follows that every countersignature has to wait on others, indefinitely, that reading has no end, but is always to-come as work of the other . . . a text never comes to rest in a unity or meaning finally revealed or discovered. This work must also be a work of mourning. In truth, only this situation allows a text to have a "life" or, as we shall say later, an "afterlife." For the moment, let us hang on to the fact that the written text presupposes this mortality of empirical writers and readers; it is therefore indifferent to their real death: to this extent the text is inhuman . . . and in its very principle exceeds the resources of any humanist analysis.[65]

Nearing the end of this chapter, we are forced to admit that we are still no nearer an answer to the question: *what is it to read?* We remain close to it, our closeness an immeasurable proximity, which names the intimacy figured by the *close* in the expression *close reading.* That figure, of being close, also whispers of what will never happen to reading: its close, its completion. So, we keep reading close, even though it gets away from us. We know that we will never have done with it, that we are unable to catch up with (what we read as) reading's promise, and knowing also that, after our deaths, there will still be reading to come. The act of close reading speaks of an ongoing performance, intimate and yet frustrated, frustrating in its irreducible propinquity: "on the streets, in the schools, reading," as Avital Ronell has it.[66] We might say that we are in its neighborhood, but we don't have reading's address.

Understanding this matter of proximal spacing, which all reading reintroduces, gives one to comprehend how, in one's relation to the other, there can be neither homogeneity nor amalgamation. Despite the desire for unity that drives a certain reading, and the self's attempt to read after this fashion, all reading only serves to bring the reader face-to-face with the experience of alterity, of difference and discontinuity. In coming to terms with the question of the vicinity of reading and, at the same time, the impossibility of ever being at home with reading, we hear one possible answer, articulated by Avital Ronell, as a possible response to the question, *what is it to read?* Reading and, as important, "teaching (how to read) remains elusive and blinding as it remains the promise of future illumination."[67] We might wish to ignore that promise, if only in order to calm things down a little, to keep something in place for a while. We might rush to read the following from Ronell as merely a biographical, confessional narrative:

> Teaching [how to read] remains elusive and blinding as it remains the promise of future illumination. But it is a future that will never have completed its task in the present. There was, for the one for whom I-write, a history consisting of many scenes of pedagogy. In fact, you learned far too many lessons. There was still never enough time to read. On the streets, in the schools, reading. Piano lessons, cosmetics, reading. The runs in your stockings, Hegel, reading. B-ball, concert tickets, reading. This opens the dossier of another scene of finitude's score, the place of a reading that starts from scratch, or from a metaleptic scream, and from the silence of one who, refusing to respond, still dwells in language. The figure of the inscribing cry, the *Schreiben/Schrei*, the cri/écrit, continues to haunt these pages.[68]

The initial impression thus received from this extract is one of a disjointed linear temporality, linearity available despite the effect of displacement, through that kind of a reading that reassembles and simplifies. Flowing from the future promise of reading to a past concerned constantly with learning to read, desiring to read, there is discernible a single narrative. Such a reading produces a unity from the trajectory of the life, the I who writes. To produce a life in this fashion would be to reduce the text to a state of unreadability, closing it off from its future reception, from that *future that will never have completed its task in the present*. The closeness, the intimacy of the reading that is put in process here would be closed were I to present a reading, for example, of the kind that reduces the effects of the figural to the biographical meaning. Such proximity, articulated in part by desire, would be closed to itself also, unavailable to Ronell for the analysis of reading. There would be no reading without a spacing and an incompletion, without figural displacement and substitution, which the translation into a meaningful unity would cancel or otherwise downplay as merely "literary" or rhetorical effect.

The writing self thus opens itself in its attempts to read and thereby remains close to its other. In the act of inscription, reading is announced even as it remains fraught with difficulties. Reading may well be an escape but "it" also escapes from the reader. There is never time for reading, never the right time, *never enough time to read*. It signals that which is left but *remains* the promise of future illumination. Reading *remains elusive* even as it countersigns the remnant as the elusive *remains* that escape, again and again, insistently. This is announced everywhere in the figural performativity of this passage, in its temporal passages. In this, the text is not simply either readable or unreadable. Rather it pushes at the limits of the reading act, negotiating between the promise of a reading and the fact that it cannot be read. It folds and unfolds itself, onto itself where *reading is part of what is read*. There is remarked in this citation of Ronell's text the strange time of reading, of that which precedes and that which is *not yet*; as we will find, this matter of reading's impossible time has returned to us.

For the moment, however, notice the figural rhythm here. Notice how it enacts the condition of the promise, how it precedes our attempt at reading while, through the iterable pulse, displaces itself within and from itself. Although there is *never enough time to read*, or, perhaps, precisely because of this lack whereby all our efforts are mistimed, reading is everywhere, while the task is never completed. Reading (dis)figures any simple temporal narrative or biographical delineation, displacing, disjointing through a manifest, serial iteration, from which the very question of the readable is indissociable. The performative and the analytical modes and motifs cannot be separated. Reading returns to haunt this passage, to disrupt its flow, as a figure to be read. As the haunting, iterable inscription belonging to both past and future, hidden and presented in the partial reading of a life, reading behaves as though it were the sign of metalepsis itself, as though in its serial returns it traced the movement of metonymic substitution of rhetorical figures, one after another. Announcing itself four times, taking place hurriedly, reading arrives too late and yet to come. Each figure of reading figures this impossible, unbearable situation. Every utterance of *reading* countersigns itself as metaleptic figure, supplement and displacement, of every other figure of *reading*. There is no origin for reading, no absolute starting point to which we can justifiably point. It is the work of the figure of reading that allows us to read this. In working in this way reading opens *the place of a reading*, while maintaining in this opening the proximity by which the hope of reading must proceed.

However, while there is *never enough time to read*, reading's metaleptic act, its performative disturbance of any simple descriptive function and its affirmation of itself as never itself, does not refer merely to those obvious figures of reading. Reading, as figural effect, allows us to attend to the way in which the I-writing speaks of its history as *scenes of pedagogy*, through the metalepsis at work through all those figures, each substituting for every other. *Hegel. Piano lessons. Concert tickets. On the streets, in the schools.* These and each of the other instances of this history are the figures that the inscribing/cry of reading puts to work as metonymic substitutions, one after another, one for another as the places of reading and as *that which remains to be read*. To this extent, Ronell's remarks, substituting the pasts and futures of reading as disfigured iterations of one another, suspends, as Peggy Kamuf puts it, "the trait of reading *in* the text and *of* the text."[69] We are thereby brought face-to-face with one of the conditions of reading and its impossibility, which is that "the unreadable is fixed only to the extent that it is apprehended as that which remains to be read, even if that reading is theorised (as it is in Derrida's work) as belonging as much to an immemorial past as to the future."[70] Nicholas Royle's argument concerning the unreadable is partly readable in, and as an effect of, the citation from Ronell's text. The citation is unreadable to the extent that it enfolds the time of reading, and the idea of reading as always to come into its own passage. Arriving after the event, as readers, we read that, in a certain past, reading was never caught up with, that it always returned, and that reading remains to come, in a future that will never be present. Reading "precedes," yet it is "necessarily still to come."[71] As we have seen, the passage plays on the troping of biographical figures so as to embed the difficulties of reading and thereby enact its "strange time, which is never proper, never *on* time," as Royle puts it.[72] It might be said then, that Ronell's text provides an exemplary performative instance of Royle's remarks concerning reading's ruined temporality.

The irreducible difference of, between, the *past* and *future* of reading, its continuous affirmation and nonfulfillment with which we have to grapple, announces in the rhythm of reading what Susan Stewart describes as "one of the strongest models of a presumed disjunction."[73] In conclusion, it has therefore to be recognized that disjunction marks every reading act; it is perhaps the only true name for reading's occasions, for the occasional possibility that reading might commence. Disjunction cannot help but countersign reading, as reading is transformative: it marks both the reader and what is being read, which, in being read, is always on the way to becoming something other, awaiting the other reader. The element of disjunction is also read in the constant, necessary return to reading, to what is impossible for us. It is signed, furthermore, and countersigns itself, in the seemingly paradoxical movement of reading, where it *is still not yet what it already is.* For all these reasons, and for many others, "reading is a rather risky business whose outcome and full consequences can never be known in advance."[74] We might even go as far as to suggest that *resistance to theory* occurs, whenever it takes place and in whatever form it manifests itself, as a recurring fear of that disjunction of the self that reading imposes on us; we find ourselves riven in and by reading.

There is another aspect of reading that divides us: its *solitude*. Reading causes us to be disjoined from our selves. The supposed unity of the self comes into question. Moreover, in reading we erase our presence, escaping into the text, "escaping in broad daylight" as Hélène Cixous maintains.[75] This is the case whether we read in private, on our own, or in full view of others. While reading has undoubtedly *inhabited the scenes of solitude,* at least since Samuel Pepys, and probably since St. Augustine also,[76] as Susan Stewart suggests, it has also hidden the reader in plain view, in what Stewart describes as "the invisible social space of reading and writing."[77]

Everything about reading intimates invisibility, not least the act itself. The "product" of reading is invisible Stewart reminds us in the place just cited, as is its trace (by the acknowledgment of which we begin to discern an abyssal structure). Writing only serves to reinforce the spacing between reading and writing, reader and writer. Reading returns this opening, though in a different manner. The shadowy figures of the absent writer and the absent reader identified by Stewart, who, caught in a process of frustrating communication, inscribe what Timothy Clark describes (in citing Derrida and thereby reduplicating the abyssal disfiguration) as *the space "of deferred reciprocity between reading and writing."*

With invisibility comes silence and "profound loneliness."[78] This latter effect of reading is all the more pronounced when reading takes place in the "social space" wherein the invisible reader exists, in "solitude."[79] The depth, the profundity of solitude, which acts of reading engender, is amplified when the scene of reading inhabits, if not the same space, then one of nearly unbearable proximity to the social. In this description, Stewart's exploration of the condition of reading unfolds a complex, intimate spatial structure wherein reading takes place, even as it displaces the self. While Cixous has identified in such solitude a freedom and excitement—*eating the forbidden fruit, making forbidden love*—Stewart's analysis of the space of reading tends toward an unresolvable melancholy.

That reading can cause one to feel both guilty pleasure and loneliness should not surprise us. Solitude, like reading, is neither one nor the other, necessarily. Yet, it is inescapably traced by the memories of both, and the infinite potential for the return of such effects. Neither are discrete, and, as we know, both are capable of slipping into the mode of the other. Indeed, solitude, or loneliness, are not themselves either simply pleasurable or melancholy. Capable of both resonances, they require the patience of a reading turning back upon itself. Furthermore, there is in that melancholy produced by solitude a pleasure peculiar to the feeling, while pleasure is equally apt to slide into melancholy of a quite different kind (if only in anticipation of the eventual loss of guilty pleasure, or the return of the memory of such pleasure in moments of solitude). Solitude as pleasure is available as soon as we open the book, as soon as we step out of the world. Yet we leave off reading and are consigned to a sense of melancholy driving our desire to return to the act of reading. All the time we are reading we know that the loneliness of reading becomes another kind of solitude, when we call a halt to reading. There is that absence, already at work in close reading, and yet there is also the absence anticipated in reading, of the moment when we will no longer read, or desire to read. For every time we close the book, put it down, abandon it, we have—even if we do not recognize it or ignore it—the intimation of a future in which there is no reading. Each occasion of reading is haunted by the promise of no more reading, no more occasions. And this is all the more pronounced when we realize that we have returned to what Stewart names that tumultuous life,[80] wherein we feel all the more lonely, all the more melancholy, because we perhaps no longer strive after the intimacy of reading. Thus, in mourning for this loss, and as a small act of responsibility, we find ourselves back where we had started, recalling the words of Louis Althusser: *we must say what reading we are guilty of.*

INTRODUCTION

1. Sarah Kofman, *Lectures de Derrida* (Paris: Galilée, 1984), 89.

2. On the subject of "introduction," and its occasions, see chapter one.

3. The argument concerning thinking the relationship between species and genus is developed in chapter eight, "Origins of Deconstruction?"

4. Jacques Derrida, "Faith and Knowledge: The Two Sources of 'Religion' at the Limits of Reason Alone," trans. Samuel Weber, in Jacques Derrida and Gianni Vattimo, *Religion* (Stanford: Stanford University Press, 1998), 1–78; 51.

5. Martin Heidegger, *Ontology—The Hermeneutics of Facticity* (1988), trans. John van Buren (Bloomington: Indiana University Press, 1999).

CHAPTER 1

1. As the *Oxford English Dictionary* reveals, the terms "occasion" and "occasional" suggest, in their etymology and definition, the necessary chance "coming together," disruptive of or inimical to any thematic organization, on which I insist throughout this chapter as a condition of those acts of reading understood as "deconstructive" responses and responsibilities. Occasion is described in the *OED* variously as "a falling together or juncture of circumstances favourable or suitable to an end or purpose, or admitting of something being done or effected; an opportunity" and "a juncture or condition of things, an occurrence, fact, or consideration, affording ground for an action or a state of mind or feeling; a reason, ground," or, "something that contributes to produce an effect, by providing the opportunity for the efficient cause to operate; a subsidiary or incidental cause." From such determinations, one might risk the supposition that "occasion" could be said to operate as a possible substitute, albeit a nonsynonymous one, for "deconstruction." Thus,

to name this volume *Occasional Deconstructions* is to say nothing more than Occasions. The title is thus excessive, wasteful, even while it seeks, somewhat economically, to suggest that deconstructions are irreducible to a principle or program of deconstruction and, moreover, that, all occasions of deconstructions being different, whatever might be said to be deconstructive, never takes place in the same way twice, given that every occasion, necessarily differing from every other, will, of course, be remarkable as a singular juncture of circumstances.

2. J. Hills Miller, *Theory Now and Then* (Hemel Hempstead: Harvester Wheatsheaf, 1991), 231.

3. Jean-Luc Nancy, *Being Singular Plural,* trans. Robert D. Richardson and Anne E. O'Byrne (Stanford: Stanford University Press, 2000).

4. Jacques Derrida and John D. Caputo, *Deconstruction in a Nutshell* (New York: Fordham University Press, 1997), 26.

5. Jacques Derrida, *Dissemination,* trans. Barbara Johnson (Chicago: University of Chicago Press, 1981), 7.

6. *Dissemination,* 9.

7. Jacques Derrida, "The Ghost Dance: An Interview with Jacques Derrida" Interview with Mark Lewis and Andrew Payne, trans. Jean-Luc Svoboda, *Public* vol. 2 (1989): 60–73; 61.

8. Nicholas Royle, *After Derrida* (Manchester: Manchester University Press, 1995). See Royle's discussion of the figure "after" and its temporal dislocation in relation to subject position in the phrase "after Derrida" (1995, 2–5). On the disruptive work of "after" see also Tom Cohen, *Ideology and Inscription: "Cultural Studies" after Benjamin, de Man, and Bakhtin* (Cambridge: Cambridge University Press, 1998), 22.

9. *Geoffrey Bennington,* "Derridabase," in Geoffrey Bennington and Jacques Derrida, Jacques Derrida (Paris: Seuil, 1991), trans. Geoffrey Bennington as *Jacques Derrida* (Chicago: Chicago University Press, 1993), 8, 15. Occasionally, throughout the present volume, page references are given to both French and English editions. Where this occurs, the first page reference is to the French edition, the second to the English.

10. Tom Cohen, *Anti-Mimesis: From Plato to Hitchcock* (Cambridge: Cambridge University Press, 1994), 1.

11. Cohen, *Ideology and Inscription, 7.*

12. Jacques Derrida, "Introduction: Desistance," trans. Christopher Fynsk, in Philippe Lacoue-Labarthe, *Typography: Mimesis, Philosophy, Politics,* trans. and ed. Christopher Fynsk (Cambridge, MA: Harvard University Press, 1989), 6–7. For an interesting discussion of Derrida's work in relation to Lacoue-Labarthe and Nancy, see Joan Brandt's *Geopoetics: The Politics of Mimesis in Poststruc-*

turalist French Poetry and Theory (Stanford: Stanford University Press, 1997). Brandt's work situates Derrida, along with Lacoue-Labarthe and Nancy, in relation to the Parisian intellectual scene of the late 1960s in general, and in relation to *Tel Quel.*

See also the discussion of Derrida's work in the milieu of *Tel Quel* in Suzanne Guerlac, *Literary Polemics: Bataille, Sartre, Valéry, Breton* (Stanford: Stanford University Press, 1997), 216–222. For further discussion of *Tel Quel* and the development of what is referred to as poststructuralism in the Anglo-American academy, see Jonathan Culler, "'Beyond' Structuralism: Tel Quel," in his *Structuralist Poetics: Structuralism, Linguistics and the Study of Literature* (London: Routledge and Kegan Paul, 1975), 241–254. Patrick ffrench and Roland-François Lack offer a short introduction to *Tel Quel,* as well as a significant selection of key articles by members of the group, in their *The Tel Quel Reader* (London: Routledge, 1998).

13. Jacques Derrida, *Acts of Literature,* ed. Derek Attridge (New York: Routledge, 1992), 62.

14. Derrida, *Deconstruction in a Nutshell,* 9.

15. Jacques Derrida, *Glas,* trans. John P. Leavey Jr. and Richard Rand (Lincoln: University of Nebraska Press, 1986), 204–205b.

16. Jacques Derrida, "Living On • Borderlines," trans. James Hulbert, in *Deconstruction and Criticism,* Harold Bloom, Paul de Man, Jacques Derrida, Geoffrey Hartman, and J. Hillis Miller (New York: Continuum, 1987), 83–84.

17. Derrida, "Living On • Borderlines," 84.

18. Jacques Derrida, "The Deaths of Roland Barthes," trans. Pascale-Anne Brault and Michael Naas, in Jacques Derrida, *The Work of Mourning,* ed. Pascale-Anne Brault and Michael Naas (Chicago: University of Chicago Press, 2001), 31–68; 35.

19. The singularity of the figure is disrupted through a partial citation, when citations are referred to not as stones, but as "little white pebbles," in Jacques Derrida, "Lyotard and Us," trans. Boris Belay, rev. Pascale-Anne Brault and Michael Naas, in Derrida, *The Work of Mourning,* 216–241; 230.

20. Derrida, "Lyotard and Us," 227.

21. Derrida, "Lyotard and Us," 227.

22. Derrida, *Deconstruction in a Nutshell,* 8.

23. Jacques Derrida, "I Have a Taste for the Secret," in Jacques Derrida and Maurizio Ferraris, *A Taste for the Secret,* trans. Giacomo Donis, ed. Giacomo Donis and David Webb (Oxford: Polity Press, 2001), 1–92; 48.

24. Derrida, *Deconstruction in a Nutshell,* 9.

25. Derrida, "Taste," 30.

26. Samuel Beckett, *The Unnameable* (1958), trans. Samuel Beckett, in Samuel Beckett, *Three Novels by Samuel Beckett* (New York: Grove Press, 1965), 414.

27. Derrida, "Taste," 31.

CHAPTER 2

1. Jacques Derrida, "Taste for the Secret," 89.

2. Theodor Adorno, "Transparencies on Film," trans. Thomas Y. Levin, *New German Critique,* 24/25 (1981/82): 56.

3. Adorno, "Transparencies," 56.

4. Adorno's memory calls to mind two different, yet related narratives. The first is a scene from Ingmar Bergman's film, *Fanny and Alexander* (1982). Alexander has among his toys a magic lantern projector. The scene with which he frightens his sisters consists of the apparition of a ghostly angel before a prisoner in a gothic dungeon. The motion of the spectre on the spectral scene and the apparatus that allows for this phantasmatic projection not only illustrates the points made by Adorno and Derrida concerning film but, in a certain performative fashion, films the return of the earlier technology of projection in a temporally disturbing instance as, if we can say this, a proleptic revenant. This return, as a discontinuous tracing of the ghostly nature of any act of representation, haunts the very idea of film in its marking of an irreducible relation between technologies of the ghost. The second narrative called to mind by Adorno's memory is that offered of phantasmagoria, magic lantern shows, and their relation to the gothic and haunting, by Terry Lovell in her *The Female Thermometer: Eighteenth-Century Culture and the Invention of the Uncanny* (Oxford: Oxford University Press, 1995).

5. Derrida, "Taste," 89.

6. David Skal, *Hollywood Gothic: The Tangled Web of "Dracula" from Novel to Stage to Screen* (New York: W.W. Norton, 1990).

7. Skal, *Hollywood Gothic,* 7.

8. Bernard Dick, *Billy Wilder* (Boston: Twayne Publishers, 1980), 150.

9. Richard Corliss, *Talking Pictures: Screenwriters in the American Cinema,* cit. S. S. Prawer, *Caligari's Children: The Film as Tale of Terror* (Oxford: Oxford University Press, 1980), 44–45.

10. Steve Seidman, *The Film Career of Billy Wilder* (Pleasantville: Redgrave, 1977), 4. More recently, and, as yet, untranslated, is Andreas Hutter and Klaus Kamolz's *Billy Wilder: Eine europäische Karriere* (Vienna: Böhlau Verlag,

1998), which provides a significant reappraisal of Wilder's Europeanness, his work as a writer in Berlin and, subsequently, as a filmmaker in Paris, as well as the influence on his work of the film circles in Berlin and, in Chapter 4 (147–212), the elements of style learnt from UFA productions discernible in Wilder's films.

11. Astruc's remarks on Murnau are cited by Brian Henderson, in *A Critique of Film Theory* (New York: Dutton, 1980), 51.

12. Ed Sikov, *On Sunset Boulevard: The Life and Times of Billy Wilder* (New York: Hyperion, 1998), 299.

13. Francesco Casetti, *Inside the Gaze: The Fiction Film and Its Spectator*, int. Christian Metz, trans. Nell Andrew with Charles O'Brien, preface to English Edition, Dudley Andrew (Bloomington: Indiana University Press, 1998), 18.

14. Casetti, *Inside the Gaze,* 18.

15. Avital Ronell, *Dictations: On Haunted Writing* (Lincoln: University of Nebraska Press, 1993), xviii.

16. Ronell, *Dictations,* xviii–xix.

17. Ronell, *Dictations, xix.*

18. Dick, *Billy Wilder,* 156.

19. Sikov, *On Sunset Boulevard, 291.*

20. See the discussion of this figural dislocation in my *Victorian Hauntings: Spectrality, Gothic, the Uncanny and Literature* (London: Palgrave, 2001), particularly the chapter concerning Thomas Hardy's *The Mayor of Casterbridge,* 110–39, and, more generally, on Freud's concept of the uncanny, the introduction to that book, 1–24.

21. In gesturing toward the picturesque here in relation to architecture, and bearing in mind the general sense provided by Wilder that Desmond's estate is being reclaimed by nature, there are readable the signs of eighteenth-century discourse on the picturesque, wholly in keeping with the film's gothic sensibility, even though, arguably, this is more immediately "inherited" from cinematic revisions of the gothic, as this chapter explores.

22. Arguably, as a screenwriter, Gillis has in mind not Dickens's novel but David Lean's highly gothic film of *Great Expectations.* Released in 1946, the film won two Oscars, for photography and art direction, and was nominated for three others: best picture, script, and director. Clearly, if not Gillis, then Wilder himself would have been familiar with Lean's movie. The movies certainly employ photography and lighting similarly, particularly in the presentation of Miss Havisham's house on the one hand, and Norma Desmond's on the other.

23. Robert Stam, *Reflexivity in Film and Literature: From Don Quixote to Jean-Luc Godard* (New York: Columbia University Press, 1992), 89. Stam's essay

suggestively and convincingly reads Sunset Boulevard as an exploration of the various crises felt by Hollywood, including the threat of television, in the 1950s (85–88).

24. Geoffrey Batchen, *Burning with Desire: The Conception of Photography* (Cambridge, MA: MIT Press, 1997), 179.

25. Jacques Derrida, *Specters of Marx: The State of the Debt, the Work of Mourning, and the New International,* trans. Peggy Kamuf, int. Bernd Magnus and Stephen Cullenberg (New York: Routledge, 1994), xviii.

26. Derrida, *Specters,* xx.

27. Stam, *Reflexivity,* 88.

28. As if to complicate matters further, there is readable in this scene another Hollywood reference, made available chiefly through the disorienting nature of the shot. The camera is positioned from within the body of the organ itself, with Max's white gloves in extreme close-up, and to the left of the screen, while, above the keys and to the right is the rest of the room, fully in focus, with Joe Gillis approaching. Arguably, in having the viewer's attention drawn so oddly to the gloves as they appear to play in some disembodied fashion, we are being invited to recall the gloved "hands" of Mickey Mouse.

29. Sikov, *On Sunset Boulevard,* 299.

30. For a commentary on the missing open scene, see Axel Madsen, *Billy Wilder* (London: BFI, 1968), 82–83. Madsen, in an interesting, if incidental, comment, points out that *Sunset Boulevard* was reviewed in the first issue of *Cahiers du Cinéma* (85).

31. In a sense, all cinema figures the death of the author, inasmuch as any film is always an ensemble work and therefore subject to transformation at the hands of numerous agents. Cinema is, seen in this light, a writing without origin and, therefore, exemplary of the status of all writing, figuring as it does a constant, potentially infinite transmission of iterable marks.

32. See Bernard Dick on this scene, 153–154.

33. Dick, 152. A small, if obvious, note. Whenever I refer to Hollywood, I primarily use the name as a metaphor for the film industry, rather than referring to the city itself. However, as Wilder seems to want to insist from his presentation of Norma Desmond's mansion, there is something gothic, if not uncanny, about both the location and the movie business.

34. Jacques Derrida, *Of Grammatology,* trans. and int. Gayatri Chakravorty Spivak (Baltimore: The Johns Hopkins University Press, 1974), 36.

35. Derrida, *Grammatology,* 36.

36. Sikov, *On Sunset Boulevard,* 298.

37. Laura R. Oswald, "Cinema-Graphia: Eisenstein, Derrida, and the Sign of the Cinema," in Peter Brunette and David Wills, eds., *Deconstruction and the Visual Arts: Art, Media, Architecture* (Cambridge: Cambridge University Press, 1994). 248–63; 252.

38. Oswald, "Cinema-Graphia," 251.

39. Madsen, *Billy Wilder,* 85.

40. Betty Short, the victim in the Black Dahlia case, was murdered in January 1947. John Gilmore gives a thorough account of the case in his *Severed: The True Story of the Black Dahlia Murder,* revised edition (Los Angeles: Amok Books, 1998). Uncannily, Raymond Chandler had written the screenplay (for which he won an Oscar) for *The Blue Dahlia,* which was released in 1946, starring Alan Ladd and Veronica Lake. There is, however, no similarity between the murder in the film and the Short case.

41. Stuart Swezey, "Publisher's Preface," *Severed* (i).

42. That Wilder enjoys the elements of pastiche and parody is attested to by his comic rendering of the gangster film in *Some Like It Hot,* which also mixes genres to the extent that it draws briefly on musicals, and is knowingly self–referential via Tony Curtis's impersonation of Cary Grant.

43. On this, see Neil Larsen, *Modernism and Hegemony: A Materialist Critique of Aesthetic Agency,* foreword Jaime Concha (Minneapolis: University of Minnesota Press, 1990), xxvi–xxxiii.

44. Larsen, *Modernism and Hegemony,* xxix.

45. Joan Copjec, *Read My Desire: Lacan Against the Historicists* (Cambridge, MA: MIT Press, 1994), 184.

46. Copjec, *Read My Desire,* 183.

47. Marie-Claire Ropars, *La Texte divisé,* cit. and trans. Peter Brunette and David Wills, *Screen/Play: Derrida and Film Theory* (Princeton: Princeton University Press, 1989), 63.

48. Copjec, *Read My Desire,* 186.

49. The disjointing effect of the voice in this film might usefully be considered, not only in relation to the recent *American Beauty,* but also to Steven Soderbergh's use of "flashback" and "flashforward" in his 1999 film, *The Limey.* Rather than employing voice-over, Soderbergh displaces the narrative temporality with a reiterative edit, whereby a shot of the film's English protagonist, played by Terence Stamp, is seen over and over. The character is sitting in an airplane. For most of the film's narrative it is impossible to tell whether this constantly returning clip comes from the past or the future. Indeed, given that the character is wearing the same clothes in the shot as he is when he both arrives in and leaves Los Angeles, the shot might be read as truly disruptive inasmuch as it plays both

the present and past instances simultaneously, a temporal dislocation that is not resolved until close to the film's end.

50. Jacques Derrida, "Above All, No Journalists!," in *Religion and Media,* ed. Hent de Vries and Samuel Weber (Stanford: Stanford University Press, 2001), 56–93; 70.

51. Derrida, "Above All," 70.

52. Derrrida, "Above All," 70–72.

53. Martha B. Helfer, *The Retreat of Representation: The Concept of Darstellung in German Critical Discourse* (Albany: State University of New York Press, 1996), 175.

54. Derrida, *Of Grammatology,* 144.

55. Derrida, *Of Grammatology,* 145.

56. Slavoj Žižek, *Looking Awry: An Introduction to Jacques Lacan through Popular Culture* (Cambridge, MA: MIT Press, 1992), 112.

57. Friedrich A. Kittler, *Gramophone, Film, Typewriter,* trans. and int. Geoffrey Winthrop-Young and Michael Wutz (Stanford: Stanford University Press, 1999), 10–11.

58. Kittler, *Gramophone, Film, Typewriter,* 13.

CHAPTER 3

1. Hubert Damisch, *Skyline: The Narcissistic City* (1996), trans. John Goodman (Stanford: Stanford University Press, 2001), 124.

2. Jacques Derrida, *Margins of Philosophy,* trans. Alan Bass (Chicago: University of Chicago Press, 1982), 330.

3. Derrida, *Margins,* 330.

4. Damisch, *Skyline,* 124.

5. Jacques Derrida, *Memoirs of the Blind: The Self-Portrait and Other Ruins,* trans. Pascale-Anne Brault and Michael Naas (Chicago: University of Chicago Press, 1993), 68.

6. Norman Page, *Muriel Spark* (New York: St. Martin's Press, 1990), 28.

7. Page, *Spark,* 31.

8. Peter Kemp, *Muriel Spark* (London: Paul Elek, 1974), 141.

9. Cairns Craig, *The Modern Scottish Novel: Narrative and the National Imagination* (Edinburgh: Edinburgh University Press, 1999), 133, 135.

10. Richard C. Kane, *Iris Murdoch, Muriel Spark, and John Fowles: Didactic Demons in Modern Fiction* (Rutherford: Fairleigh Dickinson University Press, 1988), 71.

11. Kane, *Iris Murdoch,* 65.

12. Joseph Hynes, *The Art of the Real: Muriel Spark's Novels* (Rutherford: Fairleigh Dickinson University Press, 1988), 52.

13. Hynes, *Art of the Real,* 51. On the subject of doubling, though with regard to the formal aspect of Spark's writing, Joseph Hynes remarks of Spark criticism that the tendency has been to decide on readings that emphasize either comedy as a dominant discourse or "a rather solemn sobriety" (13). Hynes insists, correctly it seems to me, on the necessity to stress the "paradoxical merger" of apparently disparate modes, rather than to "dichotomize" as a critical strategy (13). Such an argument moves toward reading Spark in terms of undecidability, on which we have commented in relation to haunting and spectrality in the introduction. Moreover, Hynes' commentary shadows my own interest in Dickens and the comic-gothic. While not suggesting that Spark is, consciously or otherwise, the inheritor of Dickens, or, indeed, heir to his spectral heritage, I do wish to emphasize, after Hynes, the necessity for pursuing the "contradictory critical" response that registers "laughter and shock" (14), without seeking to read one as being of greater significance than the other.

14. Velma Bourgeois Richmond, *Muriel Spark* (Boston: Twayne Publishers, 1984), 128.

15. Spark's biography of Shelley was first published as *Child of Light: A Reassessment of Mary Shelley* (London, n.p., 1951). All references to are taken from the revised edition.

16. Among the biographies available, two of the most interesting are Anne K. Mellor's *Mary Shelley: Her Life, Her Fiction, Her Monsters* (London: Routledge, 1990) and Emily W. Sunstein, *Mary Shelley: Romance and Reality* (Boston: Little, Brown, & Co., 1989). Neither takes much interest in Spark's biography, even though both share Spark's own interest in the separation and interanimation of life and work. In a concluding chapter that assesses biographical and critical work on Shelley, Sunstein describes Spark's biography briefly as sympathetic yet misleading (400), without suggesting why it is misleading, other than to intimate that this is the case because Spark did not have all Shelley's material available to her in 1951. The question here is one of aesthetic evaluation, and of treating the biography as "straight" biography.

17. Muriel Spark, *Mary Shelley: A Biography,* rev. ed. (New York: Dutton, 1987), x.

18. Spark, *Shelley,* x.

19. Spark, *Shelley,* 1–146.

20. Spark, *Shelley,* 149–235.

21. Derrida, *Margins,* 13.

22. Jacques Derrida, "The Rhetoric of Drugs" (1989), trans. Michael Israel, in *differences: A Journal of Feminist Cultural Studies* 5:1 (1993), 1–24. Rpt. In *Points . . . Interviews, 1974–1994,* ed. Elisabeth Weber, trans. Peggy Kamuf et al. (Stanford: Stanford University Press, 1995), 228–254; 238. On the passage from which this citation comes, see the final chapter, below, on "The New International."

23. Derrida, "Rhetoric," 238.

24. Robert Smith, *Derrida and Autobiography* (Cambridge: Cambridge University Press, 1995), 149.

25. *Perkin Warbeck* is not obviously a gothic novel. It is however an historical romance, influenced by and in the style of the Waverley Novels of Walter Scott, as Spark points out (199). The relationship of the historical romance to the gothic is made explicit by Scott himself in his introduction to what is considered the first gothic novel, Horace Walpole's *The Castle of Otranto.* Walter Scott, "Introduction to *The Castle of Otranto,*" rpt in Horace Walpole, *The Castle of Otranto,* int. Marvin Mudrick (New York: Crowell-Collier, 1963), 115–128.

26. Spark, *Shelley,* 153.

27. Spark, *Shelley,* 154.

28. Spark, *Shelley,* 153.

29. Derrida, "Rhetoric," 238.

30. Derrida, "Rhetoric," 238.

31. Rod Mengham, "1973 The End of History: Cultural Change According to Muriel Spark," in Rod Mengham, ed., *An Introduction to Contemporary Fiction* (Oxford: Polity, 1999), 123–134; 132.

32. Mengham, "1973," 132.

33. Mengham, "1973," 132.

34. Jacques Derrida, *"Khora,"* trans. Ian McLeod, in *On the Name,* ed. Thomas Dutoit, trans. David Wood, John P. Leavey Jr. and Ian McLeod (Stanford: Stanford University Press, 1995), 89–130; 91. The term "superoscillation" in the paragraph preceding the present citation is taken from the same passage in *"Khora,"* and identifies the double logic of the aporetic.

35. Smith, *Derrida and Autobiography,* 168.

36. Roland Barthes, *Roland Barthes by Roland Barthes*, trans. Richard Howard (Berkeley and Los Angeles: University of California Press, 1977), 145.

37. Which a critic with historicist tendencies may be tempted to connect to the period in which Spark first published her study of Shelley.

38. Spark, *Shelley*, 7.

39. Which arguably is still a textual intervention rather than a simple representation.

40. Mark Currie, *Postmodern Narrative Theory* (Basingstoke: Macmillan, 1998), 17. While Spark's biography is not in any obvious sense "postmodern" in the currently understood senses of that word, Currie's discussion of narrative convention is usefully broad enough for me to draw upon in making this point.

41. Smith, *Derrida and Autobiography*, 129.

42. See Roy Porter, *The Greatest Benefit to Mankind: A Medical History of Humanity* (New York: Norton, 1997), 711–12.

43. Brian Cheyette, *Muriel Spark* (Tavistock: Northcote House, 2000), 9–10. Throughout his study, Cheyette addresses forms of doubling and doubleness, both within Spark's narratives and as a formal narrative device. Although he offers no commentary on the *Shelley* biography, he remarks of Spark's fictional characters that her "central figures are often doubled and redoubled" (7), and that such doubling causes displacement, disruption, and instability. Furthermore, he comments on the trope of the ghost and figures of haunting in Spark's work, chiefly *The Hothouse by the East River,* but also in *Loitering with Intent,* Spark's sixteenth novel, published in 1981, in which there are set up "a series of displacements so that the distinction between fact, fiction and fantasy is made deliberately unstable" (103). *Hothouse,* along with other novels of the 1970s, "include[s] a version of history which helps to disrupt the certainties of the present day . . . what is clear is that her fiction is increasingly haunted by the ghosts of the past" (101), a remark that is itself an echo of an earlier comment by Cheyette: "Spark's fiction . . . is haunted by a past which refuses to be contained" (86). Such summaries clearly have resonances with the interests that are explored much earlier in Spark's biography of Mary Shelley, the figure of the uncontainable past suggesting the excesses and overflows being read in the present chapter.

44. Smith, *Derrida and Autobiography*, 146.

45. J. Hillis Miller, *Reading Narrative* (Norman: University of Oklahoma Press, 1998), 149.

46. Miller, *Reading Narrative*, 153.

47. Miller, *Reading Narrative*, 149.

48. Jacques Derrida, "'Le Parjure,' *Perhaps:* Storytelling and Lying ('abrupt breaches of syntax')," in *Without Alibi,* ed., trans., and int. Peggy Kamuf (Stanford: Stanford University Press, 2002), 161–201; 181.

49. Derrida, "'Le Parjure'," 182.

50. Hélène Cixous, "Grimacing Catholicism: Muriel Spark's Macabre Farce (1) and Muriel Spark's Latest Novel: *The Public Image* (2)," trans. Christine

Irizzary, in Martin McQuillan, ed., *Theorizing Muriel Spark: Gender, Race, Deconstruction* (London: Palgrave, 2002), 204–209; 206.

51. Hélène Cixous, *Three Steps on the Ladder of Writing*, trans. Sarah Cornell and Susan Sellers (New York: Columbia University Press, 1993), 7.

52. Cixous, *Three Steps,* 8.

53. It is possible to argue, after Harold Bloom, that Muriel Spark's "life" of Mary Shelley is an act of misprision, a strong reading or misreading, that swerves away from the documenting of a life in seeking to create as strong an effect as the writing of its subject.

54. Paul de Man, *Blindness and Insight: Essays in the Rhetoric of Contemporary Criticism* (New York: Columbia University Press, 1971), 84–85.

55. Cixous, "Grimacing Catholicism," 205–206.

56. Roland Barthes, "The Reality Effect," trans. R. Carter, in Tzvetan Todorov, ed., *French Literary Theory Today* (Cambridge: Cambridge University Press, 1982), 11–17; Naomi Schor, *Reading in Detail: Aesthetics and the Feminine* (New York: Methuen, 1987), 85; George Orwell, "Charles Dickens," cit. Schor, 160–161 n.6.

57. Schor, *Reading,* 75.

58. Barthes, cit. Schor, *Reading,* 90.

59. Schor, *Reading,* 91.

60. Schor, *Reading, 91.*

61. Spark, *Shelley,* 18.

62. Spark, *Shelley,* 19. This scene "returns," at least in part, in Spark's 1981 novel, *Loitering with Intent,* in which the principal character "loiters," as Brian Cheyette puts it, "ghostlike in a graveyard writing a poem" (Cheyette, *Muriel Spark,* 103). When Cheyette remarks of *Loitering* that the novel is divided between "the living and the dead," he could as easily be commenting on the Shelley biography.

63. Cixous, *Three Steps,* 7–9 passim.

64. Although space does not permit me to address the second part of the biography in any detail, it is important to note two instances of Spark's reinforcement of Mary's shadowy and marginal position. The tendency to subjugate Mary Shelley's position to those around her is reiterated in the form of the biography, as Spark moves to, what is for her, the greater importance of Mary Shelley's writing, thereby displacing the writing of a life with the discussion of the text. She suggests as an imperative for the reader of Mary Shelley that it is in "her writings themselves, then, [that] we must seek the imaginative complement to an 'imperfect picture'" of Mary's life (146). Of *The Last Man,* Spark writes that the novel

"most manifestly reveals her as Godwin's daughter, as Shelley's wife, and as a student of Platonic literature" (183–184). Spark's somewhat gothic rereading and reinvention in *Mary Shelley* is important in part, we would contend, because it provides a Bloomian act of misreading, which, from the evidence of Mary's life as presented by Spark, Shelley herself was never able to present.

65. Against such a reading there is, once more, an implicit caveat to be acknowledged. No biography can be written, conventionally at least, in which the principal subject of that biography can be narrated without recourse to other figures, social settings, historical events, and so on that serve in the reconstitution of that life. At the same time, however, there is of course the question of how the material is shaped by the biographer, how the subject is situated rhetorically amongst the factual, cultural, historical details. Mary's liminality in her own narrative, where she is read as simultaneously the subject of the biography and yet also a subsidiary figure to others, a reflection first of her parents and then of her husband, is noticeably pronounced. This is particularly so whenever Shelley is present. We might read here Spark's struggling with the power of the poet's character as it is consolidated in narratives about him, without ever being able to control it wholly, and her subject suffering as a result. Of course Mary may have been cast frequently into the shadows by Shelley's brilliance, especially when surrounded by his friends, but Spark's biography writes itself into this same process, figuring Mary on occasions as a supplement, a marginal detail of another narrative.

66. Spark, *Shelley,* 89.

67. Spark, *Shelley,* 33.

68. Spark, *Shelley,* 76.

69. Spark, *Shelley,* 75.

70. Spark, *Shelley,* 73.

71. Spark, *Shelley,* 72.

72. Spark, *Shelley,* 61.

73. Spark, *Shelley,* 52–53.

74. Spark, *Shelley,* 54.

75. Spark, *Shelley,* 68.

76. Spark, *Shelley,* 81.

77. Spark, *Shelley,* 98.

78. Spark, *Shelley,* 81.

79. Spark, *Shelley,* 94.

80. Spark, *Shelley,* 73.

81. Spark, *Shelley,* 78.

82. Jacques Derrida, "As If It Were Possible, 'Within Such Limits' . . . ," trans. Benjamin Elwood with Elizabeth Rottenberg, in Jacques Derrida, *Negotiations: Interventions and Interviews 1971–2001,* ed., trans., and int. Elizabeth Rottenberg (Stanford: Stanford University Press, 2002), 343–370; 360.

83. Derrida, "As If It Were Possible," 360.

84. Spark, *Shelley,* 84.

85. Spark, *Shelley,* 98.

86. Spark, *Shelley,* 98.

87. Spark, *Shelley,* 99.

88. Spark, *Shelley,* 100.

89. Spark, *Shelley,* 101.

90. Spark, *Shelley,* 106.

91. Spark, *Shelley,* 131.

92. Jacques Derrida, "Taste," 13.

93. Karl Malkoff, *Muriel Spark* (New York: Columbia University Press, 1968), 3.

94. Richmond, *Muriel Spark,* 79.

CHAPTER 4

1. John P. Leavey Jr., *Glassary* (Lincoln: University of Nebraska Press, 1986), 102.

2. Peggy Kamuf, "Deconstruction and Love," in Nicholas Royle, ed., *Deconstructions: A User's Guide* (Basingstoke: Palgrave, 2000), 151–170; 156.

3. Alain Finkielkraut, *The Wisdom of Love,* trans. Kevin O'Neill and David Suchoff (Lincoln: University of Nebraska Press, 1997), 37.

4. Kamuf, "Deconstruction and Love," 156.

5. Kamuf, "Deconstruction and Love," 151.

6. Kamuf, "Deconstruction and Love," 152.

7. Royle, *After Derrida,* 56.

8. Jacques Derrida, *The Ear of the Other: Otobiography, Transference, Translation,* trans. Peggy Kamuf (New York: Schocken Books, 1985), 87.

9. Although a common Latin phrase, I am drawing it with conscious reference to George Eliot's use in *Daniel Deronda,* ed. and int. Barbara Hardy (Harmondsworth: Penguin, 1986), 35, where Eliot uses it to designate a condition of

narrative, and to dismiss the idea of origins, sources, points of beginning and departure. Here we see how even the identity of citation can be problematic.

10. Derrida, *Points . . .* 340.

11. J. Hillis Miller, *Topographies* (Stanford: Stanford University Press, 1995), 296.

12. Royle, *After Derrida,* 133.

13. Derrida, *Points . . .* 196–216.

14. Derrida, *Points . . .* 206.

15. Derrida, *Points . . .* 205.

16. Derrida, *Points . . .* 205.

17. Derrida, *Points . . .* 205–206.

18. Derrida, *Points . . .* 340–341.

19. Bennington and Derrida, *Jacques Derrida,* 3; 1.

20. John P. Leavey Jr., "French Kissing: Whose Tongue Is It Anyway?," in Julian Wolfreys et al., eds., *The French Connections of Jacques Derrida* (Albany: State University of New York Press, 1996), 149–164; 149.

21. "Later in Algiers Omi would rather buy a veal tongue. But in Oran it was ox tongue. . . . Omi took the thing in her eminent cook's hands, hefted it, and began to transfigure it partially. First it is scalded and the thick skin that sheathes it is removed without difficulty, liberating the delicate tenderness of the flesh"; Hélène Cixous, "The Names of Oran," trans. Eric Prenowitz, in Anne-Emmanuelle Berger, ed., *Algeria in Others' Languages* (Ithaca: Cornell University Press, 2002), 184–194, 180–181.

22. Leavey, "French Kissing," 160.

23. Derrida, *Glas,* 1.

24. Cixous, *Three Steps,* 3.

25. Jacques Derrida, *The Post Card: From Socrates to Freud and Beyond,* trans. Alan Bass (Chicago: University of Chicago Press, 1987), 184.

26. Cixous, *Three Steps,* 53.

27. Cixous, *Three Steps,* 7.

28. Cixous, *Three Steps,* 5.

29. Cixous, *Three Steps,* 4.

30. Cixous, *Three Steps,* 5.

31. Cf. J. Hillis Miller on Derrida's as-yet unpublished discussion of the phrase "Je t'aime" [*I love you*] as performative speech act, from which the

quotation is taken, in his *Speech Acts in Literature* (Stanford: Stanford University Press, 2001), 134–139; 137.

32. Peggy Kamuf, ed., *A Derrida Reader: Between the Blinds* (New York: Columbia University Press, 1991), 485.

33. In this sentence I am echoing a comment of Derrida's from one of the interviews in *Points* . . . : "When a proper name is inscribed right on the text, within the text, obviously it is not a signature; it is a way of making the name into a work, of making work of the name, but without this inscription of the proper name having the value of any property rights so to speak. Whence *the double relation of the name and the loss of the name:* by inscribing the name in the thing itself . . . . by inscribing the name in the thing, from one angle, I lose the signature, but, from another, angle, I monumentalize the name, I transform the name into a thing" (365–66; emphasis mine). It is precisely this double relation that I believe is at stake in circumcision, and which is certainly at stake in *Daniel Deronda.*

34. Derrida, *Points* . . . , 120.

35. On nonknowing as opposed to secrets, see Derrida's discussion in *Points* . . . , 201.

36. Jacques Derrida, *Writing and Difference,* trans. Alan Bass (Chicago: University of Chicago Press, 1981), 227.

37. In the "envoi" Derrida appears to write Daniel Deronda as the proper name of a subject and not a work. The name is not italicized as is "proper" in the citation of novel titles. Of course the "envoi" is not supposed to be a properly constructed academic text, with full bibliographical details, notes, and so on. Is this some form of mistake? And, if so, whose fault is it? The one who writes? The translator? The editor? The typesetter or compositor? From internal evidence we cannot tell. Certainly, other titles are italicized: *Limited Inc* (1987b,14); *Beyond the Pleasure Principle* (22); *Le facteur de la verité* (53); *The Interpreter's Dictionary of the Bible* (73). This inexplicable issue seems to connect equivocation with identity (one is tempted to say unequivocally).

This particular "envoi" also ends equivocally, with the phrase *Je me trie* (16; "I sort myself"). A note on the line is appended to the foot of the page which comments that could be *Je me tue* (I kill myself). This internal note, on the equivocation of identity with which the two lines toy, points out that "the writing makes it impossible to distinguish between the two impossibilities" (16). In the English language edition of *The Post Card* there is no conventional abbreviation with this note, such as "[trans.]" or "[ed.]," to suggest that this is a commentary by Alan Bass, so it would appear to be some other voice. Curiously, this line is left open, there being no punctuation following "possibilities." This picks up the "absence" of "final" punctuation throughout the "envois."

Also, it is worth noting, in passing, the equivocal slippage introduced by translation from French to "American English," rather than "British English." In phrases such as "I am finishing writing you in the street," "I will continue to write you," and "I write you all the time, that is all I do" (16). In British English such lines would be written "I write *to* you," the preposition indicating trajectory, destination, posting, address. The American English form, while carrying the same connotation for American readers as "I write to you" does for British readers, also suggests that "I," in writing, actively construct "you" your "identity;" the other here always marks the self.

38. Derrida, *Points* . . . , 120.

39. Derrida, *Points* . . . , 365. See Peggy Kamuf's comments on Derrida, the proper name and the spider's web in her "Introduction: Reading Between the Blinds," *A Derrida Reader,* xiii–xlii.

40. Derrida, *Post Card,* 15.

41. Chase, "The Decomposition of the Elephants: Double-Reading *Daniel Deronda,"* in K. M. Newton, ed., *George Eliot* (Harlow: Longman, 1991), 198–218. See also, in the same volume, a counterargument to Chase by the volume's editor; Newton, *"Daniel Deronda* and Circumcision" (218–232), both of which are summarized and commented on in the present chapter.

42. Steven Marcus, "Human Nature, Social Orders and 19th Century Systems of Explanation: Starting in with George Eliot," *Salmagundi,* 28 (1975).

43. Chase, "Decomposition," 199.

44. Chase, "Decomposition," 209–210.

45. Chase, "Decomposition," 210.

46. Chase, "Decomposition," 210.

47. Newton, *"Daniel Deronda* and Circumcision," 220.

48. Newton, "Circumcision," 222–223.

49. Newton, "Circumcision," 226.

50. Newton, "Circumcision," 228.

51. Newton, "Circumcision," 230.

52. On the subject of the novel's "English" plot and its realism, this seems a misreading, for, as I argue elsewhere, there is much evidence to suggest a self-reflexiveness, a general level of self-conscious allusion to the theatrical and performative nature of this plot in relation to the subject of English national identity that destabilizes the illusion of realism. See Wolfreys, *Being English: Narratives, Idioms, and Performances of National Identity from Coleridge to Trollope* (Albany: State University of New York Press, 1994), 129–151.

53. Chase, "Decomposition," 210.

54. Chase, "Decomposition," 212.

55. Hélène Cixous and Mireille Calle-Gruber, "Inter Views," in *Rootprints: Memory and Life Writing,* trans. Eric Prenowitz (London: Routledge, 1997), 1–116; 16.

56. The figure of the redoubled doubling is taken most immediately from the beginning of an essay by John Sallis, "Doublings," in David Wood, ed., *Derrida: A Critical Reader* (Oxford: Blackwell, 1992), 120–137.

57. Eliot, *Daniel Deronda,* 575–599.

58. Eliot, *Daniel Deronda,* 581.

59. Derrida, *Margins,* xii.

60. Cixous, "Inter Views," 110.

61. Cixous, "Inter Views," 112.

62. Giorgio Agamben, *Idea of Prose,* trans. Michael Sullivan and Sam Whitsitt (Albany: State University of New York Press, 1995), 61.

63. Jacques Derrida, "Shibboleth for Paul Celan," trans. Joshua Wilner, in Aris Fioretos, ed., *Word Traces: Readings of Paul Celan* (Baltimore: The Johns Hopkins University Press, 1991), 3–75; 67.

64. Derrida, "Shibboleth," 67.

65. Derrida, *Glas,* 41.

66. Derrida, "Shibboleth," 67.

67. Barbara Hardy, "Introduction," in Eliot, *Deronda,* 7–30; 29

68. Eliot, *Deronda,* 854.

69. Chase, "Decomposition," 204.

70. Bennington and Derrida, *Jacques Derrida,* 1.

71. Derrida, "Circumfession," *Jacques Derrida,* 4.

72. Derrida, *Glas,* 39–41.

73. Jean-Luc Nancy, *The Inoperative Community,* ed. Peter Connor, trans. Christopher Fynsk (Minneapolis: University of Minnesota Press, 1991), 101.

74. Nancy, *Inoperative Community,* 102.

75. Eliot, *Deronda,* 857.

76. When introduced to Mrs Meyrick by Deronda, Mirah says, "I am a stranger. I am a Jewess" (241). This remark ghosts Daniel's later comment "My name is Daniel Deronda. I am unknown," but appears also to acknowledge to a greater degree that otherness is a structural condition of Jewish identity. One is never at home within such an identity; this identity cannot be fixed or determined, given its radical alterity.

77. Eliot, *Deronda,* 225–242.

78. Eliot, *Deronda,* 227–228.

79. Eliot emphasizes Mirah's beauty and the impression it makes on Daniel's mind in these paragraphs. Deronda, on returning Mirah's gaze and seeing the sorrow written into her expression, speculates on the "probable romance that lay behind that loneliness and look of desolation." There is a certain irony in the remark "there was no denying that the attractiveness of the image made it likelier to last" (228).

80. Nancy, *Inoperative Community,* 101.

81. Jacques Derrida, *Given Time I: Counterfeit Money,* trans. Peggy Kamuf (Chicago: University of Chicago Press, 1992), 172 n.32.

82. Royle, *After Derrida,* 140.

83. Nancy, *Inoperative Community,* 109.

84. Royle, *After Derrida,* 139.

85. Royle, *After Derrida,* 139.

86. Derrida, *Specters,* 7.

87. Derrida, "Shibboleth," 58.

88. Timothy Clark, *Derrida, Heidegger, Blanchot: Sources of Derrida's Notion and Practice of Literature* (Cambridge: Cambridge University Press, 1992), 186.

89. Derrida, *Post Card,* 183–184.

CHAPTER 5

1. Jacques Derrida, "Demeure: Fiction and Testimony," in Maurice Blanchot / Jacques Derrida, *The Instant of My Death / Demeure: Fiction and Testimony,* trans. Elizabeth Rottenberg (Stanford: University of Stanford Press, 2000), 13–103; 28.

2. Samuel Weber, *Mass Mediauras: Form, Technics, Media,* ed. Alan Cholodenko (Stanford: Stanford University Press, 1996), 86.

3. The aura of an artwork is discussed by Walter Benjamin in several essays, most famously in his "The Work of Art in the Age of Mechanical Reproduction," but also in "On Some Motifs in Baudelaire" (both in *Illuminations,* ed. and int. Hannah Arendt, trans. Harry Zohn [New York: Schocken Books, 1969], 217–252, 155–200), and "A Small History of Photography" (in *One-Way Street and Other Writings,* int. Susan Sontag, trans. Edmund Jephcott and Kingsley Shorter [London: Verso, 1985], 240–258).

Benjamin's consideration of aura is dictated by his concerns over what happens to the uniqueness of an artwork once it becomes reproduced, once that uniqueness, which is intimately embedded in and interwoven with the historicity of its production ("Work," 223), is erased through "reproduction-technology" (*Reproductionstechnik*) ("Work," 221). Thus, he argues, "that which atrophies, in the age of the technical reproducibility of the artwork, that is its aura" ("Work," 221). For Benjamin, technological reproducibility bears in its processes a power in copying that challenges an artwork's authenticity, detaching it from the sphere, realm or field of tradition ("Work," 221).

Yet what is aura, exactly? How does Benjamin define it? Aura, in the realm of natural objects is described as "the unique phenomenon of a distance, however close it may be" ("Work," 222); this "uniqueness" decays in the age of technological or mechanical reproducibility as a result of "the desire of contemporary masses to bring things 'closer' spatially and humanly" ("Work," 223). This question of distance is augmented in the essay, "A Small History of Photography": "What is aura, actually? A strange weave of space and time: the unique appearance or semblance of distance, no matter how close the object may be" ("History," 250). There is thus both a question of phenomenal perception involved in the determination of aura, while also a motion described by Gerhard Richter as "a ghostly interplay" (Richter, *Walter Benjamin and the Corpus of Autobiography* [Detroit: Wayne State University Press, 2000], 223), which recalls Paul de Man's consideration of the oscillation of the figure of light in the discourse of philosophy, cited earlier.

Richter also remarks that "Benjamin predicates the experience of the aura upon our openness to the spectral interplay of the presence and absence of sense" (223), while Eduardo Cadava remarks that, in the text of Benjamin, "even when the aura is understood in a positive light—which is not always the case—it is expressed primarily in its withdrawal or destruction. This is why the aura is always a matter of ghosts and specters" (*Words of Light: Theses on the Photography of History* [Princeton: Princeton University Press, 1997], 112–113).

It is not, however, only images through which one may have experience of the auratic. In a note, Benjamin remarks that "[w]ords, too, have an aura of their own. This is how Karl Klaus described it: 'The closer the look one takes at a word, the greater the distance from which it looks back'" ("Some Motifs," 200 n.17). On this, Samuel Weber comments: "[w]hat one 'sees' in the . . . word is not simply a reproduction of the same but something else, a distance that takes up and moves the beholder towards that which, though remote, is also closest-at-hand" (*Mass Mediauras*, 107).

4. Weber, *Mass Mediauras*, 87.

5. Giorgio Agamben, *Stanzas: Word and Phantasm in Western Culture*, trans. Ronald L. Martinez (Minneapolis: University of Minnesota Press, 1993, 108.

6. Jacques Lacan, *Le Séminaire livre XX* (Paris: Seuil, 1975), 70.

7. *Dissemination,* 222. Derrida employs this phrase to remark on the play of undecidability in certain strategically deployed "syncategorems" such as *différance, supplement, pharmakon,* hymen, and others in his writings, where, as a result of the "betweenness" and concomitant undecidability that such terms install, meaning, indeed the very possibility of a finite or determinate meaning, is disrupted.

8. Werner Hamacher, *Pleroma: Reading in Hegel,* trans. Nicholas Walker and Simon Jarvis (Stanford: Stanford University Press, 1998), 3.

9. Geoffrey Bennington, "X," in John Brannigan et al, eds., *Applying: to Derrida,* ed. (Basingstoke: Macmillan, 1996), 1–20, 5. Rpt. in Bennington, *Interrupting Derrida* (London: Routledge, 2000), 76–92. Further citations are from the latest version of the essay.

10. Hamacher, *Pleroma,* 3.

11. Hamacher, *Pleroma,* 3.

12. Royle, *After Derrida,* 162.

13. Theo Angelopoulos, "Make it Yellow: An Interview with Theo Angelopoulos," *Sight and Sound,* 9:5 (1999), 8–11. 10.

14. Martin Heidegger, *History of the Concept of Time: Prolegomena,* trans. Theodor Kisiel (Bloomington: University of Indiana Press, 1992), 289.

15. Peggy Kamuf, *The Division of Literature or the University in Deconstruction* (Chicago: University of Chicago Press, 1997), 171.

16. Kamuf, *Division,* 171.

17. Kamuf, *Division,* 171.

18. Bennington, "X," 78–79. In this essay, Bennington makes the following salient assessment of the function of conference titles, appropriate to this chapter: "titles of conferences are *essentially* proleptic, radically anticipatory of a content yet to come, which content they are designed to *call for* . . . . Conference organisers issue titles as a way of guiding contributors towards something that functions as a *hope* . . . . they *hope* that the title of the conference will nonetheless oblige speakers to think *towards* something. . . . The title of the conference *calls,* then, for something new to be brought to thought . . . . Hearing that call involves accepting an obligation at least to *read* the title that calls" (77–78).

19. Geoffrey Bennington, *"Inter,"* in Martin McQuillan et al, eds., *Post-Theory: New Directions in Criticism* (Edinburgh: Edinburgh University Press, 1999), 103–122. 106.

20. Thomas Pepper, *Singularities: Extremes of Theory in the Twentieth Century* (Cambridge: Cambridge University Press, 1997), 89.

21. Pepper, *Singularities,* 89.

22. Pepper, *Singularities,* 91.

23. Kamuf, *Division,* 171.

24. Hamacher, *Pleroma,* 5.

25. Paul de Man, *The Resistance to Theory,* Foreword Wlad Godzich (Minneapolis: University of Minnesota Press, 1997), 17.

26. Royle, *After Derrida,* 166.

27. Hamacher, *Pleroma,* 3.

28. Bennington, *"Inter,"* 105. In this sentence, I mark off "within" and "beyond" so as to suggest that the idea of the university as a separate or separable space or identity just is this "illusion of the university."

29. Elizabeth Grosz, "Times of Value: Deconstruction and Value," in Scott Lash et al., eds., *Time and Value* (Oxford: Blackwell, 1998), 32.

30. McCarthy cit. Grosz, "Times of Value," 33.

31. Kamuf, *Division,* 146.

32. Jacques Derrida, *Politics of Friendship,* trans. George Collins (London: Verso, 1997), 18.

33. Aristotle, *Nichomachean Ethics,* trans. Martin Ostwald (Indianapolis: Bobbs-Merrill Educational Publishing, 1983), 153.

34. Giorgio Agamben, *Means without End: Notes on Politics,* trans. Vincenzo Binetti and Cesare Casarino (Minneapolis: University of Minnesota Press, 2000), 57. I would like to thank Harun Thomas for the inspiration to consider Agamben in the light of the present topic.

35. Agamben, *Means,* 56.

36. Agamben, *Means,* 80.

37. Agamben, *Means,* 118, 116–117.

38. Royle, *After Derrida,* 160.

39. Avital Ronell, *Finitude's Score: Essays for the End of the Millennium* (Lincoln: University of Nebraska Press, 1994), 6.

40. Derrida, *Points . . . ,* 395.

CHAPTER 6

1. "Der Spuk das Zitate: '. . . . eine Serie von Kontiguuitäten . . . ,'" in Nils Plath and Volker Pantenburg, eds., *Anfuehren—Vorfuehren—Anfuehren: Das Zeitat in Literatur und Theorie* (Bielefeld: Aiesthesis Verlag, 2002), 163–175.

2. *Mosaic: A Journal for the Interdisciplinary Study of Literature,* 35:1 (March 2002): 21–34.

3. *Deconstruction . . . often consists, regularly or recurrently, in making appear . . . a force of dislocation, a limit in the totalization, a limit in the movement of syllogistic synthesis. Deconstruction . . . consists . . . in remarking, in the reading and interpretation of texts, that what has made it possible for philosophers to effect a system is nothing other than a certain dysfunction or "disadjustment," a certain incapacity to close the system . . . this dysfunction not only interrupts the system but itself accounts for the desire for system, which draws its* élan *from this very disadjoinment, or disjunction.* Jacques Derrida, "Taste," 4.

4. *Why stress spectrality here? . . .* in the first place, *because the structure of the archive is* spectral. *It is spectral* a priori. Jacques Derrida, *Archive Fever, trans. Eric Prenowitz* (Chicago: University of Chicago Press, 1996), 84, emphasis added.

5. *Basically, the difference between the two forms of writing in Plato, between* hypomnesis *and* anamnesis, *was a dispute not between speech and writing but rather between two different writings, one bad and the other good. Good writing is thus always* hanté *by bad writing.* "Taste," 8.

6. *Thus the limit always moves within the corpus.* "Taste," 9.

7. *What would* as if *mean from the moment—a revolutionary or messianic moment—that I was determining the* as if *on the basis of such exemplary phrases such as "it's as if I were alive" or "it's as if I were dead"? What would "as if" mean then, I ask.* Jacques Derrida, "A Silkworm of One's Own: Points of View Stitched on the Other Veil," in Hélène Cixous and Jacques Derrida, *Veils,* trans. Geoffrey Bennington (Stanford: Stanford University Press, 2001), 21–92; 25.

But above all else, the essential possibility of an "as if" had to be taken into account, an "as if" that affects all language and all experience with possible fictionality, phantasmaticity, spectrality. Derrida, *Negotiations,* 354.

8. *A future perfect is wrapped up in the past, once "late" means (as it always does, it's a tautology) "so late" and "too late."* "A Silkworm," 33.

9. *It didn't stop coming, apparitioning. Apparitioning carried on.*

That's what was transporting her: the step [pas] *of Apparition. Coming to See.* Hélène Cixous, "Savoir," in Cixous and Derrida, *Veils,* 1–16; 9. In not situating quotation marks throughout this chapter, I am seeking to acknowledge that something may come to be seen, that the apparition could equally step into view or not; that is the possibility of every spectral instance: that, in an ineluctable coming, in having never stopped returning in the past tense, it dislocates in its endless arrival to come. Or not.

10. On the one hand, ... *But* on the other hand, . . . On the one hand, . . . *But* on the other hand, . . . On the one hand, *But* on the other hand. . . . *Archive Fever,* 91, 92, 94, 95.

"What is . . . ?," which is to say, on the one hand, what is it in its essence? And on the other, *what is it (present indicative) at present . . . .*on the one hand, *. . . and,* on the other, . . . on the one hand, . . . and on the other . . . , "Faith and Knowledge," 34, 36, 50.

11. *The dislocation to which this work will have obligated is a dislocation without name; toward another thought of the name, a thought that is wholly other because it is open to the name of the other. Inaugural and immemorial dislocation, it will have taken place—another place, in the place of the other—only on the condition of another topic . . . . We endlessly get caught up in the network of quotation marks. We no longer know how to efface them, nor how to pile them up, one on top of the other. We no longer even know how to quote his "work" any longer, since it already quotes, under quotation marks, the whole language . . . even if it is only from the moment and because of the fact that "he" must be put in quotation marks, the pronominal signatory without authorial signature, "he" who undersigns every work. . . . If "he" is between quotation marks, nothing more can be said . . . that wouldn't require . . . a whole fabric of quotation marks knitting a text without edge. . . . There, near but infinitely distanced, the dislocation is to be found in the interior without inside of language which is yet opened out to the outside by the wholly other. The infinite law of quotation marks seems to suspend any reference, enclosing the work in the borderless context which it gives to itself.* Jacques Derrida, "At this Very Moment in this Work Here I Am," trans. Ruben Berezdivin, in Robert Bernasconi and Simon Critchley, eds., *Re-Reading Levinas* (Bloomington: Indiana University Press, 1991), 11–50; 33–34.

12. *In a phantom-text, these distinctions, these quotation marks, references, or citations become irremediably precarious; they leave only traces, and we shall never define the trace or the phantom without, ironically or allegorically, appealing from one to the other. . . . . Allegory speaks (through) the voice of the other, whence the ghost-effect, whence also the a-symbolic disjunction.* Jacques Derrida, "The Art of Mémoires," in *Mémoires for Paul de Man,* rev. ed., trans. Cecile Lindsay et al. (New York: Columbia University Press, 1989), 45–88; 80.

13. *It is thus necessary, beyond all perception, to receive the other while running the risk, a risk that is always troubling, like the stranger (unheimlich), of a hospitality offered to the guest as* ghost *or* Geist *or* Gast. *There would be no hospitality without the chance of spectrality. But spectrality is not nothing, it exceeds, and thus deconstructs, all ontological oppositions, being and nothingness, life and death—and it also gives.* Jacques Derrida, *Adieu to Emmanuel Levinas,* trans. Pascale-Anne Brault and Michael Naas (Stanford: Stanford University Press, 1999), 111–112.

14. *Yet behold this law making absolute reference to the commandment of the wholly other, obligating beyond any delimitable context.* "At this Very Moment," 34.

15. *Nearly always with him, this is how he sets his work in the fabric: by interrupting the weaving of our language and then by weaving together the interruptions themselves, another language comes to disturb the first one. It doesn't inhabit it, but haunts it.* "At this Very Moment," 18.

16. *Haunting implies places, a habitation, and always a haunted house. Archive Fever,* 86.

17. *For nearly ten years, this specter's comings and goings, unforeseen visits of the ghost. The thing spoke all on its own. I had to explain myself to it, respond to it—or for it.* Jacques Derrida, *Cinders,* trans., ed., and int. Ned Lukacher (Lincoln: University of Nebraska Press, 1991), 22.

18. *The spectre, as its name indicates, is the frequency of a certain visibility. But the visibility of the invisible.* Derrida, *Specters,* 100.

Another text, the text of the other, arrives in silence with a more or less regular cadence, without ever appearing in its original language, to dislodge the language of translation, converting the version, and refolding it while folding it upon the very thing . . . it pretended to import. It disassimilates it. "At this Very Moment," 18.

19. *In any case, the quotation marks always signal some kind of citation.* Derrida, "Geschlecht: Sexual Difference, Ontological Difference," in Peggy Kamuf, ed., *A Derrida Reader,* 390.

20. *I'm not one of the family means, in general . . . I do not define myself on the basis of elementary forms of kinship. But it also means, more figuratively, that . . . this, for me, is the condition not only for being singular and other, but also for entering into relation with the singularity and alterity of others. When someone is one of the family, not only does he lose himself in the herd, but he loses the others as well; the others become simply places, family functions, or places or functions in the organic totality that constitutes a group, school, nation or community of subjects speaking the same language.* "Taste," 27.

21. *You mustn't believe in images, especially not when they circulate "in these regions." Above all you have to wonder what other image, what other, and what other of the image is being forbidden in that case.* "A Silkworm," 79.

22. *A writer's work can be received without being read: texts have effects without being read. Evoked here, then, is a sort of culture of hallucination, a culture of telepathy in which people's thoughts and values, their ideas and beliefs, are variously determined and dictated, transmitted and inscribed, by thinkers whose work has not been read.* Royle, *After Derrida,* 160.

Few thinkers have so many disciples who have never read a word of their master's writings. Paul de Man, *Aesthetic Ideology,* ed. and int. Andrzej Warminski (Minneapolis: University of Minnesota Press, 1996), 93.

23. *The author is familiar to me, the book is new. Not just new to me, but newly published, recently written, so that it comes to me without the filter of commentary that so quickly surrounds a work when it enters the public domain; that filter through which almost everything we read is coloured and constrained.* Derek Attridge, "Expecting the Unexpected in Coetzee's *Master of Petersburg* and Derrida's Recent Writings," in Brannigan et al., eds., *Applying: To Derrida,* 21–40.

24. *Community as* com-mon auto-immunity: *no community . . . that would not cultivate its own auto-immunity, a principle of sacrificial self-destruction ruining the principle of self-protection (that of maintaining its self-integrity intact), and this in view of some sort of spectral sur-vival. This self-contesting attestation keeps the auto-immune community alive, which is to say, open to something other and more than itself.* "Faith and Knowledge," 51.

25. See note 3

26. *. . . a motif is nothing, but so singularly a nothing that it never lets itself be constituted in the stasis of a being. This word* motif *. . . has the energy of a motion.* Jacques Derrida, "To Unsense the Subjectile," in Jacques Derrida and Paule Thévenin, *The Secret Art of Antonin Artaud,* trans. and preface Mary Ann Caws (Cambridge, MA: MIT Press, 1998), 72. To this might be added the remark that *there is no essence or substance of literature: literature is not. It does not exist. It does not remain at home . . . in the identity of a nature or even of a historical being identical with itself.* Jacques Derrida, "Demeure: Fiction and Testimony," in Maurice Blanchot and Jacques Derrida, *The Instant of My Death / Demeure: Fiction and Testimony,* trans. Elizabeth Rottenberg (Stanford: Stanford University Press, 1998), 13–103; 28. These and other statements acknowledge and delineate singular examples of the uncanny disinterrance and derangement that takes place spectrally, and that resonates in singular fashion in the movement of citation, the movement that remains at work even when citation is installed.

27. *. . . the irreducible reality of an event (outside discourse but not outside text).* "Silkworm," 79.

28. *This question* arrives, *if it arrives, it questions with regard to what will come in the future-to-come. Turned toward the future, going toward it, it also comes from it, it proceeds from the future. Specters,* xix.

The context is open because "it comes" [ça vient], *because there is something to come* [il y a de l'avenir], "Taste," 13. Not only is the figure of the future haunted by the nontotalizable to come, but, in the second of the two quotations, the "there-is" gives us to understand the figure of displacement, the arrival from some other place, that citation in general figures, thereby disfiguring the coherence of the system in which it comes to be remarked.

29. *And even before the reading becomes what it already is, even before it enters the dialectical circle of cognition, even before the active consciousness*

grasps itself at work there, this reading is still not yet what it already is . . . Although the reading does not approach its test in an external fashion, it is not yet the immanent movement of self-reproduction which it already is. Hamacher, *Pleroma*, 3–4.

30. "At this Very Moment," 11–51 passim.

31. *And each time, at the same date, what one commemorates will be the date* of *that which could never come back. This latter will have signed and sealed the unique, the unrepeatable; but to do so, it will have had to offer itself for reading in a form sufficiently coded, readable, and decipherable for the indecipherable to appear in the analogy of the anniversary ring . . . . even if it appears as indecipherable.* Derrida, "Shibboleth," 20.

32. Bennington, "Derridabase," 100–110; 104–114, 140–156; 148–166 passim.

33. *Every sign . . . spoken or written . . . can be* cited, *put between quotation marks; thereby it can break with every given context, and engender infinitely new contexts in an absolutely nonsaturable fashion. This does not suppose that the mark is valid outside its context, but on the contrary that there are only contexts without any center of absolute anchoring. This citationality, duplication or duplicity, this iterability of the mark is not an accident or an anomaly, but is that . . . without which a mark could no longer even have a so-called "normal" functioning. What would a mark be that one could not cite? And whose origin could not be lost on the way?*

. . . would a performative statement be possible if a citational doubling did not eventually split, dissociate from itself the pure singularity of the event? . . . Could a performative statement succeed if its formulation did not repeat a "coded" or iterable statement, in other words if the expressions I use . . . were not identifiable as conforming *to an iterable model, and therefore if they were not identifiable in a way as "citation"?* Derrida, *Margins*, 320–321, 326.

34. *A citation in the strict sense implies all sorts of contextual conventions, precautions and protocols in the mode of reiteration, of coded signs such as quotation marks or other typographical devices used for writing a citation. The same holds no doubt for the* récit *as a form, mode, or genre of discourse, even . . . as a literary type. And yet the law that protects the usage,* in stricto sensu, *of the words* citation *and* récit, *is threatened intimately and in advance by a counter-law that constitutes this very law, renders it possible, conditions it and thereby renders it impossible. . . . The law and the counter-law serve each other, citations summoning each other to appear, and each re-cites the other in this proceeding* (process). *There would be no cause for concern if one were rigorously assured of being able to distinguish with rigor between a citation and a non-citation, a* récit *and a non-*récit *or a repetition within the form of one or the other.* "The Law of Genre," trans. Avital Ronell, in Samuel Weber, ed., *Glyph* 7 (Baltimore: The Johns Hopkins University Press, 1980), 176–232; 205.

35. *If we have been insisting so much since the beginning on the logic of the ghost, it is because it points toward a thinking of the event that necessarily exceeds a binary or dialectical logic, the logic that distinguishes or opposes ef-*fectivity or actuality . . . *and* ideality. *Specters,* 63.

36. *"Tout Autre est Tout Autre,"* in Jacques Derrida, *The Gift of Death,* trans. David Wills (Chicago: University of Chicago Press, 1995), 82–115 passim.

37. *Let us recall, to begin with, that the chain of this quoted quotation . . . displays the heritage of an immense rumour throughout an imposing corpus of Western philosophical literature . . . . it reaches us nonetheless with something of a delay—that of a quotation already.* Derrida, *Politics of Friendship,* 27, 28.

38. *Au fond, ce livre* [Specters of Marx] *est avant tout une réflexion sur cette catégorie de spectralité. . . . C'est un des motifs principaux de cet essai. Cette catégorie de spectralité peut être très féconde, et c'est donc un des fils conducteurs de cet essai.* Jacques Derrida. *Sur Parole: instantanés philosophiques.* Paris: Editions de l'aube, 1999, 121.

39. *. . . in the first place . . . the structure of the archive is* spectral. *It is spectral a priori: neither present nor absent "in the flesh," neither visible nor invisible, a trace always referring to another whose eyes can never be met. Archive Fever,* 84.

40. *What does the phrase "the ghost of my other I" say? My other I, is that myself or an other I, an other who says "I"? Or a "myself" which is itself only divided by the phantom of its double? Once there is phantom or double as revenant, the logic of identification . . . is not . . . easily appeased.* Jacques Derrida, *The Truth in Painting,* trans. Geoff Bennington and Ian McLeod (Chicago: University of Chicago Press, 1987). 373.

41. *One doubles the other, not as a countable presence, but as a ghost. The yes of memory, with its recapitulating control and reactive repetition, immediately doubles the light, dancing yes of affirmation, the open affirmation of the gift. Reciprocally, two responses or two responsibilities refer to each other without having any relationship between them.* Derrida, *Acts of Literature,* 307–308.

42. *In constructing the crypt, in letting the crypt construct and consolidate itself, the Wolf Man wants to save the living death he as walled up inside him. That is,* himself—*the lodging, the haunt of a host of ghosts.* Jacques Derrida, *"Fors:* The Anglish Words of Nicolas Abraham and Maria Torok," trans. Barbara Johnson, in Nicolas Abraham and Maria Torok, *The Wolf Man's Magic Word,* trans. Nicholas Rand (Minneapolis: University of Minnesota Press, 1986), xi–xlviii; xxiii.

43. *The sentence in quotation marks is indeed a simulacrum of a citation . . . such a "citation" is nowhere to be found.* Derrida, *Dissemination,* 197 n.20.

44. *A Spectral analysis of the* two *of the shoes should tell us how they go. . . . But as soon as they are no longer going anywhere, as soon as they are de-*

tached, abandoned and unlaced, they may no longer be a pair. The pair sepa-rates. What is then the spectrum of possibilities of the possibility of specters? Truth in Painting, 373–374.

45. *Pierrot is brother to all the Hamlets haunting the Mallarméan text. Dissemination,* 195.

46. *If one names and cites the best friends . . . . it is because this friendship comes to* illuminate. *. . . . It engraves the renown in a ray of light, and prints the citation of the friend in a convertibility of life and death, of presence and ab-sence, and promises it to the testamental* revenance *of more [no more] life, of a surviving. Politics of Friendship,* 20.

47. *For that which touches on it or that about which one speaks in speak-ing of touch is also the intangible. . . . I have just gone too quickly.* Jacques Der-rida, *"Le toucher:* Touch/to touch him," trans. Peggy Kamuf, *Paragraph,* 16: 2 (July 1993): 122–158; 141.

48. *Another way of talking about this might be through such terms as* relics, bits and pieces, remains *that act as reminders, memorials.* Dawn McCance and John P. Leavey Jr., "Translation/citation: An Interview with John P. Leavey Jr.," in *Mosaic: A Journal for the Interdisciplinary Study of Literature,* 35:1 (March 2002), 1–20; 12.

49. *Spectral errancy of words. The spectral return does not befall words by accident, following a death which would come to some or spare others. The spec-tral return is partaken of by* all *words, from their first emergence. They will al-ways have been phantoms, and this law governs the relationship in them between body and soul. One cannot say that we know this because we have ex-perience of death and of mourning. That experience comes to us from our rela-tion to this spectral return of the mark, then of language, then of the word, then of the name. What one calls poetry or literature, art itself . . . in other words a certain experience of language, of the mark or of the trait as such, is nothing perhaps but an intense familiarity with the ineluctable originarity of the specter.* "Shibboleth," 58.

CHAPTER 7

1. Ulrich Baer, *Remnants of Song: Trauma and the Experience of Moder-nity in Charles Baudelaire and Paul Celan* (Stanford: Stanford University Press, 2000), 1.

2. Jacques Derrida, "Taste," 61.

3. Dominick LaCapra, *Writing History, Writing Trauma* (Baltimore: The Johns Hopkins University Press, 2000), 47.

4. Avital Ronell, *The Telephone Book: Technology-Schizophrenia-Electric Speech* (Lincoln: University of Nebraska Press, 1989), 89.

5. LaCapra, *Writing History,* 185, 195.

6. Michael Bernard-Donals and Richard Glejzer, *Between Witness and Testimony: The Holocaust and the Limits of Representation* (Albany: State University of New York Press, 2001), 56.

7. Bernard-Donals and Glejzer, *Between Witness,* 58.

8. LaCapra, *Writing History,* 195.

9. Baer, *Remnants,* 11.

10. Baer, *Remnants,* 11.

11. Baer, *Remnants,* 9.

12. In pointing to a "psychoanalytic" or an "ethical" criticism, I am merely alluding to two of the more obvious "contexts" or frameworks, conceptual languages or institutionally recognized discourses, that someone reading this might highlight or foreground in order to "explain" the origins of the present critical act. The psychoanalytic and ethical registers are not the only ones at work here, however. Equally, the matter of history and our relation to, understanding of, the narratives we term "historical" are announced. Another way of commandeering the present chapter in terms of a master discourse might be to see it as an articulation of particular aspects of Jacques Derrida's recent work, and therefore, by the usual, wholly predictable extension, to apprehend this chapter as an example of so-called deconstruction. Such assumptions or, to be more accurate, calculations, exemplify the ways in which conceptualization proceeds, and which the introduction of this chapter seeks to unpack in relation to the motifs of "testimony," "trauma," "witnessing," and "responsibility."

13. Shoshana Felman, and Dori Laub, *Testimony: Crises of Witnessing in Literature, Psychoanalysis, and History* (London: Routledge, 1992), 52.

14. Gayatri Chakravorty Spivak, "A Moral Dilemma," in Howard Marchitello, ed., *What Happens to History: The Renewal of Ethics in Contemporary Thought* (New York: Routledge, 2001), 215–236; 221.

15. Baer, *Remnants,* 10.

16. Bernard-Donals and Glejzer, *Between Witness,* 5

17. Jacques Derrida, *The Other Heading: Reflections on Today's Europe,* trans. Pascale-Anne Brault and Michael Naas (Chicago: University of Chicago Press, 1992), 41.

18. Felman and Laub, *Testimony,* 53

19. I am borrowing the contours of this commentary from the work of Jacques Derrida, who, in *The Gift of Death,* has commented that "[t]he simple

concepts of alterity and singularity constitute the concept of duty as much as that of responsibility. As a result, the concepts of responsibility, of decision, or of duty, are condemned a priori to paradox, scandal, and aporia. Paradox, scandal, and aporia are themselves nothing other than sacrifice, the revelation of conceptual thinking at its limit, its death and finitude" (68). Elsewhere, in the same work, Derrida remarks: "I am responsible to any one (that is to say to any other) only by failing in my responsibility to all others, to the ethical or political generality, and I can never justify this sacrifice" (70).

20. Baer, *Remnants,* 9.

21. Joseph G. Kronick, *Derrida and the Future of Literature* (Albany: State University of New York Press, 1999), 15. Kronick elaborates this point from a discussion of Derrida's in the third chapter of *The Gift of Death:* "I can respond only to the one (or to the One), that is, to the other, by sacrificing that one to the other. I am responsible to any one (that is to say to any other) only by failing in my responsibility to all the others, to the ethical or political generality. And I can never justify this sacrifice, I must always hold my peace about it. Whether I want to or not, I can never justify the fact that I prefer or sacrifice any one (any other) to the other. . . . What binds me to singularities, to this one or that one . . . remains finally undecidable . . . as unjustifiable as the infinite sacrifice I make at each moment. These singularities represent others, a wholly other form of alterity: one other or some other persons, but also places, animals, languages. How would you ever justify the fact that you sacrifice all the cats in the world to the cat that you feed at home every morning for years, whereas other cats die of hunger at every instant." Derrida, *Gift of Death,* 70–71.

22. Alexander Garcia Düttman, *The Gift of Language: Memory and Promise in Adorno, Benjamin, Heidegger, and Rosenzweig* (London: Athlone Press, 2000), 97.

23. Derrida cit. Düttman, *Gift,* 99.

24. Düttman, *Gift,* 74.

25. Cathy Caruth, *Unclaimed Experience: Trauma, Narrative, and History* (Baltimore: The Johns Hopkins University Press, 1996), 3.

26. Baer, *Remnants,* 9.

27. It has to be acknowledged, of course, that the act of "secondary witnessing," a kind of working-through the trauma of others, is a problem fraught with the dangers of identification. As LaCapra remarks, "a difficulty arises when the virtual experience involved in empathy gives way to vicarious victimhood, and empathy with the victim seems to become an identity" (2001, 47).

28. Jacques Derrida, "Demeure," 47.

29. Avital Ronell, *Finitude's Score: Essays for the End of the Millennium* (Lincoln: University of Nebraska Press, 1994), 327.

30. LaCapra, *Writing History,* 49.

31. Louis Althusser, *Writings on Psychoanalysis: Freud and Lacan,* trans. Jeffrey Mehlman (New York: Columbia University Press, 1996), 103.

32. Althusser, *Writings,* 104.

33. Dianne Sadoff, *Sciences of the Flesh: Representing Body and Subject in Psychoanalysis* (Stanford: Stanford University Press, 1998), 45.

34. Sadoff, *Sciences,* 50.

35. Caruth, *Unclaimed Experience,* 1.

36. Sigmund Freud, *Beyond the Pleasure Principle,* in *The Standard Edition of the Complete Psychological Works of Sigmund Freud,* trans. and gen. ed., James Strachey (London: Hogarth Press, 1953–1974), vol. 18; rpt. as *Beyond the Pleasure Principle,* trans. and ed. James Strachey, int. Gregory Zilboorg, biog. Int. Peter Gay (New York: Norton, 1989), 24.

37. Caruth, *Unclaimed Experience,* 7.

38. Caruth, *Unclaimed Experience,* 1, 4.

39. Caruth, *Unclaimed Experience,* 2.

40. Caruth, *Unclaimed Experience,* 3.

41. Caruth, *Unclaimed Experience,* 5.

42. Caruth, *Unclaimed Experience,* 5.

43. Ronell, *Finitude's Score,* 313.

44. Ronell, *Finitude's Score,* 313–314.

45. Slavoj Žižek, *On Belief* (London: Routledge, 2001), 36–37.

46. Jacques Derrida, "Response to Daniel Libeskind," in Daniel Libeskind, *Radix-Matrix: Architecture and Writings* (Munich: Prestel, 1997), 110–115; 115.

47. Daniel Libeskind, "Mourning: Sachsenhausen, Oranienberg," in Libeskind, *Radix-Matrix: Architecture and Writings* (Munich: Prestel, 1997), 102–109; 102.

48. Daniel Libeskind, "Between the Lines," in Libeskind, *Radix-Matrix: Architecture and Writings* (Munich: Prestel, 1997), 34–56; 34.

49. Libeskind, "Between the Lines," 34.

50. Daniel Libeskind, www.daniel-libeskind.com/projects.

51. Libeskind, "Mourning," 102.

52. Libeskind, "Mourning," 102.

53. Libeskind, "Mourning," 102.

54. Libeskind, "Mourning," 102.

55. Libeskind, "Mourning," 102.

56. Dori Laub, in Felman and Laub, *Testimony,* 178.

57. Nicolas Abraham and Maria Torok, *The Shell and the Kernel. I,* trans. and int. Nicholas Rand (Chicago: University of Chicago Press, 1994). 100.

58. Nicola King, *Memory, Narrative, Identity* (Edinburgh: Edinburgh University Press, 2000), 17–19.

59. Rand, in Abraham and Torok, *Shell,* 14.

60. Abraham and Torok, *Shell,* 130.

61. Žižek, *On Belief,* 37–38.

62. Maurice Blanchot, *The Infinite Conversation,* trans. and foreword Susan Hanson (Minneapolis: University of Minnesota Press, 1993), 22.

63. Mary Shelley, *Frankenstein, or the Modern Prometheus,* ed. and int. Marilyn Butler (Oxford: Oxford University Press, 1994), 3.

64. In a possible development of this sketch of a reading of Shelley's novel, it can be argued that Shelley's comprehension of the aberrant, the traumatic, and the monstrous that inform modernity figures cultural experience in a proleptic, if not prosthetic manner, as that comes to be analyzed by Karl Marx at the beginning of *Capital.* As Thomas Keenan's persuasive analysis of Marx's opening rhetorical gestures makes plain, Marx addresses the ways in which the economic "shows itself by hiding itself, by announcing itself as something else or in another form"; wealth is figured as something monstrous, "compounded of elements from different forms . . . grown beyond the control of its creators." This monster cannot be domesticated; neither can it be rendered in as an organic unity, being "nothing but parts, unnatural and uncommon . . . [a]berrant, deviant. . . . This figure of monstrosity, living and dead (the *Wahrig [Deutsches Wörterbuch]* links *ungeheuer [enormous, immense, monstrous]* to *unheimlich, [uncanny, lit. unhomely],* unhomely monstrosity to ghostly recurrence), haunts the chapter (Keenan *Fables of Responsibility: Aberrations and Predicaments in Ethics and Politics* [Stanford: Stanford University Press, 1997], 104). Marx even quotes himself, thereby engaging in an act of mechanical grafting, according to Keenan, where this monstrous or ghostly act serves only to point further for the critic to the ways in which words themselves are "nothing but commodities, to be accumulated, moved and removed . . . transferred like *(als)* property or the mechanical limb . . . on a monster" (1997, 105). It is arguable that, while Keenan does not speak directly of trauma in the context of reading the opening passages from Marx, he does mobilize through his analysis of the monstrous and spectral rhetoric that Marx engages around the subject of the commodity, a transformative critique of the essentially traumatic effect on cultural identity (including Marx's own, given his choice of words) of capitalist economics.

65. Terry Castle provides a compelling account of the nineteenth century as a century of incorporation and internalisation, through an analysis of the figure

of "phantasmagoria" and its transformation from the literal meaning, pertaining to the technological production and representation of ghosts in exhibitions and other public entertainments to the wholly internal "successions of . . . phantasms . . . as called up by the imagination, or as created by literary description'; Castle *The Female Thermometer,* 141.

66. Caruth, *Unclaimed Experience,* 2.

67. Joseph Conrad, *Heart of Darkness,* in *Heart of Darkness with the Congo Diary,* ed. and int. Robert Hampson (London: Penguin, 1995), 1–140; 112.

68. Samuel Weber, *Mass Mediauras: Form Technics Media,* ed. Alan Cholodenko (Stanford: Stanford University Press, 1996), 149.

69. Conrad, *Heart of Darkness,* 118.

70. J. Hillis Miller, *Tropes, Parables, Performatives: Essays on Twentieth-Century Literature* (Hemel Hempstead: Harvester Wheatsheaf, 1990), 188.

71. Blanchot, *Infinite Conversation,* 314.

72. J. Hillis Miller, *Topographies* (Stanford: Stanford University Press, 1995), 57.

73. Jacques Derrida, "'A Self-Unsealing Poetic Text': Poetics and Politics of Witnessing," trans. Rachel Bowlby, in Michael P. Clark, ed., *Revenge of the Aesthetic: The Place of Literature in Theory Today* (Berkeley and Los Angeles: University of California Press, 2000), 180–207; 190.

74. Miller, *Topographies,* 74–75.

75. W. B. Yeats, *Purgatory,* in *The Yeats Reader,* ed. Richard J. Finneran (New York: Scribner Poetry, 1997), 252–259; 255

76. Yeats, *Purgatory,* 258.

77. Yeats, *Purgatory,* 259.

78. Yeats, *Purgatory,* 258.

79. Yeats, *Purgatory,* 259.

80. Derrida, "Self-Unsealing Poetic Text," 200.

81. John Felstiner's critical biography, *Paul Celan: Poet, Survivor, Jew* (New Haven: Yale University Press, 1995), provides a comprehensive introduction to Celan's writing. Clarisse Samuels examines Celan's response to the Holocaust through the aesthetic and philosophical influences of surrealism and existentialism on the poet's work in *Holocaust Visions: Surrealism and Existentialism in the Poetry of Paul Celan* (Columbia: Camden House, 1993). Shira Wolosky's *Language Mysticism: The Negative Way of Language in Eliot, Beckett, and Celan* (Stanford: Stanford University Press, 1995) relates experimentation with language in relation to questions of Christian and Judaic mysticism. She provides a reading of "Ich kann dich noch sehn" (232–234), drawing on Kabbalistic tradi-

tion and Emmanuel Levinas's consideration of one's relation to the Other, in particular the impossible encounter with the face of God; see Levinas, *Totality and Infinity: An Essay on Exteriority*, (1961) trans. Alphonso Lingis (Pittsburgh: Duquesne University Press, 1969), 187–220. *Word Traces* (1994) brings together a number of essays on different aspects of Celan's poetry, including Derrida's "Shibboleth: For Paul Celan," 3–74.

The translation of "Ich kann dich noch sehn' is my own. For copyright reasons, I cannot reproduce the original in German. A translation of this poem, with the original, is to be found in Celan's *Selected Poems*, trans. and int. Michael Hamburger (Harmondsworth: Penguin, 1990), 298–299.

82. Celan's careful choice of words makes translation difficult, if not impossible. There is a "multiplicity of layering," a "multilayered, precise concreteness," to quote Anders Olsson, "Spectral Analysis: A Commentary on 'Solve' and 'Coagula'," trans. Hanna Kalter Weiss in collaboration with the author, in Fioretos, ed., *Word Traces*, 267–279; 274. Such encryption, where even the most seemingly commonplace words—such as *noch*—pushes the readability of language to its limits, while also offering the reader a sense of the haunting resonance at which the material trace hints, and which, responsibly, reading should not attempt to control. One particular translation might be seen as contentious, where I have translated *Stelle* as passage, rather than "point" or "place." This translation immediately refers to a location in a text, but, given the poem's address, its passage, if you will, between addresser and addressee, and the poem's turning upon a movement, I have risked the more unlikely translation.

83. Derrida, "Self-Unsealing Poetic Text," 200.

84. Derrida, "Self-Unsealing Poetic Text," 200. On this transformation of address, see J. Hillis Miller, "Thomas Hardy, Jacques Derrida and the 'Dislocation of Souls'," in *Tropes, Parables, Performatives,* 171–180. In a remark that is uncannily pertinent to Celan's poem, Miller says that "[r]eading the poem, I, you, or anyone becomes its addressee, since it has no name or specified destination" (180).

85. Derrida, "Self-Unsealing Poetic Text," 184.

CHAPTER 8

1. Jacques Derrida, *Edmund Husserl's* Origin of Geometry: *An Introduction,* trans., with Preface and Afterword, John P. Leavey Jr. (Lincoln: University of Nebraska Press, 1989), 148.

2. Michel Foucault, "On the Archaeology of the Sciences: Response to the Epistemology Circle," in Michel Foucault, *Aesthetics, Method, and Epistemology: Essential Works of Michel Foucault 1954–1984, Volume Two,* ed. James D.

Faubion, trans. Robert Hurley et al. (New York: The New Press, 1998), 297–334; 306.

3. Derrida, *Husserl,* 149.

4. Foucault, "Archeology," 306.

5. The epigraph is taken from Bennington, "Derridabase," 15–16.

6. Arkady Plotnitsky, *In the Shadow of Hegel: Complimentarity, History, and the Unconscious* (Gainesville: University Press of Florida, 1993), 238.

7. Derrida, *Dissemination,* 330–340.

8. Derrida, *Dissemination,* 330.

9. "Qual Quelle," in Derrida, *Margins,* 273–306.

10. Derrida, *Margins,* 279.

11. Derrida, *Margins,* 291.

12. Derrida, *Margins,* 291.

13. Jacques Derrida, "Afterword: Toward an Ethic of Discussion," trans. Samuel Weber, in Jacques Derrida, *Limited Inc.* trans. Samuel Weber and Jeffrey Mehlman (Evanston: Northwestern University Press, 1988), 111–154; 141.

14. Derrida, "Afterword," 141.

15. Derrida, "Afterword," 147.

16. Jacques Derrida, "Letter to a Japanese Friend," trans. David Wood and Andrew Benjamin, in David Wood and Robert Bernasconi, eds., *Derrida and Différance* (Evanston: Northwestern University Press, 1988), 1–5; 4.

17. Martin Heidegger, *Aristotle's Metaphysics Θ 1–3: On the Essence and Actuality of Force,* second ed., trans Walter Brogan and Peter Warnek (Bloomington: Indiana University Press, 1995), 28.

18. Heidegger, *Aristotle's Metaphysics,* 29.

19. An obvious, though instructive difference, being that Being has been subject to inquiry, speculation, and attempted definition for far longer than deconstruction. What is instructive, however, is that approaches to the absolute or universal determination of deconstruction are "contaminated" by the same logic, the logic that makes the demand "What is . . . ?," and which also, sooner or later, desires to pursue the matter of origins.

20. *Aristotle's Metaphysics,* 29.

21. *Aristotle's Metaphysics,* 30.

22. *Aristotle's Metaphysics,* 30.

23. Arguably, the relentless structure I am describing can be seen in the situation of Foucault's comments cited at the beginning of this chapter, which belong to a response to a demand on the part of the Paris Epistemology Circle, a

demand to define "the critical propositions on which the possibility of his theory and the implications of his method are *founded*" ("Archeology," 297; emphasis added), coming as the Circle's response to *Madness and Civilization, Birth of the Clinic,* and *The Order of Things.* The words quoted here are those of the Circle, not Foucault's interpretation.

24. Martin Heidegger, "The Origin of the Work of Art," in Martin Heidegger, *Poetry, Language, Thought,* trans. and int. Albert Hofstadter (New York: Harper and Row, 1971), 15–89.

25. Heidegger, "Origin," 17.

26. "Origin," 17.

27. "Origin," 17.

28. Dennis J. Schmidt, *The Ubiquity of the Finite: Hegel, Heidegger, and the Entitlements of Philosophy* (Cambridge, MA: MIT Press, 1988), 102. Schmidt's reading continues in the same passage by pointing out how "Heidegger opposes the figure of circularity to the traditional metaphysical admiration for . . . syllogistic straight lines." Such straight lines, such unbroken linearity in general are, doubtless, those that would trace the continuity between a discourse, subject, or concept, and its origin.

29. J. Hillis Miller, *Speech Acts in Literature* (Stanford: Stanford University Press, 2001), 153.

30. Jacques Derrida, "Et Cetera . . . (and so on, und so weiter, and so forth, et ainsi de suite, und so überall, etc.)," trans. Geoffrey Bennington, in Royle, ed., *Deconstructions,* 282–305; 288.

31. Not to sound too certain about this, but it is perhaps a feature of many "discussions" of or, more accurately, polemics concerning origins (let us say, for example, those on the part of particular fundamentalist Christian constituencies) that certainty is hegemonic inasmuch as there is no place available for the possibility of discussion, debate, challenge, uncertainty, skepticism, speculation, or, indeed, any form of discourse, dialectical or otherwise, that would be able, according to the laws and rules of the discourse on origin, to question or call into question any article of faith. Nothing perhaps is more certain about a discourse that asserts certainty when nothing could be less certain than origin.

32. Michel Foucault, *The Archaeology of Knowledge,* trans. A. M. Sheridan Smith (London: Tavistock, 1972), 22.

33. Jacques Derrida, *"Finis,"* in *Aporias,* trans. Thomas Dutoit (Stanford: Stanford University Press, 1993), 33.

34. *"Finis,"* 33.

35. Nancy, *Being Singular Plural,* 10.

36. Bennington, "Derridabase," 15.

37. Nancy, *Being Singular Plural,* 10–11.

38. Nicholas Royle, "What Is Deconstruction," in Royle, ed., *Deconstructions,* 1–13; 11.

39. Royle, "What is Deconstruction," 7.

40. Andrzej Warminski, "'As the Poets Do It': On the Material Sublime," in Tom Cohen, Barbara Cohen, J. Hillis Miller and Andrzej Warminski, eds., *Material Events: Paul de Man and the Afterlife of Theory* (Minneapolis: University of Minnesota Press, 2001), 3–31; 28

41. Philippe Lacoue-Labarthe, *Poetry as Experience,* trans. Andrea Tarnowski (Stanford: Stanford University Press, 1999), 96.

CHAPTER 9

1. Jacques Derrida, "No Apocalypse, Not Now (full speed ahead, seven missiles, seven missives)," *diacritics,* 14:2 (Summer 1984): 20–32; 22–23.

2. Paolo Friere, *Pedagogy of the Oppressed,* trans. Myra Bergman Ramos (New York: Continuum, 1997), 68.

3. Karl Marx, "Theses on Feuerbach," in Karl Marx and Frederick Engels, *The German Ideology Part One,* ed. and int. C. J. Arthur (London: Lawrence and Wishart, 1970), 123.

4. Derrida, "Letter to a Japanese Friend," 4.

5. Derrida, "Letter," 3.

6. J. Hillis Miller, "Paul de Man as Allergen," in Cohen et al., eds., *Material Events,* 183–204; 185.

7. Jacques Derrida, *Right of Inspection,* photographs by Marie-Françoise Plissart, trans. David Wills (New York: Monacelli Press, 1998), n.p.

8. Derrida, *Right of Inspection,* n.p.

9. Friere, *Pedagogy,* 140.

10. Friere, *Pedagogy,* 140.

11. Friere, *Pedagogy,* 140.

12. Friere, *Pedagogy,* 156.

13. Louis Althusser, *For Marx,* trans. Ben Brewster (London: Verso, 1979), 101.

14. Karl Marx and Frederick Engels, *Manifesto of the Communist Party,* in *Economic and Philosophic Manuscripts of 1844 and the Communist Manifesto* (New York: Prometheus Books, 1988), 212.

15. Althusser, *For Marx,* 102.

16. Raymond Williams, *Marxism and Literature* (Oxford: Oxford University Press, 1977), 122.

17. Williams, *Marxism,* 121.

18. Peggy Kamuf, "Violence, Identity, Self-Determination, and the Question of Justice: On *Specters of Marx,*" in Hent de Vries and Samuel Weber, eds., *Violence, Identity, and Self-Determination* (Stanford: Stanford University Press, 1997), 271–283; 272.

19. Derrida, *Politics of Friendship,* 103.

20. J. Hillis Miller, "Paul de Man as Allergen," 187.

21. Antonio Gramsci, *Selections from Political Writings 1921–1926,* trans. and ed. Quentin Hoare (London: Lawrence and Wishart, 1978), 169.

22. Derrida, *The Other Heading,* 87.

23. Aijaz Ahmad, "Reconciling Derrida: 'Specters of Marx' and Deconstructive Politics," in Michael Sprinker, ed., *Ghostly Demarcations: A Symposium on Jacques Derrida's Specters of Marx* (London: Verso, 1999), 88–109; 89.

24. Ahmad, "Reconciling Derrida," 90.

25. Robert J. C. Young, "Deconstruction and the Postcolonial," in Royle, ed., *Deconstructions,* 190. In this essay, Young also discusses Ahmad's "characteristic method . . . of reductive *ad hominem* and *ad feminem* critique [which] betrays his claim to Marxist objectivity" (189).

26. Ahmad, "Reconciling Derrida," 90.

27. Jacques Derrida, "Marx & Sons," trans. G. M. Goshgarian, in Sprinker, ed., *Ghostly Demarcations,* 213–269; 230.

28. Richard E. Joines, "*Contretemps:* Derrida's Ante and the Call of Marxist Political Philosophy." *Cultural Logic,* 3:1/2 (2001): www.eserver.org/clogic.

29. Peggy Kamuf, "The Ghosts of Critique and Deconstruction," in Martin McQuillan, ed., *Deconstruction: A Reader* (Edinburgh: Edinburgh University Press, 2000); 198–213; 206.

30. Karl Marx, "The Fetishism of Commodities and the Secret Thereof," in *Capital Vol. 1,* trans. Samuel Moore and Edward Aveling (New York: International Publishers, 1967), 76–87; 76–77. The motif of the *fantastic* is highlighted here because, as will be obvious to some readers, its Greek etymology pertains to a literal "making visible" or, in some cases, a spectral apparition.

31. Derrida, *Specters,* 155–165.

32. Marx, "Fetishism," 76, 77.

33. Marx, "Fetishism," 76.

34. Marx, "Fetishism," 77.

35. Jacques Derrida, "Du marxisme. Dialogue avec Daniel Bensaïd," in *Sur Parole: Instantanés philosophiques* (Paris: Éditions de l'aube, 1999), 115–123; 121.

36. Derrida, "Du marxisme," 121.

37. Marx, "Fetishism," 77.

38. Gayatri Chakravorty Spivak, "A Moral Dilemma," in Howard Marchitello, ed., *What Happens to History: The Renewal of Ethics in Contemporary Thought* (New York: Routledge, 2001), 215–236; 221–222.

39. Joines, *"Contretemps."*

40. Jean Baudrillard, "Symbolic Exchange and Death" in *Selected Writings,* ed. Mark Poster (Standord: Stanford University Press, 1988), 119–149; 121.

41. José B. Monleón, *A Specter Is Haunting Europe: A Sociohistorical Approach to the Fantastic* (Princeton: Princeton University Press, 1990), 60.

42. Etienne Balibar, *The Philosophy of Marx,* trans. Chris Turner (London: Verso, 1995), 60.

43. Balibar, *Philosophy,* 43.

44. Balibar, *Philosophy,* 43.

45. V. N. Volosinov, *Marxism and the Philosophy of Language,* trans. Ladislav Matejka and R. Titunik (Cambridge, MA: Harvard University Press, 1986), 33, 34.

46. Derrida, "Du marxisme," 117.

47. Giorgio Agamben, *Means without Ends: Notes on Politics,* trans. Vincenzo Binetti and Cesare Casarino (Minneapolis: University of Minnesota Press, 2000), 116–117.

48. Agamben, *Means without Ends,* 116–117.

49. Nicos Poulantzas, *Political Power and Social Classes,* trans. ed., Timothy O'Hagan (London: Verso, 1973), 63.

50. Poulantzas, *Political Power,* 64.

CHAPTER 10

1. The injunction on the part of Martin McQuillan was to consider two passages from *Specters of Marx* that addressed directly the notion of "the New International." The passages to which contributors were directed are to be found on 84–85 and 102–103.

2. Derrida, "Marx & Sons," 214.

3. Derrida, "Marx & Sons," 228.

4. This remark is taken from Jacques Derrida, *"'As if* I were dead': an interview with Jacques Derrida," in John Brannigan, Ruth Robbins, Julian Wolfreys, eds., *Applying: to Derrida* (Basingstoke: Macmillan, 1996), 212–226, 213. The remark is made with regard to the notion of application.

5. Matthew Arnold, "Friendship's Garland," in Arnold, *Selected Prose,* ed. and int. P. J. Keating (London: Penguin, 1970), 301–339. *Geist* can mean ghost of course, although it is not limited to this interpretation. It is also haunted by the idea of spirit, an idea irreducible to the ghostly figure, and conjuring the notion of a national or intellectual spirit. Arnold's "rush" to avoid a certain discussion is a carefully constructed assumption of an identity in the letters that make up "Friendship's Garland," all of which Arnold writes as a supposed dialogue between himself and a German acquaintance, Arminius, who exhorts Arnold, and, more generally, the English to "get *Geist.*" Arnold's performance in these letters in relation to the question of *Geist* is assumed so as to address questions of Englishness critically.

6. Derrida, "Marx & Sons," 222.

7. "Quand on lit trop vite ou trop doucement on n'entend rien," cit. as epigraph to Paul de Man's *Allegories of Reading: Figural Language in Rousseau, Nietzsche, Rilke, and Proust* (New Haven: Yale University Press, 1979). For discussion of this aphorism, see Derrida, "The Art of *Mémoires,*" 88 n.3.

8. Derrida, "No Apocalypse," 21.

9. On the trope of addiction see Derrida, "The Rhetoric of Drugs," in *Points . . . ,* 228–254.

10. Derrida, "Rhetoric," 238.

11. Derrida, "Marx & Sons," 253.

12. Werner Hamacher, "Lingua Amissa: The Messianism of Commodity-Language and Derrida's *Specters of Marx,*" in Sprinker, ed., *Ghostly Demarcations* (168–212), 169.

13. Karl Marx, *The Poverty of Philosophy* (Moscow: Progress Publishers, 1978), 108.

14. Derrida, "Du Marxisme," 115–122.

15. Terry Eagleton, "Marxism without Marxism," in Sprinker, ed., *Ghostly Demarcations,* 83–87.

16. Derrida, "Du marxisme," 121.

17. Richard E. Joines, *"Contretemps:* Derrida's Ante and the Call of Marxist Political Philosophy." *Cultural Logic,* 3:1/2 (2001): www.eserver.org/clogic.

18. Fredric Jameson, "Marx's Purloined Letter," in Sprinker, ed., *Ghostly Demarcations,* 30.

19. Jameson, "Marx's Purloined Letter," 30.

20. Jameson, "Marx's Purloined Letter," 28.

21. Eagleton, "Marxism without Marxism," 84, 85, 87. Given Eagleton's fondness for alliterative comparison as a violent shorthand substitute for political analysis, an effect that, arguably, rebounds against him in his reference to "Auschwitz and Algeria" (85), one might be tempted to see in this stutter the signs of a self-congratulatory belles-lettrist, if one had the time. Perhaps, to paraphrase Eagleton on Derrida, the fact is he is hardly concerned with a dialogue of any kind (86).

22. Warren Montag, "Spirits Armed and Unarmed: Derrida's *Specters of Marx*," in Sprinker, ed., *Ghostly Demarcations* (68–82), 68–69.

23. Derrida, "Du marxisme,"120.

24. Ahmad, "Reconciling Derrida," 88–109.

25. Derrida, "Du marxisme," 117.

26. The sentence from which this phrase is taken runs as follows: "While there has been heated debate over the first two terms in *[Specters of Marx's]* subtitle ('the state of the debt', what it means to be a Marxist today; 'the work of mourning', ghosts and spectrality etc.) there has been little written concerning the third enigmatic component, 'the new international'." In response to this, it is the contention of the present letter that, in order to begin to come to terms with this "enigmatic component" it is absolutely necessary that we not feel as though we can move on beyond the question of spectrality, as though the so-called heated debate (if in fact this ever happened) had said enough on the question of spectrality. It is precisely because so much of Derrida's work touches on aspects of haunting, the phantom or phantasm, spectrality, the ghost, spirit, and so on, that, on the one hand, we cannot simply suggest that we have done with it, and move on to another aspect of that work (as though anything could be that separable or compartmentalizable, especially when it comes to the question of the spectral) while, on the other hand, because of the multiple manifestations of such figures throughout the text of Derrida, it is impossible, not to say unthinkable, to reduce haunting or the efficacity of hauntology to a single identity.

27. www.sussex.ac.uk/units/frenchthought/video/realvideo/derridavideo. html.

28. The two passages, with their ellipses, run as follows. First extract:

> "The New International" refers to a profound transformation, projected over a long term of international law, of its concepts, and its field of intervention. . . . A "new international" is being sought through these crises of international law; it already denounces the limits of a discourse on human rights that will remain inadequate; sometimes hypocritical, and in any case

formalistic and inconsistent with itself as long as the law of the market, the "foreign debt," the inequality of techno-scientific, military, and economic development maintain an effective inequality as monstrous as that which prevails today, to a greater extent than ever in the history of humanity. . . . The "New International" is not only that which is seeking a new international law through these crimes. It is a link of affinity, suffering, and hope, a stil discreet, almost secret link, as it was around 1848, but more and more visible, we have more than one sign of it. It is an untimely link, without status, without title, and without name, barely public even if it is not clandestine, without contract "out of joint," without co-ordination, without party, without country, without national community (International before, across, and beyond any national determination), without co-citizenship, without common belonging to a class. The name of new International is given here to what calls to the friendship of an alliance without institution among those who, even if they no longer believe or never believed in the socialist-Marxist International, in the dictatorship of the proletariat, in the messiano-eschatological role of the universal union of the proletarians of all lands, continue to be inspired by at least one of the spirits of Marx or of Marxism (they now know that there is more than one) and in order to ally themselves, in a new, concrete, and real way, even if this alliance no longer takes the form of a party or a worker's international, but rather of a kind of counter-conjuration, in the (theoretical and practical) critique of the state of international law, the concepts of State and nation, and so forth: in order to renew this critique and especially to radicalize it. (84–96)

Second passage:

Everywhere in the world today, the structure of the party is becoming more and more suspect (and for reasons that are no longer always, necessarily, "reactionary," those of the classical individualist reaction) but also radically unadapted to the new—tele-techno-media—conditions of public space, of political life, of democracy, and of the *new* modes of representation (both parliamentary and non-parliamentary) that they call up. A reflection on what will become Marxism tomorrow, of its inheritance or its testament, should include, among so many other things, a reflection on the finitude of a cetrain concept or of a certain reality of the party. . . . Let us put forward here with many precautions, both theoretical and practical, the hypothesis that this is no longer the case, *not always* the case (for these old forms of struggle against the State may survive for a long time); one must do away with this equivocation so that it will no longer be the case. The hypothesis is that this mutation has already begun; it is irreversible. (102–103)

The passages excised in the call for papers, in the order in which the ellipses appear, are as follows. First ellided passage:

> Just as the concept of human rights has slowly been determined over the course of centuries through many socio-political upheavals (whether it be a matter of the right to work or economic rights, of the rights of women and children, and so forth), likewise international law should extend and diversify its field to include, if at least it is to be consistent with the idea of democracy and of human rights it proclaims, the *worldwide* economic and social field, beyond the sovereignty of States and of the phantom-States we mentioned a moment ago. Despite appearances, what we are saying here is not simply anti-statist: in given and limited conditions, the super-State, which might be an international institution, may always be able to limit the appropriations and the violence of certain private socio-economic forces. But without necessarily subscribing to the whole Marxist discourse (which, moreover, is complex, evolving, heterogeneous) on the State and its appropriation by a dominant class, on the distinction between State power and State apparatus, on the end of the political, on "the end of politics," or on the withering away of the State, and, on the other hand, without suspecting the juridical idea in itself, one may still find inspiration in the Marxist "spirit" to criticize the presumed autonomy of the juridical and to denounce endlessly the *de facto* take-over of international authorities by powerful Nation-States, by concentrations of techno-scientific capital, symbolic capital, and financial capital, of State capital and private capital. (84–85)

Second ellided passage:

> For it must be cried out, at a time when some have the audacity to neo-evangelize in the name of the ideal of a liberal democracy that has finally realized itself as the idea of human history: never have violence, inequality, exclusion, famine, and thus economic oppression affected as many human beings in the history of the earth and of humanity. Instead of singing the advent of the ideal of liberal democracy and of the capitalist market in the euphoria of the end of history, instead of celebrating the "end of ideologies" and the end of the great emancipatory discourses, let us never neglect this obvious macroscopic fact, made up of innumerable singular sites of suffering: no degree of progress allows one to ignore that never before, in absolute figures, never have so many men, women, and children been subjugated, starved or exterminated on the earth. (And provisionally, but with regret, we must leave aside here the nevertheless indissociable question of what is becoming of so-called "animal" life, the life and existence of "animals" in this history. This question has always been a serious one, but it will become massively unavoidable.) (85)

Third ellided passage (second citation):

> And, of course, of its State correlative. A movement is underway that we
> would be tempted to describe as a deconstruction of the traditional con-
> cepts of State, and thus of party and labour union. Even if they do not sig-
> nify the withering away of the State, in the Marxist or Gramscian sense,
> one cannot analyze their historical singularity outside of the Marxist in-
> heritance—where inheritance is more than ever a critical and transforma-
> tive filter, that is, where it is out of the question to be for or against the
> State in general, its life or death *in general.* There was a moment, in the
> history of European (and, of course, American) politics, when it was a re-
> actionary gesture to call for the end of the party, just as it was to analyze
> the inadequation of existing parliamentary structures to democracy itself.
> (102–103)

29. The phrase is taken from Derrida's essay, "Typewriter Ribbon: Limited
Ink (2) ("within such limits")," in Cohen et al., eds., *Material Events,* 277–360.

30. Derrida, *Specters,* 85.

31. Louis Althusser, "Ideology and Ideological State Apparatuses," *Essays on
Ideology* (London: Verso, 1984); rpt. in Slavoj Žižek, ed., *Mapping Ideology* (London: Verso, 1999), 100–140.

32. Althusser, "Ideology," 121.

33. Karl Marx and Friedrich Engels, *The German Ideology,* ed. and int. C. J.
Arthur (London: Lawrence and Wishart, 1970), 47.

34. Louis Althusser, *Writings on Psychoanalysis: Freud and Lacan,* trans.
Jeffrey Melhman, ed., Olivier Corpet and François Matheron (New York: Columbia University Press, 1996), 103–104.

35. Paul Virilio, *The Art of the Motor* (1993), trans. Julie Rose (Minneapolis:
University of Minnesota Press, 1995), 140. Elsewhere in the same volume, with regard to speed, Virilio remarks that *"[s]peed* guarantees the secret and thus the
value of all information" (53). This remark opens for us the technicity of speed,
the tele-technological apparition as that which *tekhne* names, a certain letting appear. There is thus to be considered a question here of different speeds. On the one
hand there is the rapidity of the spectral, of the phantomatic apparition, which
passes quickly, and without duration, as Derrida has suggested (see the essay on
citation). On the other hand, there is also that speed, or those speeds—there are
more than one—that mark the politico-addictive commentary on *Specters of
Marx.* While realising that I have already taken up far too much time here, it is
tempting to suggest that, from a certain perspective, the rush to comment on
Specters and to discount the notion of spectrality, is a manifestation of speed, after
Virilio, aimed at maintaining the text of Marx in a certain way, as keeping it in

place for particular readings, while keeping other readings, and the other of those readings, a secret, thereby proprietorially seeking to ensure the value of the Marxian text, to keep its value, and the concomitant investment in it, at a premium.

36. Thomas M. Kemple, *Reading Marx Writing: Melodrama, the Market, and the "Grundrisse"* (Stanford: Stanford University Press, 1995), 24.

37. This and the following remarks of Plotnitsky's are taken from his essay, "Algebra and Allegory: Nonclassical epistemology, Quantum Theory, and the Work of Paul de Man," in Cohen et al., eds., *Material Events,* 49–92.

38. Jacques Derrida, *Spectres de Marx* (Paris: Galilée, 1993), 142. The phrase, *plus d'un,* is employed on a number of occasions by Derrida, with knowing acknowledgment of the displacement within its identity.

39. *Spectres,* 142–143.

40. *Spectres,* 143.

41. *Spectres,* 228.

CHAPTER 11

1. Robert Young, *White Mythologies: Writing History and the West* (London: Routledge, 1990), 1.

2. Roland Barthes, "Where to Begin?," in *New Critical Essays,* trans. Richard Howard (New York: Farrar, Strauss, and Giroux, 1974), 79–91.

3. Bennington, "Derridabase, 15.

4. Derrida, *Grammatology,* 162.

5. Derrida, *Margins,* 6–7.

6. Derrida, *Dissemination,* 316.

7. Louis Althusser and Etienne Balibar, *Reading Capital,* trans. Ben Brewster (London: Verso, 1979), 14–15.

8. Suhail Malik, "Différantial Technics," *Imprimatur* 1: 2/3 (1996): 200–203; 200.

9. Jacques Derrida, "Politics and Friendship: An Interview with Jacques Derrida," trans. Robert Harvey, in E. Ann Kaplan and Michael Sprinker, eds., *The Althusserian Legacy* (London: Verso, 1993), 183–232; 197.

10. Francis Barker, *The Tremulous Private Body: Essays on Subjection* (London: Methuen, 1984), 9.

11. "Thence homeward by coach and stopped at Martins my bookseller, where I saw the French book which I did think to have had for my wife to translate, called *L'escholle de Filles;* but when I came to look into it, it is the most

bawdy, lewd book that ever I saw, rather worse than *putanta errante* [1584]—so that I was ashamed of reading it; and so away home." Samuel Pepys, *The Diary of Samuel Pepys,* 12 vols., ed. R. C. Latham and W. Matthews (London: Harper Collins, 1995), IX, 21–22.

12. "Thence away to the strand to my bookseller's, and there stayed an hour and bought that idle, roguish book, *L'escholle des Filles;* which I have bought in plain binding (avoiding the buying of it better bound) because I resolve, as soon as I have read it, to burn it, that it may not stand in the list of books, nor among them, to disgrace them if it should be found" (IX: 1995, 57–58).

13. "Up, and at my chamber all the morning and the office, doing business and also reading a little of *L'escolle des Filles,* which is a mighty lewd book, but yet not amiss for a sober man once to read over to inform himself in the villainy of the world. At noon home to dinner, where by appointment Mr. Pelling came, and with him three friends: Wallington that sings the good bass, and one Rogers, and a gentleman, a young man, his name Tempest, who sings very well endeed and understands anything in the world at first sight. After dinner, we into our dining-room and there to singing all the afternoon (by the way, I must remember that Pegg Pen was brought to bed yesterday of a girl; and among other things, if I have not already set it down, that hardly ever was remembered such a season for the smallpox as these last two months have been, people being seen all up and down the streets, newly come out after the smallpox); but though they sang fine things, yet I must confess that I did take no pleasure in it, or very little, because I understood not the words; and with the rests that the words are set, there is no sense nor understanding in them, though they be English—which makes us weary of singing in that manner, it being but a worse sort of instrumental music. We sang till almost night, and drank my good store of wine; and then they parted and I to my chamber, where I did read through *L'escholle des Filles;* a lewd book, but what doth me no wrong to read for information sake (but it did hazer my prick para stand all the while, and una vez to decharger); and after I had done it, I burned it, that it might not be among my books to my shame; and so at night to supper and then to bed" (IX: 1995, 58–59).

14. Barker, 3–4.

15. Peter de Bolla, *The Discourse of the Sublime: History, Aesthetics and the Subject* (Oxford: Blackwell, 1989), 236.

16. Roland Barthes, *S/Z,* trans. Richard Miller, Preface Richard Howard (Berkeley and Los Angeles: University of California Press, 1974), 4.

17. Barthes, 4.

18. Bennington, *"Inter,"* 106.

19. On the accusation of "theory" in the guise of "deconstruction" as being either too political or not political enough in relation to institutions and politicized

discourse both inside and outside the academy, see Peggy Kamuf's scrupulous reading of the situation in *The Division of Literature,* 133–161. Richard Beardsworth, considering the text of Jacques Derrida, also provides a telling commentary on deconstruction's account of why "all political projects fail" (19) as well as its radical assessment of institutions and the violence they effect; Beardsworth, *Derrida and the Political* (London: Routledge, 1996), 18–25. See also Geoffrey Bennington's "Demanding History" (61–73), "Not Yet" (74–87), and "Outside Story" (88–98), all in *Legislations: The Politics of Deconstruction* (London: Verso, 1994).

20. On the "aporetic responsibility concerning the political" (68), see Richard Beardsworth, "The Political Limit of Logic," *Derrida and the Political,* 46–97.

21. Homi K. Bhabha, "The Commitment to Theory," in *The Location of Culture* (London: Routledge, 1994), 19–39; 25, 26.

22. Royle, in commenting on hostility toward the text of Derrida in general and the so–called Cambridge affair concerning the award of an honorary degree, also remarks that "there is not reading and there is not reading;" Royle, *After Derrida,* 160.

23. Hélène Cixous, "Without end, no, State of Drawingness, no rather: The Executioner's taking off," trans Catherine A. F. MacGillivray, in *Stigmata: Escaping Texts* (London: Routledge, 1998), 20–31; 20.

24. Cixous, "Without end," 20.

25. Cixous, *Three Steps,* 19.

26. Cixous, *Three Steps,* 21–22.

27. Cixous, *Three Steps,* 19–22.

28. Cixous, *Three Steps,* 21.

29. On the unreadable and the undecidable that propels reading, which commands that reading begin again, rather than bringing a halt to reading, see Royle, *After Derrida,* 159–174.

30. Clark, *Derrida, Heidegger, Blanchot,* 110–111.

31. Paul de Man, *The Resistance to Theory,* Foreword Wlad Godzich (Minneapolis: University of Minnesota Press, 1986), 17.

32. Simon Critchley, *The Ethics of Deconstruction: Derrida and Levinas* (Oxford: Blackwell, 1986), 88.

33. On this subject the reader is referred to the following remark of Peggy Kamuf's: "The fact that deconstruction can be positioned as at once too political and not political at all, as both PC and not PC, signals the terms in which the political is posed in this debate are inadequate to account for all the effects being produced"; *Division,* 146. There is an immeasurable gap between Bennington's

"not political enough" and Kamuf's "not political at all," which would make for interesting reading, or would bare careful commentary on the extent to which either "theory" or "deconstruction" remains unread and even unreadable, in conventional political terms, whether from the "Left" or the "Right," whether from a "Left–Liberalism" or a "Right–Liberalism."

34. Again, see Kamuf's *Division,* particularly chapter 5, already mentioned. Her following remark is also of interest, in that it implicitly acknowledges the limits of reading "theory," and the extent to which "theory" has stopped being read: "If it generally seems to be the case that—to use a very sloppy kind of shorthand that the academic institution not only tolerates but prefers and proliferates—"French theory" has been forced back into some kind of retreat from the shores of humanities and particularly literature departments in the United States, then this retreat has not occurred without leaving behind an offshoot that is usually called simply "theory." "French theory," in other words, may have been put under some kind of general ban, but "theory" without the qualifier has won what, for the moment at least, seems to be a respected place in catalogues of graduate literary studies" (12). The sloppiness of "French theory" has been replaced by the banality of "theory" as a catch-all identification, and what is interesting also in Kamuf's astute summation of the situation is that, to an extent, the location of "theory" in "graduate literary studies" suggests an implicit cordoning off of the reading material of theory from undergraduates to a large extent. Paul de Man's notion of resistance to theory is re-marked in precisely this organized, if tacit proscription of reading within the institution. Following the formula through, not only are undergraduates not given the opportunity to read "theory" (if we stay with the general term for the moment, if only for convenience' sake), they are also not encouraged to read in a so-called theoretical fashion. Kamuf's remarks apply specifically to the university in the United States. In Britain, it is possible to find a number of theory courses for undergraduates, although it would require statistical research to show whether these are more frequent in Britain than in North America. What can be said, however, is that, often "theory" courses are taught during the last year of undergraduate study. Effectively, this limits the extent to which the student can ask questions concerning what it means to read.

35. Shoshana Felman, *What Does a Woman Want?* (Baltimore: The Johns Hopkins University Press, 1993), 5.

36. The phrase "nonsynonymous substitutions" is employed by Derrida in the essay "Différance," *Margins,* 12.

37. Lacoue-Labarthe, *Typography,* 175.

38. Felman, *What Does a Woman Want?*, 5.

39. Felman, 5.

40. Felman, 5.

41. Felman, 5.

42. Felman, 5.

43. Althusser, *Reading Capital*, 14–15.

44. Barthes, *S/Z*, 4.

45. Bhabha, *Location*, 25.

46. Michel Foucault, "Self Writing," trans. Paul Rabinow, in *Ethics: The Essential Works 1*, ed. Paul Rabinow (London: Penguin, 1997), 207–222; 211.

47. Hamacher, *Pleroma*, 3.

48. Hamacher, *Pleroma*, 3–5.

49. Thomas Keenan, *Fables of Responsibility: Aberrations and Predicaments in Ethics and Politics* (Stanford: Stanford University Press, 1997), 102.

50. Keenan, *Fables*, 92.

51. Keenan, *Fables*, 92.

52. Sarah Kofman, *Nietzsche and Metaphor*, trans. Duncan Large (London: Athlone Press, 1993), 116.

53. De Man, *Resistance*, 17.

54. David Farrell Krell, *Infectious Nietzsche* (Bloomington: University of Indiana Press, 1996)

55. Emmanuel Levinas, *Beyond the Verse: Talmudic Readings and Lectures*, trans. Gary D. Mole (Bloomington: University of Indiana Press, 1994), 109.

56. Levinas, *Beyond the Verse*, 109.

57. This remark comes from the "Foreword" to Levinas's *Proper Names*, trans. Michael B. Smith (Stanford: Stanford University Press, 1996), in which he traces a shift to an analysis that relies on the reading of textual play without the acknowledgment of a more significant resonance: "Statements no longer succeed in putting things together."

> "Signifiers" without "signifieds" play a "sign game" with neither sense nor stakes. . . . There is a general alienation from the meaningful as posited . . . an opposition to the rigor of logical forms, adjudged to be repressive, an obsession with the inexpressible, the ineffable, the unsaid—which are sought in the awkward expression, the slip of the tongue, the scatological. Genealogy as exegesis, the dead bodies of words swollen with etymologies and devoid of *logos*, borne by the drift of the texts: such is modernity. . . . But a modernity that is already degenerating into elementary truths and fashionable banter. (4)

This is not simply a caveat against what is called "poststructuralism." Against the "irresponsible" playfulness discerned, Levinas situates the proper name, as the title of the collection suggests. For Levinas, proper names offer a provisional inscription through which the Saying of the Other is projected and sustained, for proper names "resist the dissolution of meaning" (4).

58. Levinas, *Proper Names*, 6.

59. Levinas, *Beyond the Verse*, 109.

60. Levinas, *Beyond the Verse*, 109.

61. Levinas, *Beyond the Verse*, 109.

62. Jean-François Lyotard, *The Postmodern Explained*, ed. Julian Pefanis and Morgan Thomas, trans. Don Barry et al., Afterword Wlad Godzich (Minneapolis: University of Minnesota Press 1992), 101.

63. J. Hillis Miller, *The Ethics of Reading: Kant, de Man, Eliot, Trollope, James, and Benjamin* (New York: Columbia University Press, 1987), 43.

64. Jean-Luc Nancy, *The Birth to Presence*, trans. Brian Holmes et al. (Stanford: Stanford University Press, 1993), 336–337.

65. Bennington, "Derridabase," 56.

66. Ronell, *Finitude's Score*, 7.

67. Ronell, *Finitude's Score*, 6.

68. Ronell, *Finitude's Score*, 6–7.

69. Kamuf, *Division*, 171.

70. Royle, *After Derrida*, 161.

71. Royle, *After Derrida*, 162.

72. Royle, *After Derrida*, 161.

73. Susan Stewart, *On Longing: Narratives of the Miniature, the Gigantic, the Souvenir, the Collection* (Durham: Duke University Press, 1993), 14.

74. Felman, *What Does a Woman Want?*, 5.

75. Cixous, *Three Steps*, 19.

76. We find the impossibility of assigning an authoritative beginning remarked here, in this case whether we are interested in the *private place* of Pepys, as identified by Francis Barker, or the *scenes of solitude*, beginning with Augustine's silent reading noted by Stewart (14); there is no beginning for reading, only its occasions, where it chances to take place.

77. Stewart, *On Longing*, 14.

78. Stewart, *On Longing*, 14.

79. Stewart, *On Longing*, 14.

80. Stewart, *On Longing*, 14.

WORKS CITED

WORKS BY JACQUES DERRIDA

Derrida, Jacques. *Of Grammatology.* Trans. and int. Gayatri Chakravorty Spivak. Baltimore: The Johns Hopkins University Press, 1974.

Derrida, Jacques. "The Law of Genre." Trans. Avital Ronell. Samuel Weber, ed. *Glyph* 7. Baltimore: The Johns Hopkins University Press, 1980. 176–232.

Derrida, Jacques. *Writing and Difference.* Trans. Alan Bass. Chicago: University of Chicago Press, 1981.

Derrida, Jacques. *Dissemination.* Trans. Barbara Johnson. Chicago: University of Chicago Press, 1981.

Derrida, Jacques. *Margins of Philosophy.* Trans. Alan Bass. Chicago: University of Chicago Press, 1982.

Derrida, Jacques. "No Apocalypse, Not Now full speed ahead, seven missiles, seven missives." *diacritics,* 14:2 (Summer 1984): 20–32.

Derrida, Jacques. *The Ear of the Other: Otobiography, Transference, Translation.* Trans. Peggy Kamuf. New York: Schocken Books, 1985.

Derrida, Jacques. *"Fors:* The Anglish Words of Nicolas Abraham and Maria Torok." Trans. Barbara Johnson. Nicolas Abraham and Maria Torok. *The Wolf Man's Magic Word.* Trans. Nicholas Rand. Minneapolis: University of Minnesota Press, 1986, xi–xlviii.

Derrida, Jacques. *Glas.* Trans. John P. Leavey Jr. and Richard Rand. Lincoln: University of Nebraska Press, 1986.

Derrida, Jacques. "Living On • Borderlines." Trans. James Hulbert. Harold Bloom, Paul de Man, Jacques Derrida, Geoffrey Hartman, and J. Hillis Miller. *Deconstruction and Criticism.* New York: Continuum, 1987. 75–176.

Derrida, Jacques. *The Post Card: From Socrates to Freud and Beyond.* Trans. Alan Bass. Chicago: University of Chicago Press, 1987. 184.

Derrida, Jacques. *The Truth in Painting.* Trans. Geoff Bennington and Ian McLeod. Chicago: University of Chicago Press, 1987.

Derrida, Jacques. "Afterword: Toward an Ethic of Discussion." Trans. Samuel Weber. *Limited Inc.* Trans. Samuel Weber and Jeffrey Mehlman. Evanston: Northwestern University Press, 1988. 111–154.

Derrida, Jacques. "Letter to a Japanese Friend." Trans. David Wood and Andrew Benjamin. David Wood and Robert Bernasconi, eds. *Derrida and Différance.* Evanston: Northwestern University Press, 1988. 1–5.

Derrida, Jacques. "Introduction: Desistance." Trans. Christopher Fynsk. Philippe Lacoue-Labarthe. *Typography: Mimesis, Philosophy, Politics.* Trans. and ed. Christopher Fynsk. Cambridge: Harvard University Press, 1989. 1–42.

Derrida, Jacques. "The Art of *Mémoires.*" *Mémoires for Paul de Man.* Rev. ed. trans. Cecile Lindsay et al. New York: Columbia University Press, 1989. 45–88.

Derrida, Jacques. "The Ghost Dance: An Interview with Jacques Derrida," Interview with Mark Lewis and Andrew Payne. Trans. Jean-Luc Svoboda. *Public* 2 (1989): 60–73.

Derrida, Jacques. *Edmund Husserl's* Origin of Geometry: *An Introduction.* Trans., with Preface and Afterword, John P. Leavey Jr. Lincoln: University of Nebraska Press, 1989.

Derrida, Jacques. "At this Very Moment in this Work Here I Am." Trans. Ruben Berezdivin. Robert Bernasconi and Simon Critchley, eds. *Re-Reading Levinas.* Bloomington: Indiana University Press, 1991. 11–50.

Derrida, Jacques. "Geschlecht: Sexual Difference, Ontological Difference." Peggy Kamuf, ed. *A Derrida Reader: Between the Blinds.* New York: Columbia University Press, 1991. 378–402.

Derrida, Jacques. "Shibboleth for Paul Celan." Trans. Joshua Wilner. Aris Fioretos, ed. *Word Traces: Readings of Paul Celan.* Baltimore: The Johns Hopkins University Press, 1991. 3–75.

Derrida, Jacques. *Cinders.* Trans., ed., and int. Ned Lukacher. Lincoln: University of Nebraska Press, 1991.

Derrida, Jacques. *Given Time I: Counterfeit Money.* Trans. Peggy Kamuf. Chicago: University of Chicago Press, 1992.

Derrida, Jacques. *The Other Heading: Reflections on Today's Europe.* Trans. Pascale-Anne Brault and Michael Naas. Chicago: University of Chicago Press, 1992.

Derrida, Jacques. *Acts of Literature.* Ed. Derek Attridge. New York: Routledge, 1992.

Derrida, Jacques. *Aporias.* Trans. Thomas Dutoit. Stanford: Stanford University Press, 1993.

Derrida, Jacques. *"Le toucher:* Touch/to touch him." Trans. Peggy Kamuf. *Paragraph,* 16: 2 (July 1993): 122–158.

Derrida, Jacques. "Politics and Friendship: An Interview with Jacques Derrida." Trans. Robert Harvey. E. Ann Kaplan and Michael Sprinker, eds. *The Althusserian Legacy.* London: Verso, 1993. 183–232.

Derrida, Jacques. *Memoirs of the Blind: The Self-Portrait and Other Ruins.* Trans. Pascale-Anne Brault and Michael Naas. Chicago: University of Chicago Press, 1993.

Derrida, Jacques. *Spectres de Marx.* Paris: Galilée, 1993.

Derrida, Jacques. *Specters of Marx: The State of the Debt, the Work of Mourning, and the New International.* Trans. Peggy Kamuf. Int. Bernd Magnus and Stephen Cullenberg. New York: Routledge, 1994.

Derrida, Jacques. *"Khora. "* Trans. Ian McLeod. *On the Name.* Ed. Thomas Dutoit. Trans. David Wood, John P. Leavey Jr., and Ian McLeod. Stanford: Stanford University Press, 1995. 89–130.

Derrida, Jacques. "The Rhetoric of Drugs." Trans. Michael Israel. *differences: A Journal of Feminist Cultural Studies 5:1* 1993, 1–24. Rpt. in *Points . . . Interviews, 1974–1994. Ed.* Elisabeth Weber. Trans. Peggy Kamuf et al. Stanford: Stanford University Press, 1995. 228–254.

Derrida, Jacques. *The Gift of Death.* Trans. David Wills. Chicago: University of Chicago Press, 1995.

Derrida, Jacques. *Archive Fever.* Trans. Eric Prenowitz. Chicago: University of Chicago Press, 1996.

Derrida, Jacques. "'*As if* I were dead': an interview with Jacques Derrida." John Brannigan, et al., eds. *Applying: to Derrida.* Basingstoke: Macmillan, 1996. 212–226.

Derrida, Jacques, and John D. Caputo. *Deconstruction in a Nutshell.* New York: Fordham University Press, 1997.

Derrida, Jacques. "Response to Daniel Libeskind," Daniel Libeskind, *Radix-Matrix: Architecture and Writings.* Munich: Prestel, 1997. 110–115.

Derrida, Jacques. *Politics of Friendship.* Trans. George Collins. London: Verso, 1997.

Derrida, Jacques. *Right of Inspection.* Photographs by Marie-Françoise Plissart. Trans. David Wills. New York: Monacelli Press, 1998.

Derrida, Jacques. "Faith and Knowledge: the Two Sources of 'Religion' at the Limits of Reason Alone." Trans. Samuel Weber. Jacques Derrida and Gianni Vattimo. *Religion*. Stanford: Stanford University Press, 1998. 1–78.

Derrida, Jacques. "To Unsense the Subjectile." Jacques Derrida and Paule Thévenin. *The Secret Art of Antonin Artaud*. Trans. and Preface Mary Ann Caws. Cambridge: MIT Press, 1998. 59–157.

Derrida, Jacques. *Adieu to Emmanuel Levinas*. Trans. Pascale-Anne Brault and Michael Naas. Stanford: Stanford University Press, 1999.

Derrida, Jacques. "Du marxisme. Dialogue avec Daniel Bensaïd." *Sur Parole: Instantanés philosophiques*. Paris: Éditions de l'aube, 1999. 115–123.

Derrida, Jacques. "Marx & Sons." Trans. G. M. Goshgarian. Michael Sprinker, ed. *Ghostly Demarcations: A Symposium on Jacques Derrida's* Specters of Marx. London: Verso, 1999. 213–269.

Derrida. Jacques. *Sur Parole: instantanés philosophiques*. Paris: Editions de l'aube, 1999.

Derrida, Jacques. "'A Self-Unsealing Poetic Text': Poetics and Politics of Witnessing." Trans. Rachel Bowlby. Michael P. Clark, Ed. *Revenge of the Aesthetic: The Place of Literature in Theory Today*. Berkeley and Los Angeles: University of California Press, 2000. 180–207.

Derrida, Jacques. "Demeure." Maurice Blanchot/Jacques Derrida. *The Instant of My Death/Demeure: Fiction and Testimony*. Trans. Elizabeth Rottenberg Stanford: University of Stanford Press, 2000. 13–103.

Derrida, Jacques. "Et Cetera . . . and so on, und so weiter, and so forth, et ainsi de suite, und so überall, etc." Trans. Geoffrey Bennington. Nicholas Royle, ed., *Deconstructions: A User's Guide*. Basingstoke: Palgrave, 2000. 282–305.

Derrida, Jacques. "A Silkworm of One's Own: Points of View Stitched on the Other Veil." Hélène Cixous and Jacques Derrida. *Veils*. Trans. Geoffrey Bennington. Stanford: Stanford University Press, 2001. 21–92.

Derrida, Jacques. "Above All, No Journalists!" Hent de Vries and Samuel Weber, eds. *Religion and Media*. Stanford: Stanford University Press, 2001. 56–93.

Derrida, Jacques. "I Have a Taste for the Secret." Jacques Derrida and Maurizio Ferraris. *A Taste for the Secret*. Trans. Giacomo Donis. Ed. Giacomo Donis and David Webb. Oxford: Polity Press, 2001. 1–92.

Derrida, Jacques. "Lyotard and Us." Trans. Boris Belay. Rev. Pascale-Anne Brault and Michael Naas. Jacques Derrida. *The Work of Mourning*. Ed. Pascale-Anne Brault and Michael Naas. Chicago: University of Chicago Press, 2001. 216–241.

Derrida, Jacques. "The Deaths of Roland Barthes." Trans. Pascale-Anne Brault and Michael Naas. Jacques Derrida. *The Work of Mourning*. Ed. Pascale-Anne Brault and Michael Naas. Chicago: University of Chicago Press, 2001. 31–68.

Derrida, Jacques. "Typewriter Ribbon: Limited Ink (2) ("within such limits".)" Tom Cohen et al., eds. *Material Events: Paul de Man and the Afterlife of Theory*. Minneapolis: University of Minnesota Press, 2001. 277–360.

Derrida, Jacques. "'Le Parjure.' *Perhaps:* Storytelling and Lying, 'abrupt breaches of syntax'." *Without Alibi. Ed.,* trans. and int. Peggy Kamuf. Stanford: Stanford University Press, 2002. 161–201.

Derrida, Jacques. "As If It Were Possible, 'Within Such Limits'. . . ." Trans. Benjamin Elwood with Elizabeth Rottenberg. *Negotiations: Interventions and Interviews 1971–2001*. Ed., trans., and int. Elizabeth Rottenberg. Stanford: Stanford University Press, 2002. 343–370.

OTHER WORKS

Abraham, Nicolas, and Maria Torok. *The Shell and the Kernel. I.* Trans. and int. Nicholas Rand. Chicago: University of Chicago Press, 1994.

Adorno, Theodor W. "Transparencies on Film." Trans. Thomas Y. Levin. *The Culture Industry: Selected Essays on Mass Culture*. Ed. and int. J. M. Bernstein. London: Routledge, 1991. 178–186.

Agamben, Giorgio. *Stanzas: Word and Phantasm in Western Culture*. Trans. Ronald L. Martinez. Minneapolis: University of Minnesota Press, 1993.

Agamben, Giorgio. *Idea of Prose*. Trans. Michael Sullivan and Sam Whitsitt. Albany: State University of New York Press, 1995.

Agamben, Giorgio. *Means without End: Notes on Politics*. Trans. Vincenzo Binetti and Cesare Casarino. Minneapolis: University of Minnesota Press, 2000.

Ahmad, Aijaz. "Reconciling Derrida: 'Specters of Marx' and Deconstructive Politics." Michael Sprinker, ed. *Ghostly Demarcations: A Symposium on Jacques Derrida's* Specters of Marx. London: Verso, 1999. 88–109.

Althusser, Louis, and Etienne Balibar. *Reading Capital*. Trans. Ben Brewster. London: Verso, 1979.

Althusser, Louis. *For Marx*. Trans. Ben Brewster. London: Verso, 1979.

Althusser, Louis. *Writings on Psychoanalysis: Freud and Lacan*. Trans. Jeffrey Mehlman. Ed. Olivier Corpet and François Matheron. New York: Columbia University Press, 1996.

Althusser, Louis. "Ideology and Ideological State Apparatuses." *Essays on Ideology*. London: Verso, 1984. Rpt. In Slavoj Žižek, ed. *Mapping Ideology*. London: Verso, 1999. 100–140.

Angelopoulos, Theo. "Make it Yellow: An Interview with Theo Angelopoulos." *Sight and Sound*. 9:5 (1999): 8–11.

Aristotle. *Nichomachean Ethics*. Trans. Martin Ostwald. Indianapolis: Bobbs-Merrill Educational Publishing, 1983.

Arnold, Matthew. "Friendship's Garland." *Selected Prose*. Ed. and int. P. J. Keating London: Penguin, 1970. 301–339.

Attridge, Derek. "Expecting the Unexpected in Coetzee's *Master of Petersburg* and Derrida's Recent Writings." John Brannigan et al., eds. *Applying: to Derrida*. Basingstoke: Macmillan, 1996. 21–40.

Baer, Ulrich. *Remnants of Song: Trauma and the Experience of Modernity in Charles Baudelaire and Paul Celan*. Stanford: Stanford University Press, 2000.

Balibar, Etienne. *The Philosophy of Marx*. Trans. Chris Turner. London: Verso, 1995.

Barker, Francis. *The Tremulous Private Body: Essays on Subjection*. London: Methuen, 1984.

Barthes, Roland. *S/Z*. Trans. Richard Miller. Preface Richard Howard. Berkeley and Los Angeles: University of California Press, 1974.

Barthes, Roland. "Where to Begin?" *New Critical Essays*. Trans. Richard Howard. New York: Farrar, Strauss, and Giroux, 1974. 79–91.

Barthes, Roland. *Roland Barthes by Roland Barthes*. Trans. Richard Howard Berkeley and Los Angeles: University of California Press, 1977.

Barthes, Roland. "The Reality Effect." Trans. R. Carter. Tzvetan Todorov, ed. *French Literary Theory Today*. Cambridge: Cambridge University Press, 1982.

Batchen, Geoffrey. *Burning with Desire: The Conception of Photography*. Cambridge, MA: MIT Press, 1997.

Beardsworth, Richard. *Derrida and the Political*. London: Routledge, 1996. 18–25.

Beckett, Samuel. *The Unnameable*. Samuel Beckett. *Three Novels by Samuel Beckett*. New York: Grove Press, 1965.

Benjamin, Walter. "The Work of Art in the Age of Mechanical Reproduction." *Illuminations*. Ed. and int. Hannah Arendt. Trans. Harry Zohn. New York: Schocken Books, 1969. 155–200.

Benjamin, Walter. "A Small History of Photography." *One-Way Street and Other Writings*. Int. Susan Sontag. Trans. Edmund Jephcott and Kingsley Shorter. London: Verso, 1985. 240–258.

Benjamin, Walter. "On Some Motifs in Baudelaire." *Illuminations*. Ed. and int. Hannah Arendt. Trans. Harry Zohn. New York: Schocken Books, 1969. 155–200.

Bennington, Geoffrey. "Derridabase." Geoffrey Bennington and Jacques Derrida. *Jacques Derrida*. Paris: Seuil, 1991. Trans. Geoffrey Bennington as *Jacques Derrida*. Chicago: Chicago University Press, 1993. 3–310.

Bennington, Geoffrey. *Legislations: The Politics of Deconstruction*. London: Verso, 1994.

Bennington, Geoffrey. *"Inter."* Martin McQuillan et al., eds. *Post-Theory: New Directions in Criticism*. Edinburgh: Edinburgh University Press, 1999. 103–122.

Bennington, Geoffrey. "X." John Brannigan et al., eds. *Applying: to Derrida*. Basingstoke: Macmillan, 1996. 1–20. Rpt. in Bennington. *Interrupting Derrida*. London: Routledge, 2000. 76–92.

Bernard-Donals, Michael, and Richard Glejzer. *Between Witness and Testimony: The Holocaust and the Limits of Representation*. Albany: State University of New York Press, 2001.

Bhabha, Homi K. "The Commitment to Theory." *The Location of Culture*. London: Routledge, 1994. 19–39.

Blanchot, Maurice. *The Infinite Conversation*. Trans. and Foreword. Susan Hanson. Minneapolis: University of Minnesota Press, 1993.

Brandt, Joan. *Geopoetics: The Politics of Mimesis in Poststructuralist French Poetry and Theory*. Stanford: Stanford University Press, 1997.

Brunette, Peter, and David Wills. *Screen/Play: Derrida and Film Theory*. Princeton: Princeton University Press, 1989.

Cadava, Eduardo. *Words of Light: Theses on the Photography of History*. Princeton: Princeton University Press, 1997.

Caruth, Cathy. *Unclaimed Experience: Trauma, Narrative, and History*. Baltimore: The Johns Hopkins University Press, 1996.

Casetti, Francesco. *Inside the Gaze: The Fiction Film and Its Spectator*. Int. Christian Metz. Trans. Nell Andrew, with Charles O'Brien. Preface to English Edition, Dudley Andrew. Bloomington: Indiana University Press, 1998.

Chase, Cynthia. "The Decomposition of the Elephants: Double-Reading *Daniel Deronda*." K. M. Newton, ed. George Eliot. Harlow: Longman, 1991. 198–218.

Cheyette, Brian. *Muriel Spark*. Tavistock: Northcote House, 2000.

Cixous, Hélène. *Three Steps on the Ladder of Writing*. Trans. Sarah Cornell and Susan Sellers. New York: Columbia University Press, 1993.

Cixous, Hélène, and Mireille Calle-Gruber. "Inter Views." in *Rootprints: Memory and Life Writing*. Trans. Eric Prenowitz. London: Routledge, 1997. 1–116.

Cixous, Hélène. "Grimacing Catholicism: Muriel Spark's Macabre Farce (1) and Muriel Spark's Latest Novel: *The Public Image* (2)." Trans. Christine Irizzary. Martin McQuillan, ed. *Theorizing Muriel Spark: Gender, Race, Deconstruction*. London: Palgrave, 2002. 204–209.

Cixous, Hélène. "The Names of Oran." Trans. Eric Prenowitz. Anne-Emmanuelle Berger, ed. *Algeria in Others' Languages*. Ithaca: Cornell University Press, 2002. 184–194.

Cixous, Hélène. "Without end, no, State of Drawingness, no rather: The Executioner's taking off." Trans. Catherine A. F. MacGillivray. *Stigmata: Escaping Texts*. London: Routledge, 1998, 20–31.

Clark, Timothy. *Derrida, Heidegger, Blanchot: Sources of Derrida's Notion and Practice of Literature*. Cambridge: Cambridge University Press, 1992.

Cohen, Tom. *Anti-Mimesis: From Plato to Hitchcock*. Cambridge: Cambridge University Press, 1994.

Cohen, Tom. *Ideology and Inscription: "Cultural Studies" after Benjamin, de Man, and Bakhtin*. Cambridge: Cambridge University Press, 1998.

Conrad, Joseph. *Heart of Darkness with the Congo Diary*. Ed. and int. Robert Hampson. London: Penguin, 1995.

Copjec, Joan. *Read My Desire: Lacan Against the Historicists*. Cambridge: MIT Press, 1994.

Cornell, Drucilla. *The Philosophy of the Limit*. New York: Routledge, 1992.

Craig, Cairns. *The Modern Scottish Novel: Narrative and the National Imagination*. Edinburgh: Edinburgh University Press, 1999.

Critchley, *Simon. The Ethics of Deconstruction: Derrida and Levinas*. Oxford: Blackwell, 1986.

Culler, Jonathan. *Structuralist Poetics: Structuralism, Linguistics and the Study of Literature*. London: Routledge and Kegan Paul, 1975.

Currie, Mark. *Postmodern Narrative Theory*. Basingstoke: Macmillan, 1998.

Damisch, Hubert. *Skyline: The Narcissistic City*. Trans. John Goodman. Stanford: Stanford University Press, 2001.

de Bolla, Peter. *The Discourse of the Sublime: History, Aesthetics and the Subject*. Oxford: Blackwell, 1989.

de Man, Paul. *Blindness and Insight: Essays in the Rhetoric of Contemporary Criticism*. New York: Columbia University Press, 1971.

de Man, Paul. *Allegories of Reading: Figural Language in Rousseau, Nietzsche, Rilke, and Proust*. New Haven: Yale University Press, 1979.

de Man, Paul. *Aesthetic Ideology.* Ed. and int. Andrzej Warminski. Minneapolis: University of Minnesota Press, 1996.

de Man, Paul. *The Resistance to Theory.* Foreword Wlad Godzich. Minneapolis: University of Minnesota Press. 1997.

Dick, Bernard. *Billy Wilder.* Boston: Twayne Publishers, 1980.

Düttman, Alexander Garcia. *The Gift of Language: Memory and Promise in Adorno, Benjamin, Heidegger, and Rosenzweig.* London: Athlone Press, 2000.

Eagleton, Terry. "Marxism without Marxism." Michael Sprinker, ed. *Ghostly Demarcations: A Symposium on Jacques Derrida's* Specters of Marx. London: Verso, 1999. 83–87.

Eliot, George. *Daniel Deronda.* Ed. and int. Barbara Hardy. Harmondsworth: Penguin, 1986.

Felman, Shoshana. *What Does a Woman Want?* Baltimore: The Johns Hopkins University Press, 1993.

Felman, Shoshana, and Dori Laub. *Testimony: Crises of Witnessing in Literature, Psychoanalysis, and History.* London: Routledge, 1992.

Felstiner, John. *Paul Celan: Poet, Survivor, Jew.* New Haven: Yale University Press, 1995.

ffrench, Patrick, and Roland-François Lack, eds. *The Tel Quel Reader.* London: Routledge, 1998.

Finkielkraut, Alain. *The Wisdom of Love.* Trans. Kevin O'Neill and David Suchoff. Lincoln: University of Nebraska Press, 1997.

Foucault, Michel. *The Archaeology of Knowledge.* Trans. A. M. Sheridan Smith. London: Tavistock, 1972.

Foucault, Michel. "Self Writing." Trans. Paul Rabinow. *Ethics: The Essential Works 1.* Ed. Paul Rabinow. London: Penguin, 1997, 207–222.

Foucault, Michel. "On the Archaeology of the Sciences: Response to the Epistemology Circle." *Aesthetics, Method, and Epistemology: Essential Works of Michel Foucault 1954–1984, Volume Two.* Ed. James D. Faubion. Trans. Robert Hurley et al. New York: The New Press, 1998. 297–334.

Freud, Sigmund. *Beyond the Pleasure Principle. The Standard Edition of the Complete Psychological Works of Sigmund Freud.* Trans. and gen. ed., James Strachey. London: Hogarth Press, 1953–1974, vol. 18. Rpt. as *Beyond the Pleasure Principle.* Trans. and ed. James Strachey. Int. Gregory Zilboorg. Biog. Int. Peter Gay. New York: Norton, 1989.

Friere, Paolo. *Pedagogy of the Oppressed.* Trans. Myra Bergman Ramos. New York: Continuum, 1997.

Gramsci, Antonio. *Selections from Political Writings 1921–1926.* Trans. and ed. Quentin Hoare. London: Lawrence and Wishart, 1978.

Grosz, Elizabeth. "Times of Value: Deconstruction and Value." Scott Lash et al., eds. *Time and Value.* Oxford: Blackwell, 1998.

Guerlac, Suzanne. *Literary Polemics: Bataille, Sartre, Valéry, Breton.* Stanford: Stanford University Press, 1997.

Hamacher, Werner. *Pleroma: Reading in Hegel.* Trans. Nicholas Walker and Simon Jarvis. Stanford: Stanford University Press, 1998.

Hamacher, Werner. "Lingua Amissa: The Messianism of Commodity-Language and Derrida's Specters of Marx." Michael Sprinker, ed. *Ghostly Demarcations: A Symposium on Jacques Derrida's* Specters of Marx. London: Verso, 1999. 168–212.

Hardy, Barbara. "Introduction." George Eliot. *Daniel Deronda.* Harmondsworth: Penguin, 1986. 7–30.

Heidegger, Martin. "The Origin of the Work of Art." Martin Heidegger. *Poetry, Language, Thought.* Trans. and int. Albert Hofstadter. New York: Harper and Row, 1971. 15–89.

Heidegger, Martin. *History of the Concept of Time: Prolegomena.* Trans. Theodor Kisiel. Bloomington: University of Indiana Press, 1992.

Heidegger, Martin. *Aristotle's Metaphysics Θ 1–3: On the Essence and Actuality of Force.* Second ed., trans Walter Brogan and Peter Warnek. Bloomington: Indiana University Press, 1995.

Helfer, Martha B. *The Retreat of Representation: The Concept of Darstellung in German Critical Discourse.* Albany: State University of New York Press, 1996.

Hutter Andreas, and Klaus Kamolz. *Billy Wilder: Eine europäische Karriere.* Vienna: Böhlau Verlag, 1998.

Hynes, Joseph. *The Art of the Real: Muriel Spark's Novels.* Rutherford: Fairleigh Dickinson University Press, 1988.

Jameson, Fredric. "Marx's Purloined Letter." Michael Sprinker, ed. *Ghostly Demarcations: A Symposium on Jacques Derrida's* Specters of Marx. London: Verso, 1999. 26–67.

Joines, Richard E. "*Contretemps:* Derrida's Ante and the Call of Marxist Political Philosophy." *Cultural Logic,* 3:1/2 (2001): www.eserver.org/clogic.

Kamuf, Peggy, ed. *A Derrida Reader: Between the Blinds.* New York: Columbia University Press, 1991.

Kamuf, Peggy. "Introduction: Reading Between the Blinds." *A Derrida Reader: Between the Blinds.* New York: Columbia University Press, 1991. xiii–xlii.

Kamuf, Peggy. "Violence, Identity, Self-Determination, and the Question of Justice: On *Specters of Marx.*" Hent de Vries and Samuel Weber, eds. *Violence, Identity, and Self-Determination.* Stanford: Stanford University Press, 1997. 271–283.

Kamuf, Peggy. *The Division of Literature or the University in Deconstruction.* Chicago: University of Chicago Press, 1997.

Kamuf, Peggy. "Deconstruction and Love." Nicholas Royle, ed. *Deconstructions: A User's Guide.* Basingstoke: Palgrave, 2000. 151–170.

Kamuf, Peggy. "The Ghosts of Critique and Deconstruction." Martin McQuillan, ed. *Deconstruction: A Reader.* Edinburgh: Edinburgh University Press, 2000. 198–213.

Kane, Richard C. *Iris Murdoch, Muriel Spark, and John Fowles: Didactic Demons in Modern Fiction.* Rutherford: Fairleigh Dickinson University Press, 1988.

Keenan, Thomas. *Fables of Responsibility: Aberrations and Predicaments in Ethics and Politics.* Stanford: Stanford University Press, 1997.

Kemp, Peter. *Muriel Spark.* London: Paul Elek, 1974.

Kemple, Thomas M. *Reading Marx Writing: Melodrama, the Market, and the "Grundrisse."* Stanford: Stanford University Press, 1995.

King, Nicola. *Memory, Narrative, Identity.* Edinburgh: Edinburgh University Press, 2000.

Kittler, Friedrich A. *Gramophone, Film, Typewriter.* Trans. and int. Geoffrey Winthrop-Young and Michael Wutz. Stanford: Stanford University Press, 1999.

Kofman, Sarah. *Lectures de Derrida.* Paris: Galilée, 1984.

Kofman, Sarah. *Nietzsche and Metaphor.* Trans. Duncan Large. London: Athlone Press, 1993.

Krell, David Farrell. *Infectious Nietzsche.* Bloomington: University of Indiana Press, 1996.

Kronick, Joseph G. *Derrida and the Future of Literature.* Albany: State University of New York Press, 1999.

Lacan, Jacques. *Le Séminaire livre XX.* Paris: Seuil, 1975.

LaCapra, Dominick. *Writing History, Writing Trauma.* Baltimore: The Johns Hopkins University Press, 2000.

Lacoue-Labarthe, Philippe. *Poetry as Experience.* Trans. Andrea Tarnowski Stanford: Stanford University Press, 1999.

Larsen, Neil. *Modernism and Hegemony: A Materialist Critique of Aesthetic Agency.* Foreword Jaime Concha. Minneapolis: University of Minnesota Press, 1990.

Leavey, Jr., John P. *Glassary*. Lincoln: University of Nebraska Press, 1986.

Leavey, Jr., John P. "French Kissing: Whose Tongue Is It Anyway?" Julian Wolfreys et al., eds. *The French Connections of Jacques Derrida*. Albany: State University of New York Press, 1996. 149–164.

Levinas, Emmanuel. *Totality and Infinity: An Essay on Exteriority*. Trans. Alphonso Lingis. Pittsburgh: Duquesne University Press, 1969.

Levinas, Emmanuel. *Beyond the Verse: Talmudic Readings and Lectures*. Trans. Gary D. Mole. Bloomington: University of Indiana Press, 1994.

Levinas. Emmanuel. *Proper Names*. Trans. Michael B. Smith. Stanford: Stanford University Press, 1996.

Libeskind, Daniel. "Between the Lines," Daniel Libeskind. *Radix-Matrix: Architecture and Writings*. Munich: Preste., 1997, 34–56.

Libeskind, Daniel. "Mourning: Sachsenhausen, Oranienberg." Daniel Libeskind. *Radix-Matrix: Architecture and Writings*. Munich: Prestel, 1997, 102–109.

Libeskind, Daniel. www.daniel-libeskind.com/projects.

Lovell, Terry. *The Female Thermometer: Eighteenth-Century Culture and the Invention of the Uncanny*. Oxford: Oxford University Press, 1995.

Lyotard, Jean-François. *The Postmodern Explained*. Ed. Julian Pefanis and Morgan Thomas. Trans. Don Barry et al. Afterword Wlad Godzich. Minneapolis: University of Minnesota Press, 1992.

Madsen, Axel. *Billy Wilder*. London: BFI, 1968.

Malik, Suhail. "Différantial Technics." *Imprimatur* 1: 2/3 (1996): 200–203.

Malkoff, Karl. *Muriel Spark*. New York: Columbia University Press, 1968.

Marcus, Steven. "Human Nature, Social Orders and 19th Century Systems of Explanation: Starting in with George Eliot." *Salmagundi,* 28 (1975).

Marx, Karl. "The Fetishism of Commodities and the Secret Thereof." *Capital Vol. 1.* Trans. Samuel Moore and Edward Aveling. New York: International Publishers, 1967. 76–87.

Marx, Karl. *The Poverty of Philosophy*. Moscow: Progress Publishers, 1978.

Marx, Karl, and Friedrich Engels, *The German Ideology*. Ed. and int. C. J. Arthur London: Lawrence and Wishart, 1970.

Marx, Karl, and Frederick Engels. *Manifesto of the Communist Party. Economic and Philosophic Manuscripts of 1844 and the Communist Manifesto*. New York: Prometheus Books, 1988.

McCance, Dawn, and John P. Leavey, Jr. "Translation/citation: An Interview with John P. Leavey Jr." *Mosaic: A Journal for the Interdisciplinary Study of Literature,* 35:1 (March 2002): 1–20.

Mellor, Anne K. *Mary Shelley: Her Life, Her Fiction, Her Monsters*. London: Routledge, 1990.

Mengham, Rod. "1973 The End of History: Cultural Change According to Muriel Spark." Rod Mengham, ed. *An Introduction to Contemporary Fiction*. Oxford: Polity, 1999. 123–134.

Miller, J. Hillis. *The Ethics of Reading: Kant, de Man, Eliot, Trollope, James, and Benjamin*. New York: Columbia University Press, 1987.

Miller, J. Hillis. *Tropes, Parables, Performatives: Essays on Twentieth-Century Literature*. Hemel Hempstead: Harvester Wheatsheaf, 1990.

Miller, J. Hillis. *Theory Now and Then*. Hemel Hempstead: Harvester Wheatsheaf, 1991.

Miller, J. Hillis. *Topographies*. Stanford: Stanford University Press, 1995.

Miller, J. Hillis. *Reading Narrative*. Norman: University of Oklahoma Press, 1998.

Miller, J. Hillis. "Paul de Man as Allergen." Tom Cohen, et al., eds. *Material Events: Paul de Man and the Afterlife of Theory*. Minneapolis: University of Minnesota Press, 2001. 183–204.

Miller, J. Hillis. *Speech Acts in Literature*. Stanford: Stanford University Press, 2001.

Monleón, José B. *A Specter Is Haunting Europe: A Sociohistorical Approach to the Fantastic*. Princeton: Princeton University Press, 1990.

Nancy, Jean-Luc. *The Inoperative Community*. Ed. Peter Connor. Trans. Christopher Fynsk. Minneapolis: University of Minnesota Press, 1991.

Nancy, Jean-Luc. *The Birth to Presence*. Trans. Brian Holmes et al. Stanford: Stanford University Press, 1993.

Nancy, Jean-Luc. *Being Singular Plural*. Trans. Robert D. Richardson and Anne E. O'Byrne Stanford: Stanford University Press, 2000.

Newton, K. M. "*Daniel Deronda* and Circumcision." K. M. Newton, ed. *George Eliot*. Harlow: Longman, 1991. 218–232.

Olsson, Anders. "Spectral Analysis: A Commentary on 'Solve' and 'Coagula'," Trans. Hanna Kalter Weiss in collaboration with the author. Aris Fioretos, ed. *Word Traces: Readings of Paul Celan*. Baltimore: The Johns Hopkins University Press, 1991. 267–279.

Oswald, Laura R. "Cinema-Graphia: Eisenstein, Derrida, and the Sign of the Cinema." Peter Brunette and David Wills, eds. *Deconstruction and the Visual Arts: Art, Media, Architecture*. Cambridge: Cambridge University Press, 1994. 248–263.

Page, Norman. *Muriel Spark*. New York, St. Martin's Press, 1990.

Pepper, Thomas. *Singularities: Extremes of Theory in the Twentieth Century.* Cambridge: Cambridge University Press, 1997.

Pepys, Samuel. *The Diary of Samuel Pepys.* 12 vols. Ed. R. C. Latham and W. Matthews. London: HarperCollins, 1995.

Plotnitsky, Arkady. *In the Shadow of Hegel: Complementarity, History, and the Unconscious.* Gainesville: University Press of Florida, 1993.

Plotnitsky, Arkady. "Algebra and Allegory: Nonclassical Epistemology, Quantum Theory, and the Work of Paul de Man." Tom Cohen et al., eds. *Material Events: Paul de Man and the Afterlife of Theory.* Minneapolis: University of Minnesota Press, 2001. 49–92.

Porter, Roy. *The Greatest Benefit to Mankind: A Medical History of Humanity.* New York: Norton, 1997.

Poulantzas, Nicos. *Political Power and Social Classes.* Trans. editor, Timothy O'Hagan. London: Verso, 1973.

Prawer, S. S. *Caligari's Children: The Film as Tale of Terror.* Oxford: Oxford University Press, 1980.

Richmond, Velma Bourgeois. *Muriel Spark.* Boston: Twayne Publishers, 1984.

Richter, Gerhard. *Walter Benjamin and the Corpus of Autobiography.* Detroit: Wayne State University Press, 2000.

Ronell, Avital. *The Telephone Book: Technology-Schizophrenia-Electric Speech.* Lincoln: University of Nebraska Press, 1989.

Ronell, Avital. *Dictations: On Haunted Writing.* Lincoln: University of Nebraska Press, 1993.

Ronell, Avital. *Finitude's Score: Essays for the End of the Millennium.* Lincoln: University of Nebraska Press, 1994.

Royle, Nicholas. *After Derrida.* Manchester: Manchester University Press, 1995.

Royle, Nicholas. "What Is Deconstruction?" Nicholas Royle, ed. *Deconstructions: A User's Guide.* Basingstoke: Palgrave, 2000. 1–13.

Sadoff, Dianne. *Sciences of the Flesh: Representing Body and Subject in Psychoanalysis.* Stanford: Stanford University Press, 1998.

Sallis, John. "Doublings." David Wood, ed. *Derrida: A Critical Reader.* Oxford: Blackwell, 1992. 120–137.

Samuels, Clarisse. *Holocaust Visions: Surrealism and Existentialism in the Poetry of Paul Celan.* Columbia: Camden House, 1993.

Schmidt, Dennis J. *The Ubiquity of the Finite: Hegel, Heidegger, and the Entitlements of Philosophy.* Cambridge, MA: MIT Press, 1988. 102.

Schor, Naomi. *Reading in Detail: Aesthetics and the Feminine.* New York: Methuen, 1987.

Scott, Walter. "Introduction to *The Castle of Otranto.*" Rpt in Horace Walpole. *The Castle of Otranto.* Int. Marvin Mudrick. New York: Crowell-Collier, 1963. 115–128.

Seidman, Steve. *The Film Career of Billy Wilder.* Pleasantville: Redgrave, 1977.

Shelley, Mary. *Frankenstein, or the Modern Prometheus.* Ed. and int. Marilyn Butler. Oxford: Oxford University Press, 1994.

Sikov, Ed. *On Sunset Boulevard: The Life and Times of Billy Wilder.* New York: Hyperion, 1998.

Skal, David. *Hollywood Gothic: The Tangled Web of "Dracula" from Novel to Stage to Screen.* New York: W. W. Norton, 1990.

Smith, Robert. *Derrida and Autobiography.* Cambridge: Cambridge University Press, 1995.

Spark, Muriel. *Child of Light: A Reassessment of Mary Shelley.* London, n.p. 1951.

Spark, Muriel. *Mary Shelley: A Biography.* Rev. ed. New York: Dutton, 1987.

Spivak, Gayatri Chakravorty. "A Moral Dilemma." Howard Marchitello, ed. *What Happens to History: The Renewal of Ethics in Contemporary Thought.* New York: Routledge. 2001, 215–236.

Stam, Robert. *Reflexivity in Film and Literature: From Don Quixote to Jean-Luc Godard.* New York: Columbia University Press, 1992.

Stewart, Susan. *On Longing: Narratives of the Miniature, the Gigantic, the Souvenir, the Collection.* Durham: Duke University Press, 1993.

Sunstein, Emily W. *Mary Shelley: Romance and Reality.* Boston: Little, Brown, & Co., 1989.

Virilio, Paul. *The Art of the Motor.* Trans. Julie Rose. Minneapolis: University of Minnesota Press, 1995.

Volosinov, V. N. *Marxism and the Philosophy of Language.* Trans. Ladislav Matejka and R. Titunik. Cambridge: Harvard University Press, 1986.

Warminski, Andrzej. "'As the Poets do it': On the Material Sublime." Tom Cohen, et al., eds. *Material Events: Paul de Man and the Afterlife of Theory.* Minneapolis: University of Minnesota Press, 2001. 3–31.

Warren Montag, "Spirits Armed and Unarmed: Derrida's *Specters of Marx.*" Michael Sprinker, ed. *Ghostly Demarcations: A Symposium on Jacques Derrida's* Specters of Marx. London: Verso, 1999. 68–82.

Weber, Samuel. *Mass Mediauras: Form Technics Media.* Ed. Alan Cholodenko. Stanford: Stanford University Press, 1996.

Williams, Raymond. *Marxism and Literature*. Oxford: Oxford University Press, 1977.

Wolfreys, *Being English: Narratives, Idioms, and Performances of National Identity from Coleridge to Trollope*. Albany: State University of New York Press, 1994.

Wolfreys, Julian. *Victorian Hauntings: Spectrality, Gothic, the Uncanny and Literature*. London: Palgrave, 2001

Wolfreys, Julian. "Citation's Haunt." *Mosaic: a Journal for the Interdisciplinary Study of Literature*. 35:1 (March 2002): 21–34.

Wolfreys, Julian. "Der Spuk das Zitate: '. . . eine Serie von Kontiguuitäten. . . . .'" ils Plath and Volker Pantenburg, eds. *Anfuehren—Vorfuehren—Anfuehren: Das Zeitat in Literatur und Theorie*. Bielefeld: Aiesthesis Verlag, 2002. 163–175.

Wolosky, Shira. *Language Mysticism: The Negative Way of Language in Eliot, Beckett, and Celan*. Stanford: Stanford University Press, 1995.

www.sussex.ac.uk/units/frenchthought/video/realvideo/derridavideo.html.

Yeats, W. B. *Purgatory*. *The Yeats Reader*. Ed. Richard J. Finneran. New York: Scribner Poetry, 1997. 252–259.

Young, Robert. *White Mythologies: Writing History and the West*. London: Routledge, 1990.

Young, Robert J. C. "Deconstruction and the Postcolonial." Nicholas Royle, ed. *Deconstructions: A User's Guide*. Basingstoke: Palgrave, 2000.

Žižek, Slavoj. *Looking Awry: An Introduction to Jacques Lacan through Popular Culture*. Cambridge: MIT Press, 1992.

Žižek, Slavoj. *On Belief*. London: Routledge, 2001.

INDEX OF PROPER NAMES